The Buddhist Philosophy of Universal Flux

THE BUDDHIST PHILOSOPHY OF UNIVERSAL FLUX

An Exposition of the Philosophy of Critical Realism as Expounded by the School of Dignāga

SATKARI MOOKERJEE

MOTILAL BANARSIDASS PUBLISHERS
PRIVATE LIMITED • DELHI

6th Reprint : Delhi, 2017
First Edition : Published by University of Calcutta, 1935

ISBN: 978-81-208-0737-2

Also available at

Motilal Banarsidass

41 U.A. Bungalow Road, Jawahar Nagar, Delhi 110 007
8 Mahalaxmi Chamber, 22 Bhulabhai Desai Road, Mumbai 400 026
203 Royapettah High Road, Mylapore, Chennai 600 004
236, 9th Main III Block, Jayanagar, Bengaluru 560 011
8 Camac Street, Kolkata 700 017
Ashok Rajpath, Patna 800 004
Chowk, Varanasi 221 001

MLBD Cataloging-in-Publication Data
The Buddhist Philosophy of Universal Flux
An Exposition of the Philosophy of Critical Realism as Expounded by the School of Dignāga
SATKARI MOOKERJEE
ISBN: 978-81-208-0737-2
Includes Index
I. Buddhism II. Philosophy III. Critical Realism
IV. Dignāga V. Mookerjee, Satkari

Printed in India
by RP Jain at NAB Printing Unit,
A-44, Naraina Industrial Area, Phase I, New Delhi–110028
and published by JP Jain for Motilal Banarsidass Publishers (P) Ltd.,
41 U.A. Bungalow Road, Jawahar Nagar, Delhi-110007

To

THE SACRED MEMORY

OF

SIR ASUTOSH MOOKERJEE

AS AN HUMBLE TRIBUTE

OF

GRATITUDE, LOVE AND ADMIRATION

PREFACE

The present work is substantially based upon my thesis which was approved for the Degree of Doctorate in Philosophy by the University of Calcutta in 1932. It has since been revised in many places and fresh matter introduced, the last chapter being entirely new.

Buddhist philosophy is a vast subject with a large number of ramifications. It is not possible to do full justice to the whole subject within so short a compass. I have here dealt with only a particular school. The previous writings on the subject are rather sectional and fragmentary and a systematic presentation of Dignāga's school was a desideratum.

I take this opportunity to offer my grateful thanks to Syamaprasad Mookerjee, Esq., M.A., B.L., Bar.-at-Law, *Bhāratī*, *Vice-Chancellor*, Calcutta University, for the constant encouragement I received from him in connection with my researches and for the provision he kindly made for the publication of my book by the University of Calcutta.

My sincere thanks are due to my pupil, Mr. Satindrakumar Mukherjee, M.A., for his ungrudging help in looking through the proofs and for his valuable suggestions. Mr. Gaurinath Bhattacharyya, M.A., Research Fellow, Calcutta University, who is carrying on researches under my guidance, also deserves my best thanks for the preparation of the Index. I must express my heart-felt thanks to my pupils, Mr. Durgacharan Chatterjee, M.A., P.R.S., Lecturer, Bethune College, and Mr. Makhanlal Mookerjee, M.A., Research Scholar of the University, attached to me, for their valuable help in the preparation of the Table of Contents. To Mr. Atulchandra Ghatak, M.A., Superintendent of the University Press, Mr. Bhupendralal Banerjee, Printer,

Mr. Kalipada Das, B.A., and the other members of the staff of the University Press, I offer my grateful thanks for the special care and interest they have taken in my work. The publication of the book within such an incredibly short time is entirely due to their hearty co-operation.

ASUTOSH BUILDING,
CALCUTTA UNIVERSITY.
November 7, 1935.

S. M.

ABBREVIATIONS

A.k.	Abhidharmakoṣa of Vasubandhu (ed. by Rahula)
AB.k.	
Abi. k.v.	
A.K.v.	Abhidharmakoṣavyākhyā of Yaśomitra (Bib.
Ab.k.v.	Bud.)
A.S.	Apohasiddhi—Ratnakīrti (Bib. Ind.)
A.vya. S or Sa	Antarvyāptisamarthana (Bib. Ind.)
A.V.	
Bhā.	Bhāmatī (N. S. P.)
Br. Sū.	Brahmasūtra (N. S. P.)
Din.	Dinakarī (N. S. P.)
H. I. L.	History of Indian Logic—S. C. Vidyābhūṣaṇa
K. T.	Kusumañjaliṭīkā (ed. by C. K. Tarkālaṁkāra)
K. T. P.	Kalpataruparimala of Appaya Dīkṣita (N. S. P.)
M. K.	Mādhyamikakārikā (B. T. S.)
M. K. V.	Mādhyamikakārikāvṛtti (B. T. S.)
M. K. P. P. V.	Do. Prasannapadāvṛtti (B. T. S.)
Mān. Me.	Mānameyodaya (T. S. S.)
N. B.	Nyāyabindu (Bib. Ind.)
N. B. T.	Do. Ṭīkā (Bib. Ind.)
N. B. T. T.	Do. do. Ṭippanī (Bib. Bud.)
N. K.	Nyāyakandalī (V. S. S.)
N. Ku.	Nyāyakusumāñjali (Chowkhamba)
N. M.	Nyāyamañjarī (V. S. S.)
N. R.	Nyāyaratnākara of Pārthasārathimiśra (Chowkhamba)
N. S.	Nyāyasūtra (Chowkhamba)
N. V.	Nyāyavārttika (Chowkhamba)
Ny. Ku. P.	Nyāyakusumāñjaliprakāśa (Chowkhamba)

P. M.	Parīkṣāmukhasūtra (Bib. Ind.)
P. M. S.	
P. L. S. V.	Do. Laghuvṛtti of Anantavīrya (Bib. Ind.)
P. M. L. S. V.	
P. M. L. V.	
P. Mim.	Pramāṇamīmāṁsā of Hemacandra
Pra. Mi.	
Pr. Mi. V.	Do. Vṛtti
S. B.	Śārīrakabhāṣya (N. S. P.)
SBNT	Six Buddhist Nyāya Tracts (Bib. Ind.)
S.B.N.T.	
S. D.	Śāstradīpikā—Tarkapāda (N. S. P.)
Śā. Di.	
S. D. S.	Sarvadarśanasaṁgraha (N. S. P.)
SDS	
S. D. Sam.	Ṣaḍdarśanasamuccaya (Bib. Ind.)
S.D.S.T.R.D.	Do. Tarkarahasyadīpikā (Bib. Ind.)
S. K.	Sāṅkhyakārikā
S. V.	Ślokavārttika (Chowkhamba)
T. T.	Tātparyaṭīkā (Chowkhamba)
Tat. T.	
Tat. ṭī	
T. R. D.	Tarkarahasyadīpikā (Bib. Ind.)
T. S.	Tattvasaṁgraha (G. O. S.)
T. S. P.	Do. Pañjikā (G. O. S.)
Vā. P.	Vākyapadīya (Chowkhamba)
Vā Pad.	
Vāk Pa.	

TABLE OF CONTENTS

CHAPTER II

Logical Difficulties explained

Section I

Section II.

CHAPTER VI

A Buddhist Estimate of Universals

Page

The Sautrāntika's Reply to the Realist's Charge

CHAPTER VII

The Doctrine of Apoha or the Import of Words

Page

CHAPTER VIII

The Soul-theory of the Nyāya-Vaiśeṣika School

CHAPTER IX

The Mīmāṁsā Theory of Soul

CHAPTER X

THE SOUL THEORY OF THE DIGAMBARA JAINAS

CHAPTER XI

THE SĀṄKHYA THEORY OF SOUL

CHAPTER XII

THE SOUL THEORY OF THE VĀTSĪPUTRĪYAS

CHAPTER XIII

THE THEORY OF SOUL BASED ON THE UPANIṢADS

Page

CHAPTER XIV

A Critical Estimate of the Non-soul Theory of the Buddhist Philosopher

CHAPTER XV

The Problem of After-life or Immortality of Consciousness-continuum

CHAPTER XVI

Nīrvāṇa

II

THE CONCEPTION OF *Nīrvāṇa* ACCORDING TO THE *Sarvāstivādins* OR THE *Vaibhāṣikas*

III

THE CONCEPTION OF *Nīrvāṇa* ACCORDING TO THE *Sautrāntikas*

Part II

CHAPTER XVII

Perception in Dignāga's School of Philosophy

CHAPTER XXI

THE THEORY OF PERCEPTION AS PROPOUNDED BY DHARMAKIRTI AND DHARMOTTARA

CHAPTER XXII

INFERENCE

II

THE SUBJECT-MATTER OF INFERENCE OR THESIS OR CONCLUSION

Page

CHAPTER XXIII

Members of a Syllogism (Avayava)

CHAPTER XXIV

Universal Concomitance (Vyāpti)

Page

CHAPTER XXVI

Negative Judgment

INTRODUCTION

The present work is an humble attempt to give a critical exposition of the philosophy of the Medieval school of Buddhism that was ushered into existence by Dignāga and Dharmakīrti and later on systematized and developed by Śāntarakṣita, Kamalaśīla, Ratnakīrti and other authors of repute. Of this philosophy, again, the purely idealistic side has been left untouched in the present work. The interest and character of this work are purely philosophical and critical and not historical. There have already appeared in the field several brilliant expositions and accounts of Buddhist philosophy and religion, which have dealt with the historical side with varying degrees of fullness. The monumental works of Prof. Sir S. Radhakrishnan and Prof. S. N. Dasgupta have provided an important place for Buddhist philosophy, and though, from the very nature and scope of these works, the treatment might appear not to be exhaustive, the account and exposition constitute a substantial contribution to Buddhist scholarship. The writings of Prof. Louis de La Vàlle Poussin, Prof. Stcherbatsky, Prof. Guieseppe Tucci, Prof B. M. Barua, Prof. A. B. Keith, Dr. Nalinaksha Datta, Dr. E. J. Thomas and other scholars have already provided the learned world interested in Buddhism with elaborate and fairly wide account of the growth and development of Buddhist philosophy and religion. Any attempt in that line would necessarily involve a repetition or reduplication of much the same thing, though it is not denied that there is room for expansion and elaboration even in that direction.

The present work has, however, steered clear of the historical side and is chiefly preoccupied with the dry metaphysical and epistemological sides of the *Sautrāntika* philosophy. What particularly impressed the present writer is the fact that the whole course of philosophical speculations in Indian systems of thought, Brāhmaṇical and non-Brāhmaṇical alike, from the third century A.D. down to 1000 A.D., which may be described as the adolescent and fruitful period of Indian philosophy, bears unmistakable evidence of Buddhist influence. Even Vātsyāyana and Śabarasvāmin are not immune from it. Of course, they have borrowed little or nothing from the Buddhists and their chief interest in Buddhist philosophy is only negative, all their energies being directed to a refutation of the Buddhist position. But this adverse criticism does not minimise their debt; on the other hand, it is proof positive of their obligation. It has been very aptly observed by a modern philosopher that "Every writer on philosophical subjects is indebted, beyond all possibility of adequate acknowledgment, to the great thinkers of the past.........But the debt is one which he makes for himself, or at least incalculably increases, by free and honest criticism. If the labours of those whom he criticizes have rendered his criticism possible, it is only by criticizing that he is brought to the intelligent appreciation of their work." [1] The real development of the *Nyāya* philosophy may be legitimately believed to commence with Uddyotakara, who, on his own avowal, derived his incentive to write his commentary from the hostile critics, whose sophistical (according to Uddyotakara) arguments went a long way to bring discredit on the *Nyāya* Philosophy. Uddyotakara's taciturnity in regard to names is notorious. Vācaspati Miśra has supplied the lacuna and tells us that it was the adverse criticism of Dignāga and men of his ilk that gave the much-needed fillip to Uddyotakara for writing his masterpiece. In fact, the sole justification for this attempt lay in the

[1] H. H. Joachim, Preface to *The Nature of Truth*, p. 4.

necessity of a refutation of Dignāga's animadversions which created a perilous situation for *Nyāya*.[1]

The subsequent career of *Nyāya* philosophy and of Post-Dignāga Philosophy, for the matter of that, is but a progressive record of the daring and desperate fights between these two schools, which were fought on a hundred and one battle-fields. The fight was keen and vigorous and continued with unabated enthusiasm down to the days of Vācaspati, Jayanta, Udayana and Śrīdhara, on the one hand, and Śāntarakṣita, Kamalaśīla, Ratnakīrti and their followers, on the other. But we have omitted to mention another philosopher, a towering personality and a hero of a thousand and one battle-fields, I mean, Kumārila Bhaṭṭa. Kumārila came after Uddyotakara and he was, to all intents and purposes, a greater fighter, who fought clean and hard. Uddyotakara's polemics smacked of rankling jealousy and were rather full of transparent sophistry and claptrap. So the Buddhists did not find it very hard to expose his fallacies. In Kumārila, however, they found a veritable Tartar. It is not seldom that the Buddhists were compelled to revise their old theories and to re-formulate them in the light of Kumārila's criticism.[2] In fact, a more formidable critic, so firmly posted in the niceties of Buddhist philosophy and dogmas, could hardly be imagined. Kumārila's sledge-hammer blows were telling in their effect and the replies of Śāntarakṣita, Dharmottara,[3] Ratnakīrti and subsequent writers indirectly acknowledged the

[1] yad Akṣapādaḥ pravaro munīnām | śamāya śāstraṁ jagato jagāda | kutārkikājñānanivṛttihetuḥ | kariṣyate tasya mayā nibandhaḥ ||

N. V. Intro.

Cf. yadyapi bhāṣyakṛtā kṛtavyutpādanam etat tathāpi Dignāgaprabhṛtibhir arvācīnaiḥ kuhetusantamasasamutthāpanena 'cchāditaṁ śāstraṁ na tattvanirṇayāya paryāptam ity Uddyotakareṇa svanibandhoddyotena tad apanīyata iti prayojanavān ayam ārambha iti. Tāt. ṭī., p. 2.

[2] *Vide* the chapters on *Apoha* and *Manovijñāna* in particular.

[3] *Vide* the chapter 'Negative Judgment,' Pt. II.

justice of his criticism in more places than one, inasmuch as they had to re-shape their theories in fundamental aspects.

What is, however, particularly refreshing in this tense atmosphere of fighting is the fact of the earnestness of the fighters. Though all cannot be regarded as equally honest or honourable in their methods, their earnestness and sincerity are beyond doubt or cavil. The fighting has all the freshness of life and reality. There is no air of unreality about it. In fact, they fought for what they believed to be a question of life and death. Philosophy was not a matter of academic interest in India. Change of philosophy meant the change of entire outlook and orientation in life. Victory in a philosophical debate, therefore, was essential to the preservation of one's religion and mode of life, and defeat spelt inglorious death or apostacy from the accepted faith. There was, in fact, no line of demarcation between philosophy and religion in India. A religion without a philosophical backing was unthinkable.

The cleavage between philosophy and religion is pronounced where religion is held to be a matter of unquestioning faith irrespective of a philosophic sanction. But in India the two were identical. So even the atheists had their own religion, because philosophy and religion were one. Belief had to submit to the test of logic, and a faith that was not warranted by philosophic conviction, was rightly regarded as perverse dogmatism which has no right to the allegiance of a man of sound education and culture. It is this fact of intellectual honesty and spiritual earnestness that account for the intensity and desperate character of this fighting for opinions among ancient philosophers of India. As has been aptly observed by Prof. Dasgupta with his characteristic insight, " The systems of philosophy in India were not stirred up merely by the speculative demands of the human mind, but by a deep craving after the realisation of the religious purpose of life." [1] Ignorance of this peculiarity of the Indian mind has

[1] *History of Indian Philosophy*, Vol. I, p. 71.

been responsible for the so-called charge of scholasticism that has been laid at the door of Indian philosophy. Philosophy was not the fad of intellectual circles that indulged in these metaphysical gymnastics for mere intellectual satisfaction or for the purpose of whiling away their idle hours. It was, on the contrary, the earnest quest of truth and life's purpose and nothing short of truth could give its votaries peace or satisfy their ardent minds. And the intensity of this craving was not appeased except by a thoroughgoing and meticulous application of the truth to every detail of life. Accordingly no fictitious barrier between religion and philosophy was tolerated.

If religion was not sanctioned and inspired by philosophy, it was regarded as a useless superstition. If philosophy was not lived in actual religion, it was rightly held to be a mere waste of time and a dereliction from life's true purpose and mission. As Prof. Sir S. Radhakrishnan observes with his inimitable felicity of expression, "In many other countries reflection on the nature of existence is a luxury of life. The serious moments are given to action, while the pursuit of philosophy comes up as a parenthesis. In ancient India philosophy was not an auxiliary to any other science or art, but always held a prominent position of independence."[1] The true criterion of philosophy and scholasticism therefore should be sought not in the identity of the interests of religion and philosophy, which, to my mind, far from being an occasion of halting apology, constitutes the very apex and perfection of both of them. The criterion, in my humble judgment, should be the crucial test as to whether or not the pursuit of philosophy is inspired by an unremitting and unhesitating enquiry after truth and whether it is only an after-thought, a metaphysical eyewash, or a clever subterfuge to bolster up a pet dogma. If this criterion is accepted and applied, Indian philosophy will, we believe, come out in triumphant glory. Unquestioning, blind faith may be shameful

[1] *Indian Philosophy*, Vol. I, p. 22.

superstition, but the studious endeavour to keep religion apart from philosophy is a perversity of mind, of which we should be equally ashamed. To keep up philosophy again in a water-tight compartment and to prevent it deliberately from finding its fulfilment in religion constitutes an unpardonable case of moral cowardice, insincerity of purpose and shallow dilettantism.

The purely critical outlook of Buddhism

There might be a semblance of justification or excuse for the charge of scholasticism against the course of philosophic thought in some Brāhmaṇical schools (which, we believe, we have succeeded in proving to be without foundation); but this indictment cannot be brought against Buddhist philosophy with any show of plausibility. From the very beginning Buddhism has been critical in its spirit. Lord Buddha was an intellectual giant and a rationalist above anything else. He exhorted his disciples to accept nothing on trust. "Just as people test the purity of gold by burning it in fire, by cutting it and by examining it on a touchstone, so exactly you should, O ye monks! accept my words after subjecting them to a critical test and not out of reverence for me."[1] These words of the Buddha furnish the key to the true spirit of Buddhist philosophy throughout its career. And this freedom of thought encouraged by Buddha was responsible for the schism in the Buddhist church and for division of Buddhist philosophy into so many divergent schools. This should not be regarded as a matter of regret ; on the contrary, we should read in it the signs of pulsating life. Dead level monotony and formal uniformity in a religion may have a practical value in that it may conduce to the solidarity and cohesiveness of the body of its followers. But this uniformity and solidarity may have been purchased at the cost of intellectual expansion. So the bargain is not profitable, as it may appear at first

1 tāpāc chedāc ca nikaṣāt suvarṇam iva paṇḍitaiḥ । pārīkṣya bhikṣavo grāhyaṁ madvaco na tu gauravāt ॥ Quoted in T. S. P., p. 12.

sight. Honest difference of opinion, on the other hand, need not necessarily mean faction and feud. It is undoubtedly the sign of intellectual growth. Uniformity, absolute and unqualified, can be secured only if all the members of a community reach the same level of progress or if all intellectual growth is rendered impossible. Deny the privilege of education and men will not put awkward questions. So difference of opinion and birth of diverse philosophies should not be banned, as this would prove fatal to the intellectual growth and progress of mankind. We have therefore no reason to mourn the lack of uniformity in the philosophical speculations of ancient India. They furnish the evidence of real life. Liberty of thought and difference of opinion are not incompatible with the harmonious growth or solidarity of a nation. After all, if exclusive emphasis is not laid upon the points of difference we can never fail to find out fundamental unity and a common platform in our social, political and economic relations. The differences, on the other hand, may really be a source of inspiration for philosophic thought and thus be a real factor in the development of a nation. History contains numerous and brilliant proofs of this truth. The sharp differences of the Buddhist and non-Buddhist schools of thought did not lead to any calamity; rather they stimulated and enriched philosophical thought in India. In one sense divergence of thought is the very condition of growth and development of real philosophy. A critical and sympathetic study of the history of Indian philosophies will bear out the position we have put forward.

It may be hoped that the importance and utility of the study of Indian philosophy in all its varieties and branches will not be denied by any serious student of human thought. It has all the strength and weakness of human life, and we are inclined to believe that the life of philosophy in ancient and medieval India was never languid or at a low ebb. There is a prevalent superstition that too much interest in philosophy brought about the political downfall of India. It is said that Indians were more interested in the problems of the next world than in the stern realities of present life. Things of the earth were looked upon with contempt. Like the proverbial star-gazer of old their eyes were fixed upon heaven and the result was a deterioration of physical and economic prosperity. It enervated the people and paved the way for foreign invasion. This charge against Indian philosophy has the apparent sanction of history, and the present degradation and misery of India lend an easy justification for same. But here also we beg to differ. The downfall of India is not the result of vigorous pursuit of philosophy in the past. The vulgar mind easily detects a family relationship between culture and indolence and outward appearance yields an easy support to this facile condemnation. But this very accusation carries with itself its own condemnation and a lesson for the necessity of close thinking, which refuses to be led away by appearances and dares penetrate deep below the surface. The average mind will put a premium on physical and tangible results and will ignore or slur over the hidden springs of activity. But all grand achievements of mankind have a prolonged preparation behind them. They are but the outward expression and efflorescence of a long-drawn-out intellectual discipline. Ultimately it is the brain that works and moves the body, though its activity is not apparent to the superficial observer. In point of fact all great political upheavals came after a long course of philosophical discipline. Though the causal relation is not easily discoverable, the coincidence is significant. Alexander came after Socrates, Plato and Aristotle. Candragupta and Aśoka came after the Buddha. These may be regarded as chance coincidences, pure and simple. But look at the life of the Buddhist monks, who are believed to be apostles of peace and exponents of a negative philosophy. The extra-worldly interests of the Buddhists are too well-known to need emphasis. But were they a lot of idlers ? The answer is an emphatic 'No.' These peace-loving Buddhists crossed the Himalayas and the seas, at considerable personal risk and in the face of deterring privations and discomforts, to preach the gospel of the impermanence of the world and the message of peace. The great protagonist of *Vedānta*, I mean Śaṅkarācārya, whose philosophy is believed to have weaned away the Indian masses from their worldly interests and thus hastened the political downfall of India was, however, one of the most indefatigable workers that the world knows. Were these philosophers then false to their own teaching ? The truth lies rather in the contrary supposition. There is no antagonism between a vigorous philosophy and a vigorous life. It is only when the living inspiration dies and people fall out of tune with true philosophy that they sink down to idleness. It is lack of intellectual vigour and mental lassitude that are at the root of national despair and degeneration. The vulgar mind, which will not and cannot probe deep into the bottom and through sheer inertia take the surface-appearance for the reality, causally connects the two events, though the distance of time and presence of other factors will prove the hollowness of the conclusion to the discerning student. Philosophy stirs up the intellect and disciplines the will and prepares a man for great sacrifice, without which nothing great has ever been achieved in the world. We must therefore learn to pay no heed to the croakers and Philistines who find nothing but waste of time and energy in the pursuit of philosophy. They look for direct practical results. But philosophy is slow in its results direct or indirect. Then, again, its results are more often than not apt to be affiliated to the immediate causes preceding them. Only a penetrating insight and a sturdy intellect, that can look long and far, deep and sure, can appraise them at their true worth and find out the truth. Whatever may be the case, the truth can be proclaimed from house-tops that philosophy, which trains the intellect and makes it active and alert, can never encourage idleness. It is a libel against philosophy which seems to have acquired plausibility by sheer reiteration. It will be a calamity if men are not found who will pursue the enquiry after truth irrespective of the opinion of the masses and consideration of material advantages. The present degradation of India is the result not of pursuit of philosophy but rather of the want of it. It is the result of the death of philosophy, of the unreasoning and unquestioning acquiescence in the inevitable, which all philosophy in India condemns in unqualified and unequivocal language.

We now propose to turn our attention to the special claims of Buddhist philosophy on our thought. Buddhist philosophy, particularly of the *Mahāyāna* schools, came as a challenge and as a surprise to the happy-go-lucky and self-complacent attitude of contemporary philosophers. It gave a tremendous shock to the naïve, common-sense realism of the *Nyāya-Vaiśeṣika* and *Mīmāṁsā* schools. By its bold denial of a permanent ego-principle it invited and called forth the indignant protests of the entire philosophical world. The self-complacent realism of the *Vaibhāṣikas* was unceremoniously brushed aside and covered with ridicule and contempt equally with the Brāhmaṇical and *Jaina* schools of thought. The *Yogācāra* school by advocating an extreme form of subjective idealism, with its consequent denial of the objective world, came in for vigorous attacks from the realistic and absolutistic schools alike. The climax was reached when Nāgārjuna and his followers propounded their philosophy of absolute negativism with its undisguised distrust of the empirical testimony of our sense and intellect. The result was an all-round panic and confusion. It provoked vigorous thought and spirited criticism. Whatever might be the merits of these philosophies, one thing is certain and undeniable that they produced the expected result ; they broke the placid contentment of the contemporary philosophic thought in India. They created a sense of alarm and thus gave the fillip to vigorous thinking in all schools to look out for the ways and means to protect their vested interests. But, however formidable might have been these Buddhist philosophies, the most upsetting were the dialectics of Dignāga and Dharmakīrti and their redoubtable successors. This is evidenced by the vitriolic attacks of the Brāhmaṇical and *Jaina* philosophical writings of the period.

The present work concerns itself with this school of Buddhist philosophy and logic. It is the result of long years of study and thought. The present writer has endeavoured to present the philosophy of Dignāga's school with all its strength and purity. The plan and arrangement are entirely original and a critical student of Buddhist philosophy will, it is hoped, not fail to detect in this book the working of a modern and critical mind. The subtle dialectic of the Buddhist philosophers is difficult in the extreme and demands the utmost critical thought and minutest attention from the student It will be too much to expect that these difficulties have been minimised by the present attempt. But the present writer hopes that his exposition is at least easier than that in the original works. Nowhere has there been an attempt, conscious or deliberate, to avoid the difficulties. The present writer has boldly faced the difficulties and has tried his level best to present them to the modern mind in an intelligible form. Fidelity to the original has been the watch-word and motto with his humble self and, though the thoughts and arguments have been presented in the language of a modern thinker, there has not been the slightest departure from the original. The idea has all along been to let the philosophers speak for themselves and where linguistic and verbal fidelity threatened obscurity, he has not hesitated to give a free rendering of their ideas and thoughts without regard to the peculiarities of Sanskrit idiom. Nevertheless, there are places where the technicalities of Indian philosophy and dialectic have been presented in their original form and this has been done deliberately with a view to acquainting the student with the methodology of ancient thinkers.

In conclusion the attention of the reader is particularly invited to the chapters 'The objections from the point of view of causation' and 'A critical estimate of the *Sautrāntika* theory of Causation,' 'Universals,' 'The doctrine of *Apoha,*' and '*Nirvāṇa*' in the first part and to 'Universal Concomitance' in the second part. Although the main character of this work is expository and the author has had to play the rôle of an advocate for the most part, it will be found that on some fundamental points he has not hesitated to criticize the Buddhist position where he has not been able to see eye to eye with them. In short, an attempt has been made to give a critical and dispassionate presentation of the Buddhist philosophy of Universal Flux and, in this, particular care has been taken to steer clear of a partisan spirit.

A word of explanation seems to be necessary for my designating the philosophy of Dignāga's school, in so far as it is presented in this book, as the philosophy of Critical Realism. The word 'critical' was adopted by Kant as the special appellation of his philosophy. This has not stood in the way of a school of American Realists from describing their system of philosophy as 'critical.' For similar reasons I too have not hesitated to adopt this expressive term in my designation of the realistic philosophy of Dignāga's school. I felt that to put the same label on this philosophy and on that of the *Nyāya-Vaiśeṣika* school would be inappropriate and rather misleading. In fact, the philosophy of Dignāga's school, in so far as it is realistic, will be found to have greater affinities with Kant's philosophy than with the commonsense naïve Realism of the *Nyāya-Vaiśeṣika* and *Mīmāṁsā* schools. Like Kant the Buddhist Realist thinks the categories of thought and reality as *a priori* subjective concepts and the difference lies in the latter's insistence on the evidentiary value of sensation, in which the thing-in-itself (*svalakṣaṇa*) is believed to be presented in its pure and unsullied character. Kant, however, thinks that the things-in-themselves are never revealed to the mind and as such, they are bound to remain unknown and unknowable. In spite of this fundamental divergence the two schools are found to agree in the proposition that all determinate knowledge, which is knowledge in the real sense of the term, is the result of a synthesis of an *a priori* and an *a posteriori* element. In view of this agreement with Kant and of its fundamental difference in outlook and attitude from the other Realistic philosophies of India and Europe, the designation of 'Critical Realism' may not be looked upon as an unwarrantable misappropriation of a respectable term.

PART I

METAPHYSICS

THE BUDDHIST DOCTRINE OF FLUX

CHAPTER I

The Nature of Existence

The whole universe of reals has been classified by the *Naiyāyikas* under two exclusive heads, *viz.*, *kṛtakas* (products or perishable) and *akṛtakas* (non-products or imperishable). The *Vātsīputrīyas*, an independent school of Buddhists, however, have grouped all realities under two classes, *viz.*, *kṣaṇika* (momentary) and *akṣaṇika* (non-momentary). Whatever principle of classification be adopted, the conclusion is inevitable that non-eternal entities must be momentary, as they are perishable by their very nature and constitution. Now, if a thing is perishable by its very nature and consitution, it will perish in the very next moment of its birth independently of the service of an external agent. If, however, it is not constitutionally perishable, it must be imperishable and no amount of external force, that may be brought to bear upon it, can make it cease to exist, as a thing cannot forfeit its own nature and assume that of another and yet continue to remain the same entity as before. And there is no medium between momentary and non-momentary, the two classes embracing the whole universe of thought and reality. To suppose, therefore, that a thing may be perishable by its nature and constitution and yet must be dependent upon an external agent to bring about its destruction, involves a necessary absurdity.

It has been urged that as a thing is seen to perish in a determinate place and time, its destruction must be contingent upon an extraneous cause and so long as this destructive agent does not appear, it will naturally continue to exist. The hypothesis of spontaneous destruction is opposed to experience and hence unacceptable. There is no absurdity in supposing that a thing may be perishable by nature and yet may be dependent on an external cause for its destruction, quite as much as a seed, which, though possessed of a natural aptitude for producing a sprout, is seen to effectuate a sprout subject to its association with water, air, soil, and the like and not independently. Experience also shows that hard metals like copper and the like are liquefied, when impinged upon by the flames of fire, but revert to their pristine condition of hardness when the heat communicated by fire is withdrawn. A jug continues to exist until it is crushed by the stroke of a club. So the dialectic of natural constitution—that if a thing is perishable by its nature it will perish by itself—should be accepted with a qualification, in the light of experience, *viz.*, as subject to action by a destructive agent.

The whole argument of the opponent, however, is vitiated by a misreading of facts. The analogy of the seed is pointless as the seed *per se* is not the cause of the sprout, but the particular seed-entity, vested with sprout-producing efficiency, that emerges in the final stage immediately before the sprout is produced. The hard copper is no firm and obdurate entity but is in continual flux ; and when associated with the subsidiary causes, fire and the like, it gives rise to another distinct entity liquid in nature and, when other circumstances supervene, the liquid moments disappear and hard moments manifest themselves. The theory of an external, destructive agent, on the other hand, gives rise to logical complications. The destructive agent, requisitioned for the destruction of an entity, can be posited if it has any effect on the thing to be destroyed ; but this effect will transpire to be illusory on examination. Well, what can be the nature of this effect? Is it the production of another entity or non-existence of the previous entity? On the former alternative, a destructive agent has no useful function, as a thing is brought into existence by its own proper cause, which is the immediate, antecedent entity. And to say that the cause of a succeeding event is the cause of the destruction of the previous entity is to say that destruction is self-caused and spontaneous, which is our position. The second alternative that the destructive agent causes non-existence of the previous entity is equally untenable, as only an entity can be produced and non-existence being produced will be an entity—which is absurd. And if this supposed non-existence is identical with the thing that is produced, the cause of destruction as distinct from the previous entity need not be postulated. Moreover, the destructive agent must be supposed to produce an effect on the thing to be destroyed. And is this effect something distinct from the thing on which it is produced or not distinct? If distinct, it will not destroy the thing, as there is no relation between the two. On the latter alternative, it is useless as nothing new is produced. Aviddhakarṇa, an old *Naiyāyika*, whose opinions are frequently quoted in the *Tattvasaṁgraha*, but who has been entirely forgotten by the later Brāhminical writers, has taken strong exception to the Buddhist position that destruction is spontaneous. He argues, destruction is neither contemporaneous with, nor antecedent to, an entity, but a subsequent event occurring in the next moment, as the Buddhist too would have it. And so being an event occurring at a determinate point of time it must have a cause and cannot be spontaneous.

Uddyotakara, again, has attacked the Buddhist position in the following arguments: if destruction is uncaused, it will be either non-existent like a barren woman's son or an eternal entity like ether (*ākāśa*), as no medium is possible between the two. If it is non-existent, all entities will be eternal, as they will not be subject to destruction and consequently the conception of perishability of all composite bodies will be an unfounded myth. If it is eternal, it will co-exist with all entities—an absurd position, as existence and non-existence, which is the connotation of destruction, are mutually contradictory. If co-existence is denied, there will be no birth, as eternal destruction will preclude all production.

All the objections, the Buddhist rejoins, proceed from a confusion of the meaning of the word 'destruction!' Now, this word, 'destruction' can have two possible meanings: in the first place, it may mean the fluxional nature of all entities; in the second place, it may connote absolute cessation of existence (*bhāvasvarūpa-nivṛtti*). Destruction in the first sense does not connote any negative idea; it only implies that things are in a state of continual flux, that an entity endures only for a moment, yielding place to another entity emerging into being. So if destruction means the fluxional nature of an entity, it does not militate against our position, as we also admit it to have a cause, but as the cause is inherent in its own constitution and nothing foreign to its nature, we style it uncaused. But this fluxional character is nothing distinct from the entity itself and as such cannot be regarded as a subsequent event in regard to its own self, although there is nothing to prevent it from being conceived as a subsequent event in regard to the immediately preceding entity. Destruction in this sense exists and accordingly the conception of the perishability of composite bodies (*saṁskṛta*) is not an unfounded illusion.

Destruction, in the sense of absolute cessation of existence, is, however, an unreal fiction. Pure negation is an abstract idea and has no existence and so cannot be an event, which means the coming into existence of an entity which was previously non-existent. It is as unreal as a sky-lotus and to affirm existence, previous or subsequent, of it is an absurdity. When we say that there is a cessation of existence, we only mean that a thing passes out of existence and not that non-being exists or occurs. It is a meaningless expression. What we seek to establish is that cessation of existence in the sense of pure non-being cannot be an objective category. So the contention of Uddyotakara that the negation of non-being will entail eternal existence of all entities falls to the ground, because all real beings, fluxional in nature, will pass out of existence in the second moment without any gratuitous help from an external entity. The whole contention of Uddyotakara proceeds on the assumption that negation is an objective category, but, as we have seen, it is only an ideal fiction and not a concrete fact, as the *Nyāyavaiśeṣika* school postulates.

The whole allegation of Uddyotakara, that all uncaused entities are either eternal verities or non-entities and negation being an uncaused fact will be eternal, has no force against the *Sautrāntika* philosopher. The *Sautrāntika* does not admit any eternal, uncaused category. The *Vaibhāṣikas*, however, allege that there are three eternal verities, *viz.*, *ākāśa* (space) *pratisaṅkhyānirodha* (dissociation of the mind from impurities effected by transcendental knowledge) and *apratisaṅkhyānirodha* (non-emergence due to absence of causes).[1] But these *Vaibhāṣikas* are not regarded by us as the true followers of the Buddha. They are grouped along with the other heretical schools of thought, *viz.*, the *Naiyāyikas* and the like. The *Sautrāntikas*, who maintain the doctrine of universal flux, have no place in their scheme of realities for an uncaused category. These so-called eternal verities are ideal fictions (*sāṁvṛtas*), pure and simple. Uddyotakara in fathering this doctrine upon the *Sautrāntikas* only betrays his ignorance of the Buddhist position.[2]

As regards the so-called non-perishable entities such as space, time, God and the like, they are mere fictions of imagination

[1] The import and nature of these three eternal categories of the *Vaibhāṣikas* will be elucidated in the chapter on *Nirvāṇa*.

[2] 'Yaccoktam akāraṇam bhavato dvidhā nityam asacceti, tat parasiddhāntānabhijñatayā, yato nyāyavādināṁ bauddhānām akāraṇam asadeva .... ye ca Vaibhāṣikā ākāśādivastu sattvena kalpayanti, te yuṣmatpakṣa eva nikṣiptā na śākyaputrīyā iti na tanmatopanyāso nyāyāt'—Kamalaśīla Pañjikā, p. 140, *Tattvasaṁgraha*.

and do not exist as objective realities, as the connotation of reality is causal efficiency (*artha-kriyākāritva*) and no causal efficiency is predicable of them. And if these be real entities, as you claim, they must be momentary existents, as causal efficiency is predicable only of things that are momentary. No other definition of reality except causal efficiency can be logically sound. Let us examine the definitions of reality as proposed by the *Naiyāyikas*. *Sattāsambandha* or *sattāsamavāya* (participation or co-inherence in universal existence) is not a tenable definition, as *samavāya* is a form of relation and all relations are unreal. And even if it is allowed, universality (*sāmānya*), particularity (*viśeṣa*) and co-inhesion (*samavāya*), which do not participate in the universal, will have no existence. Nor is the attribution of a *sui generis* existence to each of them a clever hypothesis, as this means too many different types of existence. Moreover, these tentative definitions are confuted by the following dilemma : Is this *sui generis* existence (*svarūpasattā*) something different from existence as such or not different ? In the former alternative, it will be non-existence and the categories concerned will be unreal. In the latter, the *sui generis* existence will be unmeaning, as there is nothing to differentiate it from existence as such and the categories will be lumped into one. So also with regard to the other categories, *viz.*, substance, attribute and action. If they are identical with existence as such, there is no excuse of their being regarded as separate categories and if they are different, they will have no existence of their own. So we see that the very categories of the *Naiyāyika* are reduced to unreal fictions by his own definition.[1] The poor *Naiyāyika* finds himself

[1] The universal (*sāmānya*) cannot participate in any other universal, as this will lead to infinite regression. The universal too cannot be attached to particularity, as in that case the particular will cease to be particular, if it becomes universal in any form. Co-inherence is regarded as one, invisible, eternal relation obtaining between the universal and the particular, substance and attribute, part and whole. There can be no universal relating to this entity, as the idea of the universal presupposes a number of concrete

in the predicament of defining existence as one that is 'existence,' which amounts to a confession of failure.[1]

But what does demarcate such unreal fictions as a rabbit's horn and the like from things which are real ? Well, it is causal efficiency alone and as these fictions cannot possess any causal efficiency, they must be set down as unreal. An objection has been raised that reality cannot be supposed to consist in causal efficiency, as causal efficiency exists even in such unreal fictions as a sky-lotus and the like. These fictions certainly generate an impression in the mind and thus have causal efficiency in that respect, but they cannot be accepted as real on that account. Moreover, in dreams and illusions, unreal things are seen to have practical efficiency. The false snake in the rope is as much a cause of trepidation as the real one, and sometimes a man is seen to develop all the symptoms of poisoning and on some occasions to die, because he was falsely persuaded that he was bitten by a snake. And a dream-elephant is seen to be as powerful as a real elephant of our wakeful experience. If you make causal efficiency the sole test of reality, you will be painfully obliged to accord reality to those fictions.

The Buddhist replies that predication of causal efficiency relates to an objective reality and does not include subjective fictions. In dreams and illusions the objects that are experienced, are not real, objective facts, but are evolved from the imagination. The contents of these experiences are but the objectified memory-impressions and have no existence, outside the experiencing mind. It will be a sheer perversion of facts to apply to these mental fictions the standard of reality, which belongs to objective facts. Such unreal fictions, as sky-lotus and

individuals sharing in it and as *samavāya* is one, the question of its being a universal cannot arise. See *Kirṇāavali*: vyakter abhedas tulyatvaṁ saṅkaro ' thā' navasthitiḥ । rūpahānir asambandho jātibādhakasaṁgrahaḥ ॥

[1] Compare in this connexion the observations of Prof. Mctaggart in his 'Nature of Existence,' Ch. I, Sec. 5.

the like, are purely subjective facts without any objective foundation and as causal efficiency has been postulated as the test of an objective reality, it cannot have any application to these fictitious representations of the imagination. When we deny causal efficiency to these ideal fictions, we deny it in the sense of their being objective realities. All these objections could be enforced if we held with Kumārila and the *Naiyāyikas* that illusions and dreams were conversant about realities.[1] But according to our theory these experiences are purely subjective and are absolutely devoid of any objective reference. Causal efficiency therefore stands unrefuted as the test and definition of reality, as reality connotes real, substantive facts and not subjective fictions.[2]

And causal efficiency is exercisable either in succession or simultaneity and as simultaneity and succession are incompatible with the supposed permanent entity, causal efficiency is restricted to the momentary, fluxional entity alone. One may legitimately enquire : Why is it that practical efficiency cannot be predicated of a non-fluxional, permanent entity ? Because it is redargued by the following dilemma : Has your "permanent" power of past and future practical efficiency during its exertion of present practical efficiency or no ? If it has such power, it cannot fail to execute the past and future actions exactly as it does its present action, because the execution of an action is the inevitable consequence of such efficiency, which it is conceded to possess. And there is no reason why there should be any delay in the effectuation of such actions as the causal

[1] Kumārila holds that even memory and dream experiences contain an objective reference like perception. The contents of these experiences are real, objective facts, though in dreams and illusions these facts are presented under a wrong spatio-temporal relation. Nothing but an existing fact can become an object of experience and so the objects of dreams and illusions even are real facts though the spatial and temporal relations are perverted, *cf.* "svapnādipratyaye bāhyaṁ sarvathā nahi neṣyate | sarvatrālambanaṁ bāhyam deśakālānyathātmakam ||" *Śloka-vārttika*, p. 242.

[2] *Vide Tattvasaṁgraha*, verses 425-427.

efficiency is present intact. The point at issue can be brought home by the following argument.

That, which has causal efficiency in respect of anything, does execute that thing without fail, as for instance the full assemblage of causes. And this entity has past and future causal efficiency (and should therefore execute the past and future actions without fail). On the second alternative (if the permanent has no such efficiency of past and future agency), it will never do those actions, as exertion of practical efficiency results from power alone. The privation of past and future efficiency in the permanant can be specifically driven home by the following syllogism: What at any time does not do anything, that at that time is incapable of doing it, as for instance, a gravel is unable to produce a sprout. And this "permanent" does not execute its past and future actions during its execution of present action (and consequently does not possess the power for the same).

It is proved beyond doubt that this supposed "permanent" has present practical efficiency, but it does not of a surety possess its past and future efficiency. And as co-existence of efficiency and non-efficiency, two contradictory qualities, is not possible in a single entity, the conclusion is irresistible that the present entity is distinct from the past and the future entity and is thus fluxional. It may be urged that causal efficiency may exist in a thing without the effect being produced and this is confirmed by the fact that the seed in the granary is regarded as the cause of the sprout, though the sprout is not immediately produced. But this objection is based upon a misconception. In ordinary parlance, a remote, possible cause is said to possess causal efficiency. But this is a loose, popular conception and cannot be made the basis of a philosophical enquiry. In reality, however, the cause of the sprout is the peculiar seed-entity that immediately and invariably produces the sprout. The seed in the granary is regarded as the cause of the sprout only in view of a remote possibility. So there is no room for confusion between a real cause, which is immediately and invariably attended with an effect, and a remote possible cause, which can be regarded as a cause only by courtesy.

But the *Naiyāyikas* and other realists demur to accept the position of the Buddhist set forth above. They urge that fluxional cause could be accepted if the invariable concomitance of causal efficiency with momentariness was established. But this is impossible. It is quite plausible that a permanent entity, though it is the sole and sufficient cause, can exercise its causal efficiency only in conjunction with subsidiaries and as these subsidiaries occur in succession, successive execution of past and future actions is not incompetent to a permanent cause. The cause does not independently produce the effect as it develops its causal efficiency only in association with its subsidiaries. The production of the effect is contingent upon the co-presence of the subsidiaries and so does not take place when the set of subsidiaries is absent. The presence and absence of the subsidiaries, however, do not at all affect the real nature of the cause, as the cause is entirely distinct from them.

The co-presence of subsidiaries, the Buddhist observes, is an idle hypothesis. If the permanent develops its causal efficiency on its own account and is not at all assisted by the subsidiaries, the latter become absolutely useless. And if the peculiar effect-producing efficiency, that manifests itself in the last moment, is identical with its past nature, nothing can prevent the production of the effect.[1] If this nature is a different one, you cannot claim the previous entity as the cause. And if you suppose that the cause has not undergone any mutation, production becomes impossible, as its previous inefficiency will persist. But it may be contended that the permanent entity is one of the causes, and not the sole and sufficient cause. It is the entire collocation of causes (*sāmagrī*) that produces the effect and not the cause alone, however powerful it might be. The relation between cause and effect is not one of mutual necessary implication (*anyayoga-vyavaccheda*), but non-separation with one term

[1] *Vide* SBNT., p. 27, 11, 6-9.

lying independent (*ayogavyavaccheda*) as in invariable concomitance (*vyāpti*). Thus, as in *vyāpti*, the *probandum* can exist without the *probans*, though the *probans* cannot, so also a cause can exist independently of the effect, though not the effect. And in this conception of causal relation the popular view and philosophers' estimate do coincide.[1]

Well, we Buddhists, have no quarrel with you on the point that several factors combine to produce a self-same effect. What we contend for is that a permanent cause cannot *ex hypothesi* stand in need of any auxiliary factors. If the invariable efficient or inefficient nature of the permanent continues, there will be either production or non-production of the effect for all times. So there is no logic in the position of the upholders of the permanent entity that it is the full collocation of causes and not a single cause, that is productive of the effect. We have it from experience that several causal factors combine to produce a self-identical effect and we do not challenge this position. But the point at issue is whether the "permanent" undergoes any mutation or not. If there is no mutation, either production or non-production will be inevitable, as indicated above. If,

[1] Tasmād vyāptivat kāryakāraṇabhāvo 'py ekatra anyayogavyavacchedena, anyatra ayoga-vyabacchedenā' va boddhavyaḥ, tathaiva laukikaparīkṣakāṇāṁ sampratipatteḥ (*op. cit.*, p. 37). *Vyāpti* is the invariable concomitance of the *probans* (middle term) with the *probandum* and this is the very ground and *conditio sine qua non* of all inference. This relation is stated in the major premiss of Aristotelian syllogism, in which the middle term is invariably distributed, though not necessarily the major term, which may be taken in its entire or partial extension according to circumstances. Accordingly *vyāpti* has been spoken of as of two distinct types, to wit (1) *samavyāpti* in which the two terms are co-extensive and (2) *asamavyāpti*, in which the *probandum* is of wider extension than the *probans*. The contention is whether the relation of causality is of necessity one of co-extensive concomitance or may be a relation of unequal extension with one term wider than, and hence independent of, the other. The Buddhist maintains the former view and the *Naiyāyika* affirms the latter possibility with emphasis.

however, the permanent mutates, it ceases to be permanent. And this dilemma is unavoidable. No reliance again can be placed on recognition ((*pratyabhijñā*), on the strength of whose testimony the unchanged identity of the cause could be established. Recognition is an unsafe guide, as we see there is recognition even in the case of growing hair and nails and the like. Apparently therefore the relation of cause and effect is one of mutual necessary implication and not non-separation with one term lying independent, as the *Naiyāyika* affirms. The analogy of *vyāpti* is inapplicable, as *vyāpti* is a relation between two concepts and not entities and as concepts are remotely related to reals, the relation is found to congrue with facts. But the cause, you posit, has a real existence as distinct from conceptual existence.[1] An objection is sometimes raised in this connection that as there is no permanent entity, according to the Buddhist, he cannot have any experience of such, much less can he make it the term of a syllogistic argument. And if he has direct or indirect experience of such permanent entity, he cannot consistently deny his own experience. When he asserts that the "permanent" cannot have causal efficiency, he admits the existence of the permanent and cannot deny it without contradicting himself. The objection is a frivolous one, but will be dwelt on at length in a separate section, because the *Naiyāyikas* have made capital out of this.[2] Suffice it to say here that the

1 tasmāt sākṣāt kārya-kāraṇa-bhāvāpekṣayā ubhayatrāpy anyayoga-vyavacchedaḥ. vyāptau tu sākṣāt paramparayā kāraṇamātrāpekṣayā kāraṇe vyāpake ayogavyavacchedaḥ kārye vyāpye anyayogavyavacchedaḥ ......vikalpārūḍharūpāpekṣayā vpāptau dvividham avadhāraṇam. SBNT., pp. 38-39.

2 *Cf.* 'The Nature of Existence:' "It has been objected to this that, *e.g.*, the fourth angle of a triangle must be real, if we can predicate anything of it with truth. And thus any predication of unreality would contradict itself. But this seems to me to be mistaken. In order to make any predication about anything, I must have an idea of that thing, and the idea—the psychical event in my mind—must be real. But a real idea of such an angle does not involve the reality of the angle." P. 1, fn. 2.

permanent in our syllogism is a hypothetical entity and not an experiential fact. What we mean by the "permanent" is this: if the nature of causal efficiency, that is evinced in the subsequent entity, be the same with the nature of the previous entity, or if the inefficient nature of the previous entity be identical with the efficient nature of the subsequent entity, there will be either production or non-production of the effect always. So we do not go beyond our experiential data, as the efficient and the non-efficient momentary entities are real objective facts. What we seek to prove is that there can be no identity between the two entities on pain of either of the undesirable issues, *viz.*, constant production or non-production.

It has been sufficiently proved that a self-sufficient permanent cause can have no need of auxiliaries, which can have no function. If, however, these auxiliaries are supposed really to assist the main cause, they can have a legitimate function and can become necessary. But if they assist, they will produce some supplementation (*atiśaya*) in the causal entity and the question naturally arises as to the nature of its relation to the causal entity. Is this supplementation something distinct or non-distinct from the thing on which it is produced? If it is distinct from the causal entity, then this adventitious supplementation will be the cause and not the non-fluxional entity; for the effect will follow, by concomitance and non-concomitance, the adventitious supplemetation.[1] In this case, causal efficiency will be possible only in the momentary, fluxional entity and not the permanent, which the opponent has sought to prove. If the supplementation is considered to be non-distinct, that is to say, identical with the permanent causal entity, we ask whether the previous inefficient nature continues or ceases to exist. On the former alternative, there will be no production, as the previous inefficiency will operate as a bar. On the second

1 "tasmin sati hi kāryāṇām utpādas tadabhāvataḥ | anutpādāt sa evaivaṁ hetutvena vyavasthitaḥ ||" T. S. Kār, p. 400.

alternative, the previous inefficient entity has ceased and a new entity identical with supplementation, designated in Buddhist technology as *Kurvadrūpa* (effect-producing object) comes into being and so the cause becomes fluxional.

The hypothesis of the permanent cause as discharging successive functions in association with successive subsidiaries, has transpired to be illusory. But there may be another alternative, *viz.*, that a permanent entity exerts its several causal efficiencies all at once and not in succession. But this will not stand the following dilemma. This "permanent," endued with the power of producing all its effects simultaneously, either continues to exist or does not continue after production of its effects. On the first alternative there will be production of all its effects just as much at one time as at another. On the second, the expectation of its permanency is as reasonable as expecting a seed, eaten by a mouse, to germinate.[1]

The *Naiyāyika* will perhaps seek shelter under his precious theory of *samavāya* (co-inherence)—a relation, which, they claim, has the miraculous efficiency of harmonising identity with difference. Certainly the subsidiaries produce some supplementation in the permanent causal entity, but the supplementation, though a distinct entity, coinheres in the causal entity and thus becomes a part and parcel of its being. But the question naturally arises that if the supplementation in question is something distinct, how can it have a relation with the basic entity without producing another supplementation. And this second supplementation, too, being a distinct entity, will hang loose and can be connected with the help of another supplementation and so on *ad infinitum*. The co-inherence theory thus transpires to be a dodge to take in the credulous, unenquiring fellows. But the never-ending series of supplementations is not the only difficulty in the theory of successive subsidiaries. There are

[1] dvitīye sthāyitvavṛttyāśā mūṣikabhakṣitabījādāv aṅkurādijananaprārthanām anuharet. SDS., p. 24.

many-sided regressions in *infinitum*. There will be infinite regressions of all the factors involved in production. Thus, the seed, the subsidiaries, and supplementation are the three necessary conditions of production. We have seen that there will be a never-ending series of supplementations and these supplementations can be produced with the help of subsidiaries. And these subsidiaries can be of help if they produce supplementation in the supplementations themselves—otherwise they will not be required. Thus, there will be an infinite chain of supplementations afforded by the subsidiaries. So with regard to the basal cause and so with regard to the subsidiaries in their mutual relations. It is plain, therefore, that nothing can be explained by relations, as these relations will for ever fall apart and infinite regressions in each and every case will be inevitable. But the theory of flux is wonderfully immune from these difficulties—as it does not posit any relation at all. The factors being momentary units stand self-contained and self-sufficient.

Relations are requisitioned to harmonise permanence with change, but we have seen how they fail. Permanence and change, being mutually contradictory, cannot be made to constitute a harmonious whole even by virtue of these relations, which have been exposed to be hollow devices.

Trilocana,[1] the teacher of Vācaspati Miśra, contends that the whole controversy of the Buddhist turns upon a false basis. The permanent cause is absolutely independent of the subsidiaries and is not at all assisted or benefited by them. It is the effect

[1] From frequent references to, and quotations of opinions of, Trilocana made by Ratnakīrti in his treatises on '*Apoha*' and '*Kṣaṇabhaṅgasiddhi*' it can be legitimately inferred that Trilocana was an author of repute and he must have written either a commentary or an independent standard work on *Nyāya* philosophy. It is certainly a pity that all his works are lost. That Trilocana profoundly influenced Vācaspati Miśra is not open to doubt, as the latter has recorded his debt to the former in unmistakable language. (*Cf.* Trilocana-gurūnnītamārgānugamanonmukhaiḥ । yathāmānaṁ yathāvastu vyākhyātam idam īdṛśam ॥ Tāt. Ṭ., p. 133.)

which is so benefited being dependent upon the subsidiaries as it cannot come into being if the set of subsidiaries be absent. For, causal power (*sāmarthya*) is of two kinds : natural and adventitious, the latter consisting in the presence of subsidiaries. There is no logical difficulty, therefore, that the cause does not produce the effect always, as the requisite power constituted by the subsidiaries is lacking. But this is mere shifting of the ground. How can the effect, which is not yet born, have any necessity for the subsidiaries? We could accept this view, however, if the effect could independently come into being. But then the subsidiaries and all that they connote become unavailing. If the effect is independent, how can the seed be the cause? And if the seed is the cause, why should it fail to produce the effect? Nor is it supposable that the effects are perverse and sometimes do not come into being inspite of the causes, as in that case they will not be the effects of those causes. But it may be contended that a particular entity is regarded as the effect of a cause, not because it happens when the cause is there, but because it disappears when the cause disappears. But this interpretation of causal relation is indefensible. Logically we can set down the absence of the effect to the absence of the cause, only if the presence of the effect is dependent upon the presence of the cause. Otherwise the effect will be independent of the cause and the disappearance of the cause will not entail the disappearance of the effect. So the presence of the cause must be invariably followed by the presence of the effect, just as much as the absence of it is followed by the absence of the other. Otherwise the so-called cause will cease to be the cause at all.[1] Nyāyabhūṣaṇa[2] however, contends that the argument, that a

[1] " tadbhāve'pi na bhāvaśced abhāve' bhāvitā kutaḥ ।
tadabhāvaprayuktaśca so'bhāva iti tat kutaḥ ॥ " SBNT., p. 41.

[2] Nyāyabhūṣaṇa is the name of a very old commentary on the Nyāyasāra of Bhāsarvajña and it exercised a very pronounced influence on the later development of Nyāya thought and perhaps created a sub-section of

cause should discharge all its future functions even while it discharges its present function, because the future causal efficiency is present in it at the time, is a case of plain self-contradiction just like the statement—'My mother is barren.' How can the future causal efficiency function in the present? If it did, it would cease to be future efficiency. Certainly causal efficiency for blue cannot result in the production of yellow.

The contention of Nyāyabhūṣaṇa, Ratnakīrti observes, is but a mere jugglery with words. If the permanent cause possesses permanent causal efficiency, why should it function at some future time and not in the immediate present, on the basis of which future efficiency is postulated? The opponent may answer, 'because, we see it actually functioning in the future.' Yes, but as this is incompatible with its permanency, you should regard it as momentary. You cannot suppose that it is the nature of the permanent to function in the future, because such a supposition is logically absurd. A thing is supposed to have a particular nature only when there is logical necessity for such a supposition; and no hypothesis, however convenient, can be accepted if it violates the canons of logic.[1] The Buddhist

thinkers, who were called Bhūṣaṇīyās. See *Bibliography of Nyāya Philosophy* by Principal Gopīnāth Kavirāj and the introduction to *Nyāya-sāra* by Dr. S. C. Vidyābhūṣaṇa.

[1] SBNT., pp. 41-42.

References:

T. S., ślս. 350-546.

SBNT., pp. 20-53.

It may be interesting to observe in this connection that Mr. Bertrand Russell arrives at the same conclusion that there is no persistence in the world, each entity being momentary and the idea of persistence is only an illusion due to continuity in the series. He takes his cue from the cinematograph and avers that not only the cinema-man, but "The real man too, I believe, however the police may swear to his identity, is really a series of momentary men, each different one from the other, and bound together, not by a numerical identity, but by continuity and certain intrinsic laws. And what applies to men applies equally to tables and chairs,

therefore concludes that as the theory of permanent cause fails to explain facts and on the contrary introduces logical compli-

the sun, moon and stars. Each of these is to be regarded, not as one single persistent entity, but as a series of entities, succeeding each other in time, *and lasting only for a brief period, though probably not for a mere mathematical instant.*" (P. 129.) The Buddhist philosophers long ago anticipated Mr. Bertrand Russell and I am tempted to believe they are more logical and consistent than Mr. Russell. Mr. Russell seems to suffer from a confusion in this respect. His abhorrence for the "infinitesimal," which he borrows from modern mathematical speculations, is responsible for this aberration. Now, moments cannot be finite divisions of time, as this means that there are no moments at all. If a span of time consisting of many smaller divisions be regarded as the unit, the smaller divisions will have no meaning. The *mathematical instant*, of which he speaks, is not an empirical fact but a logical presupposition. Nor does the introduction of the "infinitesimal" re-open the gates of the puzzles of Zeno. The Buddhist philosopher does not admit the reality of motion. Motion is only a "logical construction" or a "symbolic fiction" to quote Mr. Russell's own words. There being no permanence anywhere in the world, no single thing can be in two places. The things are different and distinct. That the "arrow in its flight is truly at rest" (p. 81) is also the finding of the Buddhist philosopher, but only subject to a proviso, *viz.*, that the arrow is not one but many arrows successively appearing in the horizon, which give rise to the illusion of a persistent identity owing to continuity of similar entities. The Buddhist emphasises the aspect of similarity as the cause of the illusion of permanence, which Mr. Russell omits to emphasize. Continuity alone cannot be credited with this capacity for producing illusion, as continuity of dissimilar things does not have this effect. The syllables of a word are quickly uttered, but the quickness of succession does not stand in the way of their being perceived as discrete and distinct entities. So by continuity we must understand uninterrupted succession of similar entities, which should be emphasised for the sake of clarity and precision. The "intrinsic laws" of which Mr. Russell speaks, are regarded by the Buddhists as the law of causality, in the language of the Buddhist, as the law of relative origination (*pratītyasamutpāda*). The superstitions of ages which have clustered round the concept of cause have been smashed into smithereens by the sledgehammer blows of the Buddhist dialectic and it has been formulated in a manner which can be accepted without prejudice to facts. Mr. Russell seems to play into the hands of sceptics, when he declares

cations, which are insurmountable, the theory of flux should be adopted as it is the happiest possible explanation of the world of reality.

the causal relation to be a mere case of probability. The failure of prophecy, by which he sets so much store, does not go against the law of causality. It is due to imperfect knowledge. The nature of the causal relation will be explained in the third chapter of the present book and to ask for a logical *à priori* explanation will lead to scepticism or idealism, as will be shown in Chapter IV. *Vide Mysticism and Logic.*

CHAPTER II

Logical Difficulties explained

Section 1

The doctrine of flux rests on the fundamental principle that co-existence of two contradictory qualities is impossible in one and the same substratum and that this fact alone constitutes the ground of difference of mutually different objects. But even this fundamental position has been challenged. It is argued that there is no logical repugnance in the fact that a thing may possess different attributes without prejudice to its integrity. The Buddhist assumes that the seed which is admittedly the cause of the germinating sprout, is the cause as well of the supplementary phenomena, *viz.*, changed soil and the like, found in association with the sprout.[1] Now, is the causal efficiency in respect of the subsidiaries the same efficiency which produces the

1 This would appear to be an unusual view, but it follows from the Buddhist theory of causation, which will be elucidated in the next chapter. But I think it to be still necessary that something should be said in advance on this knotty issue, as I am afraid that the point may escape the reader. To be brief, the Buddhist holds that several factors, the basic cause and the subsidiaries, combine to produce a self-same effect. For instance, the sprout is believed to be the joint product of seed, soil, water and the like and each of these causal factors is credited with independent productive efficiency for the same. If we look closely we cannot fail to note that the sprout is not an isolated product, though perhaps the most remarkable and most expected, but that there are other phenomena associated with it, to wit, the changed

sprout? If the two efficiencies are identical, the soil, etc., and the sprout will be identical in nature. If, however, they are different, the self-same seed will be split up into different entities, because different efficiencies, being exclusive of each other, are mutually contradictory and cannot inhere in the same entity on your own theory. Such is the case with regard to the burning lamp, which consumes oil and burns the wick at the same time. And so also with regard to the colour-form amalgam (*rūpa*), which produces an after-entity vested with colour, taste and smell. And these effects being different from each other, presuppose different causal powers, which will spilt up the causal integer into so many different causal entities. Moreover, the seed is efficient in regard to the sprout but it is inefficient with respect to the ass and the like; and efficiency and inefficiency, being contradictory, will divide even one and the same seed-entity into different entities—a contingency which even the Buddhist will demur to accept. So efficiency and inefficiency can subsist in perfect accord in the same causal entity and cannot of necessity make it different at different moments. The whole plea of the Buddhist that contradictory attributes cannot co-exist in the same substratum therefore falls to the ground and with it his theory of flux.

These thinkers, the Buddhist observes, are obviously labouring under a confusion of thought. That a particular causal entity may possess different natural powers in the shape of different attributes without detriment to its integrity is not denied. What we seek to emphasise is that different attributes

soil, fermented water and so on. Now, what would be the cause of these phenomena? Certainly, the previous entities, *viz.*, the seed and the so-called subsidiaries, each in their individual capacities, as co-operation in the sense of mutual service is denied. So the seed should be looked upon as the cause not only of the sprout, but also of the other phenomena found together, precisely in the same fashion as the subsidiaries are believed to be the cause of the sprout.

may connote contrariety, but not contradictory opposition. Contradiction is a relation which exists between two particular terms—where the affirmation of one necessarily implies the denial of the other and *vice versa*—they being mutually exclusive. Thus, the existence of a particular power is contradictorily opposed by the non-existence of that power and not by the existence of a different power. The production of sprout is opposed by the non-production of sprout and not by the production of any other entity. Besides, perceptual evidence testifies to the identity of a particular entity though it might be possessed of manifold distinct attributes or powers. Thus, for instance a single jug is seen to possess two distinct attributes—substantiality (*dravyatva*) and the generic nature of a jug (*ghaṭatva*) and there is no contradiction between them. And even two contradictory qualities, *e. g.*, efficiency and non-efficiency, can co-exist without logical opposition in one and the same entity, provided they relate to different objects. There is no repugnance in the fact that the seed is efficient in regard to the sprout and not so in respect of the ass. But the opposition is manifest if two contradictory qualities are supposed to relate to one and the same substance. Thus we cannot conceive by any stretch of imagination that the two contradictory qualities, such as efficiency and non-efficiency in relation to the self-same product, can co-exist without splitting up the identity of the thing concerned. If there is no contradiction between such exclusive attributes, there will be no contradiction anywhere in the world and all distinctions will be nugatory.

It has been urged by the opponent that though contradiction is undeniable between two mutually exclusive attributes at one and the same time, there is no reason why these two characters may not be found in the same entity at different times. There is no contradiction in the fact that the self-same seed produces sprout in one place and does not do so in another place. And if efficiency and non-efficiency can co-exist without opposition in the same entity by virtue of the different place-relations, there is no earthly reason why there should be any opposition if two mutually exclusive attributes should appear in the same substratum if the time-factors are different. The same crystal that was inactive before, may become active at a subsequent moment, and the same seed that was lying inactive in the granary, may subsequently develop causal efficiency for sprout without involving any logical absurdity. There is no logical inconsistency between permanent efficiency and inconstant production subject to variation of time.

The whole controversy, the Buddhist rejoins, is based upon an apparent misapprehension. We do not hold that difference of place is an antidote to opposition in contradiction, we only insist that there is no contradiction in such cases. Causal efficiency in a particular place is opposed by its absence in that place only and not in a different place, nor by a different sort of efficiency. But this analogy of difference in place cannot be extended to difference in time, as contradiction is a relation of opposition constituted by two mutually incompatible attributes and time and place relations have no direct bearing upon it. The principal factor of contradiction is mutual incompatibility and as permanent efficiency has been redargued by the dialectical necessity of constant production or non-production, permanent efficiency and variable production have been found to be mutually incompatible. But as there is no incompatibility in the fact that the seed produces a sprout in a particular place but is inactive outside that place, we cannot regard the seed *per se* as different entities. On the contrary, the unity of the seed is attested by strong, unmistakable perceptual experience, which must be accepted as absolutely authentic as there is no invalidating evidence, *à priori* or *à posteriori*.[1]

[1] na cai 'vaṁ samānakālakāryāṇāṁ deśabhede'pi dharmibhedo yuktaḥ, bhedasādhakapramāṇābhāvāt indriyapratyakṣeṇa nirastavibhramāśaṅkenā 'bhedaprasādhanāc ca. SBNT., p. 46.

Section 2

Concomitance of Existence with Flux

The entire theory of flux is pivoted on the truth of the proposition 'whatever is existent is momentary.' And existence has been proved to consist in causal efficiency alone and this efficiency is exercisable in succession or simultaneity. But as succession and simultaneity are not predicable of a permanent non-fluxional entity, all existents are perforce proved to be momentary. But what is the proof that causal efficiency is not competent to a permanent entity ? Because succession or non-succession, in which causal efficiency can be exercised, is incompatible with it. Permanency consists in the identity of a thing in both previous and subsequent moments and succession or non-succession implies difference of identity in different moments. And identity and change, the connotations of permanence and succession on the one hand and non-succession on the other respectively, being contradictory in nature, cannot co-exist in a permanent substratum.[1] And succession or non-succession being the condition precedent, in Sanskrit terminology *vyāpaka* (pervader or container), the absence of the former in a non-momentary entity will necessarily entail the absence of the latter, according to the rule that the exclusion of the continent implies the absence of the content.[2]

The *Naiyāyika* has raised a storm of controversy over the above position of the Buddhist. He contends that the rule—the exclusion of the continent implies the exclusion of the contained—cannot be enforced in the case of the ' permanent,' which is the subject of the syllogism advanced by the Buddhist : " whatever is

[1] " tathā hi pūrvāparayor ekatve nityatvam, kṣaṇadvaye 'pi bhede kramitvam. tataśca nityatvaṁ kramākramitvaṁ ce 'ty abhinnatvaṁ bhinnatvaṁ ce' tyuktaṁ bhavati. etayoś ca parasparaparihārasthitilakṣaṇatayā virodhaḥ. tat kathaṁ nitye kramākramasambhavaḥ." SBNT., p. 55.

[2] " vyāpakavyāvṛttyā vyāpyavyāvṛttir iti nyāyena vyāpaka-kramākramavyāvṛttyā 'kṣaṇikāt sattvavyāvṛtteḥ siddhatvāc ca." SDS., p. 20.

lacking in causal agency, in succession or non-succession has not causal efficiency, as a rabbit's horn. The supposed 'permanent' entity has no such agency (and therefore has no causal efficiency)."[1] Evidently the argument is not a hypothetical argument of the type of *reductio ad absurdum* that is employed to enforce an undesirable contingency in the adversary's position (*prasaṅgānumāna*), because the *probans*, 'the absence of successive or non-successive agency' is a proved fact and not assumed (for argument's sake) on the affirmation of the adversary and lastly, it does not tend to establish the contradictory position—all the three conditions of *prasaṅgānumāna* being conspicuous by their absence.[2] Nor can it be regarded as an independent argument (*svatantra*), as the subject (the permanent) is non-existent and a middle term unrelated to an existent subject (*āśrayāsiddhahetu*) is not competent to prove any conclusion. The subject of the present syllogism is the permanent entity, but such a thing is a chimerical abstraction on your own theory and as such cannot be cognised either by perception or by inference, as they are cognisant of real entities alone.

It may be contended that even an unreal fiction can be visualised by imaginative intuition (*kalpanājñāna*). But this imaginative intuition may be fivefold, *viz.*, (1) generated by the power of perception and bringing up its rear; (2) generated by the cognition of a characteristic mark; (3) generated by a memory-impression; (4) cognisant of a doubtful entity; (5) and lastly, cognisant

1 yasya kramākramikāryaviṣayatvaṁ nā 'sti na tat śaktam, yathā śaśaviṣāṇam. nā 'sti ca nityābhimatasya bhāvasya kramākramikāryaviṣayatvam iti vyāpakānupalambhaḥ. SBNT., p. 55.

2 nanu vyāpakānupalambhataḥ sattvasya kathaṁ svasādhyapratibandhasiddhiḥ, asyā 'py anekadoṣaduṣṭatvāt. tathā hi na tāvad ayaṁ prasaṇgāhetuḥ, sādhyadharmiṇi pramāṇasiddhatvāt, parābhyupagamasiddhatvābhāvāt, viparyayaparyavasānābhāvācca.—SBNT., p. 56. For a fuller account of *Prasaṅgānumāna* see *infra* the chapter entitled "*Prasaṅgānumāna*," Pt. II.

of an unreal fiction.[1] The first two alternatives will affirm the existence of the permanent and consequently a denial of the same will involve a necessary contradiction. The third, subject to possible aberrations, is not susceptible of sublation, as memory-impression presupposes previous experience and the latter is impossible without a real datum. The fourth is not a possible hypothesis, as neither existence nor non-existence can be categorically predicated of a doubtful entity. The fifth alternative, *viz.*, pure imagination giving purely imaginary data, is to be positively scouted, as in that case the fallacy of subject-less reason will have no *raison d'être* as an imaginary subject will be available everywhere.[2] So no inference is possible with a fictitious subject (minor term). The same argument holds good of the example also.

Moreover, it has been trotted out that there is opposition in contradiction between a permanent entity and causal agency, successive or non-successive. But opposition can be understood if the terms in opposition are apprehended quite as much as heat and cold, eternity and conditionality are known to be in opposition from concrete data as snow and fire and the like.[3] Again, negation is cognisable if there is a positive substratum actually cognised, as, for instance, the non-existence of a jug is cognised on the ground actually perceived. Perception of an actual substratum is thus the necessary condition of cognition of negation. Furthermore, a relation, whether oppositional or otherwise, is understandable if the subject and predicate, the two constituent terms, are real, concrete facts. If the non-momentary entity that is sought to be denied is known by experience, denial of it will be a contradiction. If the non-momentary be an entitative

[1] api ca tat kalpanājñānaṁ pratyakṣapṛṣṭhabhāvi vā syat, liṅgajanma vā, saṁskārajaṁ vā, sandigdhavastukaṁ vā, avastukaṁ vā. SBNT., p. 57 *et seq.*

[2] antimapakṣe tu na kaścid hetur anāśrayaḥ syāt, vikalpamātrasiddhasya dharmiṇaḥ sarvatra sulabhatvāt. *Ibid*, p. 57.

[3] *Ibid*, p. 61.

fact, negation of causal agency, which is the equivalent of existence, will be a contradictory reason. If the subject be of a negative character, there will be a subjectless middle term and also a logical seesaw ; if it be conceived to partake of a dual nature (both existence and non-existence) the reason will be inconclusive (*anaikāntikam*). So the whole argument intended to prove the contradiction of a 'permanent' with existence is vitiated by a triple fallacy.[1]

It may be contended that the non-momentary may be visualised by pure imagination and even an imaginary datum can be the term of a syllogistic argument. But this contention will not stand the dilemma : Is your imaginary datum real or unreal ? If real, you cannot deny it. If it is purely imaginary and unreal, is the opposition sought to be proved real or imaginary? The former alternative is impossible, as opposition by an imaginary opposite is not conceivable. There can be no opposition regarding a barren woman's son. And if the opposition itself be a fancied unreal opposition, the denial of existence regarding the non-momentary will not be real. And so the doctrine of flux, supposed to rest on the bed-rock of the aforesaid argument, will be thrown overboard.

Udayanācārya in his *Nyāyakusumāñjali*, Ch. III, has put forward an elaborate plea that no negation is predicable of an unreal fiction (*alīka*). Mere non-apprehension cannot prove the non-existence of anything, but only the non-apprehension of a thing competent to perception. The analogy of such unreal fictions as a rabbit's horn and the like is wide of the mark. Because even a rabbit's horn or a sky-flower has such competency subject to defects in the sense-organ and other conditions of perception. The presence of organic defect or mental aberrations and the like is the necessary condition of perception of such

[1] *Ibid*, p. 62. The logical seesaw in the second horn of the dilemma arises in this way: The non-momentary cannot be a reality because causal agency in succession or non-succession is incompatible with it and the latter is incompatible, because the non-momentary is unreal.

unreal things and, when this requisite condition is present, the perception in question is inevitable. So the denial of a rabbit's horn and the like is not possible when there is such competency constituted by the necessary conditions set forth above. And when such fictions are negated, it simply implies that the necessary condition of their perception is lacking.[1] Nor is inference competent to prove the non-existence of an absolutely unreal fiction, because negation is intelligible if the object of negation (*pratiyogin*) and the locus or substratum (*āśraya* or *dharmin*), on which the non-existence of anything is cognised, are real positive entities. Even illusory perception of an absolute non-entity is impossible. When the silver is perceived in the mother-of-pearl by illusion, the silver as such is a real entity and when true perception of the mother-of-pearl sublates the previous cognition of silver, what is sublated is the wrong spatio-temporal relation and not the reality of silver, which exists in another place and time. So the permanent non-momentary entity, the negation of which can prove the existence of the momentary, must be a real, existent fact, as nothing but a real can be negated. And if it is a real entity, absolute negation of it will be a contradiction in terms.[2] The doctrine of momentary reals, therefore, stands self-condemned.

In reply to this elaborate criticism of the *Naiyāyikas* the Buddhist points out that an imaginary, unsubstantial datum (*avastu*) is as much serviceable as a real fact. Besides in negative inference, a reference to the substratum or locus (*āśraya*) is not at all necesssary—what is needed is to show that the negation of the more general concept necessarily implies the

[1] duṣṭopalambhasāmagrī śaśaśṛṅgādiyogyatā ।
na tasyāṁ no 'palambho 'sti nāsti sā' nupalambhane ॥
N. KU., Ch. III, 3.

[2] vyāvartyābhāvavattai 'va bhāvikī hi viśeṣyatā ।
abhāvavirahātmatvaṁ vastunaḥ pratiyogitā ॥
N. KU., Ch. III, 2.

negation of the less general, which is included in the denotation of the former. The non-existence of the tree necessarily connotes the non-existence of the *śiṁśapā*, a particular species of the former, on the general maxim that the exclusion of the continent involves the exclusion of the contained, without any reference whatsoever to the place where such non-existence may be cognised.[1]

And if negation be supposed to contain a necessary reference to a substratum or locus, an imaginary substratum or locus will answer the purpose. Because the subject-predicate relation is found to be used as much in connection with a real entity as with an imaginary fiction. Thus, for instance, such propositions, as 'there is no sharpness in a rabbit's horn,' 'there is no fragrance in a sky-lotus,' 'there is no stunt in a barren woman's son,' are as much allowable as the propositions, 'there is bovine nature in a cow,' 'there is whiteness in the cloth,' and the like.[2] Moreover, your assertion that 'an unreal fiction cannot be a subject,' does not militate against our position, if you mean that it cannot be the subject of a real predicate. But if your implication is that the unreal cannot be the subject even of an unreal predicate, you contradict yourself, because by denying all predication respecting an unreal fiction, you yourself make it the subject of your denial.[3] Certainly it is sheer autocracy to forbid others from doing what you yourself do.[4] The absurdity of the adversary's position will be demonstrated by the following

[1] tasmād vaidharmyadṛṣṭānte neṣṭo 'vaśyam ihā' śrayaḥ |
tadabhāve tu tan ne 'ti vacanād api tadgateḥ || T.S.P., 145.

[2] *Vide* SBNT., p. 62, ll. 9, *et seq.*

[3] 'yenai 'va hi vacanenā 'vastuno dharmitvaṁ niṣiddhaṁ tenai 'va vacanenā 'vastuno dharmitvābhāvena dharmeṇa dharmitvam abhyupagatam.—SBNT., p. 63. The emended reading in the foot-note has been further emended as above.

[4] parastu pratiṣidhyata iti vyaktam idam īśvaraceṣṭitam. *Ibid*, p. 63.

dilemma: When you aver that the unreal cannot be the subject of a syllogistic argument, do you deny the character of subject of this unreal, or any other or of nothing at all? On the first alternative, the character of subject is not denied of the unreal, because the absence of subjecthood (*dharmitvābhāva*) is predicated of it. On the second alternative, nothing is predicated of the unreal, as the subject of predication is quite different from it. The third alternative is devoid of meaning, as the predicate 'absence of subjecthood' is not related to any subject at all. So the denial of subjecthood of an unreality is impossible in any circumstance.[1] The very statement that 'the unreal cannot be the subject of a predicate' presupposes the subjecthood of the unreal, otherwise the whole statement will be unmeaning. If you want to avoid the contradiction of making the subject of an unreality, you will be perforce reduced to silence. An unenviable position for sooth! If he keeps silent, he cannot prove his thesis; and if he chooses to speak, he contradicts himself. Perhaps the *Naiyāyika* will rejoin: 'Silence is the proper course for a logically minded person when an unreal topic is broached.' Certainly this is cleverness *par excellence.* After discoursing to the best of his ability on the nature of the unreal, he now seeks to back out by a subterfuge seeing defeat inevitable. Certainly discourse on an unreality is not prohibited by a royal mandate. It is established, therefore, that a syllogism, having the non-monentary, whether an unreality or doubtful reality, as the minor term and absence of succession and simultaneity as the middle term and non-existence as the major term, is a perfectly logical syllogism, as all the objections against it have been proved to be devoid of sense and substance.[2]

Now, a predicable attribute can be threefold in character: (1) one that is objectively real, for instance, blue and the like;

[1] *Ibid*, pp. 63-64. *Cf.* tasmād anupākhye vipakṣe hetor vyatirekanivṛttau vā vyatireke vā sahṛdayānāṁ mūkatai 'vo ' citā. Tat. Ti, p. 173.

[2] *Ibid*, pp. 63-64.

(2) one that is objectively unreal, for instance, pure unqualified negation; and (3) one partaking of a dual character, as for instance, mere non-perception.[1] That an objectively real attribute cannot be predicated of an unreal subject is perfectly reasonable. But to maintain that even the second and the third category of predicables are not predicable of an unreal subject is an evident piece of contradiction. So the charge of the fallacy of subjectless reason (*āśrayāsiddhahetu*) falls to the ground. The charge could be substantiated if the non-momentary subject could not be apprehended, as an unknown entity is not amenable to any predication. But the very fact of its denial shows that it is not absolutely unknown. The unreal, therefore, is cognisable quite as much as the real, though the nature and process of understanding is necessarily different in each case. Perceptual and inferential cognition and determinative reflection arising in the trail of perception are directly or indirectly caused by the generative power of an objective reality. But an unreal, imaginary datum has no such generative power and is conjured up by pure imaginative intuition. Certainly negation is no concrete reality, with a distinctive shape and form, that can be envisaged. But it is a concept which has a pragmatic value and this pragmatic value can be possessed even by a purely subjective concept, visualised by pure imagination.[2] Accordingly our thinking principle must be credited with this faculty of pure intuition, independent of the influence of an extra-mental reality, otherwise these purely subjective ideas will be left unaccounted for. And even the most staunch

[1] "trividho hi dharmo dṛṣṭaḥ, kaścid vastuniyato nīlādiḥ; kaścid avastuniyato yathā sarvopākhyāvirahaḥ; kaścid ubhayasādhāraṇo yathā anupalabdhimātram." *Ibid*, p. 64.

[2] "sākṣāt pāramparyeṇa vastusāmarthyabhāvinī hi vastu-pratītiḥ, yathā pratyakṣam anumānaṁ pratyakṣapṛṣṭhabhāvī ca vikalpaḥ, avastunas tu sāmarthyābhāvād vikalpamātram eva pratītiḥ, na hy abhāvaḥ kaścid vigrahavān yaḥ sākṣātkartavyo 'pi tu vyavahartavyaḥ. sa ca vyavahāro vikalpād api sidhyaty eva." *Ibid*, p. 65.

realist cannot avoid using these purely subjective concepts, as all predication about them, affirmative or negative, necessarily presupposes their existence. And as they cannot have an objective existence, they must be accepted as subjective facts or pure ideas. So there is no logical or psychological difficulty in accepting the non-momentary, permanent entity as a usable concept, though it is avowedly a pure idea and not an objective reality. The demand of the *Naiyāyika* and other realists that all our ideas are derived from experience of external objective data is extravagant and leads to self-contradiction. So the non-momentary is a possible datum and, hence, the accusation of a 'subjectless reason' falls to the ground. It has been urged that if an imaginary concept can become the subject of a predication, then the fallacy of subjectless reason will be an unreal myth, as an imaginary subject will be always and everywhere available. But the apprehension is baseless. The fallacies of reasons in relation to an unreal subject and a dubious subject (*āśrayāsiddha* and *sandigdhāśraya hetu*) occur, when a real predicable is predicated of an unreal and a doubtful subject respectively. The imaginary subject remains a doubtful real before the reason is applied and is accounted as unreal when the reason is driven home.[1] There is no room for the aforesaid fallacies, however, as the *probans* (*hetu*), the *probandum* (*sādhya*) and the subject (*dharmin*) are all imaginary concepts alike. The homologues (*dṛṣṭānta*), space, a rabbit's horn and the like are equally imaginary concepts. All the objections of the *Naiyāyika* could hold good if either the subject or the predicate were real. So the charge of the fallacy of subjectless reason cannot be brought home when the subject and the predicate are both unreal fictions and even the most rabid realist cannot deny to the mind, on pain of self-contradiction, the faculty of

[1] vikalpaś cāyaṁ hetūpanyāsāt pūrvaṁ sandigdhavastukaḥ, samarthite tu hetāv avastuka iti brūmaḥ. *Ibid*, p. 66.

pure imaginative intuition visualising even an unreal, airy nothing.[1]

The plea of Udayana that the object (*pratiyogin*) of negation must be a real, objective fact, attested by experience, has been found to be a hollow assertion. His second plea that negation can be perceived in a real substratum, actually experienced, remains to be examined.[2]

Now, the *Naiyāyika* contends that negation of succession and simultaneity cannot be apprehended except in a real substratum, and as there is no real substratum in this case, perception of non-existence of succession and simultaneity is impossible. Accordingly, non-existence of the non-momentary is equally inapprehensible, as there is no substratum

1 " tad evam avastudharmāpekṣayā 'vastuno dharmitvasya vikalpamātreṇa pratīteś cā'pahnotum aśakyatvān nā 'yam āśrayāsiddho hetuḥ." *Ibid*, p. 66.

2 *Vide* N. KU., Ch. III, 2.

It must be stated here, to avoid misunderstanding, that the view criticised by Ratnakīrti is not, historically speaking, the view of Udayana but that of Trilocana, probably the teacher of Vācaspati Miśra. Ratnakīrti has criticised Nyāyabhūṣaṇa, Śaṅkara, probably the same as Śaṅkarasvāmin the *Naiyāyika*, quoted in the *Tattvasaṅgraha* and the *Nyāyamañjarī*, Trilocana and Vācaspati Miśra, but not Udayana. Had Ratnakīrti lived after Udayana, he could not but have criticised him. We shall not, therefore, be wrong if we place Ratnakīrti before Udayana. MM. Hara Prasad Sastri thinks Ratnakīrti to be a younger contemporary of Vācaspati Miśra, which is very probable. But the date of Vācaspati cannot be 898 Śaka era, as that learned antiquarian holds, since that will make him a contemporary of Udayana, who wrote his *Lakṣaṇāvalī* in the Śaka year 905. So we should think it to be in Saṁvat and this will remove Vācaspati from Udayana by 142 years, and Ratnakīrti being his junior contemporary will be separated from Udayana by almost a century. This tallies with the tradition current among the Pandits that Udayana gave the last blow to the Buddhists, and we do not hear much of any Buddhist philosopher after the tenth century. We have represented, in the present work, this view as of Udayana on the ground that the view of Udayana very cogently represents Trilocana's views and that it is regarded, in the circle of orthodox Paṇḍits at any rate, as the original view of Udayana.

such as the surface of ground on which non-existence of the tree and the like is actually perceived. But the objection of the *Naiyāyika*, the Buddhist observes, is altogether baseless. Non-existence is not a concrete reality, which can be envisaged on its own account. The cognition of the non-existence of the tree is nothing but the cognition of a particular ground-surface out of relation to the tree, and such is the case with regard to other negations as well. In the case of succession and non-succession, again, the non-momentary subject, bodied forth by an imaginative intuition, is the substratum, which, being cognised alone without relation to succession and non-succession, is interpreted as the cognition of the latter's non-existence. And the cognition of the non-momentary without relation to causal efficiency is the cognition of the negation of the latter. The non-momentary subject is the product of pure imaginative intuition which is, however, projected outside and visualised as real by a process of intellection called *adhyavasāya* (imaginative intuition). And this *adhyavasāya* consists in an impulsive movement of the mind, generated by the force of the immediately preceding cognition, towards an object though not actually cognised. And Ratnakīrti assures us that he has established and fully explained the nature and function of this *adhyavasāya* in his work, entitled '*Citrādvaitasiddhi*.'[1] So there is no logical bar to the apprehension of the negation of succession and non-succession, as the substratum in the form of the non-momentary is present there, on which its negation can be perceived. And this condition of the perception of non-existence is satisfied as much by an unreal subjective concept as by a real objective fact.[2]

[1] 'adhyavasāyāpekṣayā cabāhye 'kṣaṇike 'vastuni vyāpakābhāvād vyāpyābhāvasiddhivyavahāraḥ. adhyavasāyaś ca samanantarapratyayabalāyātākāraviśeṣayogād agṛhīte 'pi pravartanaśaktir boddhavyaḥ. īdṛśaś cā' dhyavasāyārtho 'smaccitrādvaitasiddhau nirvāhitaḥ. SBNT., p. 71.

[2] ayañ ca nyāyo yathā vastubhūte dharmiṇi tathā 'vastubhūte 'pī 'ti ko viśeṣaḥ. *Ibid*, pp. 71-72.

It may be urged that an unreal subject cannot have any logical bearing on the question of validity, as validity can be determined on the basis of a real objective fact alone.[1] But, what is the precise meaning of this objective basis? Does it mean (1) that it must be derived even remotely from an objective datum, or (2) that it must have a practical bearing in some form or other on real data of experience, or (3) that it must have a necessary relation to a real objective substratum?

In the first alternative, there is no difficulty, as the idea of succession and non-succession and of causal efficiency is derived from real data, of which the necessary relation is cognised. The second alternative is also satisfied, as the idea of the non-momentary is the instrument of establishing the momentary nature of reals. The third alternative is not lacking either, as the non-momentary subject is a real, subjective concept, in relation to which the absence of succession and non-succession and, consequently, of causal efficiency is predicated. The non-momentary, though non-existent as an external objective fact, is yet existent as a real, subjective concept. And so the real foundation is not lacking since reality may be either subjective or objective.[2]

[1] nanv etad avastudharmi no 'payogi, vastvadhiṣṭhānatvāt pramāṇavyavasthāyā iti cet.—*Ibid*, p. 73, l. 4. The text, however, presents a different reading, which is hopelessly meaningless and can by no stretch of imagination be made to fit in with the context. We have, accordingly, emended the text as above.

[2] *Vide* SBNT., p. 73, ll. 4-17.

The term 'non-momentary' (*akṣaṇika*) may have a twofold meaning, according as the negation is understood either as absolute (*prasajyapratiṣedha*), or relative (*paryudāsa*). In the first sense, it will mean 'non-existence of the momentary;' in the second sense, it will mean 'a positive entity different from the momentary.' The latter sense is accepted here and so the 'non-momentary' is a real datum as a concept, though not as an objective fact.

The accusation of triple fallacy is baseless, since the non-momentary as '*the subject*,' 'absence of succession and simultaneity,' as the *probans*, and the *probandum*, 'non-existence'—all the members of the syllogism, are conceptual facts. The fallacies would have arisen if the terms of the syllogism were real objective facts. The argument proving non-existence in the present case stands altogether in a different category from the argument which seeks to establish 'existence.' Because the terms of the latter are all objectively real facts and not pure concepts as in the former and so all the threefold fallacies crop up.[1]

The contention of Trilocana, that opposition can be apprehended if the terms in opposition are cognised, does not affect our position as the non-momentary is comprehended as a real concept. Nor can it be maintained that all comprehension means experience alone and as there is no experience of the non-momentary, there can be no opposition regarding it.

[1] It is an established logical conclusion that 'existence' *per se* cannot be proved by inference. An argument is possible if there is an existent fact. We can prove any other circumstance of a thing except its existence, which must be accepted as the irreducible datum of inference. If the very existence of the subject, the minor term in a syllogism, is doubted, all inference will come to a standstill. Proof means the application of a middle term, but no middle term is competent to prove the existence of a doubtful subject. Thus, if the middle term is a positive fact, it will be 'unproven in respect of the subject;' in other words, it will be a subjectless reason (*āśrayāsiddhahetu*); if it be negative, it will be a contradictory reason, proving the contradictory of existence, which is the *probandum*; if it be of dual nature (positive and negative in one), it will be inconclusive, proving neither existence nor non-existence. This has been summed up in the verse: "asiddho bhāvadharmaś ced vyabhicāry ubhayāśrayaḥ | dharmo viruddho 'bhāvaś ca sa sāttā sādhyate katham ||"

This verse is an oft-quoted one, found in the *Pañjikā* of Kamalaśīla, the *Nyāyamañjarī*, the *Parīkṣāmukhalaghusūtravṛtti* of Anantavīryya and other books. The verse however is not quoted by Ratnakīrti, but obviously alluded to here, *op. cit.*, p. 74, ll. 14-21. (See N. M., p. 128., P.M L.S.V., p. 28; T.S.P., pp. 412-13.)

Because, in that case, you cannot deny the existence of a barren woman's son, as such unreal fictions are never known through experience, and such expressions as 'there is no beauty in a barren woman's son' will be an anathema to you.

The last objection, that contradictory opposition being a relation between two terms will become itself fictitious if one of the terms be unreal, will not hold water. If opposition is conceived to be an independent entity standing with one foot on each term, it would certainly become fictitious if either of the terms was unreal. But we, Buddhists, do not hold opposition to be an independent entity, connecting the terms from outside—so that with one term vanishing the relation might vanish.[1] Contradictory opposition in our view is nothing but the mutual exclusion of two contradictory terms, as that of existence and non-existence, and this opposition is absolutely real Certainly existence and non-existence do not overlap each other. The opposition between permanence and succession or non-succession is equally a real opposition. Permanence connotes uniformity and non-change in different times, and succession or non-succession implies change of nature at different moments. And change and non-change, being mutually exclusive, are contradictorily opposed, and this opposition is as much real as that of existence versus non-existence. But it may be urged that you, Buddhist, do not admit the existence of opposition independent of. and external to the 'opposites;' and as one of the opposites, at any rate, *viz.*, the non-momentary, is an unreal fiction, how can the opposition in question be real? Yes, the Buddhist does not believe that a third factor, *viz.*, opposition, is necessary to make two terms opposite to each other. Opposition is nothing apart and distinct from the terms in opposition. Any two particular terms are said to be in opposition, because the existence of one

[1] 'na hi virodho nāma vastvantaraṁ kiñcid ubhayakoṭidattapādaṁ sambandhābhidhānam iṣyate 'smābhir upapadyate vā, yenai 'kasambandhino vastutvābhāve apāramārthikaḥ syāt. *Op. cit.*, p. 75.

implies the non-existence of the other. So, opposition is nothing but the mutually exclusive nature of the terms in themselves. And if they are not by nature exclusive of each other, the relation of opposition lying outside or alongside of them cannot make them opposed.

So the *Naiyāyika* does not gain anything by positing the oppositional relation as an independent entity. On the contrary he introduces confusion. Because relations, external to and independent of the *relata*, are not intelligible. The Buddhist does not admit any relation external to the terms. If there is any relation it is internally inherent in the terms themselves. It would be logically more correct to say that 'the terms are opposed' than saying 'there is opposition between the two,' if by opposition be understood something aloof and distinct from the constituent terms.[1]

[1] "nanu nityatvakramayaugapadyavattvañ ca viruddhe vidhūya nā 'paro virodho nāma. kasya vāstavatvam iti ced, na hi dharmāntarasya sambhavena virodhasya pāramārthikatvaṁ brūmaḥ, kintu viruddhayor dharmayoḥ sadbhāve. anyathā virodhanāmadharmāntarasadbhāve 'pi yadi na viruddhau dharmau kva pāramārthikavirodhasadbhāvaḥ ? viruddhau ca dharmau, tāvatai 'va tāttviko virodhavyavahāraḥ, kim apareṇa pratijñāmātrasiddhena virodhanāmnā vastvantareṇa? " *Op. cit.*, p. 76.

CHAPTER III

Objections from the Point of View of Causation explained

Śāntarakṣita has quoted the view of an author, whom Kamalaśīla describes as Bhadanta Yogasena, apparently a Buddhist of the Hīnayāna school, who attacks the theory of flux on the ground of its failure to explain causation. The gravamen of his attack lies in the charge that even the momentary entity cannot produce the expected effect either in succession or in non-succession exactly like the non-momentary, as in either case the function of the subsidiaries remains unintelligible. The theory of flux holds that all existents are momentary, existing only for the moment and disappearing in the next moment, in which an exact facsimile of the previous entity crops up This process of duplication and re-duplication goes on for any length of time and this is the reason why entities are *prima facie* looked upon as continuous. In reality, however, there have been many entities, one similar to the other, and this similarity in appearance is mistaken for their unchanged identity. This is so far an intelligible position. The real difficulty, however, crops up when a dissimilar entity emerges, as, for instance, when the seed-series disappears and a different series in the shape of the sprout springs into being. Now, it is held that the cause of the sprout is not the same or similar seed-series, that was lying inactive in the granary, but a different entity, endued with a distinct causal efficiency (*kurvadrūpa*), that leaps into being when the full complement of subsidiaries, to wit, soil, water, air and the rest, are associated with the basic cause, *viz.*, the seed. Plainly, it is unquestionable that the seed develops its peculiar causal efficiency for the sprout not in its independent capacity, but only when it is acted upon by the subsidiary conditions. And these subsidiaries can be required only if they can assist the basal cause, for assistance means the production of a supplementation on the basal cause, *viz.*, the seed. But the basal cause and the subsidiaries, being alike momentary, can only exist side by side like the two horns on a cow's head, and mutual assistance between them is impossible. Besides, each entity is independent of the other, being produced by its own proper cause, and cannot and does not stand in need of the assistance that may be afforded by foreign auxiliaries in order to come into being. So the peculiar sprout-producing entity will be produced by the power of its own cause and the subsidiaries will be totally useless. But, then, the question arises, if the momentary subsidiaries are powerless to produce any effect on the causal entity, which is equally a momentary and indivisible unit, and if the main cause be credited with a spontaneous, innate efficiency for the sprout, why does not the seed produce the sprout always ? There can be no necessity for the subsidiaries, which are as powerless and ineffectual with regard to the momentary entity as they have been proved by the upholder of flux in respect of the permanent cause. So the momentary also cannot exercise its causal efficiency, either in succession or in simultaneity, and there being no conceivable occasion for diversity, we shall have the same seed-series and not the dissimilar sprout.[1]

So far with regard to causation. The flux theory equally fails to account for destructive opposition. Destruction is regarded to be spontaneous, as an entity being perishable by its natural constitution cannot stand in need of a foreign destructive agent. But spontaneous destruction is equally unintelligible as spontaneous production. Now, take the example of the jug, which, as the flux-theorist holds, perishes spontaneously in the second moment of its birth. But we ask, why should the jug produce

[1] kramеṇa yugapac ce 'ti yatas te 'rthakriyākṛtaḥ |
na bhavanti tatas teṣāṁ vyarthaḥ kṣaṇikatāśrayaḥ ||
sahakārikṛtaś cai 'vaṁ yadā nā 'tiśayaḥ kvacit |
sarvadā nirviśeṣai 'va tadā santatir iṣyate || T. S., Śl. 431-32.

its facsimiles and not potsherds which are also regarded to be the effect of it ? Why is it that the club is required to occasion a different entitative series (*visadṛśasantāna*)? Certainly, the club cannot produce any effect, adverse or otherwise, on the indivisible, momentary jug. The same difficulty is confronted with regard to darkness. If darkness be a positive entity and goes on producing distinct replicas of itself every moment, why should it cease to exist when the light comes in? Certainly, light cannot be regarded to cause the destruction of darkness, as destruction is spontaneous and is uncaused so far as a foreign agent is concerned. And if you hold that it is the nature of darkness, as of other things, to come to a dead extinction, why does it not do so always, but does so only when light comes in ? Perhaps, it will be said, 'Well, darkness perishes every second moment, it is the series of duplicates that continues, which, in its turn, becomes defunct when another distinct series comes to take its place.' But this is nothing but prevarication. The point at issue is, why is it that the same or similar series does not continue, if it be the nature of an entity to produce its duplicates ? Or, if it be its nature to cease to exist, why does it not do so always? Why should it go on producing duplicates in some cases and should cease to do so in other cases ? Why should there be in your terminology *santānabheda* (diversity of series) at all ? Certainly, the nature of things cannot be freakish, and if causation and destruction be freaks of chance, which the theory of spontaneous production and spontaneous destruction, the two corollaries of the doctrine of flux, make them out to be, then the whole phenomenal order will be condemned to confusion. The doctrine of flux, therefore, only leads to negation of all philosophy.[1]

[1] *Vide Tattvasaṅgraha* and the *Pañjikā*, verses 428-34. Almost similar objections have been recorded by Ratnakīrti in his '*Kṣaṇabhaṅgasiddhi*;' but it is a pity that the author does not quote the name or names of the adversaries whose opinion he criticises so elaborately. We, however, do not refrain from reproducing those arguments even at the risk of repetition of much that has been said above, because we feel that the logical cogency of

Further, causal efficiency has been proved to be incompatible with a permanent entity. But it is no more compatible with a momentary entity either, as dependence or independence, unity or multiplicity, which are the characteristics of all existents and the necessary conditions of exercise of causal efficiency, cannot be predicated of it (a momentary entity). Now, a particular seed, when planted in a well-irrigated soil, nourished by a supply of free air and other conditions, is said to develop sprout-producing efficiency by its independent natural constitution. But why is it that some particular seed should come to have this differentiating factor, *viz.*, sprout-producing efficiency, and not others, though they are to all intents and purposes absolutely similar in nature, being produced in the same field and harvested and garnered in precisely the same fashion?[1] And this supplementation is certainly not in

Ratnakīrti's writings will go a long way in placing the views of the opponent in a clear light. In fact, this is the most damaging objection that has been advanced against the theory of universal flux and we shall have to judge how far the Buddhist philosopher has been successful in rebutting it. To the credit of the latter it must be stated that he has neither shirked nor burked the discussion. He has boldly faced the opposition and has perhaps given the only possible answer. As Ratnakīrti observes in the closing part of the discussion, the opponent's arguments will only serve to prove that causation is an impossible and inexplicable phenomenon, as both the momentary and the non-momentary have been alternately shown by both the parties to be inconsistent with causation. In fact, causation is a phenomenon which is difficult to explain and Nāgārjuna and Śaṅkara have proved that causation is only an appearance, as it is not amenable to any logical explanation. But the theory of flux is wonderfully immune from many of the objections of the idealist and is thus the most approximate logical explanation of the reality of the phenomenal world. So no school of idealism can afford to leave out of account the doctrine of Universal Flux, because the limitations of this theory are the least of all, and idealism can be established on a secure foundation if the theory of flux be shown to be an impossible or unsatisfactory explanation of experience and reality.

[1] nanv ekatra kṣetre niṣpattilavanādipūrvakam ānīya ekatra kuśūle kṣiptāni sarvāṇy eva bījāni sādhāraṇarūpāṇy eva pratīyante, tat kutastyo 'yam ekabījasambhavī viśeṣo nā 'nyeṣām iti. SBNT., pp. 49-50.

evidence in any of the seed-entities before its association with the subsidiaries and comes into play when that particular association takes place. But this adventitious supplementation cannot be attributed to the influence of the subsidiaries, as the Buddhist insists that causal efficiency is innate and inherent in an entity. It may be observed that the seed develops this peculiar efficiency of its own initiative, subject, however, to the co-presence of subsidiaries. But, in whatever way it may be explained, it is undeniable that causal efficiency, though inherent in its constitution, is not in evidence when the subsidiaries are absent. The conclusion is, therefore, irresistible that the seed and the subsidiaries, being ineffective in isolation and effective when combined, are dependent on each other for the production of the sprout or for the sprout-producing efficiency. So it cannot be maintained that a momentary entity is the sole cause of production independently of the subsidiaries. But dependence also is not any more intelligible in the case of momentary entities, as there can be no reciprocity of services between two simultaneous point-events. So the first condition of causal efficiency, *viz* , dependence or independence, is not predicable of the momentary.

Let us examine the second condition of causal efficiency, which is another name for existence, *viz.*, unity or multiplicity. The final seed-entity, which independently produces sprout, is believed also to produce the other factors associated with it, *viz.*, the changed soil, the fermented water and the like. Now, if the causal efficiency with regard to the supplementary co-products is identical with the efficiency for the sprout, the sprout and the supplementaries, soil, water and the like, will be identical in nature, being the co-products of the self-same cause. It may be urged that the causal nature is different in different cases. Thus, the seed is the material cause of the sprout but ancillary cause in respect of soil and the like. But the question is whether the material and the ancillary cause are a singular entity or multiple entities. If they are singular, the causal nature in question cannot be different. If they are multiple, the question is whether they are identical with or distinct from the basic cause, the seed. If they are distinct, the seed cannot be the cause; if identical, the seed cannot but be multiple. And if, to avoid this dilemma, you say that the material cause of the soil is the previous soil-entity and the latter is but another aspect of the seed's causal efficiency, then you must admit that the seed produces the soil not independently of the soil-entity, which is conceded to be the material cause of the latter. If, however, the seed were the independent cause of the soil, the latter would not be different from the sprout. So the seed and soil are interdependent. But this interdependence is intelligible if they are serviceable to each other, as it is propounded by the Buddhist that only things which are serviceable are required. But no benefit can accrue from or to a momentary entity, which is an indivisible unit and independent in its origin.

So a momentary entity cannot be either singular or multiple, and thus the second necessary condition of existence is lacking. It may be put forward that though the ancillary conditions do not assist the main cause, they are still necessary as they are seen to function together and the effect is found to follow them both in concomitance and non-concomitance. So the dialectic of dependence or independence does not arise. But this can be said with equal force with regard to the permanent cause, which may stand in need of subsidiaries, though they are absolutely ineffective, and thus the permanent will execute its functions in succession subject to the association of successive subsidiaries. So the middle term in the syllogism, *viz.*, 'existence,' proving the fluxional nature of all entities, is inconclusive as its absence in the contradictory is doubtful, the absence of succession and non-succession from the non-momentary being an unproved assumption.[1]

[1] yadi manyetā 'nupakārakā api bhavanti sahakāriṇo 'pekṣaṇīyāś ca, kāryeṇā 'nuvihitabhāvābhāvatvāt sahakaraṇāc ca, nanv anena krameṇā

Now, in reply to the objection that interdependence is not intelligible in respect of a momentary entity, Ratnakīrti observes that inter-dependence is intelligible in three possible ways. Firstly, it may mean that a supplementation is produced on the main cause by the action of the subsidiaries and *vice versa*. Secondly, it may denote that the cause enters unaltered as a catalytic agent into combination with the subsidiaries and produces the effect. Thirdly, that the cause and the subsidiaries together produce the effect in their independent, unaided capacities without reciprocal help. The first and second alternatives are out of the question, as a momentary entity is an indivisible unit and as such impervious to any influence, friendly or hostile; and catalysis is inconceivable when all existents are constitutionally momentary and so cannot remain the same even for two consecutive moments. So interdependence is intelligible only in the third sense that the subsidiaries and the main cause combine to produce a self-same set of efficient factors without mutual assistance or benefit, as assistance is not conceivable between two simultaneous facts existing side by side like the

'kṣaṇiko 'pi bhāvo 'nupakārakān api sahakāriṇaḥ kramavatkāryeṇā 'nukṛtānvayavyatirekān apekṣiṣyate, kariṣyate ca kramavatsahakārivaśaḥ krameṇa kāryāṇī 'ti vyāpakānupalabdher asiddheḥ sandigdhavyatirekam anaikāntikaṁ sattvam kṣaṇikatvasiddhāv iti. SNBT., pp. 48-49.

The syllogism proving the momentariness of all existents is as follows:—

'yat sat tat kṣaṇikam, yathā ghaṭaḥ, santaś cā 'mī vivādāspadībhūtāḥ padārthāḥ'—'whatever is existent is momentary, as, for instance, the jug; and the things under dispute are existent; (therefore they are momentary).' As existence is identical with causal efficiency and as succession and non-succession, the necessary conditions of causal efficiency being exercised, have been proved to be incompatible with a non-momentary entity, the momentary is alone proved to be really existent. But the opponent shows that succession and non-succession are not necessarily incompatible with the non-momentary. So the middle term 'existence' is inconclusive, its non-concomitance with the non-momentary (the contradictory of the momentary) being doubtful.

two horns on a cow's head.[1] But it may be urged that if the seed develops its particular generative power in its independent unaided capacity irrespective of the service of the subsidiaries, then, why is it that it does not produce the sprout when the subsidiaries are absent? The answer is, that the particularly efficient seed-moment was not in existence at the time when the subsidiaries were absent. If it had been in existence, it could not have failed to produce the particular effect in question. The opponent may urge, 'Well, it is an unwarranted assumption that a particular seed develops a particular causal efficiency in its independent capacity and not others, when they are all alike to all intents and purposes.' But this objection is wide of the mark. Though to all outward appearance, so far as form and colour may go, they may be looked upon as absolutely similar, there is no possible means of divining that their invisible inner constitution persists to be the same or similar. It is quite supposable that things may have a quite similar structure and appearance and yet they may differ in their inner powers. In every act of production, it is admitted on all hands that two sets of causal factors are in operation, *viz.*, the seen and the unseen. Certainly, the entire collocation of all these seen and unseen powers is not cognisable by one short of omniscience.[2] And even in the theory of permanent cause, the development of the particular effect-producing efficiency is not any more explicable. You will have to infer its existence from the effect produced by it. So the momentary real is supposed to develop a particular causal efficiency on the evidence of the effect produced. And for the emergence of this efficiency the service of the subsidiaries is useless. If causal efficiency is not

[1] samasamayakṣaṇayoḥ savyetaragoviṣāṇayor ivo 'pakāryopakāraka-bhāvāyogāt. SBNT., p. 47.

[2] kāraṇam khalu sarvatra kārye dvividham, dṛṣṭam adṛṣṭaṁ ca sarvāstikaprasiddham etat. tataḥ pratyakṣaparokṣasahakāripratyayasākal-yam asarvavidā pratyakṣato na śakyaṁ pratipattum. *Op. cit.*, p. 50.

developed of its own inherent constitutional force, an external agent cannot induce this supplementation, as the natural constitution of things cannot be changed. And the supplementation will fall apart, if it does not enter into the inner constitution of the thing itself. Nor can it be supposed to enter into the essence of a thing, as the dialectic of distinction and identity will prove the hollowness of such supposition. So inter-dependence in the sense of interaction is an unfounded myth ; but if combination without interaction be meant by it, it is possible.

The second objection that singularity or multiplicity cannot be predicated of a momentary cause is equally untenable. The cause is one indivisible entity and produces its effect by one identical causal energy. It is regarded as a material and a subsidiary cause only in its different relations and those relations are conceptual fictions and do not pertain to the order of objective realities. So you cannot attribute a plurality of natures to a cause. It is one singular entity, the difference is due to relations which are ideal fictions. And the objection that an identical cause will produce an identical effect is not sanctioned by experience, as we see very often that one particular cause produces a plurality of effects. When it is affirmed that identity of cause entails identity of effect, the word 'cause' stands for the entire collocation of causes—certainly, the effect cannot vary when the collocation of causes is identical.

In reply to the criticism of Yogasena, Śāntarakṣita first elucidates the Buddhist theory of causation and shows that the subsidiaries have a determinate, assignable place in the production of an effect and yet the objections of non-relation or infinite regression, which are unavoidable in the theory of a permanent cause, do not at all affect the Buddhist position.

Now, co-operation (*sahakāritva*) can be understood in two possible senses, *viz.*, (1) combination of several independent factors to produce a self-same effect ; (2) interaction or mutual assistance. Now, things being fluxional, there can be no co-operation in the second sense and so we have to fall back upon the first alternative. The several factors of production, as for instance, the seed, water, soil and the like, when associated together for the first time, can have no action upon one another, as they have all come into being under the influence of their proper causes and stand side by side independently of one another like the two horns on a cow's head. But though devoid of interaction they are not, in spite of their structural or morphological similarity, the same or similar entities as before, but are altogether distinct entities vested with different causal efficiencies. So instead of producing their replicas, as they were doing before, they produce in the second moment distinct entities, each endowed with sprout-producing efficiency, which in the third moment give rise to the grand effect, as, for instance, the sprout. So there is no interaction at any one of the stages. But if the seed-continuum is looked upon as one identical entity, the idea of interaction becomes intelligible. In this case, the peculiar effect-producing entities, which appear in the second moment and which culminate in the production of the grand effect in the third moment, can be supposed to have been effected by interaction between the subsidiaries and the main cause, as it is undeniable that the second set of efficient factors do derive their peculiar efficiency from their immediate predecessors. But as the continuum (*santāna*) is only an ideal abstraction, the interaction cannot be regarded as real in any sense. But the makeshift of *santāna* does duty for the permanent entity of the *Naiyāyika* and is yet free from the difficulties of the dialectic of relations. The assistance of subsidiaries was requisitioned to account for the novel efficiency, which distinguishes the sprout-producing seed from its compeers. But in the Buddhist theory of causation the sprout-producing seed derives its peculiar causal efficiency not from any external auxiliaries, but from its own cause, which is responsible for its being. Such is exactly the case with the subsidiaries also. Each of them is endued with the same kind of efficiency as the seed and this efficiency they derive severally from their own causes. But though each is thus possessed of the causal efficiency requisite for the production of the ultimate effect, none of them can be supposed to be redundant, as every one of them has been generated by its own proper efficient cause. Nor can they be supposed to function in isolation, as there is no cause operating to rend them asunder at the time of their association and no such occasion arises in the succeeding moment also, as, being momentary, they will have disappeared in the next moment of their own initiative. It may be urged that this association of several co-efficient causal factors involves an unnecessary waste of energy when there is no plurality of self same effects, and the result is only a single self-identical product, for which the service of any one of them would be enough. But the Buddhist replies that this charge could be brought forward if the causal factors were intelligent entities, possessed of the power of prevision and independent choice and action. If there is waste of energy the fault is entirely due to the blindness of Nature.[1] We may be permitted to observe in this connection that modern science has discovered numerous instances of blind waste of natural forces and scientists have complained of the prodigality of Nature. The Buddhist theory of causation, therefore, cannot be shaken on the ground of redundancy or waste of energy when the whole course of Nature is found to pay scant courtesy to considerations of economy and is not afraid of being prodigal.

It has been questioned that if the peculiar causal efficiency is inherent in the very constitution of things, why is it that it becomes evident only when the subsidiaries are present and not

[1] pratyekaṁ samarthā hetavaḥ pratyekaṁ kāryaṁ janayeyuḥ, kimity ekam aneke kurvanti ? atrā 'py amīṣāṁ kāraṇāni praṣṭavyāni...... vayaṁ tu yathādṛṣṭasya vastusvabhāvasya vaktāro na paryanuyogam arhāmaḥ.........yatrai 'kam eva samarthaṁ tatrā 'pareṣāṁ ka upayoga iti cet, satyam, na te prekṣāpūrvakāriṇo yad evaṃ vimṛṣyo 'dāsate ekaṁ kāryam aparasmād utpadyata iti. N. K., p. 74.

otherwise ? Certainly this is unaccountable unless the subsidiaries can produce an effect on the main cause, but this can be possible only if the causal entity is non-momentary.

But the objection, the Buddhist observes, is a specious one. You cannot cavil at the nature of things, as you cannot pretend to be aware of all the secrets of nature. Things have powers that cannot be fully gauged ; and if some unwonted and unexpected energy is evinced by a thing in some particular circumstances, it does not lie in us to question its logical propriety. We have to record the evidence and shape our theories pursuant to such evidence. Besides, the hypothesis of the permanent cause is not in the least free from the objections levelled against the theory of flux. It is open to the question why should the seed develop its sprout-producing efficiency, even when acted upon by the subsidiaries ? If you say, 'because it is found to develop that particular efficiency and no other,' well, the same answer is possible in the case of the fluxional entity also. Questioning is allowable only up to a certain limit, but it is out of place when the ultimate nature of things is involved. You cannot question fire why it should burn and the sun why it should shine. So you cannot question why should the seed suddenly develop a causal energy for the sprout and not any other, or why should it not continue to produce its duplicates as it was doing previous to its combination with the subsidiaries, because such questions are unanswerable in any hypothesis.[1]

Now, as regards the objections raised in connexion with destruction and opposition, let us take up the question of destruction first. Destruction, in the sense of extinction of an entitative series, is certainly uncaused, as extinction of being is not an objective fact but an idea and, as such, cannot be said to be produced. But if destruction is understood to denote the emergence of a

[1] niyatācintyaśaktīni vastūnī 'ha pratikṣaṇam ।
bhavanti nā 'nuyojyāni dahane dāhaśaktivat ॥
T. S., Sl. 438.

diverse entitative series, certainly we do not deny that it has a cause. The destruction of the jug caused by the stroke of a club does not connote that non-being of the jug takes place somewhere ; it means that it is succeeded by another entitative series of an opposite character. And, certainly, destruction, in the latter sense, *viz.*, the emergence of an opposite entitative series, has a definite, assignable cause in the shape of the club and other circumstances, produced in their turn by the inherent causal power of the previous entity.[1]

As regards opposition, it should be made explicit that there is no such thing as opposition as an objective fact. In reality, however, supersession of one entity by another is logically untenable, as the inherent nature of a thing is unalterable.[2]

From experience we have it that there are two sorts of entities, though momentary alike, of which one sort is found to induce diminution of energy in the other, with which it comes in contact, as, for instance, fire and cold. But we find no such antagonism in respect of other entities, as between fire and smoke. The relation between the two sets of entities is however purely one of causality, which is mistaken for opposition or antagonism by those who cannot probe the inwardness of the situation. There can be no opposition, however, between two momentary units, which are indivisible and so impervious to any influence, friendly or hostile. But this opposition is manifested between two series of momentary reals, when one series is seen to be supplanted by another. Thus, when the moments of fire and the moments of cold are brought into relation, in the first moment fire is unable

[1] santānocchedarūpas tu vināśo yo na hetumān ।
tasyā 'nte 'pi na bhāvo 'sti tathā janma tu vāryate ॥
vilakṣaṇakalāpāder utpādas tu sahetukaḥ ।
so' py ādau jāyate nai 'va tadā hetor asambhavāt ॥
T. S., Śls. 440-41.

[2] na tu vastūnām paramārthataḥ kaścid bādhyabādhakabhāvo 'sti, sataḥ sarvātmanā niṣpatteḥ. svabhāvānyathātvasya kartum aśakyatvāt.
T. S. P., p. 157.

to remove the cold, but becomes itself incapacitated. The second moment of fire, however, renders the succeeding moment of cold inefficient, and in the third moment, fire supplants the cold-series, it having disappeared owing to loss of efficiency it has undergone in the presence of fire. So if there is opposition, it is possible in the third moment, if the operation is the earliest and quickest possible. So opposition is nothing but the occasioning of diminution of causal energy in one series of entities by another series. [1]

That such is the essential character of opposition has been enunciated by Dharmakīrti in his *Nyāyabindu* in the following words : " Opposition is understood when one series of entities is found, in spite of the fact that the entire collocation of its causes is present intact, to disappear when another series of entities supervenes." [2] Śāntarakṣita cautions us that opposition in the sense of one being sublated by another should not be confounded as a factual occurrence obtaining in the objective order of things. It is an ideal construction and is subjectively arrived at. And that this is the case is plainly deducible from the expression 'opposition is understood.' Thus, the so-called relation of opposition, being nothing but an aspect of causality, is predicable only of the series (*santāna*) and not of the individual moments. And as this series is only a mental construction [3] and has no

[1] tasmād yo yasya nivartakaḥ sa taṁ yadi paraṁ tṛtīye kṣaṇe nivartayati, prathame kṣaṇe sannipatan asamarthāvasthānayogyo bhavati ; dvitīye viruddham asamarthaṁ karoti ; tṛtīye tv asamarthe nivṛtte taddeśam ākrāmati............tato 'yam paramārthato na kṣaṇayor virodhaḥ, api tu bahūnāṁ kṣaṇānām. N. B. T., pp. 72-73.

[2] Avikalakāraṇasya bhavato 'nyabhāve 'bhāvād virodhagatiḥ.

N. B., p. 113 (B.I.).

[3] *Cf.* " Classes or series of particulars, collected together on account of some property which makes it convenient to be able to speak of them as wholes, are what I call *logical constructions* or *symbolic fictions*. The particulars are to be conceived, not on the analogy of bricks in a building, but rather on the analogy of notes in a symphony. The ultimate constituents of a symphony (apart from relations) are the notes, each of which

existence outside the individual moments, which are in their turn absolutely unrelated and independent facts, the fact of opposition is only an idea and not an objective fact.[1]

Dharmottara in his *Nyāyabinduṭīkā* joins issue with those who hold that opposition is an unreal, ideal construction. It is probable that he meant Śāntarakṣita, who certainly preceded him in time, though he does not choose to mention his adversary by name. Dharmottara's taciturnity in regard to names is notorious, as he does not even mention Vinītadeva, Śāntabhadra and Kumārila, whose opinions he obviously criticises in his commentary, as has been pointed out by the author of the sub-commentary. So his silence in this respect does not prove anything. Be that as it may, it is indisputable that he attacks that sort of view, which has been propounded by Śāntarakṣita and Kamalaśīla. Dharmottara argues that if opposition is regarded as unreal, then, one should, to be consistent, regard causation also as unreal. That opposition is not found as a fact but is only understood after an entity has disappeared is no argument for its ideality or unreality, inasmuch as causation also is not perceived as an objective fact but is only understood as an idea after an entity is seen to have been produced. And if causation is accounted to be real on the ground that the cause actually precedes the effect, the same logic holds good of opposition also, as the actual presence of fire causes privation of causal energy in the cold.[2]

lasts only for a very short time. We may collect together all the notes played by one instrument : these may be regarded as the analogues of the successive particulars which commonsense would regard as successive states of one 'thing.' But the 'thing' ought to be regarded as no more 'real' or 'substantial' than, for example, the rôle of the trombone." *Vide Mysticism and Logic*, Constituents of Matter, pp. 129-130. (The italics are mine.)

1 bādhyabādhakabhāvas tu vastuno nai 'va tāttvikaḥ I
vidyate tata evo 'ktaṁ virodhagatir ity api II

T. S., Śl. 443.

2 *Vide* N. B. T., pp. 73-74.

CHAPTER IV

A Critical Estimate of the Sautrāntika Theory of Causation

From the elaborate exposition of the theory of causation with its confused tangle of criticism and counter-criticism, that has been reproduced in the previous chapter, one cannot resist the impression that the *Sautrāntika* has failed, in spite of his logical acumen and wealth of dialectic, to carry conviction. The fact of the matter is that causation is as unintelligible in the theory of flux as in the theory of the permanent cause. Nāgārjuna and Śaṅkara have elaborately proved by their irrefragable dialectics that causation is an inexplicable phenomenon, whether the theory of *satkāryavāda* (production of a potentially existing effect) or of *asatkāryavāda* (production of a previously non-existent effect) is adopted. The *Sautrāntika* is an adherent of the latter theory and when questioned why the sesame seed should produce oil and not any other substance, though they are all equally non-existent in the causal entity, he only says in reply that there can be no questioning with regard to the ultimate laws of nature, which are unthinkable and beyond the scope of philosophy. They are to be accepted as facts without question.[1] There is no means of divining the inner powers of things by intuition ; they can be known only when the particular effects are seen to be produced. There is an unknown law which regulates the powers of things and the determinate effects that are seen to issue from particular causes are determined by this unknown law. But it has been urged that determination connotes the idea of delimitation, and when the other limit, *viz.*, the effects, is

[1] niyatācintyaśaktīni vastūnī 'ha pratikṣaṇam |
bhavanti nā 'nuyojyāni dahane dāhaśaktivat ||
T. S., Sl. 438.

absent, how can you speak of determination? It is understandable if the effects are existent in some form or other, otherwise it is only a word without a meaning.[1] The Buddhist allows the justice of the objection that the word 'determination' is inapplicable in the absence of the other limit, *viz.*, the effect. But the position he seeks to establish simply amounts to this : that the causal entity, the unique fact, which is seen to be invariably attended by another entity, styled the effect, is undeniable as a real substantive fact, though the particular expressions usually employed to characterise it may fail to convey a correct idea of its real nature.[2] Words are but convenient symbols, employed according to the taste and purpose of a speaker and are by no means to be regarded as integral parts of things-in-themselves. So the objection with regard to an expression does not touch the essential nature of things. However objectionable and defective may be the language one may use to interpret the causal relation, the existence of the two entities, one following closely in the heels of another, is unquestionable.[3] All existents being momentary, they can have neither a past nor a future history and their momentary existence is interpreted as origination by a necessary fiction of the understanding.[4]

The question of their previous existence or non-existence cannot therefore arise, as a momentary entity is, *ex hypothesi*,

1 avadhīnām aniṣpatter niyatās te na śaktayaḥ |
sattve tu niyamas tāsām yuktaḥ sāvadhiko nanu ||

Ibid, Śl. 29.

2 nai 'vaṁ teṣām aniṣpattyā mā' bhuc chabdas tathā param |
sarvopādhiviviktasya vasturūpasya na kṣatiḥ ||

Ibid, Śl., 30.

3 na nāma rūpaṁ vastūnāṁ vikalpā vācakāś ca te- |
viśvakalpāḥ pravarttante yathābhyāsam abhedini ||

Op. cit., Śl. 131.

4 vastūnāṁ pūrvāparakoṭiśūnyānāṁ kṣaṇamātrā- |
vasthāyī svabhāva evo 'tpāda ity ucyate ||

Op. cit., p. 33.

destitute of all continuity. It is, however, by a fiction of the understanding supposed to be non-existent in the past, as it is only seen to emerge closely on the heels of another entity. But in reality neither existence nor non-existence can be predicated of it, as a non-existent can never be existent or *vice versa.* The idea of one thing being the cause and another being the effect is also an intellectual fiction—a mere form of understanding called into being by the necessity of interpreting the relation of two events, which however has nothing to do with the objective order of reals. What happens in reality is that one entity follows closely after another.[1] And this is endorsed by an *ipse dixit* of the Buddha, "O thou Mahāmati (take it) that all these phenomena have no origination, as neither existent nor non-existent can be produced." [2]

But this account of the *Sautrāntika* throws overboard causation *in toto.* It reduces causation to a merely mechanical sequence and confesses its inability to explain the character of necessity, which distinguishes causal relation from cases of accidental sequence. The *Sautrāntika* plays into the hands of the *Śūnyavādin,* who declares that causation is an appearance and not reality. The *Śūnyavāda* and the theory of *Māyā* have however the virtue of logical consistency to their credit, as they make no scruple to declare that the phenomenal order of things is unintelligible and inexplicable, that the entire cosmos is a mysterious appearance of which no logical explanation is possible. But the *Sautrāntika* realist seems to hold with the hare and run with the hound by his insistent demand to regard the momentary units of existence as absolutely real, although

[1] utpādo vastubhāvas tu so 'satā na satā tathā |
sambadhyate kalpikayā kevalaṁ tva 'satā dhiyā ||
yad idaṁ vastuno rūpam ekānantaram īkṣyate |
prāg āsīn ne 'ti tad bījaṁ prāgbhūte tvi dam asti na ||
T. S., Śls. 32 and 33.

[2] anutpannā Mahāmate sarvadharmāḥ sadasator anutpannatvāt.
T. S. P., p. 32.

he denies in the same breath the reality of all relations. But if the relations are ideal constructions and not integral parts of the order of objective reality, what remains of the objective order of reals ? A universe of reals, each unique and momentary, having no relations among them to link them together into one system of reality, but marching onward to eternity, seems to be little short of a chaos. Does this order of reality give any metaphysical satisfaction ? What is this world minus its inter-relation ? If one is false, the other cannot be true. And if it be true, what does this truth really signify ? The *Sautrāntika* may rejoin that this philosophy is the most perfect possible explanation of the objective world and is absolutely immune from the logical difficulties, which are the besetting sins of other realistic philosophies. But the justice and validity of this claim have been disputed by Nāgārjuna and Śaṅkara, who have shown in unmistakable language that causation is the hidden rock on which the barque of realism has suffered shipwreck.

The problem of pre-existence of the effect is not the only logical difficulty in the theory of causation, propounded by the *Sautrāntika*, but the precise office and function of the subsidiaries also present an insuperable difficulty. The *Naiyāyika* and the *Sautrāntika*, or for the matter of that all realistic schools of thought, are unanimous that no single cause can produce an effect, but an entire collocation of all the conditions—the full complement of the subsidiaries and the main, basal cause.[1] But do the subsidiaries really assist the main cause or not ? If they do not assist, they will not be necessary, as they will have no function in the causal operation. But the idea of assistance is not any more intelligible. Assistance means the production of supplementation. But if the cause be a momentary unit, how can it be the receiver of this supplementation, as it will disappear in the next moment along with the subsidiaries

[1] na kiñcid ekam ekasmāt sāmagryāḥ sarvasambhavaḥ (Dignāga ?) T. S. P., p. 155.

and so supplementation can neither be produced nor received ? And the permanent cause also will equally fail to receive this supplementation as supplementation can be of real service to the permanent, provided there is a relation between the two and if this relation is external to the cause, it will not relate. And if this adventitious supplementation is regarded to be identified with the main cause (which is, however, impossible, as two distinct entities of contradictory nature can never be identified), the cause will forfeit its permanency and become fluxional. But this is an inconceivable position, as a thing cannot be supposed to take leave of its essential character and assume that of another without stultifying itself. The argument that the causal entity develops its peculiar causal efficiency in question in combination with the subsidiaries, though the subsidiaries are without any action on the same, is an argument of despair and fails to give logical satisfaction. If the cause develops its efficiency of its own inherent, constitutional force, why does it not do so when the subsidiaries are absent ? The subsidiaries are certainly ineffective with regard to the causal energy that is evolved by the main cause of its own inherent force. To say that such is the nature of things, which has to be presumed on the evidence of the result produced, is certainly no answer. It totally fails to carry conviction. To cite the failure of the rival theory is no proof of its correctness. The weakness of one cannot be construed, by any manner of quibbling, as the strength of the other.

Another fatal objection against the flux-theory of causation is that it does not explain the necessity of one entity being followed by another. If it be its nature to perish in the second moment, what warrant is there that it should be followed by another entity, which will be an exact facsimile of itself ? To say that experience warrants such supposition is no explanation Philosophy does not concern itself with recording experience, but with finding a meaning for it. Moreover, destructive opposition is left behind as an inexplicable mystery quite as much as in the theory of permanent cause. Between two opposite entities, one is seen to perish altogether and the other to prevail. But what is the explanation that one should become defunct and another should go on merrily in the process of reduplicating itself, though both are equally existent and have the same claim to exist in the series ? To take a concrete example, why should fire prevail in its tussle with cold, which meets with absolute doom, as continuity in the process of the series is denied to the latter ? Why should not the tables be turned? What is the reason that cold should not prevail and fire should not go to the wall ? To adduce the testimony of experience as a metaphysical explanation of the phenomenon should be scouted as unphilosophic, as the supreme task of philosophy is to give a rational explanation of experience and where such explanation is impossible, honesty requires that philosophy should take courage in both hands and declare that it is an appearance and not a reality. But the *Sautrāntika* claims absolute reality for both the terms of a causal relation and gives an explanation which is only a show of it.

CHAPTER V

Objections on Psychological and Metaphysical Grounds discussed

The Realist's Objections

Kumārila contends that if all entities are impermanent and momentary, the relation of action and its result, causality, memory and the like will become unintelligible and unaccountable. Thus, the conscious moment, which discharges a meritorious or unmeritorious action, does not continue to reap the fruits of its action and the moment, which enjoys the fruit, was not responsible for the action which necessitated the production of the result. Thus there being no common agent of these necessarily subjective phenomena, the two absurd issues, *viz.*, the loss of earned merit (*kṛtanāśa*) and the enjoyment of unearned deserts (*akṛtāgama*) become unavoidable in the theory of flux. But this is an absurd position and runs counter to universal experience and scriptural evidence as well. Certainly it is unthinkable that X would reap the fruits, favourable or unfavourable, of actions that were done by Y. Scriptural authority also debars such supposition in the following sentence: 'who else will enjoy the fruits of an action done by another?[1]

All these objections are urged assuming that freedom of activity is possible. But if we look deeper into the logical implications of the theory of flux, we shall find that it

[1] tathā hi yenai'va kṛtaṁ śubhādikaṁ tenai'va tatphalaṁ bhujyata iti loke pratītam. Na hi Devadattena kṛte karmaṇi śubhādike Yajñadattas tatphalam iṣṭam aniṣṭañ co'pabhuṅkta iti prasiddham. nā'pi śāstre, yatho 'ktam, " anenai'va kṛtaṁ karma ko'nyaḥ pratyanubhaviṣyatī " 'ti. T. S. P., p. 166.

leaves no room for voluntary activity. When everything is momentary and a man's span of conscious life is confined to the present moment, there can be no self or ego-principle, which can function as the active agent. All activity is inspired by a desire for some end, which the agent seeks to attain. But this desire and volitional urge cannot arise at all, as the conscious agent is persuaded of its utter doom in the very next moment and as such cannot be supposed to put forth exertion for an end, which will be enjoyed by another. No intelligent being can be expected to engage himself in any active endeavour, the result of which will not be his, but will accrue to another person. All activity, therefore, meritorious or otherwise, will be impossible and the law of retribution, of which the Buddhist is so loud in his protestations, will be an unfounded myth.

But this objection also proceeds by way of concession. We urged that voluntary action would be impossible in the theory of flux and the interpretation was likely that involuntary action could have a free play. But it will transpire that all activity, voluntary and involuntary alike, is rendered absolutely impossible by this theory. Neither the past nor the future agent can be supposed to discharge the present action and the present agent also, being momentary, cannot persist a moment longer, in which it can exert itself for the production of an effect. The future agent cannot be made responsible for the effect in question, as it has not yet come into being; nor is the past moment, which has become defunct, capable of producing any effect, as a non-existent cannot have any efficiency. The present moment too cannot have any better chance, as it occupies itself in coming into existence in the first moment and has no further lease of life in which it can struggle for the production of another entity. But this is also a concession on our part, so affirms the non-Buddhist. If we probe deeper into the problem, it will transpire that the present moment also will have no *raison d'être*, as it cannot have any cause which can call it into being. The immediately preceding moment has disappeared absolutely and irrevocably without leaving any trace behind as its legacy and so what is there to bring the present moment into existence? It may be contended that the cessation of the cause and the production of the effect are synchronous events like the rise and fall of the two scales of a balance ; and so the cause being present intact in the preceding moment, the subsequent entity follows as the product of this positive entity and not from a void. The law of causation requires that the cause should immediately precede the effect and not synchronise with it. But this is only an eye-wash, as there is no room left for the causal operation ; and how can an effect issue into being from an inert, passive, inoperative entity? The cause can operate if it is present in the moment of the effect's production. Causation cannot be supposed to consist in mere antecedence and sequence bereft of all operative agency. Were it otherwise, the odour of the jug would be the effect of the colour that existed in the jug in the preceding moment. But odour is never regarded as the effect of colour, though one is the antecedent and the other is the consequent. By similar logic the subsequent colour of the jug also cannot be regarded as the effect of the previous colour, though temporal succession obtains between the two. It must, therefore, be conceded that mere precedence cannot be the ground of causal relation but something deeper and more fundamental, *viz.*, causal operation. In other words, the cause is that whose active operation brings about the effect and is not one that merely precedes in time.

To sum up : if the effect is supposed to be produced from a cause that has become defunct, the effect will be destitute of a cause, as a defunct entity is a pure non-entity. And if it be conceived to be originated by a living cause, the cause must be conceded to exist for more than one moment. So the Buddhist is placed between the two horns of a dilemma. If he admits the former alternative, he cannot explain causation ; if the latter alternative is accepted, he gives up his position—the doctrine of universal flux.

The difficulty of causation is not the only difficulty in the theory of flux. This theory equally fails to explain perception. If all objects are momentary, they cannot be amenable to sense-perception. Perception requires that there should be a contact of the sense-organ with the object; but the object disappears as soon as the contact takes place and so cannot be cognised, as cognition can arise only in the second moment, but by that time there is no object to be cognised. Thus perceptual cognition is rendered impossible and as a consequence causal relation is reduced to an indeterminable phenomenon. Because, causal relation is determined by the joint processes of observation and non-observation of sequence. Thus, when a particular phenomenon is observed to be invariably followed by another phenomenon and with the disappearance of the former the latter also is observed to disappear, the impression is borne in upon us that the two phenomena are causally related. But observation has been ruled out as an impossibility, and non-observation is nothing but a case of observation, in which the locus alone is cognised as unrelated to the object which rested on it.

It has been proved that causation and its cognition become absolutely unaccountable in the theory of flux owing to difficulties lying in the very nature of the objective reality. But there are equally insurmountable difficulties from the subjective side also. Even granting that the object is amenable to perception, there is no constant subject who can connect the two successive events in causal relation. This relationing presupposes that there must be one subject who knows the two events successively. But there is no such subject, as all things including ego-consciousness, are believed to be momentary. The cognising subject varies with the cognitions and so relationing of two events, which is the pre-condition of the knowledge of causality, will be impossible.

Again, recognition as a psychical fact becomes equally unintelligible, because recognition means the cognition by one individual of the identity of two facts happening at different times and thus the continuous identity of the subject and the object is the necessary condition of recognition. But as there is no continuity either in the subject or in the object, recognition as a psychical fact becomes an impossibility in the Buddhist's scheme of philosophy. The Buddhist, however, contends that recognition does not presuppose the permanent identity of an object, as recognition takes place if there is close similarity between the objects concerned as in the case of flames, growing hair and nails. But this contention is perfectly unavailing so far as Buddhist metaphysics is concerned. Granted that the continuity of the object is not necessary for recognition, how can you dispense with the continuity of the subject ? When both the subject and the object are momentary, how can there be any recognition at all ? Besides, how can you account for the rise of desire in a man for the taste of a fruit when he sees only the colour of it ? Certainly he does not experience the taste when he sees it from a distance. It is possible if the man remembers that taste and colour were found to be associated in his previous experience. But this presupposes the functioning of memory and memory presupposes identity of the subject of the two cognitions, which the Buddhist chooses to deny. Moreover, bondage (*bandha*) and liberation (*mokṣa*) become unintelligible fictions if this theory is adhered to ; because the moment that is in the shackles of pain and passion, totally disappears in the second moment and the moment that will be emancipated, will be quite another. And there can be no legitimate aspiration or endeavour for attaining emancipation, as the spirit in bondage will *eo ipso* die out in the second moment and so emancipation will have no meaning as the subject is simply not. Bondage and release can bear an intelligible sense if they relate to an identical self and to say that one is in bondage and another is released is simply to talk nonsense. Bondage and emancipation, whether physical or spiritual, have the same connotation and are intelligible if they connote the successive states of a self-identical individual. By precisely the same logic, memory, determination, teleological plan and purposive activity, search for a thing lost or put in a forgotten place and such other phenomena, which necessarily presuppose the relationing of two experiences by a self-identical subject, will become absolutely impossible of explanation in the theory of flux. Obviously, therefore, a system of philosophy, which fails to render an intelligent account of the major part of our life and experience, must be a bankrupt one, and the sooner one withholds one's allegiance from such a philosophy, the better are the chances of one's realization of life's purpose and meaning.[1]

The Buddhist Position

In reply to this elaborate criticism of Kumārila, Śāntarakṣita and Kamalaśīla observe that the relation of action and result, memory, bondage, emancipation and the rest are all capable of explanation in terms of causality and do not contain any logical or psychological presupposition of an underlying, continuous soul-entity. As in the material, external plane the succession of seed and sprout and the like is determined by the law of causation, so also in the spiritual plane the order and succession of psychical phenomena is precisely governed by the self-same relentless law of causality and a permanent self postulated *ad hoc* as the substratum of these successive states will be an idle appendage, absolutely devoid of logical necessity. Causation, which is expressed in Buddhist terminology as dependent or relative origination (*pratītyasamutpāda*), does not imply anything more or less than pure succession of one thing by another and no permanent substratum underlying or uniting these floating phenomena is cognisable. Good or bad results are seen to issue from actions called good or bad and this is to be set down to the natural constitutive energy of the cause itself and the hypothesis of an energising principle apart from the phenomenon

[1] T. S. and Pañjikā, Śls. 476-500.

itself will be an idle abstraction. "There is action and there is the result, but no agent is found who throws over one complex and adopts another. It is nothing but a conventional formula symbolically expressed in the following terms : 'one being, another is, on the emergence of one, another emerges into being.'"[1]

But Śrīdhara in his *Nyāyakandalī* contends that without a permanent substratum such as the self, the different cognitions emerging successively one after another cannot give rise to the idea of unity of consciousness. Because the cognitions being discrete and self-contained units can have no nexus between and so will fall apart. The hypothesis of a causal relation cannot explain away the unity of conscious life, as the causal relation itself is cognisable only if there is an underlying unitary principle cognising the different cognitions happening at different times. And though cognitions are self-conscious in the Buddhist theory, and as such may be supposed to cognise their own character as cause or effect, as the case may be, this character being a part and parcel of their constitution, still the causal relationship cannot be apprehended, as the idea of relation is possible only if the relata themselves are cognised in one sweep. But cognitions being self-contained and self-regarding in reference and as such absolutely out of relation with one another, there can be no cognition of a relation and consequently no determinative conception of the same (*adhyavasāya*), which follows only in the wake of a previous perceptual cognition.[2]

1 asti karma, asti karmaphalam, kārakas tu nopalabhyate ya imān skandhān ākṣipati, anyāṁś ca skandhān upādatte, anyatra dharmasaṅketāt. tatrāyaṁ dharmasaṅketo yadutā 'smin satī'dam bhavati, asyotpādād idam utpadyata iti. T. S. P., p. 173.

2 pūrvottaradhiyau svamātraniyate kutas tasyāḥ kāraṇam aham, asyāś cā 'smi kāryam iti pratīyetām, parasparavārtānabhijñatvāt. tābhyām agṛhītaṁ kuto 'dhyavasyati, tasyā 'nubhavānusāritvāt. N. K., pp. 71-72.

Ratnakīrti in answer to a criticism of this nature observes in the *Kṣaṇabhaṅgasiddhi* that a subsequent cognition, when generated by a previous cognition, is not a simple entity, but emerges into being as impregnated with the impression of the previous cognition and so the concomitance of the two factors of causality-in-presence is easily apprehended in the form 'one thing happening another happens.' And there is no difficulty in the cognition of this concomitance in absence also. Thus, while a cognition cognising the ground-surface without a jug on it is followed by the subsequent cognition as its effect, the latter emerges along with an impression of the previous non-cognition of the jug and because the impression is there, there is no such thing as the loss of the previous cognition as it is present in the form of a memory-impression in the being of the subsequent cognition and for this no permanent underlying principle need be postulated. The cognitions are certainly self-contained and discrete, but by virtue of the causal relationship the subsequent cognition comes into being instinct with the memory-impression of the former cognition as its legacy. Moreover, if a single cognition is held to be incapable of referring to the previous and subsequent cognitions, how can there be a cognition of this sequence even if there are two distinct cognitions, as these are not mutually related in any wise. The supposition of a permanent substratum, holding the two cognitions in its fold, cannot explain this phenomenon either, unless and until it is supposed to cognise the two cognitions happening at different times by one simple cognition. So here too one cognition has to be postulated and, if so, you cannot legitimately object to the subsequent cognition cognising both itself and the previous cognitions existing in the form of an impression, which you too will have to admit. The only difference is this that you postulate a separate self apart from these facts of cognitions; but as cognitions are self-intuitive and can thus fully account for relational thoughts, the assumption of a unifying permanent self is uncalled for. The supposition, moreover, introduces logical complications in the shape of relations of the self with the discrete cognitions, and these relations, as we have proved before, are nothing but unwarranted makeshifts, running counter to all logical canons. The Buddhist's theory, however, is immune from these logical difficulties. The assumption of a permanent self as a distinct category, therefore, is not only redundant but logically absurd.[1]

The idea of unity of conscious life, Śāntarakṣita contends, is generated by the homogeneity of the contents of the series, the apparent continuum, which, however, is a false abstraction in its turn and as such cannot be pressed into requisition in the philosophical determination of the ultimate nature of things. And this psychical continuum is to be understood as absolutely devoid of an underlying unitary principle in exact parallelism to the continuum of material bodies, which, too, has no existence outside the successive units. Uddyotakara, however, sees a continuity of the causal substance in the effect; he opines that the component parts of the seed-substance, when conjoined with water and soil, enter a new phase and the water and soil too by a process of fermentation produce the juicy substance and this with the seed-components in question culminates in the germinating sprout. So it cannot be said that there is no continuation of the

1 ekāvasāyasamanantarajātam anya-
vijñānam anvayavimarśam upādadhāti ।
evaṁ tad-ekavirahānubhavodbhavānya-
vyāvṛttidhīḥ * prathayati vyatirekabuddhim ॥

evaṁ sati gṛhītānusandhāyaka evā 'yaṁ vikalpaḥ, upādānopādeyabhūtakramipratyakṣadvayagṛhītānusandhānāt.

" yadi nāmai 'kam adhyakṣaṁ na pūrvāparavittimat ।
adhyakṣadvayasadbhāve prākparāvedanaṁ katham ॥ " iti.

SBNT., p. 32.

* The reading '*vyāvṛttadhīḥ*' has been emended by me as '*vyāvṛttidhīḥ*.'

causal substance in the effect.[1] But Śāntarakṣita points out that Uddyotakara's position is absolutely untenable and is based on unwarranted assumptions. Now, Uddyotakara assumes that there is both a continuity and a change and this involves a contradiction in terms. If the soil, water and components of the seed-substance and the like do not suffer any change in their constitution, the sprout and the seed will be identical, as no case for distinction can be made out. And if they are distinct, they must be invested with distinctive characters. Change means difference of nature and this cannot be reconciled with identity. Uddyotakara's contention lays the axe at the very root of the conception of causality. If distinction of the cause and the effect is to be explained, you must say that there is no continuity. You cannot argue by halves.[2]

The contention of Kumārila, that if the cause does not continue and synchronise with the effect, the cause will be defunct and no positive effect can result from a defunct cause, is evidently based on a misconception. The truth of the matter is that the effect is produced in the second moment under the generative influence of the cause, which existed in the immediately preceding moment. The cause in the first moment is a substantive entity and remains unimpaired before the effect is produced.

1 yatho 'ktam Uddyotakareṇa, tatrā 'pi ye bījāvayavās te pūrvavyūhaparityāgena vyūhāntaram āpadyante, vyūhāntarāpattau ca pṛthivīdhātur abdhātunā saṁgṛhītam āntareṇa tejasā pacyamāno rasadravyaṁ nirvarttayati. sa rasaḥ pūrvāvayavasahito 'ṅkurādibhāvam āpadyata iti. tat kathaṁ tatra sūkṣmo 'pi nāṁśo 'stī'ty ucyate. T.S.P., p. 174.

2 yadi pṛthivyādaya uttarasmin sanniveśe varttamānā aparityaktaprāktanasvabhāvā eva varttante, tadā na teṣāṁ pūrvavyūhatyāgo vyūhāntarāpattiś co'papadyate, tādātmyāt, pūrvavat............ atha bhedo 'ṅgīkriyate 'ṅkurādīnām, tadā niyamena prāktanasvabhāvaparityāge sati kṣityādīnāṁ pūrvavyūhatyāgo vyūhāntarāpattiś cā 'ṅgīkartavyā, anyathā bheda eva na syād. T.S.P., p. 174, *ad*, T. S., Śls. 507-508.

It does not assuredly continue up to the second moment that the effect is produced, being momentary. And if it is supposed to continue, it will be perfectly useless as the effect is already produced and the continuing cause will be of no further consequence to it. Certainly the continuing cause cannot be supposed to originate the effect, as the effect has already come into existence and origination means the coming into existence of one that was non-existent. If an existent fact can again be brought into existence, there will be no end of the process. Now the vicious infinite will not be the only issue; there will be no means of distinguishing a cause from an effect, as previous non-existence, which is the characteristic of the effect, can no longer be pressed. In our view of causation, however, no such contingency arises. An effect comes into being in the second moment under the generative efficiency of the cause which exists in the previous moment unimpaired and intact. If the effect was supposed to be produced in the third moment, the objection of defunct cause could be advanced; but this is not admitted by us. Nor does the contingency of the cause synchronising with the effect arise in our position, which could arise if the effect were supposed to be produced in the first moment and if we admitted a co-existent cause (*sahabhū hetu*) like the *Vaibhāṣikas*. But we do not hold any such position, which is logically absurd.[1] Kumārila only commits the blunder of the *Vaibhāṣikas* by making the cause and the effect synchronous. But synchronism

[1] *Vide* T. S., Śls. 509-514. *Cf.* tathā hi yadi tṛtīyādiṣu kṣaṇeṣu kāryaṁ bhavatī 'ty abhyupetaṁ bhavet, yathā Vaibhāṣikair aṅgīkṛtam "eko 'tītaḥ prayacchatī" 'ti, tadā vinaṣṭāt kāraṇāt kāryotpādo 'ṅgīkṛtaḥ syāt. na cā 'yaṁ pakṣo 'smākam, ayuktyupetatvāt. Yaugapadyaprasaṅgo 'pi kadācid bhavet, yadi prathama eva kṣaṇe kāryam iṣyate, yathā tair eva Vaibhāṣikaiḥ sahabhūr hetur iṣyate, tac cai 'tad ayuktam. T. S. P., p. 175.

For a detailed exposition of the nature of '*sahabhū hetu*,' see *Systems of Buddhistic Thought* by Yamakami Sogen, p. 310, and A.K., II., 49-50.

and co-existence of the cause and the effect involve a contradiction in terms. If the cause is non-existent what could produce the effect? If the effect is co-existent with the cause, what will the causal efficiency avail?[1]

It has, however, been urged that the relation of cause and effect is one of subject and object, of agent and product, like that of the potter and the pot and so there is no contradiction in the cause being synchronous with the effect. But this is an unwarranted assumption and only seeks to obfuscate a plain situation. Neither experience nor logic gives us a warrant to suppose that the cause seizes hold of the effect after the fashion of a pair of pincers and then operates upon it; or that the effect comes into being with the cause lovingly caught up in its tight embrace.[2] There is again no logical necessity for postulating the existence of a causal operation as something distinct and apart from the causal entity. If the exercise of causal operation, on which Kumārila lays so much emphasis, is supposed to connote the existence of something distinct from the causal entity, then we must emphatically declare that the whole world of reality, material and spiritual alike, though subject to the relentless operation of the law of causation, is absolutely inert and passive and inoperative. The cause and the effect are equally passive entities in this sense. There is nothing except a succession of moments, one moment following closely upon another moment with a clock-like regularity without the slightest exchange of services. When one moment

[1] asataḥ prāg asāmarthyāt sāmarthye kāryasambhavāt |
kāryakāraṇayoḥ spaṣṭaṁ yaugapadyaṁ virudhyate ||
T. S., Śl. 515.

[2] na hi tat kāryam ātmīyaṁ saṁdaṁśene 'va kāraṇam |
gṛhītvā janayaty etad yaugapadyaṁ yato bhavet ||
nā 'pi gāḍhaṁ samāliṅgya prakṛtiṁ jāyate phalam |
kāmī 'va dayitāṁ yena sakṛdbhāvas tayor bhavet ||
T. S., Śls. 516-17.

follows another moment, the previous entity is spoken of as generating the subsequent entity and the two entities are respectively called the cause and the effect. There is no such thing as functioning of one thing into the other and when we speak of one thing as producing another thing, we mean nothing more than their pure succession. Our expressions cannot be held to represent the real state of things. Language does not conform to the rigorous nature of truth ; on the contrary, it follows the guidance of convention which is traceable ultimately to nothing but the speaker's habitual predilection for a particular mode of speech.[1]

We have seen that the hypothesis of separate function from the causal entity is not logically tenable. We cannot also discover any logical necessity for this assumption and we do not find what particular purpose may be served by this distinctive causal operation. The causal operation has been postulated to make the immediate production of the effect possible. But this is not at all necessary. The actual precedence of the cause is sufficient to account for this production ; then why should you insist on its separate functioning, which is an unnecessary and uncalled for assumption after all ? If, however, causal functioning or operation is thought to satisfy an intellectual curiosity, why do you suppose that it should be necessarily distinct from the cause itself ? The cause and the causal operation can be regarded as the same thing—its very struggle to come unto

[1] niyamād ātmahetūtthāt prathamakṣaṇabhāvinaḥ ।
yad yato 'nantaraṁ jātaṁ dvitīyakṣaṇasannidhiḥ ॥
tat taj janayatī 'ty āhur avyāpāre 'pi vastuni ।
vivakṣāmātrasambhūtasaṅketānuvidhāyinaḥ ॥

T.S., Śls. 518-19.

Cf. janayatī 'ty upalakṣaṇam, tattad āśrityo 'tpadyata ity api vijñeyam.

T. S. P., *sub voce.*

itself, its very existence can be construed as its operation.[1] In fact, the Buddhist is an advocate of the dynamic constitution of things and he seriously maintains that there is no reality which is static and stationary. Everything in his view is in perpetual motion and there is no rest and no cry for halt. What he objects to is the affirmation of a causal energy as distinct from the causal entity originally inert and passive. The thing moving cannot be abstracted from motion—the two are one indivisible whole and the idea of abstract motion is but an intellectual fiction. It may, however, be urged that if there is no causal functioning, then how could the idea of dependence be explained? The effect is said to depend upon the cause for its origination and the cause is regarded as conditioning the effect. Quite so; but this dependence is nothing but the invariable sequence of the cause and the effect. The fact that an effect invariably follows the cause is construed into a relation of dependence; but this is only our interpretation of this invariable sequence and is no argument for its objective existence.[2]

Again, what is the factual basis of this supposition of causal functioning as a distinct factor in causation? Certainly, it is the invariable sequence of the cause and the effect, on which this hypothesis is grounded. You posit a separate causal operation when you see that a particular effect invariably accompanies

1 janmātiriktakālena vyāpāreṇā 'tra kiṁ phalam |
sattai 'va vyāpṛtis tasyāṁ satyāṁ kāryodayo yataḥ ||
T. S., Śl. 520.

Cf. also a Buddhavacana,
tatre 'dam uktaṁ Bhagavatā,

'kṣaṇikāḥ sarvasaṁskārā asthirāṇāṁ kutaḥ kriyā |
bhūtir yai 'ṣāṁ kriyā sai 'va kārakaṁ sai 'va co 'cyate ||
Quoted in the T.S.P.

(The reading '*yeṣām*' is obviously a misprint or a scribe's error. The reading '*yai'ṣā*' found in some books is also sensible, p. 11.)

2 ya ānantaryaniyamaḥ saivā 'pekṣā 'bhidhīyate |
kāryodaye sadā bhāvo vyāpāraḥ kāraṇasya ca ||
Ibid, Śl. 521.

another entity called the cause and you assume that without this causal operation functioning independently or as an integral part of the basal cause, the causal factor is inefficient regarding the effect to be produced. But the fundamental datum of this assumption is not anything more or less than the invariable concomitance of the two factors in question attested in a number of instances under observation. In the circumstances we do not see any necessity for postulating the existence of a *tertium quid*, a separate causal operation apart and distinct from the basal cause. Nor do we visualise any harmful issue if we suppose that it is the cause in question, which produces the effect ; on the other hand, we have the full sanction of experience on our side. When the full complement of causes and conditions is present, the effect is seen to be produced invariably and without fail. We certainly do not pretend to any occult powers whereby we can envisage the existence of the functioning or operation distinct from the entities themselves. Nor do we see any logical necessity for inferring this additional factor. But the näive realist may assert that a cause, static and inoperative, is as good as non-existent and if it is to be efficient, it must energise and this is possible if there is an energising operation over and above. We admit the plausibility of the hypothesis. But we elect to enquire of Kumārila if this 'energising function' produces the effect independently of another operation or not. If it requires another operation, that will require a third and the third will require a fourth and so on to infinity ; it must be admitted for avoiding this contingency that 'energising' is self-sufficient and independent of any external help. And if this be so, what is the harm if you think the causal entity to be the self-sufficient cause of the effect ? On the contrary, you will not have to posit any invisible agency—an altogether gratuitous assumption. Certainly you do not gain anything by positing the existence of an unnecessary *tertium quid*, but on the other hand, you offend the Law of Parsimony which requires us to suppose the fewest possible factors for explanation of a phenomenon. We, however, demur to subscribe to the *Naiyāyika's* contention that causal operation can be distinctly envisaged. We forswear all pretentions to any such extraordinary powers of vision.

The logical absurdities of the position of the näive realists can be brought home by a dilemma. Is this causal operation or energising, which has been heralded by Kumārila with such a flourish of trumpets, something distinct or non-distinct from the causal factors themselves? If it is something distinct, you should believe this to be the cause and not the previous entity, say, the seed. It may, however, be contended that the previous entity as informed with this energising is the cause and neither the cause nor the energising in isolation has any efficiency. So neither of the two is superfluous. But this interpretation will only make the hypothesis open to dialectical difficulties. If these two factors, to wit, the basal cause and the energising, are really two distinct entities as you posit, how could there be any relation between them? For the relationing of the cause and the effect you had to assume a *tertium quid, viz.*, the energising, as the connecting link. But as this energising is equally a distinct fact, it will also hang loose unless there is another 'energising' to bring them together. And so an infinite number of causal operations or energisings will have to be assumed and yet the effect will not be produced. If, on the other hand, this energising or operation is supposed to be something non-distinct, it will be an idle appendage to the causal entity. So neither logic nor experience gives any warrant to postulate the existence of causal operation in contradistinction to the causal entity and so no case has been made out against the fluxional entity becoming a cause in its own right.

Moreover, Kumārila cannot consistently insist upon the proposition that an unfunctioning cause cannot have any efficiency, since he admits that our cognitions do not require a separate functioning or operation to cognise their objects. These cognitions apprehend their objects as soon as they are born, since our states of consciousness are momentary and so cannot last a moment longer, in which they could exercise their operative efficiency. Kumārila has to make an exception in favour of cognitive states, which he admits in common with the Buddhists to enjoy only a moment's existence. But the argument applies to all causes alike, as the momentary nature of all entities has been proved to the hilt and so causal functioning or energizing, by which Kumārila laid so much store, is only an inconsequential hypothesis without any bearing whatsoever upon causality.[1] The next objection of Kumārila—that if mere antecedence bereft of operative efficiency is regarded as the determinant of causal relation, it will make the odour of the jug an effect of the colour preceding it—has no force against the Buddhist theory of causation. If the whole series of successive moments be ideally comprehended as a continuum, the colour and the odour can be believed to be causally related. We do not, however, regard mere antecedence as the determinant of causal relation, but invariable and unconditional antecedence. So there is absolutely no necessity for supposing that an antecedent as exercising a causal operation in the second moment is the cause of the subsequent entity so operated upon, since an invariable and unconditional antecedent will meet the situation.

Again, the objection that perception of external reality will become impossible of explanation, because the object and its cognition are not synchronous, does not affect the Buddhist position in particular. It is a common epistemological difficulty and its solution will be of a piece with that proposed by other schools of thought. The problem of perception as to how the mind can take stock of the external objective reality is an eternal problem and is neither enhanced nor minimised whether the reality is

[1] buddher yathā ca janmai 'va pramāṇatvaṁ nirudhyate |
tathai 'va sarvabhāveṣu taddhetutvaṁ na kiṁ matam ||
kṣaṇikā hi yathā buddhis tathai 'vā 'nye 'pi janminaḥ |
sādhitās tadvad evā 'to nirvyāpāram idam jagat ||

T.S., Śls. 528-29.

regarded as permanent or fluxional. There are two possible theories which have been advocated by different schools of thought. One theory maintains that our consciousness is clear like a clean slate and does not depart an inch from its intrinsic purity even when it apprehends the external reality. Consciousness is an amorphous substance and remains so in all its activities. It is like light and reveals the object with its form and qualities without undergoing any morphological articulation in its constitution. This is called the theory of formless perception (*nirākāra-jñāna*).[1] It may be designated for the sake of convenience as the theory of presentative perception. There is another theory, which may be called the theory of representative perception (*sākāravijñānavāda*). The latter theory holds that knowledge of external reality is made possible by virtue of the objective reality leaving an impress of its likeness on the mirror of consciousness. The *Sāṅkhya*, *Vedānta* and the *Sautrāntika* Buddhists are advocates of the latter theory. It appears, however, from the *Tattvasaṅgrahapañjikā* that there was a class of Buddhist thinkers who held the opposite theory of presentative perception. Kumārila and the *Nyāya-Vaiśeṣika* school regarded perception as non-representative in character, as they thought that the representational theory gave a convenient handle to the subjective idealists for denial of external reality altogether. Perception is held to be direct awareness of the reality and to be without any content on the subjective side. The contention of the idealist, that awareness and its content are one inseparable whole and so are intuited together, was thus made out to be a groundless assumption. All external perception is thus awareness of something, distinct from and external to the subjective awareness, which was held to be amorphous (*nirākāra*) in nature. The form and configuration perceived belong to external reality

1 *Cf.* "ākāravān bāhyo 'rtho nirākārā-buddhiḥ."

Quoted in the T. S. P., p. 101.

and these have no representative or counterpart in the psychosis, which is formless and amorphous.[1]

Śāntarakṣita and Kamalaśīla observe that both these theories have their advocates in the camp of the Buddhists and the theory of flux has no special difficulty in either case. If perceptual knowledge, or all knowledge for the matter of that, is regarded as a contentless, pure, amorphous awareness and as taking stock of the objective reality directly and immediately, the Buddhist can accept this theory without prejudice to his metaphysical position, *viz.*, the doctrine of momentariness of things. The particular cognition of an object is to be supposed to be engendered by a common set of causes and conditions, which ushers into existence the object and the cognition as co-products at one and the same time. The cognitive relation between the two factors is to be explained by a law of harmony or mutual affinity inherent in the constitutional peculiarity of the subjective and the objective factor. And this is the only possible explanation of the etiology of perceptual knowledge and the Buddhist shares the difficulties or advantages of this theory equally with the non-Buddhist schools. If, on the other hand, perception is believed to be representational in character, it would be a perception of the likeness or image of the objective reality as imprinted on the perceptual cognition by the reality itself. In this case, however, the perceptual knowledge will be cognisant of the likeness or the mental portrait of the objective reality in the first instance and this perception of the likeness forming the mental content is to be vicariously regarded as perception of the objective reality itself. The so-called perception of the external object will be nothing more than a perception

[1] *Cf.* "All the sciences united are nothing but the human understanding, which remains one and the same however varied be the objects to which it applies itself, and which is no more altered than is the light of the sun by the variety of the objects it illumines." *Regulae*, I (XI, p. 202). Quoted in "Studies in the Cartesian Philosophy," by Norman Smith, p. 22.

of the likeness or the copy of the object imprinted on the mental canvas and as such may be regarded as mediate and indirect in character.[1] Moreover, it has been urged that this theory of representative perception not only makes perception vicarious and indirect, but it also degrades consciousness into the position of a variegated canvas, impressed as it will be with all the forms and colours of the external objects. And in the opposite theory also, the relation of awareness and the object cannot be explained, as there is no connecting medium between the two. Awareness will be pure, indeterminate awareness and not awareness of this or that, unless the two are supposed to be brought together. If you seek to explain the difficulty by an appeal to the specific individuality of the two factors and by postulating the operation of a law of harmony or fitness, the Buddhist philosopher will also have recourse to some such theory. And if the difficulties of the representational theory are sought to be explained away by regarding the likeness or the portrait to be a fictitious articulation, or by holding the two factors, *viz.*, the awareness and its content, as one and the same thing being essentially spiritual alike, the Buddhist also will offer this explanation. The objection, that the object of cognition has passed out of existence when the cognition is supposed to come into being and so the cognition will have no reference to the object, is based on a misconception of the representative theory itself. In this theory the object of direct perception is no longer the external uncompromising reality, but only a likeness or image of the same imprinted on the consciousness. So what is perceived is a content of consciousness itself and the existence of the external object at the time of perceptual cognition does not give any

[1] "na hi mukhyato yādṛśam jñānasyā 'tmasaṁvedanaṁ tādṛg evā 'rthasye 'ṣṭam, kiṁ tarhi? svābhāsajñānajanakatvam evā'rthasya saṁvedyatvam." T.S.P., p. 570, under Śls. 2034-2035.

Also, "sākārajñānapakṣe ca tannirbhāsasya vedyatā."

Loc. cit.

advantage. The presence of the content is only necessary for perceptual knowledge and not of the external object, which will have served its purpose if it has left an impress of itself on the mind. And so even if the object is believed to persist and thus to synchronise with the perceptual knowledge, this synchronism, apart from the question of its logical relevancy, will have no bearing on the psychology of perception, as explained by us. So Kumārila only fights with a shadow.

As regards the objection of loss of earned merit and enjoyment of unearned deserts, it must be stated that no such contingency arises in the Buddhist theory of causation. There would be loss of earned merit if the productive efficiency of the previous agent was absolutely lost with the disappearance of the agent, which, however, is not the case. The productive efficiency, whether of good or evil, is transmitted in and through the series of moments until it matures and exhausts itself in the production of the effect in question. It is not necessary that the agent should continue in order to make the production of the effect possible, as the continuity of the series will serve the purpose. But the effect actually takes place as soon as the causal efficiency reaches maturation and so there is no loss of earned deserts. Similarly, the argument of enjoyment of unearned deserts could be brought home if there had been no productive factor in the series. But this is denied by us, the Buddhists. No effect is produced unless there has been a potent cause for it in any one of the constituent moments of the series. Though the particular moment, which discharged the meritorious action, has disappeared, it leaves behind a legacy of its merit in the shape of an unconscious driving impulse (*vāsanā*) which runs down in and through all the moments of the consciousness-series until finally it exhausts itself in the production of the expected result. The moments of our conscious life are not simple entities, but have unsuspected powers and potencies, which discover themselves only by their results. Śrīdhara urges that an unstable consciousness, existing only for a moment, cannot either receive or retain this *vāsanā* in its being and so we have to postulate a permanent, continuous substratum, which can hold and retain this for an indefinite length of time. But this objection cannot stand examination. We do not see how a permanent substratum can be of any help. Certainly the supposed permanent agent, when it discharges a meritorious act, does not continue to be the same unchanged entity as before. On the contrary, it must be supposed that the permanent agent has come to be vested with a different property by reason of which it ultimately enjoys the fruits of its meritorious action. But this can be possible of explanation if the conscious agent undergoes material change of nature, and if, on the other hand, it continues in its previous unblest condition, no explanation of the enjoyment of reward can be offered. Paradoxical though it may appear, it is the theory of flux which can explain the law of retribution—this theory of reward and punishment. If the agent is supposed to be a permanent, unchanging soul-entity, there can be no activity, voluntary or involuntary, on its part, far less the enjoyment of fruits of its labour. The theory of reward and punishment, a corollary of the law of retribution, which has been postulated by all schools of thought as the only explanation of the variety and inequalities of the world-order, will thus collapse like a house of cards, if the doctrine of a permanent, unchanging self is adhered to, as the permanent is not amenable to any activity.

Kumārila, however, pleads that the complaint of loss of earned merit and enjoyment of unearned deserts is not based on the loss of merit acquired by an agent, as the Buddhist does not recognise any agent at all. The objection rests on the fundamental assumption that the action, responsible for the result, is lost completely and irrevocably and the result is supposed to emerge without a causal basis. But we, Buddhists, plead guilty to the charge and our apology is that no such continuity is either logically necessary or defensible. The law of causality governing a particular psychical continuum is adequate to explain this phenomenon and the continuation of the agentive moment does not facilitate, nor does its discontinuation frustrate, the operation of this causal law. It will do if a particular result has a predecessor in the series, possessing generative efficiency for the same. What is necessary is this generative efficiency and it continues unimpaired in the series, being born anew with each resultant factor. That the two moments, the agentive and the enjoying factors, are distinct and discrete entities is acknowledged by us and if this be the gravamen of his complaint, we welcome the issue as an inevitable consequence of the law of causality. If you seek to avoid this consequence, you can do so on the pain of denial of the law of causality, which is tantamount to denial of all attempts at a philosophical explanation of experience and reality.

The next objection of Kumārila is that voluntary activity will be impossible if all things, the subjective consciousness included, are momentary, because the subject, convinced of his utter doom in the next moment, will have no incentive for action, as the consequences will not be enjoyed or suffered by him. But this objection is devoid of all substance. Now, there are two classes of persons, who engage in a voluntary action, to wit, in the first place, the enlightened, who have realised the fluxional nature of all existence, and, in the second place, the unenlightened, who have not yet attained to this transcendental knowledge. So far as the latter are concerned, there is absolutely no ground of apprehension of any such crisis. The unregenerate person is in the grip of delusion and is absolutely persuaded of the unity and permanence of his ego-consciousness. And this idea of a permanent ego-principle is due to his mistaking the apparent continuum of the conscious states for an undivided unitary self. In reality, however, our consciousness does not possess any unity at all; it is nothing but an ever-flowing, unimpeded procession of unique conscious moments, each sharply divided from the other. The unity of consciousness is only an illusion, generated by the homogeneity of the conscious units coupled with their uninterrupted career, their ceaseless continuum, which experiences no check and never comes to an abrupt end. But the unregenerate person, deluded by the surface-appearance of things, is not convinced of the illusory nature of his egoism and so engages in all pursuits with a view to ulterior results, which he hopes to enjoy for himself. To him it makes no difference whether the ego-consciousness is a momentary phantom or a permanent fixture, because he is under the hypnotic spell of ignorance (*avidyā*) and is not in a mood to philosophise. As regards the enlightened soul, who has realised that all existents are momentary and the ego-consciousness is an unreal phantom, for him, too, there is absolutely no difficulty or bar to be engaged in active pursuits for the deliverance of unregenerate persons. He is aware that the world of reality, both subjective and objective, is governed by the inexorable law of causality, under the influence of which a good and meritorious action eventually results in the good and well-being of all sentient beings and it is out of a super-abundance of love and an innate irresistible charity of heart that the enlightened being engages himself in this active humanitarian mission. Such a spirit, though free and illuminated himself, does not feel happy so long as the world is unfree and is caught up in the eddy of universal misery. He takes up the burden of the misery of the entire world upon his own shoulders and throws himself heart and soul into a long drawn-out campaign against this universal suffering. Though personally (if we can use such an expression regarding the enlightened being who has seen through the illusion of personalised existence), the *Bodhisattva* has no cause of misery, he identifies himself with the whole order of suffering creatures and poignantly feels the sting of misery that is tormenting the whole world. So far from enjoying the blessedness of isolation and peace of impersonalism, which is his due, he becomes one of the busiest and the most miserable of all living beings. Personal motivation plays no part in his mission of universal love and he is the antithesis of the wicked person who feels an impersonal pleasure in doing evil. The wicked man scatters misery all over the world and makes it a mission of his life. The *Bodhisattva* is his counterpart and his mission of universal love and selfless service is equally an impersonal motivation.[1]

As regards the objection respecting memory, recognition, and the like, there is absolutely no difficulty in the theory of flux. These psychical phenomena are strictly governed by the law of causation and they appear in that psychical continuum (*santāna*), in which a previous cognition took place at some past moment. It is neither logically nor psychologically necessary that the remembering moment must be identical with the cognising moment, as the identity of the subjective continuum will do. That the said memory does not appear in a different subjective centre is due to the regulative power of this law of causality and for this a permanent ego-principle need not be postulated, as the ego-principle logically fails to connect these phenomena in the unity of a whole.[2] And when an explanation, consonant with the principles of logic, is possible, it is certainly unwarranted that an illogical hypothesis should be entertained. Memory therefore is not impossible of explanation in the theory of flux and recognition, enquiry and such like psychical phenomena, which presuppose a relationing of two independent cognitions and thus proceed from memory, are likewise explicable in the light of causality.

[1] ahīnasattvadṛṣṭīnāṁ kṣaṇabhedavikalpanā । santānaikyābhimānena na kathañcit pravartate । abhisambuddhatattvās tu pratikṣaṇavināśinām । hetūnāṁ niyamaṁ buddhvā prārabhante śubhāḥ kriyaḥ । T.S., śls. 541-42.

cf. 'yāvac cā 'tmani na premṇo hāniḥ sapadi naśyati । tāvad duḥkitvam āropya na ca svastho 'vatiṣṭhate । mithyādhyāropahānārthaṁ yatno 'saty api bhoktarī' ti । Pañj., *ad ibid.*

[2] The failure of a permanent soul to cement all the diverse experience units by a common bond lies in the dialectical difficulties of reconciling permanence with change, continuity with diversity. This will become manifest in our examination of the different soul-theories.

As regards bondage and emancipation, they, too, do not relate to an identical subject. Bondage is nothing but consciousness in the grip of ignorance, the fountain-head of passions and defilements which vitiate the conscious life in the phenomenal plane. Emancipation is the dissociation of consciousness from these overgrowths of *avidyā* (ignorance or nescience), and once disentangled from the shackles of these imperfections, consciousness shines in its undimmed glory and absolute purity and this is emancipation in our view.[1] Furthermore, there is no example which shows that bondage and emancipation are the successive stages of one and the same person, as every thing is subject to change and so physical bondage and physical release even relate to two distinct entities. On the contrary, the very idea of bondage and emancipation is incompatible with the idea of a permanent ego-principle, because the permanent self will not be subject to any change, which this difference of condition involves and indicates. If liberation connotes an appearance of a novel character, it will not relate to the permanent unchanging soul. If, however, the soul is conceived to be identified with this novel phenomenon, it will be momentary like the latter. If, on the other hand, it is conceived to hang apart and not to relate to the soul, the soul will continue in its pristine inglorious and unregenerate condition and will not be emancipated. So the opponent is compelled to accept our theory of universal flux if he attempts to give a rational explanation of the theory of bondage and emancipation, which we have proved to be absolutely incompatible with the idea of a permanent self, that was trotted out by the opponent as the fundamental presupposition of this universal doctrine of religion. The interests of religion and metaphysics are therefore safe in the keeping of

[1] kāryakāraṇabhūtāś ca tatrā 'vidyādayo matāḥ |
bandhas tadvigamād iṣṭo muktir nirmalatā dhiyaḥ | T.S., śl. 544.
cf. cittam eva hi saṁsāro rāgādikleśavāsitam |
tād eva tair vinirmuktaṁ bhavānta iti kathyate |
T.S.P., *ad ibid.*

this doctrine of universal flux and the theory of permanent cause and permanent self is only a false guardian and a false philosophy.

To sum up: we have seen that the difficulties and objections, advanced by the philosophers of rival schools against the theory of universal flux, are imaginary and fanciful and are based upon a short-sighted logic and surface-view of reality. They do not at all affect the solid foundations of the doctrine of flux ; on the contrary, they find their solution in it, which other systems have failed to afford.

Reference:

1. Tattvasaṅgraha and the Pañjikā, ślś. 476-545, pp. 166-85.
2. Kṣaṇabhaṅgasiddhi in the six Buddhist Nyāya tracts, pp. 20-77 (28-32 pages particularly relevant).
3. Nyāyakandalī, pp. 71-82.
4. Nyāyamañjarī, pp. 444-67.
5. Śloka-Vārtika, pp. 728-845.

CHAPTER VI

A Buddhist Estimate of Universals

The philosophers of the *Nyāya-Vaiśeṣika* school have postulated two different types of universals or genuses (*jātis*), *viz.*, (1) Existence (*sattā*) and (2) Substantiality and the rest. The first is the highest universal, the universal *par excellence*, the summum genus (*parā jāti*), because it only serves to bring all existents together under one category and emphasises their community of nature without any reference to their mutual differences. A universal has been defined as a unitary (*ekam*), eternal (*nitya*) principle underlying and informing a number of individual beings.[1] Different individuals are grouped under one category by virtue of this unitary principle which inheres in them, one and all. Its supreme function is assimilation. The highest universal, *viz.*, existence, exercises this function *par excellence*. The other universals, *viz.*, the substance-universal (*dravyatva*), the quality-universal (*guṇatva*), the action-universal (*karmatva*), are minor universals (*aparā jātis*), because they not only assimilate different individuals into one class or group, but they also serve to differentiate one class and the members thereof from another class and its constituent members. Thus these universals have a double function and a double aspect, *viz.*, assimilation and differentiation. The highest universal exercises the function of assimilation alone, which is the proper function of a universal. Hence it is called the highest and supremest of all universals.

These philosophers further maintain that these universals are objective entities and are envisaged in perceptual cognitions

[1] nityam ekaṁ anekānugataṁ sāmānyam. The words, *sāmānya* and *jāti*, are synonymous.

as much as individual objects, as the idea of universals arises on the operation of sense-object contact. And the existence of these universals can be demonstrated by a regular syllogistic inference also. Our perceptual experience is not of the particular cow, but contains a reference to another distinct principle, which is not confined to the individual concerned, but continues in other individuals in the same manner and in the same degree. Had this experience been cognisant of the particular individual alone, the reference would have been different in different individuals, as in the case of a cow and a horse. But this is not the case ; there is a sameness of reference in our cognitions of different cows and this identity of reference, linguistic and psychological alike, can be accounted for only on the assumption of a universal element super-added to particulars.[1] The existence or non-existence of an objective reality can be determined by the arbitration of experience alone and the dictum that 'excess in knowledge pre-supposes a corresponding excess in the objective order,'[2] should be accepted by all believers in extra-mental reality. So the particular and the universal should be accepted as equally true and equally real and there is no contradiction or logical incompatibility in these two factors coalescing in one substratum. Logic becomes a tyrant when it arrogates to itself the power of dictating terms to experience *ex cathedra*. You cannot dictate that the universal and the particular are mutually contradictory and so cannot be found together. After all, what constitutes incompatibility and contradiction ? Well, we consider a position incompatible, which has not the sanction of valid experience, or in other words, which has not been cognised by means of any of the recognised instruments of knowledge. And we regard any two things to be mutually contradictory when we do not find them to co-exist in one substratum. When there is

[1] tasmād ekasya bhinneṣu yā vṛttis tannibandhanaḥ I sāmānyaśabdaḥ sattādāv ekadhikāraṇena vā I S. V., Ākṛtivāda.

[2] viṣayātiśayam antareṇa pratyayātiśayānupapatteḥ. N. M., p. 314.

contradiction between two things, there can be no co-existence ; on the contrary, one of them is superseded by another. Light and darkness are regarded to be contradictory, because they are not found to co-exist. But if co-existence of two things is attested by uncontradicted experience, there is no earthly reason why they should be regarded as mutually contradictory. And in the present case of the universal and the particular there is absolutely no contradiction or logical incompatibility as they are found to co-exist in perfect amity and peace. Nor can this experience be challenged, as there is no other experience to contradict its truth. The experience of silver in the mother-o'-pearl is regarded as false, as it is sublated by a subsequent experience of the mother-o'-pearl. So the co-existence of the universal and the particular is neither incompatible, as it is attested by undisputed experience ; nor is it contradictory as there is no sublative experience to prove its falsity.[1] The doctrine of universal flux, which maintains that all existents are momentary, cannot be accepted as it fails to render an adequate explanation of the class-concepts, which cannot be denied an objective foundation unless the position of extreme subjectivism is seriously maintained. The subjective idealists (*Vijñānavādins*), who regard the whole objective world to be a phantasmagoria conjured up by a diseased imagination, have at any rate the virtue of consistency to their credit ; but the *Sautrāntikas*, the so-called critical realists, have

[1] yad apy abhihitam itaretaraviruddharūpasamāveśa ekatra vastuni no 'papadyata iti tad api na samyak,

parasparavirodho 'pi nāstī'ha tadavedanāt |
ekabādhena nā 'nyatra dhīḥ śuktirajatādivat |

yatra hi virodho bhavati tatrai 'katararūpopamardena rupāntaram upalabhyate, prakṛte tu nai 'vam iti ko virodhārthaḥ. chāyātapāv api yady ekatra dṛśyete, kiṁ kena viruddham abhidhīyate, adarśanāt tu tad viruddham uktam, na cai 'vam ihā 'darśanam ity avirodhaḥ. N. M., p. 311.

Also, 'anupapannam iti naḥ kva sampratyayo yan na pramāṇenā 'vagatam, viruddham api tad budhyāmahe, yad ekatra niviśamānaṁ na paśyāmaḥ,'—*Ibid*, p. 547.

not got this redeeming virtue. Their philosophy is at best a compromise between honest realism and honest idealism and like all compromises it is but a hopeless failure. They choose to deny reality to relations and class-concepts, which, according to them, are as much unreal and fictitious creations of the morbid imagination as they are in the idealist's scheme, and yet they believe in the reality of the extra-mental world. But this realistic concession is neither here nor there. It satisfies neither the idealist nor the realist. It is not a healthy philosophy, whatever else it might be.

The Sautrāntika's Reply to the Realist's Charge.

Śāntarakṣita and Paṇḍita Aśoka, whose works have come down to us in their original form, have given crushing replies to the realist's charges. The idea of a continuous identity underlying all the different individuals, by which the *Naiyāyika* has laid so much store, will appear on strict examination to be a pleasant illusion of the realists. There is not only not a shred of evidence in favour of the existence of such objective categories, but there is, on the other hand, incontestable proof against this supposition. The contention of the *Naiyāyika* that ideas of universals arise immediately on the operation of the sense-object contact is not true, because such ideas are conceptual in character and conceptual thoughts can emerge only after the name-relations are remembered. First of all, there is the sensuous presentation immediate and direct and divested of all foreign reference. Secondly, a mental energising towards the recalling of the verbal association; thirdly, the remembrance of the name. So the mind has travelled far away from the immediate datum of presentation and the idea of the class-character arises only after a series of psychical operations, which have little bearing on the immediate objective datum. To say therefore that class-ideas are sensuous presentations is to betray psychological ineptitude and uncritical reading of experience. The class-idea is formed only when there is a reference through memory to past objects and so this idea is but the result of a confusion between a past object represented by memory and the presentation of a sense-datum. The unreality of these conceptual constructions will be proved to demonstration in the chapter on perception.

It may be urged that if the class-character is not an objective entity envisaged in perception, then, how could such ideas arise at all ? The particulars are absolutely distinct from one another and have nothing in common according to the Buddhist's theory ; and so the idea of community cannot be generated by them. The particulars may have efficiency in regard to their own ideas and as this efficiency varies in each individual, the idea of the universal cannot be accounted for by reference to these particular efficiencies either.[1] But this objection has no substance. Though the particulars may be absolutely distinct and discrete, still they can generate, owing to a determinate constitutive energy inhering in each of them, a common idea, an identical concept. This fact of one uniform efficiency is found in distinct individuals. Thus, the myrobalan, the *āmalakī* fruit (*dhātrī*) and other substances are seen to cure diseases of the same sort. Now these substances are admittedly different from one another and yet they are found in experience to possess a common efficiency. It cannot be supposed that these different medicinal herbs and fruits possess a common nature, that is to say, they are informed and enlivened by a permanent universal, which exercised this common efficiency; because in that case, the efficiency would be absolutely invariable and identical in respect of time and magnitude. But this is not the case ; one is seen to afford speedy relief, another to be sluggish in operation and the magnitude of efficiency also is seen to be variable in different substances. Had there been one unalterable rigid principle underlying them all, these differences in operation and efficiency could not be expected. Nor can these variations be set down to the action of other

[1] *Vide* S. V., śls, 15-17, Chapter on Ākṛtivāda.

factors, *e.g.*, difference of time and place of production of the medicinal herbs and fruits. Because, these differences cannot have any effect, either in the way of detraction or of supplementation, on an unalterable, eternal verity, which, on pain of self-destruction, must be impervious to all such external influences. Exactly on the analogy of the above cases, different individuals possessing a uniform psychological efficiency can be accepted as a reasonable hypothesis. And as regards the linguistic usage, too, there is no difficulty whatsoever. When causal efficiency in its widest and most comprehensive sense is intended to be understood, such expressions, as 'entity' (*sat*), 'thing' (*vastu*) and the like are applied to all existents. Particular expressions, horse, cow and the like, are employed to designate peculiar sets of causal efficiency, such as ploughing, carrying, milk-yielding and the like. And as has been set forth above by the analogy of the common medical action of different herbs and plants, particulars, though discrete and distinct, may produce a common psychological action. The concept of the universal is nothing but an intellectual fiction, an adumbration of the mind, which, however, is hypostatised as an objective reality existing in its own right, independently of the thinking mind.[1] These conceptual fictions have a pragmatic value no doubt ; but this pragmatic utility is due to the particular objective reality, of which the universal is a remote derivative.[2]

The contention of the realist that our perceptual cognitions contain a distinct reference to the universal apart from the form and configuration of the individual is a hollow assertion unsupported by experience. The underlying universal is described by you to be an entity devoid of form, colour and verbal association ; but our cognitions have invariably these attributes as

[1] antarmātrāsamārūḍhaṁ sāṁvṛtam avalambya te |
bahīrūpādhyavasitaṁ pravarttante 'ṅkuśādikam | *Ibid.*, śl. 735.
antarmātrā—buddhiḥ. T. S. P., *ad ibid.*

[2] T. S., śls. 728-29.

their contents. A universal, amorphous and colourless, is never envisaged in perceptual cognitions. Śaṅkarasvāmin,[1] however, opines that the universals are not amorphous entities, but they have the same perceptible qualities, form and colour, etc., as the individuals. The universal of 'blue' has the features of the individual 'blue' and so the different individuals are referable to one catagory. But this view is equally untenable and makes no improvement. If the universal is believed to have the same characteristics with the individual, there is left no means of distinguishing it from the individual in question. And if the two are supposed to be presented as an undistinguishable whole, with its contents lumped together, then, how could there arise the distinct verbal and psychical references, on which the *Naiyāyika* laid so much stress? The entire argument of the realists is pivoted on the supposition that class concepts and identity of nomenclature will be unaccountable if the objective existence of universals is not admitted and this supposition is a necessary corollary of the more fundamental assumption that all our knowledge is derived from sense-data presented in perception.[2] Our consciousness is but a receptive medium without any constructive faculty or power to conjure up an idea, which is not ultimately derived from objective experience. In fact, this is a fundamental attitude of mind and has divided philosophers into rival schools. So there is no reason to be optimistic that one day all philosophers will sink their differences and profess one philosophy. Philosophy is not so much a question of conviction or carrying conviction as it is a question of mental attitude and outlook of thought and habit of thinking. It will

[1] Śaṇkarasvāmī tv āha—sāmānyam api nīlatvādi ṇīlādyākāram eva, anyathā hi nīla ity evam anuvṛttipratyayo na syāt. T.S.P., pp. 243-44.

Vide also śls. 740-42, T.S.

[2] *Cf.* Essays in Radical Empiricism, p. 42. The same tendency is seen to be at work in the Empiricism of James, though the conclusions which he deduces from this fundamental postulate are widely at variance from those reached by the *Naiyāyika* realist.

be therefore better and more consonant with truth to say that the task of philosophers is rather conversion than logical conviction. The phenomenon of rival schools of thought holding contradictory views and constantly fighting with one another, however unphilosophical it may appear, will not be a thing of past history, because the fundamental attitudes of mind, the bias of our thought-movement, cannot be changed or destroyed. But ratiocination is the accredited instrument of all philosophy and there is a common modicum of rationality in all human beings and so the proselytising activity in philosophical circles will never come to an end, the failures of the past notwithstanding. So we must try to clinch the issue on logical grounds.

Even granting that class-concepts are grounded in objective reality still it cannot be proved that there is an eternal, undying universal running through the discrete individuals, because in that case its cognition would not be contingent on the cognition of particulars, which are admittedly impermanent. But this objective foundation is purely a figment of the imagination. What objective foundation can be trotted out for such concepts as 'thing' or 'entity'? You cannot postulate the existence of a higher universal, to wit, thingness, because that only shifts the difficulty to 'thingness' itself. The concept of thingness would require another universal and that again another and so on to infinity. To avoid this vicious infinite series the *Naiyāyika* has to assume that universals are a class of *sui generis* categories and that they do not participate in other universals. The sameness of verbal and psychological reference, *i. e.*, the identity of expression and idea in the case of universals, is not sought to be explained by reference to another universal, but is believed to be self-contained. Even the *Naiyāyika* has to concede that there is no ontological foundation for these concepts. Such concepts as 'cook' (*pācaka*), 'non-being,' etc., are without any factual basis. There is no such universal as 'cookhood' or 'non-beingness,' yet there is no difficulty in the matter of referring to different individuals by a common name and a common concept.

In the case of 'non-being,' there are four cases of such, *viz.*, previous non-being (*prāgabhāva*), posterior non-being (*pradhvaṁsābhāva*), reciprocal non-being (*anyonyābhāva*) and lastly absolute non-being (*atyantābhāva*),[1] and all these cases are referred to by the generic name of 'non-being.' But there is no universal of non-being, as universals are believed to be entitative in character. And such fictitious appearances as cloud-mansions in the horizon and illusory silver perceived on the mother-o'-pearl are even referred to by the common name and concept of house or silver. But this nomenclature and conceptual thought cannot be made the ground of supposing the existence of an objective universal in these fictions. Cooks and tailors may form a professional class by themselves and thus may be referred to by a common name and concept. But nobody, possessing even a modicum of sense and sanity, would think of according an objective universal to these professional interests. Action cannot be supposed to be the ground of this conceptual thought, the uniting bond of the stray, discrete particulars, inasmuch as action varies with each individual. The action of one is not the self-identical action of another and as continuity and identity are the characteristic features of the supposed universals, action cannot be a universal. And if

[1] The non-existence of the cloth before its production is a case of previous non-being. This type of non-existence is without beginning and continues until the cloth is produced. The destruction of the cloth constitutes a case of posterior non-being, which takes place as an event at a definite point of time. It has a definite beginning unlike the former and thus has a previous limit, but it continues as such through all the time and thus has no end or lower limit. The difference of one thing from another is a case of reciprocal non-being. A table is not a chair and *vice versa*. The last type of non-being, *viz.* absolute non-being, is one that is timeless. It has neither previous nor subsequent history, but continues uniform and unaffected. The non-existence of such fictions as a barren woman's son or a horned horse is absolute without any reference to time-limitation. The non-existence is not relative to a particular division of time or of space, and is not contingent on any extraneous condition. Hence it is called absolute and unconditional non-being (*atyantābhāva*).

action, though variable and inconstant, be believed to be the cause and ground of the conceptual thought, there is no reason why the individuals should be denied this efficiency. Moreover, action, say for example, 'cooking' being an accidental fact and so being discontinuous, a person would not be called a cook, when he does not actually perform the cooking operations. Neither can the past nor the future action be responsible for this conceptual thought, as they are simply non-existent. So no objective basis can be discovered for this conceptual thought and permanent nomenclature. But the *Naiyāyikas* as a class are noted for their tenacity and Śaṅkarasvāmin has found an objective living universal in cooks and tailors and thus holds out a hope for the perennial preservation of amenities of civilized life—no doubt a consolation for legislators and social workers! He avers that the individual actions may be variable, but the universal of action (*kriyātvajāti*) is imperishable and this becomes the ground of the class-concept. This argument reminds us of the drowning man catching at the straw. How could the universal remain when its medium of expression, *viz.*, the individual action, has ceased to exist? And even if it did exist, how could it be perceived, as universals on your own hypothesis reveal their existence in and through the individuals alone? Nor can its apprehension in the past in any locus be the reason for the continuation of the notion in futurity. The idea of staff-bearer does not continue when the man in question does not carry the staff. Your argument, however, assures the continuity of the idea, but this is falsified by experience. And if you posit a distinct universal, say for example, cookhood and the like, a cook should have been recognised as a cook even when he was born, as the universal is there for all time. But if for some inscrutable drawback the universal and the child fail to be united, the union will never take place, as neither of them, permanent entities as they are, will depart from their original state. So the concept of cookhood should never arise at all. And if the individual may possibly transcend this drawback, being subject to change, no such contingency however can be supposed to happen to the universal, which is immutable by its very nature. Uddyotakara however realised the absurdity of the above position and so came forward with a more plausible explanation. He asserts that universals are no doubt the cause and ground of class-conceptions, but the converse of the proposition is not true. There may be class-conceptions even without an objective universal, as, for instance, in the case of cooks as a class, since there is no such universal as cookhood. The connotation of cook is the chief agency of the act of cooking and as this agency is found to continue in other individual cooks, the class-notion is not ungrounded. But this only smacks of prevarication. What this chief agency exactly connotes is not explained. If it means efficiency (*śakti*), it does not avail in the least, as efficiency is peculiar to each individual and does not continue. If it means the individuality (*svabhāva*) of the substance, or of the attribute or of action, it leaves the matter where it was, as individuality is peculiarly individualistic and never functions as a unitive principle.

Thus all attempts at finding an objective basis for the class-ideas having failed in the aforesaid instances, it must be supposed that the ideas of these universals are conceptual constructions from their exclusiveness of the opposite entities. The idea of the cook-universal arises from the fact that cooks, individual by individual, are sharply distinguished from all that are not cooks. So the cook-universal as a concept is ultimately resolvable into exclusion of non-cooks and so can be logically equated with the idea of 'not-not-cook.' The use of nomenclature too is purely a matter of convention, ultimately referable to this negative idea. So for the explanation of conceptual thought and linguistic usage it is not at all necessary to postulate the existence of objective universals. These universals are thus subjective fictions, fondly hypostatised by the habitual tendency of the mind to localise ideas in external reality—the realistic bias of thought, which is the bane and obsession of the *Naiyāyika*. It is proved therefore that class-concepts and class-names are not necessarily grounded in an objective universal. They are purely subjective constructions and have no reference to an objective, continuous principle, in other words, to a universal. Such at any rate is the case with ideas of negation (*abhāvavijñāna*). A negation cannot have a universal attached to it, as a universal can exist only in positive entities.

Śaṅkarasvāmin, however, seeks to explain the concept of negation by reference to the universal of the object of negation. A negation is always understood as negation of this or that, of the jar or cloth or table and the like. So though negation may not have a universal, the universal of the object negated will be the cause of the conceptual thought. But this only seeks to confound the real issue. We can understand the position of the realist when he seeks to explain the concept of jar by reference to the universal of jar. But how can the universal of one have a bearing on the concept of another, passes our understanding. The concept of negation is entirely a distinct concept having no relation, direct or indirect, to the jar universal, which exists only in the individual jars. If the mere existence of a particular universal can give rise to various concepts, as it is imagined in the case of jar, which not only originates the concept of the jar but also of the negation of the jar, then, there will be no necessity to postulate different universals, as one universal will have the power to give rise to all possible concepts. Bhāvivikta however thinks that there is no difficulty in the fact that the universal of one gives rise to the concept of a different sort. There is no such restriction that our ideas should always conform to the nature of the object, that idea and object should be commensurate in all respects. Thus the idea of an army, which is the idea of a unit, or the idea of a forest is not generated by any unitary principle, but by another thing, the plurality of the individual soldiers or trees. The idea of one beverage is not due to any unitary principle either ; it is generated by the admixture of various ingredients. If our ideas had to conform, as a matter of necessity, to the nature of the objective reality, these ideas would be ideas of distinct units conjoined together and not unitary in reference. We, Buddhists, fully endorse the above position that ideas and objects are not always commensurate, and precisely for this reason we think that there is no logical or metaphysical necessity to suppose that our ideas of universals should be affiliated to corresponding objective principles. These ideas can be supposed to have been generated by the particulars, distinct and discrete though they are. By the way, the universals were postulated on the hypothesis that our ideas should have corresponding objective realities as their cause. But when idea and reality are admitted to be at variance, in some cases at any rate, it is better and more reasonable to accept our theory. We, Buddhists, do not admit any objective universal over and above the particulars. And if we analyse the psychological process of conceptual thought, we shall find nothing beyond the particulars. Thus a particular is first experienced and then it is at once assimilated to other particulars under the impetus of the law of association and thus a generic idea is formed to which a symbolic expression, a name, is attached by a pure caprice of will; and this name becomes a conventional symbol of the generic concept and a convenient medium of communication of ideas, which, though purely subjective constructions, have a pragmatic value, as these ideas are remotely related to objective facts, being ultimately derived from them.[1]

It has been urged that though some conceptual thoughts are seen to arise without an objective universal, that is no reason that all conceptual thoughts should be unfounded illusions. The concept of negation is a case in point. It is said to be a subjective construction, because negation cannot have a universal attached to it. But there is no such logical bar in the case of other concepts and so to lump them together with these admittedly

[1] bhedajñāne satī 'cchā hi saṅketakaraṇe tataḥ | tatkṛtis tacchrutiś cā 'syā ābhogas tanmatis tataḥ | anvayavyatirekābhyām idam eva viniścitam | samarthaṁ kāraṇaṁ tasyām anyeṣam anāvasthitiḥ | T. S., 773-74.

subjective creations is not logically tenable. You could with equal logic deny validity to all our experience, because some particular experiences were found to be wrong. We admit the plausisibility of the argument of the realist. But our contention is that we do not repudiate the objectivity conceptual thoughts on the analogy of concepts which are admittedly false. We only emphasised that the realist's position that all our knowledge must be derived from objective experience was not invulnerable. This is a positive gain on our behalf. Now we deny the existence of universals because there is no proof in their favour. Universals are posited to account for conceptual thoughts. But no causal relation canbe discovered between concepts and universals. Causal relation is understood by means of the Joint Method of Agreement and Difference. But universals being eternal verities and conceptual thoughts being occasional events, there can be no causal relation between them. The non-emergence of a particular concept cannot be due to the absence of the universal concerned, as universals without exception are present always. Nor can the occasional emergence of a conceptual thought be causally affiliated to a universal, because the universal is ever present and if it had any such efficiency, it would generate the idea always. So nothing is gained by postulating universals. If, however, the cognition of universals is supposed to be contingent on the cognition of the particulars in question, we do not see what these effete universals will avail. Our conceptual thoughts are seen to arise even without them.

The concepts of negation have been proved to be unfounded in objective universals. Kumārila however contends that even in negation there is an objective universal, as negation is nothing but a positive entity, bereft of a particular determination. Thus, the prior negation of curd is nothing but the milk existing in its pure state.[1] This contention may hold good in case of negation of

[1] nanu ca prāgabhāvādau sāmānyaṁ vastu ne 'ṣyate |
sattai 'va hy atra sāmānyam anutpattyādirūṣitā ||
S. V., Apoha, śl. 11.

objective realities, but it has no force in negation of fictions of imagination. The position of the realist that negation presupposes prior existence of the thing negated is only a hollow assertion. When we say that there was no such person as Kapiñjala [1] or Hamlet in reality, we do not see how can the concept of negation be affiliated to an objective universal even of the object of negation. The plea of Kumārila that negation always refers to a positive entity divested of a particular determination falls to the ground in these negations of fictitious persons and things. Hamlet or Kapiñjala is not a real entity under any circumstance. And what about the negation of doctrines or of categories maintained by the rival school of philosophers ? Kumārila would say that there is no such thing as *Pratisaṅkhyānirodha*. But does this negation imply a positive fact in any wise ? If not, how could the concept of negation arise at all in these cases, as in these cases there is no positive entity, far less a universal attaching to it. If you answer that negation in these cases relates to a subjective concept, which has no objective reality, then, for the sake of consistency at least you should admit that our concepts and expressions without exception are alike devoid of objective reference ; in other words, they are subjective fictions, pure and simple, their pragmatic value notwithstanding.[2]

Furthermore, even granted that these universals are objective categories existing in their own right, it cannot be conceived how they are related to particulars. The universal and the particular cannot be distinguished by perception, as they are not distinctly perceived. But distinct things are perceived as distinct from one another. The universal is supposed to exist in a number of particulars in the same fashion and in the same form. But they are not felt as such. You might say that the universal is not perceived independently of the particulars, as it exists in them ; but its mode of existence cannot be logically

[1] A minor hero in the Kādambarī, a romantic novel by Bāṇa Bhaṭṭa, a protégé of Emperor Harsavardhana of Northern India, who was the patron of the celebrated Chinese pilgrim, Hiuen Tsang.

[2] T. S. P., p. 255, under śl. 788.

conceived. Existence is ordinarily understood to be non-forfeiture of one's nature. A thing is said to exist when it does not lapse from its own nature, or in other words, when it maintains itself intact. But for this self-maintenance or self-assertion a thing must rely on its own independent resources and must not be dependent on extraneous help or favour. And if the universal is an independent entity, it must exist by its own nature and for this a medium is useless. If, on the other hand, it does not possess such powers of maintaining or asserting its existence, a medium cannot be of any help to it. A medium is seen to be necessary to prevent a thing from falling down, as for instance a basket is needed for the holding together of fruits and vegetables. But the universal is not a gravitating body ; it is on your own assumption a passive entity devoid of locomotion and gravitating tendency. If, however, the universal is supposed to exist in the particular mediums by the relation of co-inherence (*samavāya*), it does not make any improvement on the situation; on the contrary, it further complicates the issue. The universal is a bold assumption in itself and to justify this you are making another assumption which is equally absurd. One absurdity necessitates another absurdity, just as one lie requires an infinite number of lies for its justification, but all this to no purpose. Co-inherence is a relation, but unlike other relations it does not bring together two terms existing independently of one another. It obtains between two things, which are never found to be dissociated in nature. But this is a case of plain self-contradiction. A relation between terms which are conjoined by their very nature is absolutely unavailing. If there is a relation, the terms must be supposed to have existed separately and if they were never separate, no relation can be necessary or possible. So the relation of co-inherence cannot be accepted as a satisfactory explanation of the relation of the universal and the particular. The position taken up by the realist that there is no contradiction in experience, unless it is shown to be contradicted by another experience, is not a logically sound position. When there is a divergence in the interpretation of experience itself, the issue can be decided by an appeal to logic only. The present dispute affords a case in point. Our perceptual experience is believed by the *Naiyāyikas* and the *Mīmāṁsakas* to be cognisant of the particular and the universal both at one sweep. But the Buddhist does not think that the idea of one continuous principle is directly derived from perceptual data.[1] So the strength and validity of experience cannot be determined otherwise than by a logical examination. The falsity or invalidity of an experience is determined by a contradictory experience no doubt ; but that is not the only means. Those who are possessed of a philosophic insight do not rest satisfied with the *prima facie* verdict of experience, but seek to test it by logical canons. Experience, no doubt, is the final arbiter, but it must be attested and approved by logic. The disregard of this procedure will only land us in rank empiricism.[2] Co-inherence as formulated by the *Nyāya-Vāiśeṣika* school thus fails to render an explanation of the relation of the universal and the particular. Kumārila maintains that the relation of the universal and the particular is one of identity in difference. A reality is a concrete whole of which the universal and the particular are two aspects. So a cow is both identical with and different from another cow. It is identical in respect of the universal, but different in respect of the particular variation. But this is an absurd position and does not even deserve a refutation. How can one thing be one and many, eternal and non-eternal ? It is a contradiction in terms. Kumārila however would turn round and say that there is no contradiction in it, as it is found to be so in uncontradicted experience. But this appeal to experience is an argument of despair and we have just proved the hollowness of this position.

[1] ḍṛṣṭatvān na virodhaś cen na tathā tadavedanāt ।
uktaṁ hi nā 'nuvṛttārthagrāhiṇī netradhīr iti ॥ N. M., p. 301.

[2] dṛḍhādṛḍhatvam akṣuṇṇam aparīkṣyai'va saṁvidām । na ne'ti pratyayād eva mithyātvaṁ kevalaṁ dhiyām । kiṁ tu yuktiparīkṣā, pi kartavyā sūkṣmadarśibhiḥ ॥ *Op. cit.*, p. 301.

It may be supposed that the relation is one of revealer and revealed. The universal is revealed in the particular and it is for this reason that they are found together. But this too does not take us nearer the solution. If the universal is possessed of the efficiency to generate a cognition of itself, the revealing medium will have no function in this respect. And if the universal does not possess this efficiency, then, too, the medium will be useless, as an eternal verity cannot be supposed to change its nature. If the universal is supposed to develop this efficiency in association with the particular media, the universal must be supposed to be fluxional, as the existence of contradictory attributes in one substratum is impossible unless the supposed integer is split up into diverse entities. But this amounts to the negation of the universal.

Again, let the relation of the universal and particulars be one of co-inherence. But does the universal exist in its entirety in each of the particulars or in its partial extension in them? If the universal exists in a particular in its entire extension, it will be exhausted in one such particular and so cannot exist in other particulars. But universals are *ex hypothesi* supposed to exist in all its particulars in the same fashion and in the same degree. And if a universal is supposed to exist in each of the particulars in its partial extension, the universal will exist in none of them in its totality and so the idea of the universal cannot be supposed to relate to any one of these particulars. Moreover, the universal is supposed to be an impartite whole and so we cannot conceive that the universal exists part by part in the particulars just as in a garland the connecting thread exists part by part in the individual flowers.[1] Again, the question arises whether universals are ubiquitous like space or soul of the *Naiyāyika* or they exist only in the particular individuals belonging to them. If they are

[1] piṇḍe sāmānyam anyatra yadi kārtsnyena vartate | tatrai 'vā 'sya samāptatvān na syāt piṇḍāntare grahaḥ | ekadeśena vṛttau tu gotvajātir na kutracit | samagrā 'stī 'ti gobuddhiḥ pratipiṇḍam katham bhavet || N. M., p. 298.

supposed to be ubiquitous, all universals will exist together and the horse-universal will be cognised in the cow and the cow-universal in the horse and so with regard to all other universals. Thus there will be confusion and no determinate concept can arise. Nor can it be legitimately supposed that the individual members of a class will exercise a regulative influence and so the cow-universal alone will be revealed in the individual cows and not the horse-universal or other universals, because such supposition could be possible if universals were not thought to be impartite entities. So a universal once revealed will be revealed in its entirety and thus should be cognised to be ubiquitous. The individual is supposed to reveal the existence of the universal like light ; but as light does not reveal its own self alone or its qualities alone, the individual should reveal the universal not only as it exists in it, but as it is by its nature, that is to say, the universal should be revealed as ubiquitous and all-pervading. But this is not our experience and we do not see how such universals can be of any help, the question of logical propriety apart.

Of course, none of these difficulties arises if we suppose like Praśastapāda that a universal exists in its own particular members only and not also in the intervening spaces. But Praśastapāda's theory is open to equally damaging objections. If the universal exists only in its proper individuals, we cannot conceive how the universal can attach itself to a thing which is not born as yet. The cow-universal existing in the living cows cannot be supposed to unite itself to the cow that is just born, because it is inactive and stationary. If it is supposed to move from one subject to another, it will cease to be a universal, because only a substance (*dravya*) can have activity. And even supposing that universals are active principles, we cannot conceive how it can move forward without deserting its former locus and if it is supposed to leave its previous loci, the latter will be lifeless entities bereft of the universal. Furthermore, the relation of the universal and the particular is peculiarly embarrassing. The universal pervades the particular from top to bottom, inside and outside, in a complete and thoroughgoing fashion, but it does not touch the ground whereupon the individual rests. This is certainly a very strange position. The universal does not move forward to join the individual which is just born ; it was not there before, because the individual was not in existence ; but it is found to exist in the individual after the latter has come into existence.[1] The Realist makes these absurd assumptions one after another with a sangfroid which befits a bravado and calls upon us to accept his position without scruple or questions. And if we refuse to take him at his word, he accuses us of infidelity to experience and ultra-rationalism. But there are limits to human credulity and each man has his own experience and his own interpretation to rely upon. When there is a divergence about the interpretation of experience itself, the dispute can be terminated by an appeal to logic only. But logic is not a thing which finds favour with the realist.

To sum up: we have seen that the universals are but subjective constructions, pure and simple. The fault of the realist lies in his believing these subjective fictions to be ontological realities existing in perfect independence of thinking minds. The absurdity of the realist's position has been thoroughly exposed and further argument is useless and unnecessary, as argumentation is nothing but a waste of energy when a person is determined not to understand.

[1] anyatra vartamānasya tato 'nyasthānajanmani I tasmād acalataḥ sthānād vṛttir ity atiyuktatā I yatrā 'sau vartate bhāvas tena sambadhyate na tu I taddeśinaṁ ca vyāpnoti kim apy etan mahādhutam I na yāti na ca tatrā 'sīd asti paścān na cā 'ṁśavat I jahāti pūrvaṁ nā 'dhāram aho vyasanasantatiḥ I S. D. S., p. 27.

Reference :

1. Tattvasaṅgraha, śls 708-812.
2. Sāmānyadūṣaṇa in the Six Bnddhist Nyāya Tracts.
3. Ślokavārtika, pp. 5456-5.
4. Sarvadarśanasaṅgraha, Bauddhadarśana.
5. Nyāyavārtika, pp. 314-34.
6. Do. Tātparyaṭīkā, pp. 477-95.
7. Nyāyamañjarī, pp. 297-317.

CHAPTER VII

THE DOCTRINE OF APOHA OR THE IMPORT OF WORDS

The Realists of the *Nyāya-Vaiśeṣika* school and the *Mīmāṁsakas* maintain that words have direct reference to objective realities and as words relate to universals in the first instance, these universals should be looked upon as stern realities existing in their own right and not subjective constructions, as the Buddhists would have it. The subject and the predicate in a proposition are equivalent with real facts and affirmation or negation, whatever the case may be, really connotes a factual relation subsisting between real objective facts. The factual foundation of our linguistic usage is daily and hourly attested by our practical experience inasmuch as in all normal cases word and fact are found to be congruent. This congruence would otherwise become unaccountable except on the supposition of an actual objective basis. Now there is a wide divergence of opinion in relation to the question as to what is the direct and exact connotation of a word—whether it is the universal or the particular or both. In the last alternative again there is room for controversy as to the relation between the universal and the particular, as to whether it is the universal as qualified and determined by the particular or the particular as the substantive with the universal annexed as an adjunct. But this will be treated of more fully in the following pages.

The Buddhist, however, roundly denies the fundamental assumption of the realist that words contain an objective reference, in all its aspects and bearings. The Buddhist maintains that words have no reference to reality in any sense. Words in their opinion deal with concepts and these concepts are purely subjective constructions. We have proved in the previous chapter that universals are intellectual fictions and their pragmatic value is due to their remote extraction from objective facts, which however are uncompromising particulars, discrete and distinct and without any continuity or nexus between one and the other. The best way to prove our contention will be by examining the actual and probable theories of the rival thinkers and to see how far these theories are tenable. Now a word cannot denote the self-contained, unique particular which is alone real, as has been proved by us. And these particulars are momentary entities and so do not continue up to the time that conventional relation is apprehended. Apart from the question of its momentariness, particulars are self-contained facts and even if the word-relation is supposed to relate to these distinct entities, it will be of no avail with regard to other particulars, which were not taken into account when the verbal convention was cognised. So the word 'cow' would mean only a particular cow and not any other. But this will serve no purpose. And it is humanly impossible that a man should apprehend this conventional relation with regard to all the individual cows that are and have been and will be in existence. If it is supposed that all the individuals are conceptually apprehended and labelled by a common name, then it should be admitted that the conventional relation is apprehended with regard to a conceptual construction and not real individual facts, distinct and discrete that they are. It may not be out of place to observe in this connexion that the theory of transcendental contact with all the possible and actual individuals in and through the medium of the universal in question (*sāmānyalakṣaṇasannikarṣa*), which has been propounded by the latter-day *Naiyāyikas*, equally fails to explain the factual incidence of the verbal convention, for which it was postulated.[1]

[1] na hy adṛṣṭeṣv atītānāgatabhedabhinneṣv ananteṣu bhedeṣu samayaḥ sambhavaty atiprasaṅgāt. vikalpabuddhyā vyāhṛtya teṣu pratipadyata.

We have hitherto contended that verbal relation is not comprehensible with regard to particulars, either collectively or individually, because of their infinite number and the suggestion was not unlikely that the relation could be apprehended individual by individual. But this also is impossible. The conventional relation can be apprehended only after the name-relation is remembered and the name-relation is remembered after the individual has been perceived, but the individual being momentary will have passed out of existence when the conventional relation can be apprehended. Nor can it be apprehended with reference to the facsimile-individual that comes into existence in the individual-continuum, because the conventional relation that is recalled had reference to the first moment and not to the later moments. It may be contended that the moments being closely similar and homogeneous in structure and appearance, they can be conceived to give rise to a concept of identity and the name-relation is apprehended with reference to this conceptual identity. But in this view, also, the name cannot relate to the self-identical individual moment, but to a conceptual construction. If words had reference to objective entities, then we could expect the self-same full-blooded apprehension as in sense-perception. Take for instance the case of fire ; the word does not express the full individuality of fire with all its heat and light that is revealed in perceptual knowledge. What is expressed by the name is only a bloodless concept. And as regards configuration (*ākṛti*), it is nothing but a case of conjunction of component parts and conjunction as distinct from the componental factors is only an intellectual fiction. So this too cannot be the objective of word-relation. As regards the universal or its relation, neither can be the connotation of a word, as universals have been proved in the preceding chapter to be hollow abstractions and relation has no existence apart and distinct from the *relata*. So the

eve'ti cet. evaṁ tarhi vikalpasamāropitārthaviṣaya eva śabdasanniveśanam, na paramārthato bhedeṣv iti prāptam. T. S. P., p. 278.

contention of the *Naiyāyika* that universal (*jāti*), individual (*vyakti*) and configuration (*ākṛti*) are the connotation of words falls to the ground, because these conceptual vagaries are unsubstantial fictions, pure and simple. Equally indefensible is the position of those who think that words have reference to the conceptual image, in other words, the ideal content, because the ideal content is a self-contained particular like the objective facts and so does neither continue in other concepts nor relate to objective reality. Moreover, these ideal contents are purely subjective facts existing inside the mind of the subject and as such cannot have the pragmatic efficiency that is possessed by real objective entities. So this too cannot be supposed to function as the connotation of words, much less as the subject-matter of verbal convention.[1]

There are some theorists who hold that the essential meaning of all words is undefined and unspecified 'existence' (*astyartha*) and not any specific determination. When the word 'cow' is heard, it simply connotes that something exists to which the name 'cow' is affixed and no form or determination enters as a content into this purely existential reference. The determinate content of this reference is purely a matter of belief or pre-conception of the subject in question. So even words which have a reference to visible and perceptible objects are on the same level with words which refer to unknown and unverifiable objects. Thus, for instance, such expressions as 'heaven,' 'merit' or 'demerit' do not bring home to the understanding any specific content, but only convey a vague existential reference and our ordinary work-a-day expressions too do not connote anything

[1] vācyaṁ svalakṣaṇam upādhir upādhiyogaḥ |
sopādhir astu yadi vā ''k kṛtir astu buddheḥ |
ādyantayor na samayaḥ phalaśaktihāner |
madhye 'py upādhivirahāt tritaye na yuktaḥ |
Apohasiddhi, p. 18.
Vide T. S., śls. 869-84, and the Pañjikā thereunder.

more than this. But this view too does not make any improvement upon the previous theories. If words do not present any definite meaning but only a vague reference to mere existence, then linguistic usage would become absolutely abortive, as there will be no variation in meaning and the content. The word 'cow' and the word 'horse' would mean the same thing, if they mean nothing more than 'existence, pure and simple.' But if they are supposed to contain a reference to an objective individual, unique and distinctive, or to some concrete universal or to an ideal representation, then the theory will make itself open to all the charges levelled against the previous theories. It may be contended that the connotation of the word 'cow' is not unqualified existence, but existence as determined by the particular word 'cow' and the universal of 'cowhood,' and because the specific attributes and individual characteristics are not understood in this reference, it is held that words are existential in their import. The word 'cow' connotes 'that something exists,' but this something is not an indefinite concept, but has in it the cow-universal and the cow-expression as its content determining it. But even this interpretation does not make it more sound and intelligible. It only restates the position of the *Naiyāyika* who holds that words have a reference to the universal-in-the-individual, the individual as defined and determined by the universal. But universals have been proved to be unreal intellectual fictions and so this theory shares in the absurdity of the *Nyāya* theory *in toto*.

Others again hold that words denote 'an undefined group or totality' without any reference whatsoever either to the individuals comprising it, or to the specific attributes constituting the class-concept. They connote a group or a totality without any emphasis, either on its distributive or its collective character. But this 'group' or 'totality' is nothing but the well-known 'universal' of the realists masquerading under a different verbal expression and as such is liable to all the objections attaching to the universal. There are some other thinkers who maintain that the connotation of words is but a complex of word and an objective fact coalesced together and this is evidenced by the fact that all our reference to an objective fact is carried on by the machinery of words. Word and fact are always found to be associated in the relation of identity and this is the connotation of word. But the Buddhist thinks that this view is based on a confusion of a subjective idea with an objective fact, which is absurd on the face of it. If any objective reality, either individual or universal, were denoted by a word, then there could be a remote possibility for a confusion of a word and a fact. Besides, the verbal reference, out of which capital is sought to be made, is purely a subjective idea and has absolutely nothing to do with an objective reality. So this view does not make any advance on the theory of those who hold the subjective ideal content to be the meaning of words. But the latter view has been thoroughly demolished, as an idea is not anything different from consciousness and being momentary alike, it fails to synthesise the different individuals, supposed to be denoted by a word.

There is another theory which holds that word has a reference to the subjective content, the idea or mental image, which is occasioned by an external object and this idea or image is believed to be the external reality itself by being superimposed upon it. So long as the idea is believed to be a subjective fact, which it is in reality, it does not and cannot lead to any activity, as subjective fictions are not actionable. So the idea is impinged upon the reality which causes it and this complex identity of idea and object is the import of words. This theory may be easily confounded with the Buddhist theory of *Apoha*, but there is a fundamental difference between the two. The Buddhist too believes that the import of words is a subjective idea hypostatised as an objective fact, but this objectivity is a purely intellectual construction and is an ungrounded illusion, because it is neither subjective nor objective, but a fiction, pure and simple. The present theory, on the other hand, holds that the idea is a correct measure of the reality and is actually superimposed upon an objective datum to which it refers. If the external objective reference is believed to be a projection of the conscious principle, absolutely ungrounded in an objective reality and the synthetic class-concept is thought to be an ideal construction, engendered by the exclusion of opposite entities, shared in common by a set of individuals, then and then alone can this theory be equated with the Buddhist theory of *Apoha*. The Buddhist denies that words possess a factual meaning, be it subjective or objective. Now what is the import of a word ? It is certainly what is presented in a determinative verbal cognition. But this determinate presentation is not of a subjective idea, but of an external objective fact possessed of practical efficiency. And this objective fact referred to is not an actual reality, as it lacks the distinctive features of a living reality, which is unique and self-identical and as it is not confined to one individual, but comprises in its reference all the possible individuals. Nor can it be a universal, since a universal has been proved to be a conceptual fiction. So the import of a word is neither a subjective idea nor an objective fact and ultimately transpires to be an illusory projection. And when we refer to the denotation of a word, we mean this illusory projection and nothing else.

There is still another theory which holds that words do not signify any real object at all, nor do they convey any determinate idea. Words are but symbolic values and stand on the same level with signs and gestures. They produce an indeterminate and contentless intuition (*pratibhā*), which comes to be associated with objective facts by repeated usage. They are destitute of definite presentative content and are only vaguely suggestive of facts and actions, as is seen in the case of children and animals. And even this suggestion has no direct bearing on definite objective data. Had it been directly grounded in an objective reality, there would have been no occasion for the conflicting interpretations of texts or contradictory expositions ; and fictions and stories

15

could not have been possible.[1] Now the implications of this theory have got to be thoroughly threshed out. If this suggestion (*pratibhā*) is supposed to have reference to an objective fact, then how can a particular word give rise to various suggestions in various minds, when the objective reality is uniform in character ? And if the verbal suggestion of intuition have absolutely no bearing on an objective datum, then also they would be unmeaning nonsense and as such could not lead to any volitional activity, which is however the actual fact. If it is supposed that the subjective suggestion is erroneously believed to be an objective fact, then the import of words would be an illusory fiction and the ideation and volitional activity would be a case of unmitigated subjective illusion. But this illusion must have a *raison d'etre*, otherwise an uncaused illusion can emerge always and everywhere and no case for its limitation can be made out. If however the illusion is traced to the peculiar distinctive nature of individual entities, which sharply distinguishes it from entities of contradictory nature and which thus cumulatively gives rise to the idea of a generic universal, then this theory of suggestion will have nothing to differentiate it from the Buddhist theory of *Apoha*.

There are some other theorists, again, who maintain that the subjective idea and the objective fact are structurally and qualitatively close analogues like two twin brothers ; and though the objective reality is not the significate of a word, still the subjective idea leads to the objective fact by reason of its close analogy. But this theory fails to explain the invariable objective reference of verbal cognition. The analogy of twin brothers does not help the issue. It is not a fact that one twin will be invariably

[1] yathai 'va hy aṅkuśābhighātādayo hastyādīnām arthapratipattau pratibhāhetavo bhavanti, tathā sarve 'rthavat-sammatā vṛkṣādayaḥ śabdā yathābhyāsaṁ pratibhāmātropasaṁhārahetavo bhavanti, na tv arthaṁ sākṣāt pratipādayanti. anyathā hi kathaṁ parasparaparāhatāḥ pravacanabhedā utpādyakathāprabandhāś ca svavikalpoparacitapadārthabhedadyotakāḥ syur iti. T. S. P., p. 286. Vā. P., II, 119 ; T. S., śls. 892, 902-905.

confused with the other. The real person intended may be understood and so the subjective image may not be invariably confounded with the objective fact and sometimes may be correctly apprehended as subjective and in that case the activity bearing on the objective fact will be impossible of explanation.[1]

All these different theories can be summarily dismissed by this dialectic : Is the import of words a reality or not ? If it be a reality, is it fluxional or permanent ? If the former, it cannot have the synthetic reference, and if the latter, then the emergence of successive ideas would be unaccountable. And so the theory of the *Vaibhāṣikas* who postulate the existence of a word-entity (*nāmakāya*) and of an objective generic character (*nimitta*) existing as part of the reality signified by a word is equally indefensible. If the word-category and the meaning-category be something momentary or non-momentary, then they would be absolutely unavailing.[2]

We have seen that words have no objective reference. Neither the individual nor the universal can be actually signified by a word, because the individual is self-contained and has nothing to do with any other individual, similar or dissimilar and as such cannot be the subject of verbal convention (*samaya*); and

[1] atha mataṁ yo vivakṣāviparivartī rūpādir artho yaś ca bāhyas tayoḥ sārūpyam asty ataḥ sārūpyād acodite bāhye pravṛttir bhaviṣyatī yamalakavad ity ata āha—sārūpyāc ca śruter vṛttiḥ kathaṁ vā 'śabdacohite । sārūpyād yamalakavat । (Śl. 908). T. S. P., p. 289.

N.B. Most of these theories have been alluded to in the *Vākyapadīya* of Bhartṛhari and the T. S. and the *Pañjikā* have taken them from that work. Of course the criticism is entirely original. *Vide* Vā. Pa., Ch. II, śls. 118-134.

[2] *Vide, The Central Conception of Buddhism*, p. 106.

Cf. yo 'pi Vaibhāṣikaḥ śabdaviṣayaṁ nāmākhyaṁ nimittākhyaṁ cā 'rthacihnarūpaṁ viprayuktaṁ saṁskāram icchati, tad apy etenai 'va dūṣitaṁ draṣṭavyam, tathā hi tan nāmādi yadi kṣaṇikaṁ tadā anvayāyogaḥ, akṣaṇikatve kramijñānānupapattiḥ.

T. S. P., p. 290.

the universal is a chimerical abstraction and a subjective fiction, pure and simple. Now the question is relevant that if words do not signify any real object, then what is its signification ? Words certainly have got a meaning and an objective external reference too and this cannot be accounted for if words are supposed to signify a subjective idea existing internally within the mind. A subjective idea cannot be reconciled with an extra-subjective reference. The Buddhist however rejoins that what is signified by a word is neither a subjective idea nor an objective reality, but something fictitious and unreal, which is neither here nor there. The fact of the matter is that both the speaker and the hearer apprehend in fact and reality a mental image, a subjective content and not any objective fact ; but the speaker thinks that he presents an objective fact to the hearer and the hearer too is deluded into thinking that the presented meaning is not a mental image, but an objective verity. The speaker and the hearer are both labouring under a common delusion like two ophthalmic patients who see two moons and communicate their experience to each other. So the connotation of words is but a subjective idea, a mental image, which however is hypostatised as an objective reality existing in its own right independently of the thinking mind.[1] And as this mental image is found to have a distinctive character of its own which marks it out from other such mental representations and thus to contain a negative implication, we characterise it by a negative expression, *viz.*, 'negation of another' (*anyāpoha*). The connotation of a word therefore is a subjective notion, a mental image in the first instance, which is a positive idea no doubt. But as it has an exclusive reference by implication and as this negative implication gives the verbal import its

[1] tasmād eṣa vikalpaviṣayo na jñānākāro nā 'pi bāhya ity alīka evāstheyaḥ, yathā " ha Dharmottaraḥ, " buddhyā kalpikayā viviktam aparair yad rūpam ullikhyate | buddhir no na bahir " iti.

Tāt. ṭī., p. 485.

distinguishing character, its real significance and force, the connotation of a word is rightly looked upon and designated as a fundamental negation. The negative characterisation has a four-fold *raison d' etre* ; in the first place, because the mental content, the ideal representation, which is occasioned by a word and which as such should be regarded as its meaning and import, has a distinctive individuality and this individuality will have no meaning if it does not negate and exclude other such ideal contents. That it is a definite idea means that it is not any other and this definite individuality cannot have a meaning and a *raison d'etre* unless it negates what it is not. So negation constitutes its fundamental individuality ; negation is its very life and soul, without which it will be an empty nonsense. Secondly, because the verbal idea leads to the attainment of a real individual entity, which has a self-identity peculiarly its own. The real is something which is detached and severed from all other individuals, similar or dissimilar. So the reality from which word and its meaning derive their significance and utility being something essentially negative in character, the word-meaning should be looked upon as essentially negative in function. Thirdly, because the ideal representation is directly caused by a self-identical real, which is exclusive of other individuals. Lastly, because vulgar people regard the ideal concept, the verbal import, as identical with the self-contained reality, which possesses an exclusive identity. So the negative character of a verbal import has a twofold meaning and justification, one essential and the other incidental, according as it is grounded in its essential individuality, as well as from its source of origin and ultimate reference.

And this negation has a twofold aspect according as it is relative or absolute. An absolute negation is an unqualified pure negation and has no positive reference, remote or direct. For example, 'the cow is not not-cow' is a negative judgment, pure and simple. A relative negation on the other hand has primarily a positive reference and its negative value is only indirect and implied inasmuch as it comes into relief only in reference to an *other*. It is an affirmation in and by itself and only in relation to an *other* it becomes negative in force. For instance, the concept 'cow' is in and by itself a positive fact, but in relation to a horse, it is a negative concept. And this relative negation may be again twofold, *viz.*, a concept and a fact. The import of words is a relatively negative concept and is neither a fact nor an absolute negation. It is not an absolute negation inasmuch as it is a conceptual construction positive in character, but it is not regarded as a true measure of reality, because it carries a factual objective reference, though it does not possess any objectivity in itself. As a concept it is a purely subjective phenomenon and is true and real *quâ* subjective ; but it has an objective external reference and that constitutes its falsity. But though false and unreal it is only a concept that is generated by a word and it is this concept which is regarded as the meaning of that word. So the denotative relation of word and meaning is at bottom a relation of causality between a fact (word) and a concept, or to be precise, between one concept and another concept. But this concept is not a pure negation and is as much positive as anything. But though positive in appearance, it has a negative implication, as negation is its determinant and formative principle, as set forth above. So when Dignāga declared that word imports a negation and neither an objective universal nor a particular, he only emphasised this negative implication of verbal import. He did not mean that negation was the primary and apparent connotation. But Uddyotakara and Kumārila misunderstood the real significance of Dignāga's doctrine and raised objections which were uncalled for and irrelevant. All their objections and criticism proceed upon the assumption that Dignāga regarded pure negation as the connotation of words and when they say that pure negation without a positive basis is unintelligible nonsense, this does not affect the central position of the master and only fights with a shadow of their own creation. The connotation of a word is a positive concept and when Dignāga characterised it as a negation, he only emphasised its essential negative implication which makes the verbal import significant and meaningful. Uddyotakara argues, " Is this ' negation of the opposite ' itself the expressible meaning of the word ' negation '? If it is the expressed meaning, then the position should be surrendered that negation is the signification of words. At any rate, the expression ' negation of the opposite ' signifies something which is not a negation of an *other*. If it were so, there would arise a *regressus ad infinitum*, because the negated other, ' the non-negation ' would require another negation and so on. And if negation is not its signification, then something else should be assigned as its meaning and that being non-negation would transpire to be something positive. And if 'negation' itself be the signification of the expression ' *apoha* ' (negation) and not ' negation of an *other*,' then the proposition that ' a word signifies its meaning by negating the meaning of other words ' would come to mean ' that a word signifies an *other* without signifying it '—which is a case of plain contradiction."[1] But this argument of Uddyotakara, apart from its sophistry, is based upon a misconception. Uddyotakara has been carried away by the *prima facie* meaning of the position. We have observed before that the relation of denotation is a relation of causality. When a word is said to denote an object, it does not do anything more than this : the word only generates in the subject's mind a conceptual image, which is distinct and different from other concepts and this conceptual image is believed to be an external reality existing ahead and independently of the thinking mind. And denotation of meaning by a word is nothing but the production of this conceptual image by a word. The negation is not directly connoted but is only understood by implication. The word ' cow ' only engenders a conceptual image of the reality

[1] N. V., pp. 328-29, Tāt. ṭī, p. 492.

'cow,' but as this conceptual image has a self-identity distinct from that of other concepts, its distinctive character is felt and distinction means negation of what it is not. So the criticism of Bhāmaha—that if the connotation of the word 'cow' be contingent on 'not-cow,' then some other word would be in request to signify the positive cow—does not affect our position, as the word does not connote the negative idea in the first instance. As the proposition 'Devadatta is fat but does not dine at day' conveys a negative meaning in the first instance, but has a positive implication, 'He certainly takes a hearty meal at night, otherwise how could he be fat ?' and as these two positive and negative judgments conveyed by a self-identical proposition do not offend against the law of contradiction, exactly so a word can occasion a positive and a negative concept, one by its denotative power and the other by implication. So the objection of Bhāmaha does not arise at all, as we, Buddhists, do not hold that a word denotes the negative idea first. The word has a meaning in the positive concept and the negative import is a resultant cognition.[1]

And this conceptual form is regarded as the universal informing and underlying all the individual members, because it is conceived to be the common factor of all perceived individuals. But this universal is but a conceptual construction and though not an objective entity it is regarded as such owing to the influence of nescience inherent in every conscious subject. And this conceptual form is variously designated as 'negation of the opposite' (*anyāpoha*) by the Buddhist and as an objective universal by the Realist. This universal is nothing but a conceptual

[1] bāhyārthādhyavasāyena pravṛttaṁ pratibimbakam ।
utpādayati yene 'yaṁ tenā 'he 'ty apadiśyate ।
tasya ca pratibimbasya gatāv evā 'nugamyate ।
sāmarthyād anyaviśleṣo............
divābhojanavākyāder ivā 'syā 'pi phaladvayam ।
sākṣāt sāmarthyato yasmān nā 'nvayo vyatirekavān ।

T.S., śls. 1017, 1019, 1020.

construction and has no existence outside the subjective consciousness. And though it has no existence outside consciousness, it is fondly hypostatised as an objective category by the inherent illusory tendencies of the subject. But it is not an unfounded illusion for that, as the idea is remotely derived from an objective datum. The conceptual forms however are regarded as unreal fictions, because they are not objective facts with which they are supposed to be identical and so far as their objectivity is concerned, they are regarded as illusory fictions. Now a question is raised, 'Well, if there is no objective universal and all reals are self-enclosed and self-contained particulars, each distinct and different from the other, then how is it that they should give rise to a conceptual image, which is not particularistic in its reference but comprises all the discrete and distinct individuals in its fold ? And how again a common name is affixed to all the individuals and it should denote not this or that individual, but all the individuals, possible and actual ? If an objective universal is postulated over and above the individuals, then such ideas and such verbal usage become intelligible and not otherwise.' But the Buddhist answers that our ideas are not exact copies of external reality and it has been proved in the chapter on universals that ideas need not be contingent on corresponding objective realities at all. There is no impossibility in the fact that individuals, though discrete and distinct, should give rise to an identical concept. It is a matter of experience that some individuals, though distinct and different from one another, discharge an identical action and this uniform causal efficiency is the ground and *raison d'etre* of common appellation and common concept. The individual jars are each distinct and different, but they are labelled with a common name 'jar,' because they possess a uniform causal efficiency with regard to drawing of water and the like. In the preceding chapter we have mentioned the case of medicinal herbs and minerals, as an instance in point as to how they are referred to by the common name of 'purgative,' though they have nothing in common. But a difficulty has been raised in this connexion: 'Well, there can be no identical causal efficiency in different individuals. The drawing of water and the like which is discharged by the individual jars is not identical, but varies from individual to individual and the cognition of each such individual and of its action too is variable in each case. So the identical efficiency, on which you would base the conceptual thought, is an unfounded assumption.' Yes, we reply. The activity of individuals is variant in each case, nay, in each moment and its cognitions too are not identical. But still they possess the capacity for generating an idea of an identity. It may be argued that this efficiency for identical conception too is not anything distinct from the individual entities and so the conceptual thought should also be variable in each case. And then there would be no ground for this identical concept and nomenclature. Yes, we admit the justice of these objections; but we do not base our position on the identity of the actions or of the cognitions. The actions and the cognitions are no doubt variant and have no nexus or identity between them. We do not rely on any such identity. We only speak of the identical reference. The cognitions of individual jars, though different *per se* in each and every case, still the determinate judgment, which follows in its trail, contains an invariable reference to an identity, though this identity is only an illusory construction from discrete particulars.[1]

Jayanta Bhaṭṭa, however, has put forward an elaborate contention against this interpretation of conceptual knowledge. Jayanta contends, "Well, it is a dogmatic assertion that the

[1] T.S., Śls. 1034, 1036-37. *Cf.* yo 'sau pratyavamarśapratyayas tasyā 'pi svalakṣaṇabhedena bhidyamānatvād ekatvam asiddham. tataś ca tasyā 'py ekatvasiddhaye param ekākārapratyavamarṣakāryam anusarato 'navasthā syāt. tataś cā 'navasthitaikakāryatayā na kvacid ekaśrutiniveśaḥ siddhyet. nai 'tad asti, na hi pratyavamarśapratyayasyai 'kakāryatayai 'katvam ucyate. kiṁ tarhi? ekārthādhyavasāyitayā, tena nā 'navasthā bhaviṣyati. T. S. P., p. 325.

conceptual judgment (*vikalpa*), which arises in the trail of perceptual knowledge, should cognise only that negative aspect of the reality, which distinguishes it from dissimilar things and not the other side which distinguishes it from similars too. It may be contended that if the full individuality, exclusive of similar and dissimilar entities, is supposed to be cognised in the conceptual knowledge too, then there would be nothing left to distinguish it from the original perceptual experience and so the conceptual knowledge will be reduced to an effete and ineffectual repetition of the perceptual experience. But Jayanta says that this contingency is not to be avoided by the Realists, who think that the conceptual knowledge has a definite objective in the universal. And even if it be regarded as a useless repetition of the perceptual experience, that need not be a deterrant barrier against this possibility. Because there is nothing repugnant in the fact that two cognitions should cognise one and the same thing. Our cognitions do not proceed with a view to necessity and they require no justification by utilitarian considerations. And this repetition should not be treated as a peg to hang this theory on. A man whose thirst has been satisfied may not have any use for a glass of ice-water, but that is no excuse that he should regard it as a piece of silver for that. We cannot be persuaded to believe that conceptual knowledge proceeds by halves, that it should take note of one aspect and not of the other. The negative side of the individual is not anything different from the individual itself and negation of similars is as much a part of its essence as negation of dissimilars. Then why should there be any bias in favour of the latter aspect and the former should be ignored with contempt? If however the full negativity is apprehended in the conceptual knowledge, all our knowledge will be knowledge of particulars, but this will sound the death-knell of linguistic usage and inferential knowledge, which proceed on the knowledge of universals. And if the negation of opposites, from which the Buddhist works out the knowledge of universals, be an objective fact, it will only reinstate the universal under another name. If the negation be traced to a subjective memory-impression (*vāsanā*), then also the objective universal has got to be postulated, as memory is not an ultimate fact but presupposes an original experience, which must have an objective datum as its cause So the novel interpretation of *apoha* of the later Buddhists, which sought to save the doctrine of Dignāga from the onslaughts of Kumārila, has not succeeded in finding for it a haven of peace and security.'' [1]

Jayanta further contends that the reference to an identity, on which the Buddhist has sought to base the synthetic conceptual knowledge is an ungrounded assumption. It may be contended that the content of conceptual knowledge which follows upon the perception of a black cow is not different from the content of another conceptual knowledge which follows upon the perception of a yellow cow and this identity of content of all conceptual cognitions is the ground of synthesis of distinct cognitions and of the particular individual objects referred to by it. But this argument of the Buddhist is more ingenious than convincing. The conceptual cognitions are distinct and separate one from the other, being momentary like the principle of consciousness from which it is not anywise distinct. As regards the contents of such conceptual cognitions, which are regarded as non-distinct in all such cognitions, we ask, is the content distinct from the cognitions or not ? If it is distinct, it is an objective universal with only a different name affixed to it, there being no reason to regard it as an unreal fiction. If however the content is not anywise distinct from the conceptual cognition, it should be different with different cognitions and so cannot be supposed to be identical, on the strength of which you would explain the synthetic reference of such cognitions. [2]

[1] N.M., pp. 316-17.

[2] vikalpollikhyamānākārabhedānavagamād vikalpānām aikyam yādṛśam evai 'kaśābaleyādisvalakṣaṇadarśanānantarabhuvā 'pi vikalpeno

These objections of Jayanta have been boldly and squarely faced by Ratnakīrti in his '*Apohasiddhi*' and they have been effectively refuted by him. The power of generating the idea of one universal, which is the content of conceptual cognitions, is certainly not distinct from the cognitions themselves and so an objective universal has no logical justification to be posited apart from and independent of the subjective ideation. The generative efficiency is non-distinct from the individual cognitions and as such cannot but vary with varying individual cognitions. But that does not detract from its invariable identical reference. If one thing is equally efficient with another thing, what is there to find fault with? And what about your universals? Does not one universal generate the self-same synthetic concept as another universal does, though they are distinct from one another and have no other universal underlying and synthesising them? So our individuals, though particular and discrete, can with equal cogency be supposed to generate a selfsame concept without any gratuitous aid from an external universal, existing in and outside of them. The universals are all labelled by a common name, *viz.*, as universal and because they lack another universal, they are on the same level with particularistic individuals, as universals in relation to one another are no less particularistic than individuals. And if in spite of their particularistic character, there is no difficulty in the matter of their competency with regard to an identical concept and nomenclature, what earthly reason is there that a ghost of doubt should be raised with regard

'llikhita ākāro gaur iti tādṛśam eva gopiṇḍāntaradarśanānantarajanmanā 'pī 'ti viṣayābhedāt tadaikyam ucyate.........tad etad api na hṛdayaṅgamam abhidhīyate. vikalpas tāvad vijñānakṣaṇasvabhāvatvād anyonyam bhinnā eva bhavanti—yas tu vikalpollikhita ākāro 'nupalabhyamānabhedas tebhyo vyatirikto 'vyatirikto vā. vyatiriktaś cet syāt sāmānyam eve 'dam nāmāntareṇo 'ktaṁ bhavati. avāstavatvakṛto viśeṣa iti cen na, avāstavatve yuktyabhāvāt. avyatiriktaś cet sa ākāras tarhi vikalpasvarūpavad bhidyata eve 'ti kathaṁ tadaikyam kathaṁ vā tadaikye bhinnānām api darśanānāṁ miśrīkaraṇam avakalpate? N. M., pp. 314-15.

to particulars? If lack of a universal underlying and informing the distinctive individuals be regarded as a condemnation, then the realistic universals should be equally condemned.[1] And the other objection of Jayanta,—that conceptual knowledge should take cognisance of the full individuality, with its twofold negative implication and not alone the negation of dissimilars as negation of similars, too, is as much an integral part of the reality as the other negation, namely, of dissimilars,—is an objection which is neither fair nor worthwhile. The objection can be raised against the *Naiyāyika* too. It can be equally legitimately asked why should not the primal indeterminate cognition take note of the universal and if it is supposed to cognise the universal, then, why should it not be explicit like the determinate conceptual judgment? If it is supposed that the explicit relational reference is due to the remembrance of name-relation, the Buddhist too can have recourse to the self-same explanation. The conceptual judgment is regarded as distinct from the perceptual experience not from any fear of repetition or lack of utilitarian value, but from the variation of contents. So Jayanta's censure and logical sermonisings are equally uncalled for. It may be asked, why this preference for one aspect of truth to the exclusion of the other? Why this playing by halves? Our answer is that there is no favouritism in our theory and if it savours of undeserved preference, it is the fault of human psychology and not of our theory. The idea of the universal does not arise in the primal sense-experience, because the conditions are lacking in it. When the primal sense-experience is reinforced by a memory of the

[1] nanu sāmānyapratyayajananasāmarthyaṁ yady ekasmāt piṇḍād abhinnam. tadā vijātīyavyāvṛttaṁ piṇḍāntaram asamartham. atha bhinnam, tadā tad eva sāmānyam, nāmni paraṁ vivāda iti cet? abhinnai 'va sā śaktiḥ prativastu. yathā tv ekaḥ śaktasvabhāvo bhāvas tathā 'nyo 'pi bhavan kīdṛśaṁ doṣam āvahati? yathā bhavatāṁ jātir ekā 'pi samānadhvaniprasavahetur anyā 'pi svarūpeṇai 'va jātyantaranirapekṣā, tathā 'smākaṁ vyaktir api jātinirapekṣā svarūpeṇai 'va bhinnā hetuḥ. A. S., p. 13.

previous experience of another individual, then and then alone the concept of the universal arises in the mind. But this universal is a hollow subjective creation and is not an objective reality, as supposed by the Realist.[1] We have thoroughly proved the worthlessness of the claims of these universals to being regarded as objective categories and the arguments need not be repeated here.

Jayanta has contended that if the negation of opposites be traced to a memory-impression, it would end in proving the existence of objective universals, as memory presupposes an original experience and experience is impossible without an objective datum. But this is only an assumption based on analogy. The memory-impressions of universals etc., have an infinite past history and they cannot be assigned a definite beginning. So the objection does not touch our central position that universals are ideal constructions and not facts. And when we speak of words as denotative of universals, we mean nothing more than their efficiency for generating a conceptual image with its implicit negation of dissimilar entities and concepts.[2] The conceptual contents are erroneously believed to be objective facts and this objective reference has proved a veritable snare for the Realists, who mistake the false appearance for a reality. If however a word really denoted a living fact, then, all predication would be unaccountable. The Realist holds that the subject and the predicate in a proposition are equated with objective facts, but this is opposed to reason. If the word 'cow' really denoted an actually living cow, no predication about it would be justifiable. In the proposition 'the cow exists,' the predication

[1] yat punaḥ sāmānyābhāve sāmānyapratyayasyā 'kasmikatvam uktam, tad ayuktam. yataḥ pūrvapiṇḍadarśanasmaraṇasahakāriṇā 'tiricyamānā viśeṣapratyayajanikā sāmagrī nirviṣayaṁ sāmānyavikalpam utpādayati. A. S., p. 12.

[2] tatra sāmānyavacanā uktāḥ śabdā ghaṭādayaḥ |
vijātīyavyavacchinnapratibimbaikahetavaḥ |
T. S., śl. 1038.

of 'existence' is redundant if it relates to a living cow actually in existence. Neither can 'non-existence' be predicated, as that would involve a contradiction in terms. If the 'cow' is supposed to refer to a cow not in existence, that too does not improve the situation, as affirmation of existence with reference to a non-existent cow would be a case of self-contradiction and denial of existence would involve a useless tautology. So the very fact of subject-predicate relation proves that words stand for conceptual fictions and not objective entities.[1] All reals are momentary point-instants, exclusive of all similar or dissimilar entities and there can be no relation between them. Nor can there be any split of the integer of reality into a quality and a substance. But linguistic usage proceeds on the assumption of such relations of synthesis and analysis, integration and division, which are not possible between two real objective facts. For instance, the word 'forest' denotes a number of trees integrated into one whole, but in reality, the trees, individual by individual, are absolutely detached from one another and have no objective nexus between one and the other. Again when we speak of a 'blue flower,' the two things 'blue' quality and the 'flower' substance are understood to be distinct entities brought together. But in reality, the flower and the blue are one and the same thing, the division is only a conceptual construction without any factual basis.[2] Let alone the function of words in the rôle of subject and predicate, which proceeds on conceptual integration and division, even the direct import of words should be regarded as conceptual in character. Sometimes these concepts have a

[1] kiñ ca svalakṣaṇātmani vastuni vācye sarvātmanā pratipatteḥ, vidhiniṣedhayor ayogaḥ. tasya hi sadbhāve 'stī 'ti vyartham, nā 'stī 'ty asamartham. asadbhave nāstī 'ti vyartham, astī'ty asamartham. asti cā 'styādipadaprayogaḥ. A. S., pp. 7-8.

[2] saṁsṛjyante na bhidyante svato 'rthāḥ pāramārthikāḥ ।
rūpam ekam anekaṁ ca teṣu buddher upaplavaḥ ।

T. S. P., p. 228 under 1049.

remote bearing on objective reality being derived from it, but there are others which refer to a fiction or they are such as to relate to a fact and a fiction in the same fashion. Thus, the word 'blue' connotes a real fact, the word 'rabbit's horn' refers to a fiction and such expressions as 'amorphous' are indefinite, being referable to a fact, *viz.*, 'consciousness' and a fiction, *e.g.*, 'a rabbit's horn.' So the content of words should be regarded as conceptual constructions conjured up from the store of subconscious impressions deposited from beginningless time.[1]

The Realists have found a crux in this situation and have not been able to give a satisfactory explanation of this phenomenon consistently with their theory. Vācaspati and Jayanta Bhaṭṭa hold that the connotation of a word is neither exclusively a universal nor exclusively a particular, but a particular as determined and qualified by a universal. But when pressed with the question, how can there be any predication of either existence or non-existence with reference to such concrete facts, which are supposed to be living objective facts, Vācaspati gives up his original position and adopts another view that words denote universals and, though eternal by nature, they are amenable to affirmation, or negation, being subsistent in an infinite number of individuals widely distributed in infinite space and time. So when existence is predicated, it means that the universal is related to a present individual and negation of existence only emphasises that the universal is related to a past or a future individual as opposed to a present, living individual.[2] Jayanta

[1] anādivāsanodbhūtavikalpapariniṣṭhitaḥ | śabdārthas trividho dharmī bhāvābhāvobhayāśrayaḥ | bhāvāśrayo yathā nīlam iti, abhāvāśrayo yathā śaśaviṣāṇam iti, ubhayāśrayo yathā amūrtam iti, amūrtaṁ hi bhavati vijñānaṁ bhavati ca śaśaviṣāṇam. Tāt. ṭī., p. 497.

Cf. tasmāc chabdapratibhāsasya bāhyārthabhāvābhāvasādhāraṇyaṁ na tadviṣayatāṁ kṣamate. A. S., p. 8.

[2] tasmāj jātimatyo vyaktayo vikalpānāṁ śabdānāṁ ca gocaraḥ...... na ca śabdārthasya bhāvābhāvasādhāraṇyaṁ no 'papadyate. sā hi svarūpato nityā 'pi deśakālaviprakīrṇānantavyaktyāśrayatayā bhāvābhāva-

too observes that as a word primarily denotes exclusively a universal without any reference to its existence or non-existence, the fact of existence or non-existence is predicated of it to satisfy an intellectual demand and to emphasise its definitive existence. It may savour of repetition, but this repetition is necessary for the sake of emphasis. For instance, when we make a statement like this—'The jar is a jar and not a cloth,' there is a repetition no doubt, but this repetition only emphasises the exclusive identity of the subject and so is not unjustified.[1]

Ratnakīrti observes that Vācaspati here contradicts himself and apart from contradiction or surrender of his position, which is more or less a question of personal aberration, he has been forced to concede that a word cannot denote an 'individual' and also that predication is not competent to an individual and this is evident when he throws the entire weight upon the 'universal.' And as these universals are conceptual fictions, he practically accepts the Buddhist position and even if they be regarded as objective entities, predication of existence or non-existence is equally untenable with reference to these universals. When he says that the predication of existence means the relation of universal to a living individual, he only seeks to avoid the logical absurdity by a subterfuge. Existence or non-existence always relates to an individual, because individuals are alone possessed of practical efficiency and as such are alone amenable to predication. We can quote Jayanta Bhaṭṭa in this connexion to expose the fallacy of Vācaspati's position. Jayanta observes that a universal is

sādhāraṇī bhavaty astināstisambandhayogyā, vartamānavyaktisambandhitā hi jāter astitā, atītānāgatavyaktisambandhitā ca nāstitā.

Tāt. ṭī., p. 487, A. S., p. 8.

[1] sarvasya gaur ityādiśabdajanitasya jñānasyā 'tītatvādy anapekṣya sāmānyamātraviṣayatvād ākāṅkṣānirākaraṇāyā 'sti nastī 'ti padāntaraṁ prayujyamānaṁ sambadhyate. niyatārūpitāniścitanijarūpe vastuni vastvantarasya vyavacchedabandhanam iṣyata eva ghaṭo ghaṭa eva na paṭa iti. N. M., p. 317.

neither an agent, nor possesses differences of sex, nor is it amenable to numerical variation, but these are invariably the connotation of words and suffixes. So the universal cannot be supposed to be the denoted meaning of a word.[1] And the view, which takes the universal-in-individual to be the denotation of a word, is fully exposed to the objections advanced against the individual. If the individual be the meaning of a word, no matter whether qualified by a universal or not, the objections lying against the 'individual' will apply with full force against the theory.

We have seen that the import of a word is primarily and naturally a conceptual construction and not an objective fact, whether individual or universal. This conceptual construction is however hypostatised as an objective reality by an inherent subjective illusion and this becomes the intended import of a word. It is affirmative in character and reference, but is characterised by the Buddhist philosopher in terms of negation on the ground of its logical negative implication. But the negation is only a logical pre-supposition and is not psychologically felt in the first presentation. Dignāga seems to be the first philosopher who promulgated this theory. Words have a synthetic and comprehensive import, but as particulars are alone real in Dignāga's school of thought, and as particulars are absolutely distinct and discrete without any connecting link, or nexus, the universal of the Realist was equated with a negative concept and words were held to denote this negative concept and not any positive fact. There are indications which warrant us to suppose that Dignāga put forward the theory of *apoha* as a pure negation without any positive reference and so his theory came in for ruthless animadversion first in the hands of Uddyotakara and then of Kumārila.[2] Kumārila dealt sledge-hammer blows and demolished the theory *in toto*. Later Buddhists, notably

[1] ....kārakaṁ liṅgaṁ saṅkhyā ca, na cai 'tat tritayaṁ prātipadikārthe jātāv anveti, na jātiḥ kārakaṁ, na ca jāteḥ strīpuṁnapuṁsakavibhāgo, na cā 'sya dvitvādiyoga iti. *Ibid*, p. 322.

[2] *Vide* the footnote 1, p. 138.

Śāntarakṣita, gave altogether a new orientation to the theory and we find this position again attacked by Vācaspati and Jayanta Bhaṭṭa. Ratnakīrti came after Vācaspati Miśra and refuted the objections advanced by Vācaspati and others and veered round to the old position of Dignāga. From the historical point of view, we may be justified in surmising three distinctive landmarks in the eventful career of the doctrine of *apoha*. (1) In the first place, *apoha* or *anyāpoha*, as formulated by Dignāga, had its natural meaning of pure negation, so far at least as its comprehensive reference was concerned. It had no positive content or reference. (2) In the second place, '*apoha*' was given altogether a new interpretation. *Apoha* was supposed to stand for a positive conceptual construction, a purely subjective idea, fondly objectified by the realistic bias of our psychological constitution. This realistic reference was traced to the working of previous sub-conscious impressions lying embedded in the subliminal region of consciousness from a beginningless time. But still it had a negative implication and this negative aspect, though not psychologically felt, was regarded to be the fundamental keynote of verbal import. The universal of the Realist was demolished by a powerful dialectic and the subjective concept was ushered into existence to do duty for the objective universal. The negative character, though dethroned from the psychological sphere, was installed with all the pomp and paraphernalia of regal majesty in the domain of logic with all its sovereign rights restored. (3) In the third place, we find Ratnakīrti entering the arena with his subtle dialectic and forceful diction. He does not subscribe to the position of Śāntarakṣita, who held that word conveyed a positive meaning in the first instance and a negative import by logical implication. There were some other Buddhist thinkers, we guess from the words of Ratnakīrti, who thought negation to be the primary meaning and the positive aspect of negation was supposed to be understood by a logical construction.[1]

[1] Yat tu goḥ pratītau 'na tadātmā parātme ' ti'sāmarthyāt (*Cf.* prasa-

Ratnakīrti differs from the latter theory also. He maintains like the *Naiyāyikas* that the connotation of a word is a complex, being a conceptual image as qualified by a negation of the opposite entities. The meaning of a word is therefore neither purely positive nor purely negative with contrary logical implication, but even psychologically a distinctive concept with the element of distinction or negation as a part of the felt content. The word 'cow' is conventionally affixed to the distinctive cow-concept felt as divorced from not-cows. Though the negative element is not distinctly articulated in words it is there as a felt content none the less. Just as the concept of 'blue-lotus,' to which the word '*indīvara*' is affixed by convention, is a complex of blue and lotus and the 'blue' is felt as much as the 'lotus' in one sweep, so in the case of such expression as 'cow,' which gives rise to a complex concept of 'cow-as-distinct-from-non-cow.' Here the non-cow is felt as much as the cow—the negative and the positive factor being present alike. Ratnakīrti refuses to believe that the negation is understood by logical implication from the positive content or that the positive reference is a deduction from primary negation. If the negative aspect is not comprehended as a part and parcel of the verbal concept, we cannot explain the selective and exclusive character of the volitional activity following upon it. Why does the subject avoid the horse and address himself to the cow 'when he is directed to tether a cow?' This exclusion of non-cow and adoption of the cow is proof positive that the negative aspect of the concept is comprehended as much as the existential reference in the first conceptual knowledge generated by a verbal expression.[1] Ratnakīrti thus restored '*apoha*' (negation) to its

jyapratiṣedho 'pi sāmarthyena pratīyate । na tadātmā parātme 'ti, T.S., 1013-14) apohaḥ paścān niścīyata iti vidhivādinām matam, anyāpohapratītau vā sāmarthyād anyāpoḍho 'vadhāryata iti pratiṣedhavādinām matam. A. S., p. 3.

[1] *Ibid*, pp. 3-4. 'anyathā yadi śabdād arthapratipattikāle kalito na parāpohaḥ, katham anyaparihāreṇa pravṛttiḥ. tato gām badhāne 'ti codito 'śvādīn api badhnīyat.' *Ibid.*

pristine position of psychologically felt content and rescued it from the logical domain, to which it was relegated by Śāntarakṣita.

The attacks of Kumārila were therefore avoided and not returned, as the primary presentation was materially altered. But the fundamental position—that words do not convey any reference to an objective reality, particular or universal alike, and their pragmatic value is only vicarious and derivative—was neither abandoned nor abated by any Buddhist philosopher. The meaning of a word is a positive concept, which though subjective is hypostatised as an objective fact. And affirmative or negative predication does not really appertain to the concept, because the concept being a part of subjective consciousness is attested by self-intuition and as such cannot be negated. Moreover, it is not a subjective concept that is understood to be meant by a word, but something objective. But no predication again is competent to the objective reality, as the objective reality is not presented in the verbal cognition at all. What then does the predication relate to? It does not of a certainty relate to the concept either logically or psychologically and the objective reality, too, logically speaking, is untouched by it. The answer is that all predication, affirmative or negative alike, refers to the concept psychologically felt as an objective fact—in other words, to the hypostatised concept. When the cow is said to exist, it only affirms this objectivity of the concept and the 'negative predication only denies this supposed objectivity. In reality, however, a word has no meaning, but only a false meaning.[1]

Now a difficulty has been raised by Vācaspati Misra that if the external reality is not presented in the conceptual knowledge, then, how could such knowledge lead to the actual attainment of the reality by creating a volitional urge towards it? Even the determinate conceptual knowledge, which follows upon sense-perception directly cognisant of the particular real, is not conversant

[1] *Ibid*, p. 18.

with the real because the real can be cognised by a non-relational experience alone. It may be supposed for the sake of argument that being immediately preceded by the primal simple experience the conceptual knowledge seems to take cognisance of the reality as it is and hence the volitional urge follows upon it. But this supposition, too, is precluded in the case of verbal knowledge because it does not necessarily follow upon a perceptual cognition. It cannot be supposed that the conceptual image is not felt to be distinct from an objective reality and so comes to be regarded as identical with it and the volitional activity therefore follows as a matter of course. The fact is that mere non-cognition of distinction cannot originate a confusion of identity, far less a volitional urge. The conceptual image is not felt as distinct not only from the objective reality relevant to it, but from the whole world of reality as well. So if non-apprehension of distinction be supposed to have a bearing upon volitional activity, then the activity need not be selective and exclusive in character. It could lead to activity in any direction and towards any object. If however conceptual knowledge, whether following upon perceptual experience or not, be supposed to take note of the objective reality as it is, then there is no room for confusion of activity or for inactivity, which is inevitable in the Buddhist theory.[1]

Ratnakīrti accepts the challenge of Vācaspati and assures us that there is no difficulty whatsoever in the Buddhist theory of conceptual knowledge (*adhyavasāya*). Though the objective reality is not presented as a datum in the conceptual knowledge, still it is a reality which is conceived and this conception of reality means that the volitional activity is directed towards it. Well, the crux of the problem lies in this, how can there be any volitional urge towards an object not directly felt in experience? Even if it is conceded that the conceptual image is not differentiated from the objective reality, this non-differentiation cannot be the cause of any activity, it being purely privative in character.

[1] Tāt. tī., pp. 488-90, N. M., p. 317.

It could inspire activity only if the concept and the reality were identified, but this false identification even is possible only if the two factors are present ; and if the reality is actually felt in the conceptual knowledge, then this identification need not be postulated, as the felt reality can inspire the activity and identification would be useless. So the explanation of Dharmakīrti that activity is inspired by a false identification of a concept with a fact falls to the ground, even if identification is interpreted as non-cognition of difference.[1] Ratnakīrti however argues that though the objective reality, which is aimed at by the volitional activity, is not presented to the conceptual knowledge, the mere fact of non-presentation does not put it on a level with the whole world of unpresented data. There is this distinction—that one is aimed at by a volitional activity and others are ignored. There is no room for confusion even, because a conceptual thought has a distinctive structure and a distinctive capacity, being generated by a definitive collocation of causes and conditions and so the concept of water inspires activity towards water alone and not to horse and the like, though both are equally unpresented data. The concept of water has a bearing upon water alone just as smoke has a bearing upon fire. You cannot question, why should it be so and not otherwise? Nature does not permit of any such curiosity and keeps her ultimate secrets hidden from the limited understanding of man. Whom would you reprove that fire only burns and not the sky? We do not say that there is any identification between a concept and a fact on the ground of their similarity and so the rebuke does not touch us. How does then the volitional activity arise regarding an external fact, though not presented to the mind? The answer is that the relevant memory-impression, when it is fully matured

[1] idaṁ tad ekīkaraṇam āhur dṛyśavikalpayor bhedo yan na gṛhyate, na punar bhinnayor 'abhedādhyavasāya ekīkaraṇam iṣyate. dṛśyakalpāvibhagajño loko bāhyaṁ tu manyate. N. M., p. 308.

T. S., śl. 1078.

and stimulated, springs up as a conceptual image and this conceptual image inspires activity towards the outer object by virtue of an inherent power, though there is no factual relation between the two. It is an illusory relation, but it has a remote bearing upon the objective fact, being conditioned by it at some stage of experience. Conceptual knowledge, though false *quâ* its objective reference, leads to the actual attainment of the object and in respect of pragmatic value it can be equated with such 'working errors' as perception of the jewel's light misconstrued as the perception of the jewel itself. In verbal knowledge too what is immediately present to the subjective consciousness is but a conceptual image, but this is misjudged to be the objective reality. If pragmatic satisfaction be regarded as the adequate measure of truth, verbal concepts can be taken to be true. But as the test of truth is not pragmatic satisfaction alone, but correspondence and consistency of fact and knowledge and as pragmatic success is only symptomatic of such truth, conceptual knowledge is regarded as false knowledge as it lacks the said correspondence and consistency.[1]

We have seen that the exact connotation of a word is not grounded in an objective reality. A word only generates a conceptual image in the mind of the subject and this conceptual image is hypostatised as an external fact. But as a concept even is possessed of a definitive content, it is naturally demarcated from other concepts and this negative aspect is regarded as constitutive of its individuality and significance. Though opinions differ about the exact position of the negative content as to whether it is a part of the felt content or a deduction from the positive meaning, there is no difference whatsoever about the fact that the connotation of a word is a concept, subjective in fact though objective in reference. Though Dignāga did not expressly

[1] pratibhāsaś ca śabdārtha ity āhus tattvacintakāḥ |
tattvataś ca na śabdānāṁ vācyam astī 'ti sādhitam | T. S., śl. 1078-79.

declare that by the negative import of words he meant only subjective concepts and though he expressly denied that word had a positive meaning,[1] and Uddyotakara was acquainted only with this theory of pure negation as verbal import, the theory was revised at not a distant date and the conceptual character of the word-import with negative implication was emphasised. Kumārila refers to this conceptual image being regarded by certain thinkers as the verbal connotation and Kamalaṣīla expressly states that the view in question was of some other thinkers.[2] Whatever may be the case, later Buddhists have invariably declared that the verbal import is a conceptual construction and not an objective fact. Now the question arises, if the meaning be only a subjective concept, then how could it be communicable to one another ? The concept of one is not the concept of another and so cannot be known by any two persons, simply because concepts and ideas are not amenable to perception by a different subject. How could then verbal convention be apprehended with regard to these concepts, simply because no two persons can have the same concept and even if it be possible, there is no means of knowing that the concept of one is possessed by another ? Śāntarakṣita replies that the difficulty would have been actually in-urmountable if the conceptual image wás confined within its limits and had not

[1] Kamalaśīla raises the doubt that if word had a positive meaning then, why did the author (Dignāga) deny this positive connotation in the *Hetumukha?* Śāntarakṣita saves the situation by declaring that the Master denied positive import on the ground that word had not, from the logical standpoint, any reference to an objective reality and not that he meant negation to be the direct import. 'kathaṁ tarhi Hetumukhe lakṣaṇakāreṇa 'asambhavo vidher' ity uktam?......'asambhavo vidher uktaḥ sāmānyader asambhavāt । śabdānāṁ ca vikalpānāṁ vastuto 'viṣayatvataḥ' । T. S., śl. 1097.

Pañj., p. 339.

[2] ye tv āhur vikalpapratibimbakam eva sarvaśabdānām arthas tad eva cā 'bhidhīyate vyavacchidayata iti co 'cyata iti tān pratī 'dam āha' jñānākāraniṣedhāc ca nā' 'ntarārtho 'bhidhīyate.'

T. S. P., p. 313. S. V., p. 605, śl. 145.

extra-subjective reference. Though in reality the speaker and the hearer are conversant with what is their private possession, both of them think that they understand the objective reality, and the cause of illusion being similar in both, there is no difficulty in intercommunication, just as two persons suffering from ophthalmia see two moons and when one communicates his experience to the other, his word is believed to refer to an actual fact. Language is therefore a convenient instrument for communication of concepts, which however are fictitious representatives of reality.[1]

[1] T. S., Śls. 1210-11, and the Pañj. thereunder.

Reference:

1. Tattvasaṅgraha and Pañjikā, pp. 274-366, śls. 867-1212.
2. Apohasiddhi-Six Buddhist Nyāya Tracts, pp. 1-19.
3. Nyāyavārttika, pp 320-331.
4. Tātparyaṭīka, pp. 478-491.
5. Sloka-Vārttika-Apohavāda, pp. 566-614.
6. Nyāyamañjarī, pp. 302-317.
7. Vākyapadīya, Ch. II, śls. 118-154, pp. 131-148.

CHAPTER VIII

THE SOUL-THEORY OF THE NYĀYA-VAIŚEṢIKA SCHOOL

The philosophers of this school postulate the existence of a soul-entity, which is eternal and ubiquitous like space and though unconscious in itself is the background and support of thinking, feeling and willing. The soul, though unconscious in and by itself, develops consciousness when acted upon by the sense-object contact, which in its turn is brought about and determined by an unseen destiny operating in the soul. Thus, though eternal, it comes to discharge the function of an agent, when it develops cognitive and volitional activity and is again looked upon as an enjoyer, when it experiences pleasure and pain. And it is regarded as undergoing a birth, when it comes to be invested with a physical system, in which a new order of cognitive and volitional experiences is exercised by it. The dissolution of a present physical system with its corresponding psychical complex is regarded as death. And any injury done to the physical system is construed as an injury to the self, connected with it. Thus the soul or self, though distinct and eternal and as such not subject to origination or decay, comes to possess all these various processes, when it is associated with a psycho-physical organism and this association is brought about and determined by an unseen destiny, *i.e.*, merit and demerit, acquired through previous actions.[1]

Now there is no difference of opinion between the Buddhists and the *Nyāya-Vaiśeṣika* school of thinkers that consciousness is a distinct principle apart from the physical system and the organs of sense. But the Buddhist demurs to accept the position that

[1] sadehasya manoyogo dharmādharmābhisatkṛtaḥ. T.S., 175. *Vide* T.S., 171-176.

this thinking principle is something different and distinct from the states of consciousness and as such is an eternal verity, which owns the psychical processes that occur therein. The Buddhist also denies that this thinking principle or the self is an all-pervading substance (*vibhu*). Thus the theory of soul of the *Nyāya-Vaiśeṣika* school postulates three things that the self is something distinct from the passing psychical states, of which it is a substratum or receptacle ; secondly, that this self is an eternal, unchanging verity; thirdly, that it is all-pervading (*vibhu*) like space (*ākāśa*). The Buddhist denies all these three assumptions and we propose to examine the arguments, both for and against this theory, as advanced by the respective schools.

The *Vaiśeṣika's* arguments can be summed up as follows :—

(1) There must be a separate and distinct soul-entity, standing behind the psychical phenomena, which are cognised by it. A cognition has got to be perceived in its turn like other objects and this cogniser must be the 'self,' that cognises the different cognitions which form the sumtotal of our life of experience.

(2) Our cognitions, feelings and conations, being either products or actions must inhere in some substratum like colour produced by heat, which is seen to inhere in a substratum, say, a jug. If the cognition is looked upon as an action, it also must have a supporting base like the action of cutting and that wherein it inheres is the self.[1]

(3) The fact that our different cognitions are all referred to and held together by a common ego-principle, which is the unifying factor of these varying states, shows that there is a distinct category, *viz.*, the self. Unless a common unifying principle is

[1] jñānaṁ kvacid āśritaṁ kriyātvāc chidi-kriyāvat, yatre 'dam āśritaṁ sa ātmā. N. K., p. 71.

Also, icchādayaś' ca sarve' pi kvacid ete samāśritāḥ I vastutve sati kāryatvād rūpavat sa ca naḥ pumān I T.S., 178.

postulated, the different cognitions would fall asunder, and the fact that these discrete, successive psychical facts are synthesised in a subjective experience-whole proves the existence of an independent soul, which owns them up.[1]

(4) The fact that a totally distinct word such as 'self' or 'soul' has to be employed for denoting 'self,' which has nothing to do with the accepted synonyms of 'intellect,' 'understanding,' 'sense organs' and the like, proves that the self is a distinct principle which is not covered by the expressions denoting varying psychical facts and the like.

(5) The self must be postulated to account for the exercise of vital functions by a physical body. If there be no self in the living organism, it will be like a lifeless body as dead and unconscious as a jug or a plate.

The last three arguments have been put forward by Uddyotakara in support of the soul as a distinct entity.

Praśastapāda in his *Padārthadharma-saṅgraha* and Śrīdhara in his *Nyāyakandalī* have also advanced elaborate arguments in support of the existence of a self as the basic support of the psychical and vital activities. The arguments are summed up as follows :—

(1) There must be an operator to guide and operate the sense-organs, which are so many instruments of knowledge like ordinary instruments. And as instruments have no autonomous activity, these sense-organs must have an intelligent operator, which is the self.

(2) The different cognitions of sound, smell and the like must have a cognising subject, who will possess them and exercise them.

[1] Devadattasya rūparasagandhasparśapratyayā ekānekanimittā, mayeti pratyayena pratisandhīyamānatvāt. pratisandhānaṁ punar mayā dṛṣṭaṁ mayā śrutam ity evam-ādīnām.........ekajñātṛnimittatvena ghaṭanam...... ......sarvathā pratisandhānam ucyate yad ekam arthaṁ nimittīkṛtya pratyayānāṁ sambandhanam.' T. S. P., p. 81.

(3) Our physical activities are planned and directed by an intelligent agent with a view to acquisition of what is good and avoidance of what is evil. Without an active, intelligent guide these activities will occur haphazardly and will fail to express a well-regulated, teleological plan, which we find in a living organism.

(4) The vital activities of a physical organism, which manifests growth and development and the capacity for healing wounds and abrasions, point to the existence of an intelligent owner, who improves and repairs his tenement.

(5) From the contact of the mind with the sense-organs, which occurs at regular and stated intervals, we can infer the existence of an intelligent, active self, who moves them and connects them with the desired object.

(6) The unity of this conscious subject is established by the fact that after the visual perception of the colour and form of an object, there often arises in the mind a desire to experience the taste of it. This proves that the agent, who sees the colour, is the same as that once enjoyed the taste of it. So the self cognising through the two sense-organs has been compared to a spectator, who sees through two windows. And this common subject of two different cognitions cannot be the sense-organs, even granting that they are intelligent. Because each of the sense-organs would perceive separately only the taste or the colour, for which it is competent and the integration of the diverse items of experience in a separate judgment would be left unaccounted for.

(7) Pleasure, pain, desire, aversion and effort are so many qualities and always associated with an ego-consciousness as in the expressions, 'I am pleased,' 'I am pained' and the like. And as this 'ego-consciousness' cannot refer to the body or the sense-organs or the mind, it must be taken to relate to a permanent substratum, *viz.*, the self.

These arguments, it is apparent, stress three points, *viz.*, the synthetic unity of our conscious life; secondly, the teleological character of our physical, biological and psychological activities ; thirdly, that these activities, being of the nature of qualities and actions, must inhere in a substratum.

As regards the two other characteristics of the self, *viz.*, permanence and ubiquity, Aviddhakarṇa, an older *Naiyāyika*, has put forward the following arguments :—

(1) All the different cognitions beginning with the first cognition of the new-born baby must be held to be cognised by a common subject, because they are regarded as cognitions of a particular subject. This shows that the subject must be a permanent unitary principle, cognising as it does the different cognitions occurring at various periods of time.

(2) All objects, existing far or near, must be connected with my 'self' like my body, because they are corporeal. This shows that the self must be ubiquitous.

The ubiquity of the 'Self' has been proved by Śrīdhara in his *Nyāyakandalī* by the following arguments :

'The ubiquity of the self can be inferred from the upward flaming of fire and the slanting motion of wind. These motions are certainly caused by an unseen destiny (merit and demerit) and this destiny cannot be operative, unless it is directly connected wiih the substances (fire and wind), which are the receptacle of these actions......Nor is it possible for the unseen destiny, which inheres in the soul, to be connected with other substances unless they are connected with the soul, which is its substratum. This proves that the soul is all-pervading, because it is connected with all material substances.

But it may be objected that the upward motion of fire is due to its nature and not to any unseen destiny. But what is this precious nature ? Is it the distinctive individuality of fire (*vahnitva*) or its burning power or its particular colour ? If it were any one of these, we could expect this character in the red-hot iron also. If it be supposed to consist in the fact of its being produced from a particular fuel, we would not find this in lightning and the like, which are independent of any fuel. If as a last resort it is supposed to be something supersensuous, which being present in some cases of fire, produces the upward flaming in them, then why should you refuse to regard it as a quality of the self, particularly when it is supported by the following argument: An action, which is not caused by gravity, fluidity or velocity, is produced by a specific quality of the self, as the movement of the hand is effected by an effort of the self. And as regards the upward flaming and slanting motion of the fire and wind respectively, they cannot be set down to the agency of gravity and the like, as they are absent in the substances concerned and as they would on the contrary produce other results. So these should be regarded as effected by a specific quality of the self and this would be impossible unless the self is ubiquitous so that it can be connected with all material substances.[1]

Now after having summed up the arguments of the *Nyāya-Vaiśeṣika* school, we propose to give the Buddhist position particularly on the points raised by the former.

The first argument that our cognitions are cognised by a distinct cogniser does not affect our (Buddhist's) position as we too admit that the omniscient saint or even a thought-reader can cognise the cognitions and feelings of another person. But if the argument seeks to make out that the cognitions as such have to be cognised by a distinct principle before they can be operative, we agree to differ, because we maintain that all cognitions are self-revelatory and self-cognisant and as such do not stand in need of a second cogniser to illumine them. Not alone the cognitions of another person, which are independent of such extraneous illumination from a foreign subject, but even our own cognitions are self-revealing. We do not see what particular purpose will be served by this gratuitous assumption of an independent knowing subject. On the other

[1] *Vide Nyāyakandalī*, p. 88.

hand it introduces logical complications. Certainly a cognition, which is unrevealed and unillumined by itself, cannot reveal the object. It would be tantamount to holding that a candle, unlighted and unillumined in itself, will make other objects visible. And if for the illumination of the primary cognition, a second cognition is requisitioned, this 'second' again will require a third exactly like the first, as it equally lacks original light and so on to infinity. The result will be that no knowledge will be possible. If to avoid this difficulty it is supposed that some ultimate cognition will be self-illumined, then the whole argument will fall down like a house of cards. If one cognition can be independent of the aid of a foreign subject as the supplier of its light, all cognitions should be certified to be so independent. If however the ultimate cognition is supposed to be unillumined like the first it will be equally inoperative.

The *Nyāya* theory of perception maintains that when sense-object contact takes place, the object becomes revealed, and in this, sense-perception itself remains uncognised, which, however, is cognised by a separate mental perception. You cannot formulate the proposition that the cause of the cognition concerned should be also cognised, as we see that this rule breaks down in the case of the sense-organ, which is universally admitted to be the cause of sense-perception, as sense-organs operate though uncognised. But this is a case of false analogy. The sense-organ cannot be regarded to cause the revelation of the object, it is the cognition concerned that reveals it. And the question is how can a cognition, though unrevealed in itself, reveal a foreign object ? We do not see any such instance. The light of the candle reveals other objects, only when it shines and reveals itself. If it were otherwise, we could expect the light to reveal other objects, even when it be hidden under a cover. So a cognition, which is believed to reveal other objects that come within its range, cannot be uncognised. The objection that the same thing cannot be the subject and the object, the revealer and the revealed of the same action, is also baseless. Because, the nature of cognition is to shine and this means self-revelation. So we see there is no force in the contention of the *Naiyāyika* that a cognition has got to be cognised by a cogniser, and this cogniser will be the self (*Ātman*).

The argument that cognitions, being of the nature of either products or actions must have a supporting base has no force either. If by this supporting base it is meant that these cognitions must have a cause of their own, it does not affect our position. We also admit that a cognition is produced by the combination of four causes.[1] If however it is meant that these must have a substratum or a receptacle, it will be an idle hypothesis, because these cognitions are not gravitating objects like plums and the like, which would fall asunder unless there were a receptacle to hold them together.

The next argument that our cognitions are not discrete elements but are synthesised by reference to an ego-principle and this ego-principle is the 'self' is not conclusive enough. This synthesis and unification is due to a false abstraction and cannot be made the ground of a philosophical argument. That this idea of unity of consciousness is an illusion will be fully explained hereafter. If the different cognitions be held to be the products or states of an eternal ego-principle, the sequence of these states will be unaccountable. The cause of cognitions being eternally present, there is no reason why these cognitions should not take place all at once. Certainly an eternal principle cannot stand in necessity of other factors, because being eternal, it cannot be subject to any supplementation or detraction that may be occasioned by external auxiliaries.

Furthermore, it has been argued that the very fact that altogether a new and a distinct word is employed to designate the self is indicative of the self as a distinct category, which can-

[1] For an account of this fourfold cause see the chapter on "The Buddhist theory of 'Causal' factors in Perception," Part II, Caturbhiś cittacaittā hī 'ti vacanāt, T.S.P., p. 84.

not be subsumed under any psychical or physical phenomenon. But we do not see much force in this argument of nomenclature. Names are fictions, pure and simple; and the identity of designation cannot be seriously put forward as an argument for the identity of the thing designated. Sometimes distinct objects are designated by an identical name in view of their identical or similar practical efficiency. Thus, myrobalan, sodibicarbonate, and magnesium salts are all designated by the common name of 'purgative;' but no body is ever deluded into regarding them as identical. So also the self in question is nothing but a particular conscious state, as qualified by the impression of unity due to the similarity of the conscious units. Nor do we think that the self cannot be subsumed under any one of the psychical phenomena, because the self is nothing but a conscious state modified by ego-consciousness, which is an illusory idea. Moreover, we shall prove in our Chapter on Perception that words are mere symbols and have nothing to do with reality as such. The meanings of words are determined by convention and convention is nothing but an arbitrary agreement, dependent entirely upon the wish of the persons concerned.

As regards the inference of the existence of the self from the vital functions, we need only observe that it proves nothing. If there were any established relation between the self and vital functions, the absence of the self might entail the absence of the latter. But so long as this relation is not established, the argument is inconclusive, proving neither one nor the other. Let us consider the nature of the relation that may subsist between the self and vitality. This relation may be either identity of essence or causality. It is not identity of essence, to be sure, as the self is conceded to be eternal and ubiquitous, while vitality is exactly the reverse of these. Nor can the self be regarded as the cause of vital functions, as in that case the cause being eternally present, the effect, *viz.* vital functions, will invariably and eternally follow. And the argument that desire, aversion, effort, pleasure, pain and cognition are the properties of the self and as such indicate the existence of the self is equally hollow. How can these psychical phenomena be indicative of the existence of the self, unless they are proved to have mutual relation? And this relation, we have seen in the case of vital functions, can neither be identity nor causality. So one cannot be indicative of the other. These psychical phenomena are not identical with the self, as they are regarded as the attributes of the latter. Nor can they be supposed to be causally related, as in that case they will emerge invariably and all at once, as the cause in the shape of the self is present intact, being eternal. Nor can the successive appearance of auxiliaries be held responsible for the successive emergence of these phenomena. Because an eternal cause can have no necessity for auxiliaries, as they can have no effect upon it. So these arguments of quality and substratum have no substance and they prove nothing. As regards the teleological argument of Praśastapāda, it is also not worth much. The teleological plan can prove the existence of an unseen destiny and this unseen destiny is admitted by the Buddhist also.

As regards the two other characters of the Self, *viz.*, ubiquity and eternality, they need not require any refutation, as the very self of which they are regarded as characteristics, has been proved to be an illusion. Certainly no body cares to prove either existence or non-existence of the beauty of a barren woman's son.

Uddyotakara, Bhāvivikta and Śrīdhara[1] on the other hand maintain that the self (*ātmā*) is an object of direct perception. The ego is directly perceived by means of the mind and this ego is the Self. But this is evidently a piece of misconception. The ego cannot stand for the self as conceived by Kaṇāda and

[1] *Vide* T. S. P., p. 90 and *Nyāyakandalī*, p. 71. anyair ityādinā punar apy Uddyotakara-Bhāviviktāder matam āśaṇkate. T. S. P. "yady apy ātmā 'haṁ mame'ti svakarmopārjitakāyakaraṇa-sambandhopādhikṛta-kartṛtva-svāmitva-rūpa-sambhinno manasā saṁvedyate, tathāpy atra apratyakṣatvavācoyuktir bāhyendriyābhiprāyeṇa." N. K., p. 71.

Akṣapāda who hold that the self is eternal and ubiquitous. Certainly the ubiquity and eternity of the self are not cognised in the ego-consciousness. On the other hand, the ego-consciousness is always mixed up with physical attributes as in the expressions 'I am fat,' 'I am fair', 'I am confined in this room' etc. Certainly these attributes which are mixed up with the ego can never pertain to the self, as in that case the self will be of limited dimension and impermanent like the body. And such usages cannot be regarded as figurative expressions, as there is no incompatibility of the primary sense experienced by us. Nor can such expressions as 'my body' and the like be put forward as proof of the ego as a distinct and a separate entity from the body. Because, even such usages as 'my soul' are also not rare. So the idea of the self as something distinct from the body cannot be derived from direct intuition of the ego, which is never dissociated from the body.

Śaṅkara and Vācaspati Miśra in the *Śārīraka-bhāṣya* and the *Bhāmatī* respectively have proved that the expressions 'I am fair,' 'I am fat' and the like are natural expressions and cannot be held to be figurative. Figurative usages are possible only when there is a knowledge of the difference of the primary and the secondary meanings, as in the expression 'The boy is a lion.' But there is no such idea of the ego, as distinguished and disentangled from bodily attributes. The expressions 'my body' and the like on the contrary should be regarded as figurative, as ego-consciousness can never be dissociated from physical attributes. This is proved by the fact that even the man, who uses such expressions as 'my body,' points with his finger to his own body, when questioned about his identity. Were the self an object of direct perception, there could arise no dispute about its existence.

It may be contended that the existence of the self is a matter of positive proof, the dispute arises only with reference to its real nature, just as in the case of perception, though the blue is perceived, its momentary character is disputed. But the analogy is not on all fours. The momentariness is not certified as known by the determinate perception and so arises the dispute. But the self is certified as known by a determinate perception on your own showing and there can be no false imposition regarding an object, which is known by a deliberate determinate cognition. So it must be admitted that the self as conceived by the *Nyāya-Vaiśeṣika* school is an abstract idea and is not supported by perceptual or inferential evidence.

The conclusion therefore is irresistible that the different acts of feeling, willing and knowing, emerging as they do in succession, do not relate to a permanent self but are self-subsistent. Were it otherwise, these would arise simultaneously and all at once as the cause is present intact. The momentary character and selflessness of our internal conscious life can be inferred exactly like those of external phenomena from their existence, as existence means causal efficiency and the latter is impossible in a permanent substratum. The self as an eternal principle proves to be an illusory myth, conjured up by the false ideas of the heretical thinkers.

Uddyotakara has raised a difficulty, which is more linguistic than philosophical, that negation of the soul or the self is impossible without an implict affirmation of its existence. But the Buddhist rejoins that the objection is futile. That material objects like pots and plates are without any animating principle in them is the proposition of the *Naiyāyika*. So soullessness is not an unknown idea and the Buddhist only affirms this fact of soullessness of all phenomena on the analogy of pots and plates. Whatever exists is momentary and is governed by the law of causation. So the self as an eternal category outside the range of causation is nothing but an illusion. Moreover, the contention that negation presupposes previous affirmation is to be accepted with a qualification. If this previous affirmation be intepreted as an evidence of its real existence, we enter our emphatic protest, because a thing existing as a verity, cannot be non-existent, which is the implication of negation. Only an unreal fiction, supposed to be existent, is capable of being negated. Even when we negate the existence of a pen in a particular place and time we negate not the objective reality but only a conceptual fact, falsely imagined as a real object. So when we deny the self or the soul, we deny it in the sense of a false idea fondly believed to be an objective fact. Furthermore, the conception of *ātman* (the self) is logically absurd. The soul is posited to function as the background of the psychical complex, the manifold of feeling, willing and knowing, which are supposed to be produced in the self by the action of twofold, threefold or fourfold contact (*catuṣṭaya-sannikarṣa*),[1] as the case may be. Now, unless these psychical phenomena are related to the self, the self cannot be regarded as a necessary condition of knowledge. And how can these psychical facts be related to the self, unless they enter into the constitution of the self and become identified with it ? If they are identified, the self will be a transitory event like the cognition. If however the cognition remains distinct, it will not be related and the self need not be posited as a condition of it. Likewise, pleasure and pain are looked upon as qualities of the self ; but being transitory modifications they cannot belong to the self and if they could belong to it, then the self being modifiable would become non-eternal. The explanation of Śrīdhara that the emergence and disappearance of pleasure and pain do not affect the real nature of the self and so there is no incongruity about it is only a pious hope and has no

1 Praśastapāda speaks of fourfold contact as a necessary condition of sense-perception. This fourfold contact is the contact of the soul, the mind, the sense-organ and the object. *Vide Padārtha-dharmasaṅgraha*, p. 136 and the *Nyāyakandalī*, antareṇā 'tmamanaḥsaṁyogam, manaindriyasaṁyogam indriyārthā-saṁyogaṁ ca pratyakṣābhāvāc catuṣṭayasannikarṣaḥ kāraṇam, p. 189. ' As sense-perception is not possible without the contact of the self with the mind, of the mind with the sense-organ, of the sense-organ with the object, fourfold contact is the cause thereof.'

logic in its support.[1] These qualities will either belong or not belong to the self. On the first alternative, the self cannot but be a fluxional entity like pleasure and pain ; on the second alternative, the hypothesis of a self as the ground and condition of the psychical manifold will be absolutely unnecessary.

---

[1] "nanu sukhaṁ duḥkhaṁ ce 'mau vikārāv iti nityasya ātmano na sambhavataḥ, bhavataś cet so'pi carmavad anityaḥ syāt ; na, tayor utpāda-vināśābhyāṁ tadanyasyā'tmanaḥ svarūpāpracyuter abhāvāt. nityasya hi svarūpavināśaḥ svarūpāntarotpādaś ca vikāro ne 'ṣyate, guṇanivṛttir guṇāntarotpādaś cā 'viruddha eva." N.K. p. 85.

CHAPTER IX

The Mīmāṁsā Theory of Soul

The *Mīmāṁsaka* philosopher conceives the self (*ātman*) as an eternal, continuous principle of the nature of pure consciousness, and as self-subsisting and self-revealing like light.[1] But as the self is not anything distinct from the faculty of intellect (*buddhi*), as the *Sāṅkhya* school affirms, it is held to be a dynamic principle incessantly changing with the change of states, yet maintaining its identity intact through all its diverse stages of transition. The dual character of change and continuity is not incongruous in the least, as it is observed in the case of a serpent, which remains identical in the midst of its various changes of posture. The serpent remains a serpent, whether it is coiled or erect or extends itself. Likewise the self remains the self as consciousness unmodified through all the different states of pleasure or pain, which happen to it in its career through metempsychosis. It neither totally disappears with any of its passing states, as the Buddhists hold, nor does it remain absolutely unmodified, as the *Naiyāyikas* would have us believe. In the Buddhist's theory of total destruction, there would arise the

[1] "......ātmā kena prakāśyate | ātmanai 'va prakāśyo'yam ātmā jyotir itī'ritam" S.V., P. 725, śl. 142.
also, "svasaṁvedyaḥ sa sambhavati, nā 'sāv anyena śakyate drasṭum, aśakyatvāc ca nā 'sāv api śakyate nidarśayitum......pareṇa na gṛhyata ity atrā 'pi Brāhmaṇam bhavati, 'agṛhyo na hi gṛhyata 'iti pareṇa na gṛhyata iti tadabhiprāyam etat, kutaḥ, svayaṁjyotiṣṭvavacanāt" Śabarabhāṣya, p. 22, ll ; 1 and 20. 'The self is self-cognisable and cannot be cognised by another. The *Brāhmaṇa* text, which speaks of it as incognisable, is to be understood in relation to other subjects and not to its own self, otherwise the text, which speaks of it as the self-shining light would be unmeaning.'

fallacy of lost deserts (*kṛtanāśa*) and unearned enjoyment (*akṛtāgama*), and in the *Naiyāyika's* doctrine of absolute unchange, the transitional experiences of pleasure and pain would be unaccountable.[1] So the two extremes of absolute change and absolute continuity are to be avoided and the *Mīmāṁsaka* accordingly defines the self as a continuity, subject to change of states and moods.[2] The agent and the enjoyer both are the continuing self and not the changing moods, which have no independent status of their own. So there is no apprehension of the fallacy, which threatens the Buddhist position.[3]

The existence of the self is a matter of direct proof, being clearly attested by recognition of the ego-principle in such judgments as 'I know,' 'I have known,' and so on. This gives the lie direct to the doctrine of seflessness of the Buddhists.[4] Besides,

1 syātāṁ hy atyantanāśe hi kṛtanāśākṛtāgamau ।
sukhaduḥkhādibhogaś ca nai 'va syād ekarūpiṇaḥ ।
S. V., p. 694.

2 tasmād ubhayahānena vyāvṛttyanugamātmakaḥ ।
puruṣo'bhyupagantavyaḥ kuṇḍalādiṣu sarpavat ।
S. V., p. 695.

3 na ca kartṛtvabhoktṛtve puṁso 'vasthāsamāśrite ।
tenāvasthāvatas tattvāt kartai 'vā ''pnoti tatphalam ।
S. V., p. 695, śl. 29.

Compare the following observations of Pārthasārathi Miśra regarding the statement of the scholiast that 'the self and cognition (*buddhi*) are eternal and directly perceptible, which raises a difficulty, as in the *Mīmāṁsā* theory of knowledge cognitions are not amenable to perception but can be known by inference. Pārthasārathi solves the difficulty by saying that cognitions as the moods of the self are imperceptible and transitory, but here the word '*buddhi*' stands for the self, which is both eternal and perceptible, as it is consciousness itself (and as such self-revealing).'

nanu caitanyasyā 'pratyakṣatvāt kathaṁ pratyakṣavacanam, satyaṁ, citiśaktir apratyakṣā, atra tu caitanyasvabhāvaḥ pramātai 'va buddhiśabdeno 'cyate. sa ca pratyakṣo nityaś ca, tasya jñānākhyo vikāro'pratyakṣo 'nityaś ce 'ti ! S. V., *Nyāyaratnākara*, p. 835.

4 tenā 'smāt pratyabhijñānāt sarvalokāvadhāritāt ।
nairātmyavādabādhas syāt. S. V., p. 724.

the no-soul theory fails to explain the egoistic references in our knowledge. What is indeed referred to in the judgment 'I know' by the I-cognition? The 'I' refers to the knower and the issue is whether the knower is the self or the momentary cognition, which perishes irrevocably in the second moment. If it is the self, the whole history of consciousness is at once put on an intelligible basis. If the momentary cognition is believed to be the subject, the whole thought-life becomes shrouded in an inexplicable mystery. We can possibly conceive the knowing subject to consist in either (1) the existing cognition, or (2) the past cognition, or (3) both, or (4) the series. In the first alternative, the judgment should be in the form 'I know' and not 'I have known,' because the present cognition did not exist in the past. In the second alternative, the judgment will be 'I have known or did know' and not 'I do know,' because the past cognition does not persist in the present. The third alternative equally falls to the ground, because the past and the present do not co-exist and so there can be no reference to an identical Self. The fourth alternative cannot be entertained either, as the series is an unreal fiction and has no existence outside the individual moments. So the subjecthood of the momentary cognition in all its alternatives being ruled out of court, the ego-consciousness must be supposed to refer to an eternal ego-principle, the underlying, continuous self, which can become the subject of the past, present and future judgments.[1] That this subject is an eternal principle is proved by the following arguments: The subject of the past ego-judgment is the subject of the present judgment also. Because, it is referred to equally by the past and the present ego-judgment. Or, the past and present cognitions in a particular subject-series do certainly relate to an identical self, because they all have a reference to a common subject.[2]

1 *Vide* T. S., śls. 229-37, and S. V., pp. 719-24.

2 vyatītāhaṅkṛtiś cādyo jñātā 'dyā 'py anuvartate |
ahaṁpratyayagamyatvād idānīntanaboddhṛvat | —S. V., p. 831,
T. S., śl. 238.

It may be legitimately urged that if the self is an eternal, unitary principle, then cognition (*buddhi*) also will become eternal and one, as the latter is regarded by the *Mīmāṁsakas* to be identical with the self. But this is plainly opposed to their theory, as the scholiast Śabara expressly states that cognition is momentary and does not last up to the moment of another cognition. It also goes against Jaimini's position, who defines perception to be a cognition, which is originated by sense-object contact. Certainly origination does not congrue with its eternity. Moreover, if cognition is one simple entity, the six-fold classification of *pramāṇas* will have no meaning.

Kumārila has anticipated these objections and says that the self and cognitions must be admitted to be one and eternal fact, as cognitions have no existence outside the self. The multiplicity of cognitions is not due to any intrinsic diversity of nature, but is purely accidental, being superposed by the diversity of objective data.[1] It cannot be urged that the intellect, being one and eternal and having no constitutional diversity, should cognise all the cognisable objects in one sweep and not in succession. Because though its cognising capacity is present intact for all time, it cognises only those objects that are presented to it through the sense-channel. And this is due to the limitation of the physical organism, in which it is imprisoned for the time being in consequence of its past deeds. That permanent efficiency and occasional functioning are not inconsistent is proved by the behaviour of natural objects as well.

We know fire possesses permanent capacity for combustion; but this capacity comes into play only when combustible objects

ekasantānasambaddhajñātrahampratyayatvataḥ ।
hyastanādyatanāḥ sarve tulyārthā ekabuddhivat ।
—S. V., p. 724, T. S., śl. 240.

1 buddhīnām api caitanyasvābhāvyāt puruṣasya ca ।
nityatvam ekatā ce 'ṣṭā bhedas tu viṣayāśrayaḥ । —S. V., p. 833, T. S., śl. 242.

are thrown into it. A clean mirror and a spotless crystal have the natural aptitude for catching the reflection of all material objects; but they reflect the image of those objects only, which actually come within their range.[1] So the self, which is held by us, unlike the *Sāṅkhya* philosophers, to be identical with the cognitive faculty (*buddhi*), cognises those objects alone, which are presented through the medium of sense-organs, though it is, by its very nature, all-pervading and all-cognisant, being consciousness itself.[2] The cognitive faculty too, being one with the self, is equally eternal, but appears to emerge and disappear like a perishable entity owing to its association with the sense-organs, whose activites are perishable. The limitation of its cognising capacity is also due to the limitation of the sense-organs, whose powers are circumscribed by their very constitution. The eternal nature of the intellect, or the self for the matter of that, is however proved by the continuity of its conscient nature through all the diverse acts of knowledge. The diversity, as has been observed before, is that of the data and as such is purely accidental. Those thinkers (the Buddhists), who concentrate their attention on and thus emphasise the diversity of contents, are deluded into thinking that consciousness is a varying manifold. But they obviously ignore the aspect of real continuity, which becomes apparent when the diversity of contents is overlooked, and so are liable to the charge of partial observation.[3] It is, therefore, as a matter of logical necessity that we shall have to postulate the

[1] svarūpeṇa yathā vahnir nityaṁ dahanakarmakaḥ। upanītaṁ dahaty arthaṁ dāhyaṁ nā 'nyaṁ na cā 'nyathā। yathā vā darpaṇaḥ svaccho yathā ca sphaṭiko 'malaḥ। yad yan nidhīyate dravyaṁ tac-chāyāṁ pratipadyate। tathai 'va nitya-caitanyāḥ pumāṁso dehavṛttayaḥ। gṛhṇanti karaṇānītān rūpādīn dhīr asau matā। Ś. V., p. 834 śls. 405-407. *Cf.* na hi śaktir astī 'ty etāvatā sarvadā kāryaṁ kartavyaṁ, śaktasyā 'pi sahakārisācivyasannidhy-apekṣālambanena kāryakaraṇakramopapatteḥ.' *Nyāyaratnākara*, p. 834.

[2] *Ibid.*

[3] sai 've 'ti no 'cyate buddhir arthabhedānusāribhiḥ। na cā 'sty apratyabhijñānam arthabhede' nupāśrite। S. V., p. 835, śl. 410.

existence of the self as an eternal principle consisting of pure consciousness, and as all-pervading, capable of tenanting any number of bodies in its course of metampsychosis.[1]

The Buddhist's position

The Buddhist observes that the *Mīmāṁsaka's* conception of the self or consciousness as an identity in diversity or a continuity in change, savours of mysticism for its defiance of logical canons. Diversity, it is alleged, belongs to the objective data and not to the consciousness in its own right. So continuity is its essential nature and diversity is only an accidental superposition of the objective data. But what about the illusory perception of elephants, horses and the like in a place, where they do not actually exist ? The diversity of cognitions in these circumstances cannot be explained away by reference to objective data, which do not certainly exist in the place and time concerned. But we forget that Kumārila holds that even such abnormal experiences as dreams and illusions are conversant about real objective facts, which, however, are presented in a wrong spatio-temporal relation.[2] So here too the diversity of consciousness is due to the influence of objective data. But this is cleverness *par excellence!* The time and place, to which these experiences refer, admittedly do not belong to the data of these experiences, even granting that these data are real objects. But why should, we humbly enquire, these data, real facts that they are, appear in a place and time which are apparently not their own ? At any rate, the time

1 jñānaśaktisvabhāvo' to nityaḥ sarvagataḥ pumān | dehāntarakṣamaḥ kalpyaḥ so' gacchan neva yokṣyate । S. V., p. 707, śl. 73. *Vide Nyāyaratnākara* for a detailed exposition of the logical necessity.

2 svapnādipratyaye bāhyaṁ sarvathā na hi ne 'ṣyate । sarvatrā '' lambanaṁ bāhyaṁ deśa-kālānyathātmakam । S. V., p. 242, śl. 107½ to 108½. *Cf.* 'bāhyam eva deśāntare kālāntare vā' nubhūtam eva svapne smaryamāṇaṁ doṣavaśāt sannihita-deśakāla-vattayā'vagamyate, ato 'trāpi na bāhyābhāva iti. N. R., pp. 242-43.

and place in question are unreal impositions of the imagination. If you hold that the time and place also are real facts, only they are presented in a different setting, the past being confounded with the present and the distant with the near, we cannot help believing that you have parted company with common sense and reason. How can anything be presented as another, or in a setting which is actually different from its own ? If that be the case, anything could be presented as any other thing and we must withhold our trust in the evidentiary value of our knowledge. The result will be confusion and the death of all selective activities, which can proceed on the basis of real distinctions, really discriminated.[1]

Kumārila, again, cannot regard these experiences as objectified ideas, as ideas, according to him, are destitute of articulate forms, which, he opines, can belong to objects and not to ideas.[2] And these objects are certainly absent in the place, where they are actually experienced. The plea of the presentation of real objects in a wrong spatio-temporal setting has been beaten hollow. So it must be admitted that these experiences are absolutely independent of objective data and are purely subjective (*nirālambana*). The diversity of consciousness, therefore, is intrinsic and real and not due to the accidental association of the data. And this diversity being incompatible with continuity, consciousness, or the self for that matter, must be accounted as diverse and discrete, in other words, fluxional.[3] It may be contended

1 nanu taddeśasambandho nai 'va tāsāṁ tathāsti tat I kim iti pratibhāsante tena rūpeṇa tatra ca I T. S., śl. 251, *Cf.* 'na hy anyena rūpeṇā 'nyasya pratibhāsanaṃ yuktam atiprasaṅgāt. evaṁ hi sarvam eva jñānaṁ sarvaviṣayaṁ prasajyeta. tataś ca pratiniyatārthavyavasthoccheda eva syāt.' T. S. P.. p. 101.

2 bhavanmate hi nā 'kāro buddher bāhyas tu varṇyate I
na vivakṣitadeśe ca gajayaṣṭyādayaḥ sthitāḥ I T. S., śl. 252.
Cf. ākāravān bāhyo'rtho nirākārā buddhir iti vacanāt. T. S. P., 101.

3 'tataś ca yaddeśakālasambaddhās te gajādayas taddeśasambandhitvenai 'va pratibhāseran. svavirahiṇi tu deśāntare kālantare ca kim iti pratibhāsante. tasmān nirālambanā evai 'te pratyayāḥ paramārthato 'saṁkīrṇas-

that though the individual cognitions, that vary at every moment, may be fluxional, still the subject, of which they are so many passing moods or states, does continue unchanged and unmodified as consciousness. But this is mere quibbling with words. Consciousness and cognition are the same thing ; they differ only in name. Certainly difference in name alone does not connote difference in nature. If consciousness is eternal and unchanging, cognitions also will be the same. If cognitions are allowed to be momentary, consciousness also will be momentary, as consciousness and cognitions have been proved to be identical and things identical cannot logically be supposed to have mutually contradictory characters.[1] And the identity of consciousness and cognitive states has been admitted by Kumārila also.

The absence of objective data in illusions and dreams thus proves fatal to the continuity of the self, as propounded by Kumārila. It also demolishes his theory of knowledge, which holds that knowledge is imperceptible *per se*. Because, the contents of illusions, being purely subjective facts, are not distinct from the cognitive consciousness, and unless consciousness is self-cognised, the contents also cannot be cognised, being identical with the former. So what is presented in illusion is nothing but a projection of subjective ideas (which are but the copies of external data imbibed in previous perceptions). And consciousness being self-luminous, the idea reveals itself ; but as this idea is nothing distinct from consciousness, illusion is held by us to be a case of self-presentation or self-intuition (*ātmakhyāti*). Kumārila's

vabhāvāś calātmānāś ca kādācitkatvād iti siddham ; tatsvabhāvasya ca puṁso 'nityatvānekatve ca siddhe.' *loc. cit.*

1 syān mataṁ pratyayas tasya puruṣasya dharmaḥ. tena tasya bhede 'pi na puṁso bhedo dharmitvāt tasye 'ti, tad ayuktam. pratyayaś caitanyaṁ buddhir jñānam ity anarthāntaratvāt. na hi nāmabhedamātreṇa vastūnāṁ svabhāvo bhidyate. kiṁ ca nāmabhede'pi teṣāṁ pratyayānāṁ caitanyātmakam ekam anugāmi rūpam iṣṭam eva. tasya ca caitanyasyā 'bhede pratyayānām api tatsvabhāvānām avibhāga eva, anyathā hi viruddhadharmādhyāsād aikāntiko bheda eva syāt. *loc. cit.*

theory of knowledge ignominiously fails to render an account of these experiences, because consciousness being *eo ipso* imperceptible in his theory, illusion cannot be regarded as experience of a subjective idea, as idea and consciousness are not distinct entities. On the other hand, it cannot be regarded as a case of objective cognition either, since the object is absent.[1]

Moreover, if all-cognising consciousness is present intact and for all time, then, what is there to prevent the appearance of all the cognitions at once? If the cognition of sound is the selfsame cognition that apprehends taste, colour or the like, then these cognitions should arise all at once, because the cognitive consciousness is present with its efficiency unimpaired. If, however, the sound-cognition is not admitted to be same with other cognitions, you yourself admit diversity in consciousness. The example of fire is not relevant at all, because fire has not the power to consume everything at all times; had it been otherwise, the whole world would have been reduced to a heap of cinders. The truth of the matter is that fire develops its combustive power only in association with a combustible substance, and it is for this reason that simultaneous combustion of all things does not take place. As regards mirror and crystal, etc., they too are fluxional and so change every moment; and when related to objects like blue lotus and the like, they develop the power of reflecting their images. If they remained constant and unmodified in their nature, they would either reflect the images always or not at all. Moreover, the use of the imagery of the mirror and the crystal as an aid to the understanding of the nature and functioning of consciousness is out of place and only obfuscates the matter at issue. Because, the image, that is

[1] 'etenai 'va nirālambanapratyayapratipādanena apratyakṣatvaṁ buddheḥ pratyuktam. tathāhi sa parisphuran nākāro na bāhyo gajādir iti sādhitam, tataś ca taṁ tathā parisphurantam ākāram ātmabhūtam eva pratipadyamānā buddhayaḥ svayaṁprakāśarūpatvāt svasaṁvidrūpāḥ sidhyanti.'

T. S. P., p. 101, under śl. 252.

supposed to be superimposed on the surface of the mirror, is only an appearance and not a real thing. It cannot be supposed that the image is a real object that effects an entry into the body of the mirror, because mirror is a compact substance and not porous, and two corporeal substances cannot occupy the same space, which is, however, felt to be the case. The crystal, too, does not enclose within itself the image of an object. This is evidenced by the fact that though in association with a scarlet flower, it looks red when seen from the front, it is found to be entirely white by persons looking at it from two extremities. And even if this receiving of image had been real, the receptive crystal would vary with every single act of reflection. So the image and its reflection must be set down as an unreal appearance occasioned by the peculiar nature of the receptive substances concerned. But this reception of image is out of the question in consciousness, because no illusion is possible with regard to its own self. Since the image reflected in consciousness will be identified with it, consciousness itself will be infected with illusion and there being no other consciousness to apprehend it, the illusory image will remain unknown. Neither can it be known by itself, as consciousness in your theory is *eo ipso* imperceptible; nor can it be cognised by another consciousness as consciousness is regarded as one identical entity. The false appearance of the image in a crystal or a mirror, however, is not an unlikely phenomenon, because the mirror and its cognition remain distinct and separate. But in the case of consciousness, the basis of reflection and the cognising subject being one, the illusion cannot possibly be felt. In the Buddhist theory of illusion, however, no such difficulty arises, as the particular illusory cognition emerges with the stamp of illusion as an altogether novel phenomenon under the influence of its proper causes and conditions and being self-cognisant, illusion is felt. But as consciousness is held to be an eternal substance in the Mīmāṁsā system, Kumārila cannot accept this explanation offered by us.[1]

[1] *Vide* T.S. and the *Pañjikā*, śls. 259-262.

The continuity of conscient nature in all the different cognitions and feelings has been interpreted by Kumārila as proof of the permanence and unity of consciousness *per se.* But by adopting this view Kumārila ignores the diversity of contents, which is very real and which cannot be explained away as accidental superposition of objective data, as in illusion and dream there are no objective data, but diversity is still there. The conclusion is irresistible that the different cognitions, the diverse units of experience, are absolutely distinct and discrete entities and have no underlying unity in them. The feeling of unity of our conscious life must therefore be explained by reference to a fundamental character, which characterises the diverse knowledge units without exception; and this fundamental characteristic is to be found in their common difference from non-conscious entities. The unity or homogeneity of consciousness is thus a negative conception at bottom.[1]

If the self be an eternal, uniform principle of the *Mīmāṁsā* pattern, then, there could be no diversity of states, such as pleasure, pain and the like in its nature. If on the other hand these diverse states really appertain to the self, then the self must forfeit its uniformity and eternality. In order to avoid this unpleasant predicament, Kumārila has come forward with his theory that the self is neither absolutely uniform nor absolutely variable. Thus, though the self passes through diverse states of pleasure and pain and is variable to that extent, it does not abandon its substantiality and conscient nature, but maintains its existence all throughout its chequered career. As

[1] abodharūpabhedaṁ tu samānaṁ sarvabuddhiṣu |
āropya pratyabhijñānaṁ nānātve'pi pravartate.—*Ibid*, śl. 263.

Cf. 'avaśyaṁ cai 'tad vijñeyaṁ—yan nānātva eva sati vijātīyavyāvṛttikṛtam etat pratyabhijñānaṁ na punar anānātva eve 'ti. tathā hi nirālambanāsu samāropabuddhiṣv arthabhede 'nupāśrite 'py apratyabhijñānam asty eva, na hi tatrai 'vaṁ bhavati, yai 'va gajabuddhir āsīt sai 'va turaṅgasyandanabuddhir iti..........tena yad uktaṁ—'na cā 'sty apratyabhijñānam arthabhede' nupāśrita 'iti tad asiddham.' T.S.P, p. 105.

regards the states or moods, they also do not absolutely cease to exist. What happens is this—the previous mood only subsides and gets merged in the existence of the self to make room for the emergence of the subsequent mood and there is no such thing as absolute cessation of existence. The individual moods or states, taken by themselves, are certainly antagonistic to each other. But they lose their antagonism in the whole, which embraces them all in its capacious bosom. And this is attested by experience that the self runs through all the diverse and antagonistic psychical phenomena, which are owned up by it. So the antagonism or contradiction amidst the individual moods is either suspended or reconciled in the existence of the self, of which they are passing phases or moods.[1]

Śāntarakṣita observes that Kumārila's desperate attempt to reconcile unity with diversity looks like an attempt to patch up the parts of a hopelessly broken reed and will not stand a moment's scrutiny. If these passing moods are not absolutely different from the self, then the self will be subject to emergence and cessation like its moods. If, however, these incidents are supposed to belong to the moods only and not to the self, the self and the moods will be absolutely distinct entities, as the criterion of distinction is the possession of contradictory attributes alone. If this criterion is not accepted, one self cannot be distinguished from another self, as they are regarded as distinct entities only by virtue of their mutually contradictory character. So Kumārila's conception of the self as a variable constant has to be abandoned, as it is fraught with self-contradiction. To say that experience warrants such supposition is to betray a vicious lack

[1] sukhaduḥkhādy avasthāś ca gacchann api naro mama । caitanyadravyasattvādirūpaṁ nai 'va vimuñcati । na cā 'vasthāntarotpāde pūrvā 'tyantaṁ vinaśyati । uttarānuguṇārthā tu sāmānyātmani līyate । svarūpeṇa hy avasthānām anyonyasya virodhitā । aviruddhas tu sarvāsu sāmānyātmā pratīyate । S.V., pp. 695-96. *Cf.* 'nanv avasthānām audāsīnyakartṛtvādīnāṁ mitho virodhāt pūrvasyāṁ dharmiṇy eva vyavasthitāyām uttarasyāḥ kathaṁ niṣpattiḥ, ata āha svarūpeṇe 'ti.' N.R., p. 696.

of critical judgment. Experience is of a certainty the ultimate court of appeal in a philosophical dispute, but not uncritical experience. Experience has to be tested and assayed in the furnace of logical thought before its true import can be realised; in default it will land us in uncritical empiricism. Experience, therefore, cannot be a solvent of self-contradiction. So the idea of the self as a variable constant must be abandoned.[1]

As for the plea that there is no absolute loss of any particular mood, which only gets merged in the existence of the self, when another mood emerges, the less said about it the better. If the particular moods merge their individuality in the self, then pain should also be felt when pleasure emerges. Certainly this merger can be understood if there is complete identification of one with the other, otherwise it will be only a word without a meaning. And if this identification is conceded, the self also will be subject to birth and dissolution like the moods, because things, which are identical, cannot possibly have contradictory attributes. As regards the other plea (which has been put forward to avoid the so-called fallacy of loss of earned deserts and acquisition of unearned fruits), *viz.*, that the agent of action and the enjoyer of its fruits are the self and not the passing moods of it, it will suffice to say that it stands self-condemned. If the self remains the same unaltered entity, it cannot presumably assume the rôle of an agent, much less of an enjoyer, which connotes the emergence of novel attributes. It has been pertinently pointed out by the venerable doctor, Dignāga, that if the self undergoes any modification on the emergence of a cognition, it will be impermanent ; if it remains unaltered as before, the self cannot be conceived to be a cogniser.[2] Kumārila, however, has answered that so far as the qualitative aspect (*i.e.*, the passing moods) of the self is concerned,

[1] T.S., śls. 268-71.

[2] buddhijanmani puṁsaś ca vikṛtir yady anityatā | athā'vikṛtir ātmākhyaḥ pramāte 'ti na yujyate | Dignāga quoted in T. S. P., p. 108.

the self may be called impermanent, but that does not affect the fundamental reality of consciousness *quâ* consciousness, which remains uniform and unchanged.[1] But this only confounds the issue. We have proved that no such line of cleavage subsists between consciousness and its moods; and so consciousness *per se* is to be accounted as variable. If it had been a question of naming only, we could also say that consciousness might be called a continuous entity, if its continuity in the series is contemplated. But this nomenclature does not arrest the fluxional nature of consciousness *per se*, which totally ceases to exist in the second moment, in which a new cognition emerges in its place.[2] The analogy of the serpent, which has been trotted out in defence of the permanence of the self, is based on a positive misconception. Because, the serpent too is fluxional and hence its change of postures is possible. If it had been absolutely fixed and unalterable, no such transition could have been possible. Change of moods connotes nothing less than change of nature, absolute and irrevocable.

The argument that ego-consciousness must centre round a permanent self and not any individual conscious state, which being transitory cannot account for its persistence and continuity, also proceeds on a false assumption. Ego-consciousness in reality is absolutely unfounded and as such cannot be affiliated to any ontological principle. Its *raison d'etre* is to be found in the beginningless false tendencies inherent in our consciousness—tendencies which are apt to see reality in unreality, permanence in change. Our ego-consciousness is thus an illusion, which is the product of these tendencies. It cannot be questioned as to why should these tendencies work in some particular consciousness-series and not in others? Because, such questioning is not

[1] nā 'nityaśabdavācyatvam ātmano vinivāryate | vikriyāmātravācitvān na hy ucchedo'sya tāvatā |

[2] na nityaśabdavācyatvam ātmano vinivāryate | svarūpavikriyāvṛttvāt tadvyucchedo'sya tāvatā | T. S., śl. 273.

precluded in the theory of permanent self also. Why should a particular ego-consciousness relate to a particular self and not other selves ? If this delimitation is to be explained by the peculiar individuality of the selves concerned, the same explanation is possible in the theory of flux, as the series or the continuum (*santāna*) does duty for the permanent self and so comes to have all the incidents that happen to the latter.[1]

The opponent may contend, 'Well, you may explain the delimitation of ego-consciousness to a particular subject-series by an appeal to the peculiar individuality of the former. But it does not follow that ego-consciousness should be an unfounded illusion for that! The answer is that no such foundation can be posited for this ego-consciousness. If it is affiliated to a permanent self as the cause and ground of it, then all the various ego-ideas should be produced all at once. There can be no reason why these ego-ideas should emerge in a graduated scale, as the sole and sufficient cause of these is present intact in the shape of the permanent self. Nor can an eternal verity have any necessity for other auxiliary circumstances, which, we have proved ever and anon, can have no effect on it. Nor again can ego-consciousness be regarded as a single, individual fact. The very fact that such ego-consciousness emerges occasionally is sufficient to prove its multiplicity and plurality. We do not have any ego-consciousness in dreamless sleep, in swoon and in fits of intoxication. If, on the other hand, this ego-consciousness is supposed to be affiliated to the individual conscious units, then ego-consciousness should be as distinct and pronounced as the individual cognitions, *e.g.*, visual and auditory cognitions, etc., are. But as this is neither of one kind nor of another, it is futile to search for its foundation, which is nowhere.[2]

1 T. S., ślo. 275-277.

2 nityālambanapakṣe tu sarvāhaṅkṛtayas tataḥ | sakṛd eva prasūyeran śaktahetuvyavasthiteḥ | anityālambanatve'pi spaṣṭābhāḥ syus tataḥ pare | ālambanārthasadbhāvaṁ vyarthaṁ paryanuyuñjate | T.S. śls. 278-79.

Kumārila, however, has opposed the theory of unfounded egoism on the ground that *vāsanās* (tendencies), being memory-impressions or sub-conscious desires, generated by experience, can never go wrong with reference to their objects. The memory-impression of the ego-idea, too, cannot be erroneous with reference to the ego-principle, which is its object. The reason is that memory is possible if there is an original experience behind its back, and this original experience must be an authentic one, as even error is made possible if there is a previous experience, which must be authentic in the final analysis. So if there is a memory-impression (*vāsanā*) of the self, it must refer to the real self and not a fictitious self, as the Buddhists would have us believe. And there is no warrant or occasion for our supposing this egoistic reference to be unauthentic, as it has not been sublated as yet by any stronger evidence.[1]

Śāntarakṣita observes that this egoistic reference, out of which Kumārila seeks to make capital, has been proved to be opposed to reason. So it does not permit to be said that ego-experience is an uncontradicted and unerring evidence of the existence of the self. The contention, that memory-impression (*vāsanā*) cannot go wrong so far as its objective reference is concerned, is baseless and hollow. It is a matter of common knowledge how persons, religiously inclined, conjure up false ideas of God as the First Cause of the world, as an omniscient and omnipotent being and so on and so forth. Kumārila, too, is sane enough not to believe in these superstitious vagaries. But what is the root of these ideas ? Certainly false impressions, which have been fostered by false teaching and false practices.

[1] jñātari pratyabhijñānaṁ vāsanā kartum arhati । nā 'tasmin sa iti prajñāṁ na hy asau bhrāntikāraṇam । tan nā 'haṁpratyayo bhrāntir iṣṭo bādhakavarjanāt । S. V., p. 720, śls. 124-25.

Cf. smṛtihetur hi saṁskāro vāsanā, sā'nubhūte'rthe smṛtim janayatī 'ti yuktaṁ, na tv asau bhrāntihetuḥ, yenā 'tasmin tadgraho'nayā syād iti, N. R. under the above.

If these ideas are allowed to be unfounded in an objective reality, why should you make a difficulty in the case of ego-consciousness? We have proved by logic that the latter cannot have an objective foundation, be it an eternal self or a transitory cognition. Kumārila is obviously labouring under an obsession in his endeavour to prove the existence of an eternal self, but he has only built a castle in the air.[1]

Concluding Remarks

Before bringing this dissertation to a close, the present writer feels it imperative to make a brief observation with regard to the presentation of the Bhaṭṭa theory of soul in some of the orthodox Brāhminical works. Vidyāraṇya observes that the self according to the followers of Bhaṭṭa is a multiple entity with a twofold aspect of consciousness and unconsciousness. So it has been compared to a fire-fly for having darkness and illumination both in its constitution.[2] It may be brought into line with Kumārila's conception of the self, if the self is taken to include the concrete whole, both its essential nature and its qualitative contents, the former being self-revealing and the latter being imperceptible. This conception of the soul of the Bhaṭṭa school as a compound of spiritual and unspiritual factors is a logical construction of the Vedāntist critics and is not the orthodox presentation. This is deducible from the remarks of the *Nyāyaratnāvalī*, "The self (*sic.* of the Bhāṭṭas) is a compound

[1] nā 'nantaroktayā yuktyā tasya bādhopadarśanāt I īśvarādiṣu bhaktānāṁ taddhetutvādivibhramāḥ I vāsanāmātrabhāvācca jāyante vividhāḥ katham I nirālambanatā cai 'vam ahaṅkāre yadā sthitā I tan nā 'haṁpratyaye grāhye jñātā kaścana vidyate I tataḥ sarvapramāṇeṣu na dṛṣṭānto' sti siddhibhāk I hetavaś cā 'śrayāsiddhā yathāyogam udāhṛtāḥ I T. S., śls. 281-284.

[2] *Vide Pañcadaśī*, Ch. VI, śls. 95-97.

of a spiritual and an unspiritual factor. By the former it functions as a cognising subject and by the latter, it undergoes modifications as cognition, feeling and the like and also becomes the object of the judgment 'I know myself.' "[1] The second set of functions is possible in an unspiritual substance, as spirit or consciousness is impartite and unmodifiable according to *Vedānta*. Nārāyaṇa Paṇḍita, the author of the second chapter of the *Mānameyodaya*, which deals with the metaphysics of the Bhaṭṭa school, on the other hand, has given us a definition of the self, which is of a piece with that of the *Nyāya-Vaiśeṣika* school.[2] This obvious departure from Kumārila is to be set down to the influence of the *Śāstradīpikā*, in which Pārthasārathi Miśra emphatically denies the essential spirituality of the self and defines it as the substrate of consciousness, etc. The plain texts of Kumārila which speak of the soul as pure consciousness and absolute bliss have been unceremoniously brushed aside as concession to unorthodox views (*Paramata*). It is curious that the same writer in his commentary on the S. V. has plainly admitted the spirituality of the self.[1] It is therefore gratifying to observe that Śāntarakṣita and Kamalaśīla have given an accurately correct account of Kumārila's theory, which has been either misunderstood or badly presented by some orthodox writers, who should have known better. This fidelity to a formidable opponent, whom they have subjected to a scathing criticism,

1 *Cf.* ātmano'sty aṁśadvayaṁ, cidaṁśo 'cidaṁśaś ca ; cidaṃśena draṣṭṛtvam......acidaṁśena jñānasukhādipariṇāmitvaṁ, mām ahaṁ jānāmī'ti jñeyatvañ ca'. See also P. Sastri, *Intro. to the P. Mīmāṁsā*, p. 95.

2 (P. 155, F.N. 3 *ante*). P. Sastri attributes this anomaly to the author's resentment of the *Advaita Vedānta* doctrines. But I think that quite the contrary is the case, as the position of the S. D. has been accepted by later Mīmāṁsā writers, to wit, Nārāyaṇa and Gāgābhaṭṭa, as the orthodox *Mīmāṁsā* doctrine. *Vide Mānameyodaya*, p. 80 *et seq.*, *Bhāṭṭa-cintāmaṇi*, p. 56, Ben. ed., *Intro. to P. Mīmāṁsā*, p. 99., *Śāstradīpikā*, p. 129, *Tarkapāda*, Bom., ed.

instinctively inspires our respect for Śāntarakṣita and his worthy disciple and commentator. The intellectual honesty of these two authors is an object of sincere admiration, particulary when we consider that authors of even outstanding merit have sometimes failed to do justice to their rivals and sought to gain a cheap victory. But Śāntarakṣita is too great to have love for claptrap and easy triumphs, gained by not very scrupulous means.

CHAPTER X

THE SOUL THEORY OF THE DIGAMBARA JAINAS

Like the followers of Jaimini the *Jainas* of the *Digambara* school postulate the existence of a self, of the nature of pure consciousness, having the twofold character of continuity and change in accordance with its dual nature as substance and modes. As substance consciousness continues uniformly through all the diverse states and as modes it varies at every transition. The consciousness that continues is the substance and the states of pleasure and pain are the modes. And these are not distinct and discrete, because the modes happen in consciousness and the two are never found to be dissociated. Thus the self combines the two-fold character of continuity and diversity, uniformity and change and there is no contradiction, as it is attested by direct experience. The *Jainas* hold that there can be no contradiction in experience, which is the final court of appeal in the matter of validity. A proposition is thought to be invalid, if it has not the sanction of experience and not otherwise. The *Jainas* accordingly dictate us to change our idea of contradiction in the light of experience and not submit to any *a priori* abstract principle. The abstractionistic tendency of our intellectual thought, which attaches absolute logical value to one of the aspects of reality, is a vicious superstition, as truth is multiform and has many facets, in which no one aspect should be given absolute value to the exclusion of the rest.[1]

[1] nanu bhedābhedayoḥ parasparaparihāreṇā 'vasthānād anyatarasyai 'va vāstavatvād ubhayātmakatvam ayuktam iti cet—tad ayuktaṁ, bādhe pramāṇābhāvāt. anupalambho hi bādhakaṁ pramāṇaṁ, na so 'sti. samasteṣu vastuṣv anekāntātmakatvasya syādvādino mate suprasiddhatvād ity alam. S. D. S., p. 69.

The *Jainas* further maintain that substance and its modes are neither absolutely different nor are they absolutely identical. They are found to be identical in respects of time, place and nature ; thus, the table and its form and colour and the like occupy the same place and time and they have the same essential nature, *viz.*, materiality. And in view of this fundamental unity they cannot but be regarded as identical. But they cannot for that reason be regarded as absolutely identical, as they differ in other respects, to wit, in number, (*saṅkhyā*), differentia (*lakṣaṇa*), name (*saṁjñā*), and function (*artha*). Thus, the substance is one, but the modes, *e.g.*, pleasure, pain and the like in the case of consciousness, are multiple ; this constitutes the difference in number. They differ in specific differentiae also, thus, continuity is the character of substance, while transition (break of continuity) is the character of the modes. The difference of name also is significant, thus the substance is called the self or the jar, as the case may be, whereas the modes are styled 'colour' or 'pleasure,' etc. The difference in function is equally a distinguishing trait, thus, the pot functions as drawer of water, while colour has such uses as dyeing of clothes and the like. The same line of demarcation can be drawn between the self and its varying moods. Thus we shall have to accept on the authority of experience the twofold character of all things, identity and difference, and certainly we cannot repudiate experience on the ground of their supposed contradiction at the dictate of abstract logic.

But the Buddhist refuses to subscribe to the dictum of the *Jainas* and asks him pointblank if the self that relates itself with the diversified states, makes any departure from its pristine nature or not in the process of relationing. In the former alternative, it will cease to be eternal, because there is no continuing principle in the various states. In the latter, the self cannot be regarded as a changing principle, as it does not undergo any modification but remains fixed and uniform in all the successive states. Because, modification spells a departure from the original state.[1]

The Buddhist has strongly denounced the interpretation of experience by the *Jainas*. Certainly experience has to be accepted as the ultimate tribunal, but experience has to be interpreted by logical thought. We cannot abandon our mental constitution and adopt convenient ways of thinking at the dictate of the *Jainas*. The demand is preposterous in all conscience ; it could as well ask us to suspend all thinking. So if there is identity of nature, they must be identical ; and if they are identical they cannot be different. Because, identity and difference are contradictory and as such cannot coincide. Either of them can be real and not both. So you should say that substance and moods are different and distinct ; and if you insist on regarding them as identical in spite of their contradictory character, you must repudiate all distinctions in the world and the consequence will be that even blue and yellow will be one and the same.[2]

1 tatrā 'py avikṛtaṁ dravyaṁ paryāyair yadi saṅgatam ।
na viśeṣo'sti tasye 'ti pariṇāmi na tad bhavet ।
T. S, Sl. 312.

2 svabhāvābheda ekatvaṁ tasmin sati ca bhinnatā ।
kathañcid api duḥsādhyā paryāyātmasvarūpavat ।
T. S., Sl. 316.

Cf. also ".........bhede'pi yady ekatvaṁ tat kvacid api nīlapītādau bhedo na syāt. uktaṁ hi, ayam eva bhedo bhedahetur vā yad viruddhadharmādhyāsaḥ kāraṇabhedaś ce'ti " *Kāvyaprakāśa*, Ch. V.,—p. 244 (Jhalkikar's edn).

The 'Law of Contradiction' and the 'Law of Excluded Middle' have been formulated by Udayana in his *Kusumañjali* in the following couplet :

parasparavirodhe hi na prakārāntarasthitiḥ ।
nai 'katā 'pi viruddhānām uktimātravirodhataḥ' ।
III. 8.

" Between two terms exclusive of each other, there is no third term possible. Nor can there be any identity between the two, as it is a contradiction in terms."

Thus there can be no compromise between continuity and change which are the connotations of substance (*dravya*) and modes (*paryāya*). And if they are identical, your so-called substance must be transitory like the modes, because two identical things cannot possibly have contradictory attributes or in the alternative the so-called modes will be continuous like the so-called substance, they being absolutely identical. You cannot have it both ways, as that involves a contradiction in terms. So the idea of a continuous underlying self or substance has to be abandoned and the states of consciousness;[1] are to be regarded as absolutely fluxional, each perishing irrevocably when the other succeeds. Or the idea of variable modes has to be surrendered and things are to be regarded as absolutely immutable and fixed, as mutation and continuity cannot be predicated of one and the same thing.[2]

The statement that the underlying, continuing entity is known by direct perception is a baseless error. Because, no such entity is perceived as something distinct from the transitional modes. And as it is posited that the self is an entity and is

A thing can be supposed to be 'A', or not 'A', or both, or neither. The last two alternatives are impossible.
'na prakārāntarasthitiḥ, na nobhayātmakatvaṁ nai 'katā'pi na bhāvābhāvātmakatvam api'—Haridāsa. 'na prakārāntarasthitir ity asya vivaraṇaṁ na nobhayātmakatvam iti, nobhābhyām anyatvam ity arthaḥ, na bhāvābhāvobhayabhinnatvam iti yāvat.' K. T., C. K. Tarkālaṅkāra.

1 *Cf.* Huxly, "Consciousnesses" would be a better name, but it is awkward. I have elsewhere proposed *psychoses* as a substantive name for mental phenomena" Hume by Huxly. Ch. II. p. 62. F. N. 1.

2 tato nā'vasthitaṁ kiñcid dravyam ātmādi vidyate |
paryāyāvyatiriktatvāt paryāyāṇāṁ svarūpavat |
na co 'dayavyayākrāntāḥ paryāyā api kecana |
dravyād avyatiriktatvāt taddravyaniyatātmavat |
tato niranvayo dhvaṁsaḥ sthiraṁ vā sarvam iṣyatām |
ekātmani tu nai 'va sto vyāvṛttyanugamāv imau |
T. S., Śls. 319-21.

competent to direct cognition, we must set it down as a purely illusory idea like that of a sky-lotus or a barren woman's son, because if it was a real existence, it could not but be perceived. The *Jaina's* demand that it is perceived by him must be dismissed with scant courtesy, as in that case there could arise no dispute about the existence of the self.[1]

It may be legitimately urged, however, that if there is no substance as a unitary principle underlying all the manifold modes, then why should there be such distinctions as of number, name, differentia and functions? If an underlying reality over and above the plurality of modes is posited, then these distinctions become intelligible. But the Buddhist answers that such distinctions are purely intellectual fictions and they have no being in the real existents. The entities, though absolutely distinct and different entities in and by themselves, have two sets of functions and practical uses, one common and another specific. When emphasis is laid upon the common nature of the functions concerned, these entities, in spite of their mutual differences, come to be labelled with a single epithet for the sake of convenience by an intellectual fiction. On the other hand, when attention is paid to their specific functions, they are designated by different names. The distinction of number and name is thus a matter of convenience, absolutely imposed by the intellect. The distinction of functions is due to an analogous operation of the intellect ; thus, when the similarity of the common functions is emphasised, the function is conceived to be one and when the diversity of the specific functions is accentuated, they are regarded as different and manifold. The distinction of differentiæ is also purely conceptual, arising from the operation of the 'Law of Causation.' Thus, the structure of the pot is reduplicated in all the various stages ; the black pot in its unbaked

[1] na co 'palabhyarūpasya paryāyānugatātmanaḥ |
dravyasya pratibhāso'sti tan nā 'sti gaganābjavat |
Op. cit., śl. 822.

state and the red one are absolutely two distinct entities. But the structural similarity gives rise to illusion of identity and so continuity comes to be regarded as its differentia. And when the transition of colours is contemplated, the difference and diversity come to be regarded as the differentiating character of these modes.[1] In reality, however, there is no continuity at any one of the stages and so the entities are diverse and discrete every moment. But there is an innate tendency of the intellect to synthesise those diverse aspects, which have a similar look, into one category. The similarity is only apparent and does not imply any continuity whatsoever. So the *Jainas* by adjudging the nature of reality from surface appearances of things, which are created into a category by the abstractionistic tactics of the intellect, only betray sad lack of philosophical insight and logical ineptitude.

It has, however, been urged that the twofold character (*dvirūpa*) of substance and modes is merged in one concrete whole, and this whole being one impartite identity like the man-lion deity, the distinctive individuality of the two characters escapes detection. But this involves a contradiction in terms. If the whole is one impartite identity, it cannot have a twofold character, as character means distinctive individuality and two characters would imply of necessity two individual existences and certainly an identical entity cannot have two distinct existences, as it is manifestly absurd. And the analogy of the man-lion is quite irrelevant, as the man-lion too is not one substance with two distinct individualities. The man-lion is an aggregate of manifold atoms and so having a plurality of natures, it appears as twofold.

To sum up: the *Jaina* theory of soul as a multiple entity with a duplicate nature of continuity and change is vitiated by

1 vividhārthakriyāyogyās tulyādijñānahetavaḥ |
tathāvidhārthasaṅketaśabdapratyayagocarāḥ |
Op. cit., śl. 323.

self-contradiction. It can be accepted if we give up or revise our idea of the 'Law of Contradiction.' But as the constitution of our minds cannot be changed, we cannot accept the theory, which flagrantly violates a fundamental law of thought. And so long as our logical sense refuses to be coaxed or coerced into acceptance of a contradictory proposition, the *Jaina* metaphysics must remain an intolerable and unacceptable system, though it might excite our admiration as a monument of philosophical sophistry or imagination gone mad.

CHAPTER XI

The Sāṅkhya Theory of Soul

The *Sāṅkhya* philosophers posit the existence of the self, which is of the nature of consciousness, pure and simple, as a distinct principle from intelligence, called *buddhi* or *mahat*. The *buddhi* is the primary transformation of *Prakṛti* or primordial matter, which is the material cause of the world order. *Prakṛti* is dynamic in nature and is ever changeful. *Buddhi*, being the first evolute of *Prakṛti*, inherits the dynamic character of the latter in full, the difference being the preponderance of the *sattva* principle, which makes it extremely supple and transparent. In fact, *buddhi* is the highest attenuated matter, which in transparency makes the closest possible approximation to the spirit, whose nature is pure illumination. Now when the spirit and *buddhi* are brought together, the latter receives the full reflection of the spirit and becomes spiritualised to all intents and purposes. Whatever passes in the *buddhi* becomes illumined at once by the light of the spirit and knowledge in the real sense of the word takes place. But this is not all. The transformations of *buddhi*, again, are imaged in the self or the spirit, by virtue of which the self is said to enjoy the pleasure and pain, which are only superposed on it and which in reality are the modifications of *buddhi*. Thus, though there is no modification in the self, the self assumes the rôle of experiencer of pleasure and pain and suffers bondage, which is nothing but the defilement of its native purity by the false ascription of these modifications. The *Sāṅkhya* philosopher, however, denies all active initiative to the self even in this false sense. The self is the enjoyer (*bhoktṛ*), though not an agent (*kartṛ*).

But the Buddhist refuses to subscribe to the eternal, unitary consciousness of the *Sāṅkhyas*. If consciousness is one, then why should there be such a variety and multiplicity of cognitions, such as cognitions of word, taste, colour and so on ? And these cognitions cannot be lumped into one category, because they are distinct and separate. Moreover, it is said that the self is the enjoyer of pleasure and pain, as presented by the *buddhi*. But when the self is one and eternal, how can it be said to enjoy pleasure and pain, without forfeiting its uniformity ? And why should it wait for the services of *Prakṛti* for its enjoyment ? Certainly an eternal principle can have no such dependence on an external agent. Again, there is no obligation that *Prakṛti* should minister to the self according to its needs ? Granting that *Prakṛti* has a disinterested mission in pursuance of which it caters to the needs of the self, does the self undergo any modification in the process of enjoyment ? If it does, the self cannot but forfeit its eternal uniformity. If it does not swerve from its native purity, it cannot be supposed to be an enjoyer, which denotes a change of state and change of state means modification.

But it has been said that enjoyment on the part of the self is not to be taken literally. It happens in this way : first *buddhi* undergoes a modification by being transformed into the shape of the object and this transformation of *buddhi* is imaged on the self. This reception of the image is interpreted as its enjoyment and in this the self does not undergo a modification in the least. But this is only a hoax. If the image gets merged into the identity of the self, the self will have all the incidents of the image, *viz.*, origin and dissolution. If however there is no such identification, the self cannot be supposed to be an enjoyer even by way of fiction. Again how can the unconscious *Prakṛti* shape its activity according to a well-regulated plan and programme ? If it is conceded to have such purposive activity, it is passing strange that it cannot enjoy the fruits of its labour. Certainly a person, who knows to prepare delicious dishes, should also know how to enjoy them.[1]

It has been observed that *buddhi* is an intelligent principle and so there is nothing inappropriate about it that it should shape its activity according to the requirements of the self. But this is begging the question. If you grant that *buddhi* has this intelligence, you cannot consistently affirm that it is unconscious, because intelligence is the invariable characteristic of consciousness. We have no warrant to suppose that the self is something distinct from intelligence and our experience at any rate contradicts such a hypothesis. The example has been trotted out that unconscious milk flows from the cow's udder with a view to the nourishment of the calf and no prescience can be suspected in this purposive activity. Precisely unconscious *buddhi* also can follow a teleological plan. To suppose that God guides such activity is to make an unwarranted and uncalled-for assumption. Because the activity of all intelligent persons is motivated either by self-interest or by pity, and God, who has no unsatisfied need cannot have any incentive for creative activity on the score of self-interest.[2] Nor can He be actuated by pity, because before creation there is no occasion, *e.g.*, suffering, to call for his pity. And if God is really merciful and is responsible for creation and if He has a foreknowledge of the eventual suffering of the created beings, He should have desisted from such activity, as you suppose that without his guidance no activity in unconscious matter is possible. If you say that the world-process is a beginningless cycle, and God has to order and arrange the creation of the world in conformity with the deeds of creatures in their previous lives, well, you should dispense with the superfluous

[1] kartuṁ nāma vijānāti pradhānaṁ vyañjanādikam ı
bhoktuṁ ca na vijānāti kim ayuktam ataḥ param ı T. S., 300.

[2] *Cf.* Ślokavārtika—
prayojanam anuddiśya na mando'pi pravartate ı
jagac ca sṛjatas tasya kiṁ nāma na kṛtaṁ bhavet ı

appendage in the shape of God and accord supreme power to *Karman*. So there is no absurdity in thinking that unconscious *Prakṛti* can work according to a teleological plan for emancipation of the self, which is the highest good for the self. This has been the argument of Vācaspati Miśra.[1] But the analogy of milk's activity is not germane in all essential particulars to the creative activity of *Prakṛti*. The milk in question does not move of its own initiative, but is activated by a combination of causes and conditions which come to pass at a particular time. But *Prakṛti* stands altogether in a different category. Being an eternal principle, uncontingent on any other factor, it should function always and not occasionally. But in that case *Prakṛti* should produce enjoyment and emancipation without break—an absurd issue which even the *Sāṅkhya* philosopher must hesitate to accept in spite of his undying love for *Prakṛti*.

It is, however, contended that *buddhi* has to be posited to account for origination and dissolution, which cannot appertain to consciousness. But this involves *a petitio principii*. There is no contradiction between consciousness and origin and death. On the contrary, if consciousness be an eternal *fait accompli*, the function of sense-organs will be deprived of all meaning, as the sole purpose of sense-organs is to produce knowledge, but this is already there. Certainly there cannot be any necessity for fuel, if fire is present for eternity.[2]

The argument that all composite things have to subserve the interests of another principle and the ultimate principle, which will be so served, cannot but be a spiritual substance, is acceptable

1 *Vide* S. T. K. under
vatsavivṛddhinimittaṁ kṣīrasya yathā pravṛttir ajñasya ।
puruṣavimokṣanimittaṁ tathā pravṛttiḥ pradhānasya ।
S. K. Śl. 57.

2 akṣyarthādy aphalaṁ tu syāc caitanyaṁ śāśvataṁ yadi ।
na bhaved indhanenā 'rtho yadi syāc chāśvato' nalaḥ ।
T. S., 306.

so far.[1] But it fails to take into account that this spiritual principle must be capable of receiving supplementation from its accessories, otherwise these accessories cannot render any service to it. And if this spirit derives benefit from these auxiliaries, it cannot afford to be an unchanging static principle. We have no experience of a changeless substance being benefited by others. Even examples of bed and cushion and the like that have been cited to bring home the argument are only helpful because the beneficiary is actionable and so changeful. An unactionable and unchanging spirit cannot have any necessity for accessories, because the latter cannot have any effect on the former. And if the spiritual substance is thus conceded to be capable of change, it will be a fluxional entity which is the position we hold.[2]

---

1 ''saṅghātaparārthatvāt triguṇādiviparyayād adhiṣṭhānāt ।
puruṣo'sti bhoktṛbhāvāt kaivalyārthaṁ pravṛtteś ca । ''
-Sāṅkhya Kārikā, śl. 17.

also, puruṣo 'sty avyaktāder vyatiriktaḥ, kutaḥ? saṅghātaparārthatvāt, avyakta-mahadahaṅkārādayaḥ parārthāḥ, saṅghātatvāt, śayanāsanābhyaṅgavat. *Sāṅkhyatattvakaumudī.*

2 pārārthyaṁ cakṣurādīnāṁ yat punaḥ pratipādyate ।
śayyāsanādivat tena saṅghātatvena hetunā ।
ādheyātiśayārthatvaṁ yady eṣām upapādyate ।
iṣṭasiddhir yad iṣṭās te' smābhir jñānopakāriṇaḥ ।
avikāryupakāritvasādhane sādhyaśūnyatā–
dṛṣṭāntasya calasyai 'va yuktās te'py upakāriṇaḥ ।
T. S., śls. 307-09.

CHAPTER XII

THE SOUL-THEORY OF THE VĀTSĪPUTRĪYAS

The *Vātsīputrīyas*, who profess to be followers of the Buddha, do strangely postulate the existence of the self under the name of *pudgala* (the principle of individuality), which they affirm as neither identical with, nor different from, the psychical aggregates, called *skandhas*. The *pudgala* (individual) is not held to be a distinct entity from the aggregates, because that would amount to acquiescence in the position of the heretical schools. Nor can it be held to be non-distinct from the *skandhas* either, as in that case the individual will be split up into a multiplicity. So the individual is described as an indefinable and inexpressible principle. Thus, if the individual is something absolutely distinct from the psychical elements, it will of necessity be an eternal verity; but this is logically unsound, as an eternal verity, being unamenable to any modification like space, cannot possibly discharge the functions of an agent and enjoyer, the very functions for which an individuality is postulated. And this would be directly in opposition to the teaching of the Master, who has denied an eternal soul. If, on the other hand, it is regarded as absolutely non-distinct from the psychical complexes, the individuality will stultify itself being reduced to a plurality of psychical factors. Moreover, it will be momentary like the psychical phenomena and will be subject to absolute extinction like them. But this will involve the absurdity of loss of *karman* and the consequent negation of metempsychosis, a contingency which is opposed to reason and the Master's teaching alike. So with a view to avoiding the two extremes of absolute existence (*śāśvatavāda*) and absolute extinction (*ucchedavāda*), which have been condemned by the Master as absurd, the Vātsīputrīyas have advocated a principle of individuality, called the *pudgala*, which has the metaphysical virtue of explaining the continuity of the empirical ego to the avoidance of the fallacy of the eternal self, posited by the heretical thinkers. The contradiction of identity and difference, involved in the conception of the *pudgala*, need not deter us, as experience and metaphysical necessity alike call for such a conception.

The *Sautrāntika* philosopher has, however, opposed this doctrine with all the emphasis he could command. Śāntarakṣita, an exponent of the former school, observes that this *pudgala*, which has been ushered into existence with so much pomp and ceremony by the *Vātsīputrīyas*, is but a metaphysical fiction like the sky-lotus. Because, a thing which cannot be described either as identical with, or different from, another is nothing but an unreal idea, a logical and a psychological fiction. Identity or difference can be predicated of a reality and not an unreal fiction. So this *pudgala*, which is neither identical with, nor different from, the psychical complexes will be an absolutely hollow, unreal voidity and to claim objective reality for such a figment of imagination betrays a sad lack of even elementary logical thought. Such a thing can exist in the imagination of a morbid mind, but not in reality. To say that a *pudgala* is different and non-different from the aggregates is a contradiction in terms. If it is different, it cannot be non-different ; if non-different, it cannot be different. So when you say that the *pudgala* is not different from the aggregates, you at once admit the identity of the two. When again you say that, that the *pudgala* is not the aggregates, you admit they are distinct and different. When things are found to be possessed of mutually incompatible attributes, they are set down as different and distinct,

1 skandhebhyaḥ pudgalo nānya ity eṣā 'nanyasūcanā | skandho na pudgalaś ce ti vyaktā tasye'yam anyatā | viruddhadharmasaṅgo hi vastūnāṁ bheda ucyate | skandhapudgalayoś' cai 'va vidyate bhinnatā na kim |

T. S., 343-44.

as the criterion of difference is the possession of contradictory attributes, and this is incompatible with the identity of the substratum. You say that the *pudgala* is indescribable either as identical or as distinct. But the aggregates are describable as distinct from each other; thus, the aggregate of 'physical elements' or sense-data (*rūpa*) is different from that of feelings (*vedanā*). The aggregates again are describable as impermanent, but not so the *pudgala*. So the *pudgala* and the aggregates as a class apart, are absolutely distinct categories, because they are possessed of mutually contradictory attributes, *viz.*, the fact of being describable or indescribable. The *pudgala* therefore must be set down as an absolute unreality, having no *locus standi* except in the coloured imagination of the *Vātsīputrīyas*. The impossibility of predication of identity or difference with respect to the *pudgala* does not alone prove its unreal, imaginary character; its unreality is also brought home by the fact that it cannot be described as momentary either. We have proved beyond the shadow of doubt that existence means causal efficiency and this causal efficiency, it has been demonstrated by irrefragable logic, is restricted to momentary reals.[1] So a thing, which cannot be described as momentary, must be set down as a fiction, pure and simple. How can a non-momentary thing have causal efficiency ?[2]

It may be contended that as causal efficiency is incompatible with a non-momentary thing, a non-momentary cannot be a real entity. But this *pudgala* is not accepted by us as absolutely non-momentary. What we contend is that the *pudgala* cannot from its very nature be described either as momentary or non-momentary. If we categorically affirmed its non-momentary character, the charge of unreality could be

1 arthakriyāsu śaktiśca vidyamānatvalakṣaṇam | kṣaṇikeṣv eva niyatā tathā 'vācye na vastutā |

T.S., 347.

2 'anityatvena yo'vācyaḥ sa hetur na hi kasyacit.'

Quoted in T.S.P., p. 128.

brought home to us. But as we neither affirm nor deny the non-momentary or momentary nature with regard to the *pudgala* the charge cannot be substantiated. If we categorically affirmed it to be non-momentary, causal efficiency could be denied of it. But we admit its momentary character as well; so there is nothing to prevent its exercising causal efficiency. But this only seeks to draw a red herring across the line of real dispute. The indubitable and irrefutable fact remains that there is contradiction between the two incompatible attributes of momentariness and non-momentariness. If one is true, the other must be false. If one is false, the other cannot but be true. There is no half-way house between two mutually exclusive terms. A thing cannot be permanent and non-permanent both. What is the connotation of permanence? Obviously it is the fixed and unalterable nature of a thing. A thing is said to be eternal, which does not perish at any time.[1] The non-eternal is that which does not persist always, but ceases to exist at some point of time. So, how can an identical thing be conceived as existing for all time and again ceasing to exist at some point of time? This is sheerly an inconceivable situation. The affirmation of one presupposes the denial of another and *vice versa*. You cannot have it both ways or neither. If it is eternal, it must be admitted to be an unreal fiction like a rabbit's horn. If momentary, it cannot be an unreal existence, which, however, is claimed by the *Vātsīputrīyas* with a shameless naïvete. So when the *pudgala* is not categorically a momentary entity, it must be devoid of causal efficiency, as causal efficiency is the invariable concomitant of the momentary.

As for the seeming scriptural and textual discrepancies, they have been fully explained by the noble Vasubandhu in his *Abhidharmakoṣa* and *Paramārthasaptati*. The curious reader is advised to consult those works. We are here concerned with the metaphysical issues involved in the position of the *Vātsī-*

1 nityaṁ tam āhur vidvāṁso yaḥ svabhāvo na naśyati. *Ibid*, p. 129.

putrīyas and we have shown that the whole doctrine is vitiated by a flagrant breach of the 'Law of Contradiction.' It betrays slipshod logic from top to bottom and can be held out as the best illustration of the heights of absurdity to which a man can be led by a pet superstition.

About the teaching of the Master, one word is sufficient to indicate the method which was adopted by him. The sermons of the master were inspired by the enquiries of inquisitive persons and the Master had to consider the intellectual calibre and equipment of these enquirers before giving answers to their queries—otherwise his words would become incomprehensible to them. This point has been explained (by Kumāralābha) thus: "The Buddha was pleased to construct his doctrine concerning the elements of existence (with the greatest caution), like a tigress who holds her young by her teeth (her grasp is not too tight in order not to hurt him, nor is it too loose in order not to let him fall)."[1] So when the Buddha said, "There is a being spontaneously born,"[2] it must be understood to mean the continuity of the stream of

[1] *The Soul Theory of the Buddhists* by Th. Stcherbatsky, *vide* p. 847.

Cf. "daṁṣṭridaṁṣṭrāvabhedaṁ ca bhraṁśaṁ cā 'vekṣya karmaṇām ǀ deśayanti jinā dharmaṁ vyāghrīpotāpahāravat." quoted in the T. S. P., p. 129.

[2] 'asti sattva upapādukaḥ' Prof. Stcherbatsky renders it by 'apparitional spontaneous self-birth.' The learned Professor has translated Hiuen Thsang's version as follows:—" ....if the five *skandhas* (of the intermediate state) proceed to a new life, which begins neither in the womb, nor in an egg, nor in warm moisture, then the result is called transfigurated being." *Ibid*, pp. 844 and 957. "In this way are born: gods, the inhabitants of hell and all men in the intermediate state between death and a new birth, *i.e.*, without a seed, not from previous elements, as the *Vāts* (*the Vātsīputrīyas*) believe." *Op. cit.*, p. 946. *Cf. Amarakoṣa*, "divyopapādukā devāḥ," Bhānuji comments: "nārakavyāvṛttaye divyapadam. mātāpitrādidṛṣṭakāraṇanirapekṣā adṛṣṭasahakṛtebhyo 'ṇubhyo jātā ye devāḥ, te divyopapādukā ucyante." We have it from Prof. Stcherbatsky, "The whole theory of apparitional or miraculous self-births is exposed and discussed in the III Section." *Op. cit.*, p. 966.

conscious life after death in other regions. This does not lend any support to the existence of an eternal ego-principle. The Buddha did not point-blank deny the existence of the soul, as that might be misconstrued by inferior intellects as denial of all post-mortem existence.

The *Vātsīputrīyas* have made capital out of the sermon of the Master, which is in the following terms—" O Brethren, I will explain to you the burden, the taking up of the burden, the laying aside of the burden and the carrier of the burden. Of these, the burden is the five aggregates, which are the substrates (of personal life) ; the taking up of the burden is the craving for a continuation of life, accompanied by a sense of satisfaction ; the laying aside of the burden is emancipation ; and the carrier of the burden is the individual.'' They have stressed in it the distinct mention of the individual apart from the aggregates, and have taken care to point out that unless the individual is recognised to be a distinct principle from the aggregates which have been described as the burden of life, the burden and the burden-bearer will be the same thing, which is absurd on the face of it.[1]

But such an interpretation of the parable, though to all appearances it seems to be in conformity with the text, cannot be accepted as embodying the real intention of the master. Because, the individual spoken of as the carrier of the burden is nothing distinct from the aggregates : the preceding aggregates which culminate in the production of the succeeding aggregates, are called the burden and the latter are the burden-carrier, being the inheritors of all that has gone before. That this is the sense intended is apparent from the very epithets with which the *pudgala* has been hedged round. Thus, the individual (*pudgala*)

[1] 'bhāraṁ vo bhikṣavo deśayiṣyāmi, bhārādānaṁ bhāranikṣepaṁ bhārahāraṁ ca, tatra bhāraḥ pañcopādānaskandhāḥ, bhārādānaṁ tṛptiḥ, bhāranikṣepo mokṣo, bhārahāraḥ pudgalā iti.'

I have adopted the translation of Prof. Stcherbatsky with slight alterations.

has been spoken of as the subject, bearing such and such a name, such and such a caste, coming of such a family, living on such food-stuffs, experiencing such pleasure and pain, and having such a span of life allotted to him and so on. Certainly these adjectives are ill-adapted to an eternal self or any real self, having a distinct existence apart from the elements of consciousness.[8] So this sermon cannot be interpreted as evidence of a soul-entity.

This should be a clincher to the *Vàtsīputrīyas*' contention. But Uddyotakara, to suit his purpose, has gone out of his way to seize hold of another text and has twisted it so as to make it appear as evidence of the existence of a distinctive soul-principle. The text is as follows : "' O Venerable sir, I am not colour ; and so again I am not feeling, name, conformation and cognition. Likewise, thou too, O monk, art not the colour ; nor art thou any more the feeling, name, conformation and cognition.''[9] ' The specific negation of the aggregates,' argues Uddyotakara, ' element by element, as the object of ego-consciousness, shows that there is a self apart and aloof from the contents.' If negation of the self as such had been the purport, it could have been conveniently expressed by a categorical negation of the self ' as thou art not.' But the specific negation of the aggregates, one by one, points to the existence of an independent self, as for instance, the statement ' I do not see with my left eye ' indicates that he sees with the right eye. If seeing as such was to be negated, the specific negation of the instrumentality of the left eye would be unmeaning. So it follows by way of implication that there is a self distinct from the psychical complexes, no matter whether it be an indefinable entity as the *Vātsīputrīyas* would have it or any other variety.[10]

[1] ata eva Bhagavatā, 'Bhārahāraḥ katamaḥ pudgala' ity uktvā 'yo'sāv āyuṣmān nevaṁnāmā, evaṁjātiḥ, evaṁgotra, evamāhāraḥ, evaṁ-sukha-duḥkhaṁ pratisaṁvedī, evaṁ dīrghāyur' ityādinā pudgalo vyākhyātaḥ.

[2] & [3] T. S. P., pp. 130-31.

But the contention of Uddyotakara is based on a misunderstanding of the real purport of the text. The sermon was addressed to persons who had these particular misconceptions with a view to their enlightenment. So the purport of the text is purely negative and cannot in any way be construed as an affirmation of the self, express or implied.[1]

---

1 viśeṣapratiṣedhaś ca taddṛṣṭīn prati rājate. T. S., śl. 349.

For a thorough-going and detailed exposition of the soul theory of the Vātsīputrīyas, *vide 'The Soul Theory of the Buddhists'* by Prof. Stcherbatsky, and Prof. Louis de La Vallee's *Abhidharmakoṣa* and his brilliant exposition.

CHAPTER XIII

The Theory of Soul based on the Upaniṣads

The Vedāntists, who hold to the doctrine of absolute monism, consider the world of reality as an unsubstantial appearance floating over an eternal spiritual principle, which is absolutely homogeneous and destitute of all distinctions, subjective or objective whatsoever. As the Absolute *Brahman*, which is pure consciousness and pure existence, is the only reality and the multiplicity of the phenomenal world, both subjective and objective, is only an appearance as unsubstantial and unreal as an illusion or a dream, there can be no distinctions—external or internal in the spirit, which is one, uniform, unchanged and unchangeable, homogeneous Being. The subject-object distinctions are thus purely fictitious, as the objects have no reality outside the Absolute Consciousness.

The Buddhist idealist (*vijñānavādin*) holds to an analogous doctrine as according to him also the objective world has no reality whatsoever outside the thinking minds. The subject-object distinctions are equally false creations of the conscious principle. But though thus they are fundamentally agreed on the reality of consciousness alone, they differ in a very material respect. The Vedāntists are certainly wrong in holding this consciousness to be a homogeneous, unitary principle. If this consciousness were one eternal substance, then why should there be any diversity in our ideas? Certainly colour-consciousness is not the same thing as sound-consciousness and if they are different, you connot consistently hold the doctrine of unitary, eternal consciousness. If they had been one and eternal, all these diverse cognitions should arise all at once and not in a graduated scale as they are found to do. Nor can these different cognitions be regarded as so many modes or determinations of one eternal consciousness, because modes cannot be regarded as absolutely distinct from the substance and so the substance will vary with its modes. The result will be a multiplicity of conscious units, which is our (Buddhists') position.

Moreover, no line of demarcation can be drawn between cognitions and consciousness as such, as they are found in experience to be absolutely indivisible. And if the diverse cognitions are distinct from one another, what is there to be conceived as one? The Vedāntist position of one eternal consciousness, on the other hand, renders bondage and liberation absolutely impossible. If bondage be its essential nature, there can be no emancipation and if consciousness is *eo ipso* emancipated, bondage will become equally untenable. But in the Buddhist theory, no such contingency arises, as in a consciousness-series, each moment of consciousness being absolutely different and distinct, there is no incompatibility if one moment is impure and another is divested of its impurity. The fact of the matter is that bondage is nothing but consciousness as defiled by passions and ignorance, and emancipation is nothing but consciousness in its native purity, purged of all impurities, by a course of rigorous discipline. Had bondage or emancipation been *eo ipso* the nature of consciousness, all discipline would have been unavailing.[1] If, however, bondage and liberation be held to be false superimpositions of ignorance, a praxis of yogic discipline will be devoid of all purpose, because there will be nothing to avoid or to attain. So the theory of the eternal consciousness is logically absurd and ethically a dangerous doctrine.[2]

[1] tathā hi—yadi viparyastasvabhāvam ekaṁ jñānaṁ sadā, tadā parasyā 'vasthāntarasyā 'bhāvān na mokṣavyavasthā syāt. athāviparyastaṁ tadā nityaṁ pariśuddhasvabhāvatvān na bandhaḥ syāt. asmākaṁ tu santānabhedena vijñaptiḥ saṁkliṣṭā śuddhā ce 'ṣyata iti yuktā bandhamokṣavyavasthā yatho 'ktam—"saṁkliṣṭā ca viśuddhā ca samalā nirmalā ca sā | saṁkliṣṭā ced bhaven nā 'sau muktāḥ syuḥ sarvadehinaḥ | viśuddhā ced bhaven nā 'sau vyāyāmo niṣphalo bhavet"—iti.

T. S. P., p. 124.

[2] kiṁ vā nivartayed yogī yogābhyāsena sādhayet |
kiṁ vā na hātuṁ śakyo hi viparyāsas tadātmakaḥ |
tattvajñānaṁ na co 'tpādyaṁ tādātmyāt sarvadā sthiteḥ |
yogābhyāso'pi tenā 'yam aphalaḥ sarva eva ca |

T. S. śls. 334-335.

CHAPTER XIV

A Critical Estimate of the Non-soul Theory of the Buddhist Philosophers

The Buddhists of the *Sautrāntika-Yogācāra* school have vehemently opposed the existence of a permanent self behind the psychical phenomena either as their substratum or as their condition. But they postulate the existence of pure, absolute consciousness, though momentary, bereft of subject-object determinations in the state of *Nirvāṇa*. Though the possibility of total extinction of all conscious existence is found to be adumbrated in the *Tattvasaṅgraha* and alluded to in the writings of rival schools, we shall not however concern ourselves in this context with the metaphysical merits or drawbacks of this theory, as it will be fully discussed and examined in the chapter on *Nirvāṇa*. Śāntarakṣita tells us that the gap between the Buddhistic and the Vedāntic conception of consciousness as the ultimate principle is but very narrow, though it is fundamental. The Vedāntists too have denied the existence of individual soul-centres (*Jīvātman*) as metaphysical entities and in this they are at one with the Buddhists. The issue of debate hangs upon the permanence or impermanence of consciousness. There is absolutely no difference of opinion regarding the impersonal and impartite character of consciousness too. The Buddhists hold consciousness to be of momentary duration, albeit the stream of consciousness-units is one unbroken and uninterrupted procession and in this respect of eternal duration, there is agreement, too, between the two schools of thought. The continuum of consciousness as an ontological reality whether in the series or in the unity is accepted as a fundamental reality and so for all practical purposes the two positions do not differ in a material respect.

But practical considerations are not the only thing that carry weight with philosophers. The difference of metaphysics is far too deep and uncompromising, though to the commonplace mind, it would perhaps appear to be a distinction without difference. The difference between the two philosophies is therefore based upon a fundamental ground and neither of them can be expected to capitulate to the other, as this would imply the entire change of outlook and philosophic orientation. But a dispassionate critic, when confronted with a metaphysical tangle of this type, has got to make his own decision and to pronounce an unbiassed verdict either in favour of one or against the other. It is very seldom that the critic can come with offers of compromise, as compromise proves very often to be suicidal to philosophy. Compromise is a virtue in practical life, because it ensures the harmonious co-operation of the members of a community, which disagreement and difference would render impossible. But difference of opinion does not spell any such danger, if it does not involve a fundamental antagonism in ethics and social life. So the practical work-a-day man of the world has no reason to sound the tocsin of alarm if philosophers differ between themselves, as decent philosophy does never stoop below wordy warfare.

Now, the Buddhist maintains that consciousness must be believed to vary with its contents. Thus, the consciousness of red is different from the consciousness of blue. If they were one undivided consciousness, then, the contents should be felt all at once and not in a graduated series, which is the actual fact. Nor is there any warrant either from experience or from logic to suppose that consciousness is a principle apart and distinct from its contents, because we feel the two together and as identical. So one consciousness must be held to be distinct from another consciousness and the apparent unity and identity of self-consciousness must be explained as a psychical fiction, generated by the homogeneity of the consciousness-units. The *Sāṅkhyas* put forward their epistemological theory that cognitions are processes and affections of a thin, attenuated intelligence-stuff (*buddhi*), which are as much material and unspiritual as any other material changes, but these are quickened and illuminated and thus spiritualised by the light of the spirit reflected upon it. The Vedāntists, too, with minor differences among themselves, which are negligible for our purpose, almost unreservedly accept this epistemological device of the *Sānkhyas* and the objective of all this is to maintain the supposed integrity of the spirit, standing aloof from the psychical processes. But this is only an expedient, ingenious though, devised to maintain a pet theory, which has no logical or psychological evidence to support it. If the contents of consciousness were really different and distinct from consciousness *per se*, the knowledge of these contents would become absolutely unaccountable. What is the criterion of knowledge ? What is the explanation that one thing is known and another is unknown save and except this that one thing enters into consciousness and becomes identical with it ? But how can a thing, material and unconscious in itself, come to be identified with consciousness, which is its complete anti-thesis ? The *Sautrāntikas* tide over this common difficulty of all epistemology by positing the existence of an intermediary, *viz.*, the image or likeness of the material object imprinted on consciousness. The process is something like photography.

The Vedāntists, on the other hand, think that these Buddhists have come very near the truth, but their philosophy suffers shipwreck at the very sight of the harbour. We admit, the Vedāntists argue, that knowledge of a fact cannot be explained if the fact stands in its sacred aloofness from consciousness. There must be some relation between the two and the relation of causality or objectivity (*viṣayatā* or *uddyeśyatā*) which is requisitioned by the Realists, cannot adequately explain the intimacy and immediacy of the relation involved in knowledge. There may be a case of causality between two material facts and yet there is no resultant knowledge. And a material object may be the aim and objective of our physical endeavour, but such endeavour fails to remove the cover of ignorance that envelops it.[1] You may plead that the relation is unique and the fact of illumination proceeds from consciousness to the object and so knowledge becomes possible. Yes, but this is the very crux of the problem. Your explanation only states the problem and assumes the very fact which you are called upon to explain. The Buddhist thinks that this relation is one of complete identity (*sahopalambhaniyamād abhedo nīlataddhiyoḥ*). But this is opposed to the testimony of experience. The contents cannot be believed to be absolutely identical with cansciousness, because they are felt to be distinct, external and possessed of a long or short magnitude, whereas consciousness is felt inside and as an amorphous principle without any geometrical dimension. So the two cannot be lumped together. But unless they are identified, they cannot be supposed to be illumined and revealed. Illumination is the property, nay, the very self of consciousness and unless the contents are supposed to be taken into and integrated with it, they cannot be known. Knowledge is a peculiar relation—it is neither one of complete identity nor of complete difference. It is a peculiar relation—something indescribable. There is difference between consciousness and its contents, but the difference is not real. There must be identity between the two, no doubt, without which no knowledge can be supposed to be possible. But this identity cannot be a real, absolute identity. It is something equally indescribable. Consciousness is self-luminous and as such can illumine its own identity and with regard to external objects it is

[1] hānādijananād hānādibuddhīnām arthaviṣayatvam, arthaviṣayahānādibuddhijananāc cā 'rthasaṁvidas tadviṣayatvam iti cet, tat kiṁ dehasya prayatnavadātmasaṁyogo dehapravṛttinivṛttihetur arthe ity arthaprakāśo 'stu. jāḍyād dehātmasaṁyogo nā 'rthaprakāśa iti cet, nanv ayam svayaṁprakāśo' pi svātmany eva khadyotavat prakāśaḥ, arthe tu jaḍa ity upapāditam. Bhā. *ad* Br. Sū. 1.1.1., p. 36.

Cf., dṛśyavargasya saṁvidbhinnatābhyupagame saṁvidaḥ svātmānaṁ prati prakāśatvaṁ hy abhedasaṁbandhenai 'va kḷptaṁ iti taṁ prati sā jaḍarūpā dehātmasaṁyogatulyā na prakāśarūpā. K. T. P., *ad ibid.*

perfectly unilluminative. So the very possibility of knowledge demands that the two must be brought together in a relation of identity, but this identity cannot but be illusory and fictitious[1]

Now, the Buddhist philosopher argues into the momentariness of consciousness on the ground of the variation and the fluxional nature of the contents of consciousness and he bases his conclusion upon the relation of identity between consciousness and its contents. And he explains away the felt unity of consciousness as a psychological fiction by an appeal to the palpable variability of these contents. But these are pure assumptions which militate against sound logic. It has been proved that the relation of consciousness and its contents is neither one of absolute identity nor one of absolute difference, as both these are equally felt in experience to be the case. But identity and difference cannot both be predicated of the same phenomenon, as it infringes the fundamental laws of thought, *viz.*, the Law of Contradiction and the Law of the Excluded Middle. The said relation therefore transpires to be an unreal, illusory superimposition just like the illusory superimposition of silver upon the shell. The relation of consciousness to its superimposed contents is therefore one of illusory identity and the difference of one content from another is equally false and illusory. And a false identity and a false difference cannot be made the basis of a philosophical argument. There is a felt difference between one cognition and another, but this difference is purely fictitious

[1] na ca prakāśasyā 'tmāno viṣayāḥ, te hi vicchinnadīrghasthūlatayā 'nubhūyante, prakāśas cā 'yam āntaro 'sthūlo 'naṇur ahrasvo 'dīrghaś ce 'ti prakāśate. tasmāc candre 'nubhūyamāna iva dvitīyaś candramāḥ svaprakāśād anyo 'rtho 'nirvacanīya eve 'ti yuktam utpaśyāmaḥ. Bhā. *ad* 1.1 1, pp. 36-37.

Cf. saṁvit svaprakāśe 'ti tasyāḥ svābhinna eva prakāśarūpatvasya kḷptatvāt svābhinne dṛśyavarge tasyāḥ prakāśarūpatā na sambhavati, tāttvikaś ca dṛgdṛśyayor abhedo na yujyate, ato dṛśyavargasya saṁvidvivartatayā 'nirvacanīyena tadabhedena prakāśamānatā.

K.T.P., *ad ibid*, p. 37.

and a fictitious difference cannot entail a substantive difference in consciousness. A fictitious difference cannot affect the integrity of the reality, much less can it induce a real distinction. The shell may erroneously be perceived alternately as silver or as lead. But the distinction of lead and silver does not touch the identity of the shell and so cannot split it up into two. By similar logic the difference of contents, which have been proved to be illusory superimpositions, cannot be legitimately supposed to introduce a real distinction into consciousness. Consciousness, therefore, should, in deference to the demands of logic, be regarded as a simple identity, an impartite whole, an eternal verity, with no ontological difference in itself. It is a self-illuminative principle without origin, decay and death, existing as the sole witness and illuminator of the cosmic panorama, which hangs as a pall and as a cloud over it. Ontologically speaking, it is nothing short of a vain show, a mysterious appearance, an idle phantasmagoria—the creation of an equally illusive and unreal *avidyā* (nescience), which however is not a psychological phenomenon nor a logical fiction, but an elusive category that cannot be described in metaphysical terms either as an absolute aught or as an absolute naught.

Experience too does not lend support to the Buddhist conception of multiple consciousness-units. The consciousness of red is felt to be distinct from the consciousness of blue, no doubt; but distinction is not the only note in it, the identity of consciousness is equally a felt fact. The Buddhist believes this felt unity of consciousness to be an illusion and he bases this belief upon the apparent multiplicity of contents. With equal logic one might explain away the multiplicity of contents as fiction and establish the unity of consciousness to be the reality. So appeal to experience is perfectly unavailing and its testimony is inconclusive and conflicting. The two opposite characters—unity and difference—cannot both be true, as they involve a contradiction in terms. Which of the two then is to be believed as the reality and which again as false appearance? Difference and non-difference cannot both be true and if one of them is to be discarded, we must give up the aspect of difference as false appearance over the basic foundation of unity or non-difference, because difference cannot arise except on the foundation of two units, which are in their nature simple unities. If one of the two units be absent, the concept of difference becomes impossible, as each of the units constitutes its foundation and pivot, and if the foundation be lacking, how can it subsist ? But the case of unity is quite different. It is perceived in and by itself and without any reference to any other unity. Difference however is contingent upon unity and without unity its existence is inconceivable. And if we are faced with the alternative of rejecting one, we must perforce reject the aspect of difference as false superimposition and accept the factor of unity as the basic reality, because unity is the pre-supposition of difference and even if difference be accepted to be the final truth, unity will have to be accepted, as difference without unity as its basic support is a chimera. So between unity and difference we must accept unity as the reality since unity cannot be rejected as it is the constituent factor and is the *raison d' etre* even of difference. The Buddhist philosopher commits the blunder of unpardonable abstraction when he seeks to explain away the unity of consciousness on the basis of difference of contents, which in its turn, we have seen, presupposes the fact of unity as its very foundation and essence.

CHAPTER XV

The Problem of After-Life or Immortality of Consciousness-continuum

The philosophers of the *Lokāyata* school, who believed consciousness to be a product of physical elements and as such ceasing to function with the death of the physical body, opposed the Buddhist doctrine of the immortality of consciousness-series in very violent language. They argue: when the Buddhist believes this life of consciousness to be nothing but a congeries of distinct and discrete conscious units without any real, underlying unity in the shape of the self, then how could they believe in disembodied existence of consciousness? Consistency requires that they should subscribe to the *Lokāyata* doctrine of absolute extinction of consciousness after death and they should hold with the materialists that consciousness is nothing but a bye-product of the four physical elements, earth, water, fire and air held in certain juxtaposition in a physical organism. It therefore stands to reason that consciousness should come to absolute doom, when these elements are separated by physical death, no matter whether consciousness be regarded as a bye-product or as an epiphenomenon of the same.[1] And as regards the physical organism, sense-organs, and objects of perception, they also are nothing but peculiar combinations of these elements,

[1] 'paralokino 'bhāvāt paralokābhāva' iti, a *sūtra* of the *Lokāyata* system quoted in T. S. P., p. 520.

'pṛthivy āpas tejo vāyur iti catvāri tattvāni tebhyas caitanyam' iti. (another *sūtra*). tatra kecid vṛttikārā vyācakṣate utpadyate tebhyaś çaitanyam, anye 'bhivyajyata ity āhuḥ.' *Loc. cit.*

as there is no reality outside these elements found by experience.[1]

It might be argued that the consciousness in a pre-existent body is the substantive cause of consciousness in a subsequent body and so there is no break in the continuity of consciousness even on the death of a particular body. But such a causal relation between consciousness-centres located in different bodies is absolutely unthinkable, as we find the consciousness of an elephant and of a horse to be absolutely distinct and independent. Besides, there is no instance of one subjectivity producing another in a different body, on the strength of which we could suppose this relation to obtain in a past and a future organism. The theory that consciousness is the cause of another consciousness should thus be abandoned and it should be held that consciousness emerges as a product of the living physical organism.[2] It is a bold proposition to assert that consciousness exists even in the embryonic stage. How could there be any cognition of an object in the absence of sense-organs and certainly consciousness without a content is a contradiction in terms. Likewise, there can be no consciousness in fits of swoon and the like, when sense-organs cease to function. Nor can consciousness be supposed to exist in such circumstances in the shape of a potential energy, because potentiality can exist, if at all in a substratum and as the Buddhist denies with the materialist the existence of the Self, acting as a substratum of consciousness, the organism should be regarded as the substrate and with its death, consciousness should be held to become defunct, as there is no other

1 sanniveśaviśeṣe ca kṣityādīnāṁ niveśyate—
dehendriyadisañjñe 'yaṁ tattvaṁ nā 'nyad dhi vidyate ||
T. S., 1860.

cf. tathā ca teṣāṁ sūtram—" tatsamudaye viṣayendriyasaṁjñā' iti.
T. S. P., p. 520.

2 kāyād eva tato jñānaṁ prāṇāpānadyadhiṣṭhitāt |
yuktaṁ jāyata itye 'tat Kambalāśvataro 'ditam || śl. 1864.

cf. tathā ca sūtram—' kāyād eva ' iti. T. S. P., p. 521.

organism in which consciousness could function. The hypothesis of an intermediate astral body, working as the medium of the departed consciousness, has been thoroughly exposed by Vindhyavāsin and so far as the *Lokāyata* is concerned, it is simply an idle supposition as there is no positive proof of it. Moreover, this intermediate astral body which is supposed to originate and disappear all on a sudden, cannot be supposed to act as a vehicle of the departed consciousness, because, consciousness being devoid of locomotion, cannot be transferred to this astral body even.[1] And even if this be granted, it cannot be conceived how it should deposit consciousness in another organism, as this will necessitate the existence of consciousness in an embryo, a contingency too bold to be regarded with equanimity.[2] So the Buddhist finds himself to be placed tightly between the two horns of a dilemma: either he should accept an eternal Self like

[1] 'astīha sattva upapādukaḥ '—Buddha.

[2] The entire argument put in the mouth of the materialist is bodily taken *mutatis mutandis* from Kumārila's *Śloka-vārtika*. The *Ślokas* from 1865 to 1868 are reproduced *verbatim* and Śls. 1869 to 1871 are but a summarised version of Kumārila's *Ślokas*, 59-64 and 69 to 73, *Ātmavāda*, S. V., pp. 703-07.

Śrīdhara in his *Nyāyakandalī* employs similar arguments to prove the impossibility of metempsychosis in the Buddhist theory of Soul or rather no-Soul. Śrīdhara opines that the theory of momentary consciousness would land the Buddhist in rank materialism, which denies post-mortem existence of the Soul or conscious life, to be accurate. We are tempted to believe that Śrīdhara has borrowed his arguments from Kumārila whom he quotes with great respect in other places. It is strange that the editor of the *Tattvasaṅgraha* has failed to enumerate the *Ślokas* 1865 to 1868 in that work in the list of quotations from Kumārila, given as an appendix. Perhaps the omission to mention Kumārila as the author of the same by Kamalaśīla is responsible for this overt omission on the part of the editor. It is absolutely necessary that these *ślokas* should be noticed in the appendix of the *Tattvasaṅgraha*.

Vide Nyāyakandalī, p. 81.

the *Mīmāṁsaka* or in the alternative deny metempsychosis like the materialist.[1]

Śāntarakṣita observes that the whole problem of *after-life* hinges on the correct determination of the meaning of the expression '*after-life.*' Now, if by after-life or post-mortem existence is meant something distinct from the continuity of consciousness-series, then the denial of such an existence by the materialist will not affect the Buddhist in the least. The Buddhist holds the life of consciousness to be a beginningless, never-ending continuum, in which each precedent conscious moment is followed by a subsequent conscious moment, which derives its existence from the former and goes on producing its duplicates without end. Thus, so far consciousness *qua* consciousness is concerned, it is an eternal, timeless process without a definite beginning or an abrupt end. The conception of this life or after-life is but a relative idea, according as it is considered in relation to a conventional time-standard. Thus, consciousness-continuum as delimited by a period of a hundred years or its neighbourhood is conventionally regarded as the present life and its survival after this fictitious limit is considered to be after-life or post-mortem existence. In reality, however, the procession of consciousness being a time-less existence, such standards of time-limitation are not applicable to it *per se*, which do apply to the physical organism, which is however an accidental adjunct to the conscious life.

It may be urged that the so-called continuum, which is said to be one, eternal fact in this connexion, is nothing but a fictitious idea and the problem of post-mortem existence consequently cannot be solved in terms of this fictitious convention, however useful it might be in other contexts. Yes, the continuum (*santati*) *per se* is an unreal fiction, but this does not affect the

[1] ekajñānāśryas tasmād anādinidhano naraḥ |
saṁsārī kaścid eṣṭavyo yadvā nāstikatā parā ||
T. S., Śl. 1871.

reality of the conscious units, which never come to an abrupt end but continue producing replicas of themselves to all eternity. These conscious moments are absolutely real entities and when taken in their totality they are designated by such expressions as series, continuum and the like as a matter of convenience. This series has no independent reality outside the constituent moments, just as a forest has no existence apart and distinct from the trees, still these expressions have a pragmatic value inasmuch as they give us an idea of the entire collection in one sweep. Though the series is thus a mere name, a logical fiction quite as much as the series of sky-lotuses, since it is not conceivable either as identical with or as distinct from its constituent factors, yet there is no logical difficulty for the conscious units to form an ever-recurring, never-ending procession. Moreover, the eternity of conscious existence is a matter of logical proof. Thus, the first conscious moment in a body may be regarded either as (1) an uncaused event ; or (2) as the product of an eternal conscious principle, *e.g.*, God and the like, or (3) as an eternal self-existent entity; or (4) as a product of the material elements ; or (5) lastly, as the effect of a different consciousness-series. The first advent of consciousness in the fœtus cannot be conceived to be an uncaused event, as it is a historical event, distinctly assignable to a point of time. This would be impossible, if the first consciousness is a causeless event, since an uncaused entity being independent of external factors, would continue always and not occasionally. Neither can it be regarded as the effect of such eternal categories as God, space, eternal mind, etc. Because, an eternal cause would produce an eternal effect always. The third alternative involves a preposterous issue, since consciousness cannot be regarded as an unitary, eternal entity, the diversity of cognition of colour, sound and the like being manifestly a matter of direct experience. The fourth alternative of consciousness being a product of the physical elements is open to the self-same logical difficulties, as the elements are *ex hypothesi* eternal, obdurate, unchanging entities. The successive occurrence of auxiliaries cannot be trotted out as an excuse, as an eternal entity cannot have any necessity for them. And if these elements are regarded as fluxional, this would be surrendering their own position. But even the acceptance of the elements being momentary will not help the materialist. Because the existence of extra-mental physical elements is logically untenable. So if the *Cārvāka* does not hesitate to surrender his position of eternal elements in the interests of logic, he should end by regarding them as mere ideas, consubstantial with consciousness. The unreality of the material world is proved to demonstration by irrefutable logic.

We think we can quote with profit in this connection the views of a comparatively modern thinker about the relation of thought and matter, particularly of our psychological operations with cerebral functions. " Surely no one who is cognisant of the facts of the case, nowadays, doubts that the roots of psychology lie in the physiology of the nervous system. What we call the operations of the mind are functions of the brain, and the materials of consciousness are products of cerebral activity. ....It is hardly necessary to point out that the doctrine just laid down is what is called materialism......But it is nevertheless true that the doctrine contains nothing inconsistent with the purest idealism. For, as Hume remarks (as indeed Descartes had done long before) :—

' 'Tis not our body we perceive when we regard our limbs and members, but certain impressions which enter by the sense ; so that the ascribing a real and corporeal existence to these impressions, or to their objects, is an act of the mind as difficult to explain as that (the external existence of objects) which we examine at present' (1, p. 24).

" Therefore, if we analyse the proposition that all mental phenomena are the effects or products of material phenomena, all that it means amounts to this ; that whenever those states of consciousness which we call sensation, or emotion, or thought, come into existence, complete investigation will show good reason for the belief that they are preceded by those other phenomena of consciousness to which we give the names of matter and motion. All material changes appear, in the long run, to be modes of motion; but our knowledge of motion is nothing but that of a change in the place and order of our sensations, just as our knowledge of matter is restricted to the feelings of which we assume it to be the cause.

"It has already been pointed out, that Hume must have admitted, and in fact does admit, the possibility that the mind is a Leibnitzian monad, or a Fichtean world-generating Ego, the universe of things being merely the picture produced by the evolution of the phenomena of consciousness. For any demonstration given to the contrary effect, the 'Collection of perceptions' which makes up our consciousness may be an orderly phantasmagoria generated by the Ego, unfolding its successive scenes on the background of the abyss of nothingness; as a firework, which is but cunningly arranged combustibles, grows from a spark into a coruscation, and from a coruscation into figures, and words, and cascades of devouring fire, and then vanishes into the darkness of the night.

"On the other hand, it must no less readily be allowed that.........there may be a real something which is the cause of all our impressions; that sensations, though not likenesses, are symbols of that something, and that the part of that something, which we call the nervous system, is an apparatus for supplying us with a sort of algebra of fact, based on those symbols. A brain may be the machinery by which the material universe becomes conscious of itself. But it is important to notice that, even if this conception of the universe and of the relation of consciousness to its other components should be true, we should, nevertheless, be still bound by the limits of thought, still unable to refute the arguments of pure idealism." [1]

[1] Huxly's Hume, Ch. III, pp. 80-82.

Kamalaśīla observes that even if the four physical elements, which are the only stock-in-trade of the *Cārvāka*, are granted to be momentary and fluxional, the materialist will not succeed in making out his case that consciousness is a product of these fourfold elements, combined in various proportions. There is no proof whatsoever in favour of the position that the two sets of phenomena are causally related. Well, the causal relation is comprehended by an observation of concomitance, in agreement or difference, of a special type and not by mere presence or absence. When causal relation is to be determined by concomitance in agreement, it must be laid down as a necessary condition that the effect in question must be perceptible and known to be non-existent before ; otherwise if it is imperceptible its non-existence prior to the operations of the cause will be a matter of doubt and so the causal relation cannot be ascertained. If previous non-existence is not regarded as a criterion, things already in existence, *e.g.*, the house and its furniture and the like, could be misconstrued to be the effect of the cause in question. Again the concomitance in absence or difference can be ascertained only if other likely causes are found to be present and the absence of a particular phenomenon is found to be invariably accompanied by the absence of another phenomenon. Mere concomitance in absence is incompetent to determine the causal relation, as there is room for doubt that the absence of the effect might be due to the absence of some other unobserved fact. Thus, we cannot establish any causal relation between the growth of date trees and the custom of marriage within prohibited degrees of consanguinity, though it is found that date trees do not grow in a land where such custom does not obtain. The fact of the matter is that the concomitance in question, whether in agreement or in difference, must be unconditional, else the causal relation cannot be established. Let us examine if such unconditional concomitance is found to obtain between the physical organism and consciousness. Concomitance in agreement is not ascertainable, as the antecedence of the physical organism to the advent of consciousness in the fœtus cannot be perceived by one's own self, as such perception presupposes the existence of consciousness in it. Nor can it be ascertained in other organisms, as consciousness is by its nature incompetent to perceptual observation. So concomitance in agreement is impossible of ascertainment. Concomitance in absence too does not stand any better chance. For, the absence of one's own bodily organism prior to the disappearance of consciousness can be determined if there is a consciousness, but this is sought to be eliminated in the process. Nor again can such concomitance be ascertained in the organism of another person. Because, consciousness in a different organism being invisible by its very nature, its non-existence on the cessation of the organism cannot be positively asserted. Nor can such non-existence be ascertained by means of inference on the strength of absence of all activity in inorganic bodies. Because, there is no such restriction that the cause should function always. Moreover, it is quite supposable that the absence of the activities may be due to the absence of perverted volition and desire, which are regarded as the cause of association of consciousness with a physical organism. So it cannot be proved that organised physical elements are the cause of conscious life.[1]

It may however be urged that though there may not be any positive argument for consciousness being a product of physical elements, there is no evidence either against this possibility. But this is not the case, as argument in favour of the independent existence of consciousness as an immaterial principle is not lacking. In dreams and pure imagination (*vikalpa*) the mind is found to work independently of any external stimulus, either through the nervous system or through the sense-channels. And

[1] parispandādikāryādarśanād apy abhāvaniścayo na yuktaḥ, nā 'vaśyaṁ hi kāraṇānāṁ kāryabhāvattvam, api ca dehaviśeṣaparigrahahetos tṛṣṇāviparyāsalakṣaṇasya svakāraṇasyā 'bhāvāt kiṁ tatra buddher abhāvaḥ, āho svid dehavyatirekād iti saṁśayaḥ. T.S.P., p. 526.

even in reflective thought, which arises in the trail of sense-perception and interprets the perceptual experience, the mind contributes its own quota, which is not derived from an external source. All these facts which will be described in full in the course of our dissertation points to the independence of the mind existing in its own right. The problem of life after physical death is purely a spiritual problem and our spiritual existence is independent of any physical trapping, which is only an accidental appendage and which is adopted by it either as a matter of choice or of necessity, determined by its own law of existence.

Now, let us proceed to examine the thesis of the *Cārvāka* that consciousness is a product of the physical organism in all its bearings and aspects. Is the organism as a whole the cause of consciousness, or is it as an aggregate of manifold atoms, or is it as endowed with sense-organs or independent of sense-organs the cause of consciousness? Again, if it is a cause, is it the material cause or an auxiliary cause of the same? Now, the organism as one whole cannot be the cause of consciousness, as there is no such thing as an organic whole, which, though believed to be an objective existence independent of the component parts, is held to be an intellectual fiction by the Buddhist. Moreover, if the whole is an organic unity constituted of the four elements, it will have a fourfold constitution, which is incompatible with its unitary character. Nor can the aggregate of manifold atoms be regarded as the cause of consciousness. Is each of the atoms constitutive of consciousness or the entire collection of them? Not the former, because in that case there will be as many consciousnesses as there are atoms in the body just as there are as many sprouts as there are seeds. Nor can the entire collection be productive of one single consciousness, as in that case there will be no consciousness, if there is a diminution of any part, say, a breach of the nose or a severance of the arm, because it is a matter of common observation that there is a failure of sprout, if any of the constitutive factors, say, soil, water, the wind or the season, is absent. If it is contended that all of them contribute to the production of the sprout and the absence of any one factor or factors cannot preclude the functioning of others, then, there will be a consequent variation of consciousness in a cripple and sound body ; but no such variation in consciousness is noticeable in a man, who has suffered loss of some member of the body. His culture and education persist intact as before. And in this theory, we are to expect a bigger intellect in an elephant than that in a man, because the increase or decrease of the cause is concomitant with similar increase or decrease of the effect. But as such concomitant variation is found to be absent, we shall safely repudiate any causal relation between them. Nor, again, can the body as endowed with sense-organs be responsible for the emergence of consciousness. The question is, whether the sense-organs are individually or jointly the cause of consciousness ; if consciousness be the cumulative product of all the sense-organs, then, consciousness will fail to emerge or will abruptly disappear if there is absence or loss of any one of the sense-organs, as we observe that the absence of even one of the accessories entails non-production of the effect. Nor can the sense-organs be individually productive of consciousness, because consciousness is seen to continue unimpaired even if there is loss of a sense-organ. For instance, we see that even a paralytic possesses an alert consciousness, though his active organs are rendered inactive by palsy. Certainly, a thing, whose variations are not followed by similar variations in another, cannot be regarded as the cause of the same. Besides, consciousness as the product of the sense-organs will be subject to all the limitations, incidental to the sense-organs, to wit, capacity for cognising particular types of objects and for recording indeterminate, non-relational cognitions, in other words, knowledge of particulars alone and lastly functioning in relation only to present objects. The upshot is that conceptual and relational knowledge and memory and imagination will be reduced to unaccountable mysteries. Nor can unorganised matter, destitute of sense-organs, be regarded as the cause of consciousness. Because, we do not see any indication of consciousness in an arm severed from the body. If the body as an organic whole be held to be the cause, it will be one endowed with sense-organs, because an organism devoid of sense-organs is a contradiction in terms. But the sense-organs have been weighed in the scale and found wanting in the capacity credited to their account.

The last two alternatives remain to be examined. Is the organism the material cause of consciousness ? The question can be answered if the essential nature of a material cause is determined and understood in its proper perspective. The material cause is that which bequeaths its essential nature to the effects, which, though differing in inessential matters, are found to agree in their fundamental constitution. The unfailing characteristic of a material cause which follows as a corollary from its essential character, is this that no modification in the effect is possible without a corresponding modification of the cause. Thus, for instance, a lump of clay is the material cause of the pot. Now, the production of the pot can be obstructed if there is effected some modification in the lump of clay itself. So an effect can be injured or modified only by producing an injury or modification in the material cause. If the material cause remains absolutely unhurt or unmodified, there can possibly be no change in the effect, as the effect is bound up with the material from which it is produced. So it must be laid down as a universal proposition that an effect is injured or affected only if it is preceded by a similar affection in the material cause, which means the inducement of diminution in the causal energy. Consequently, there is no possibility of any injury or benefit being rendered to the effect directly and independently of the material cause—in other words, such service or disservice is possible through the medium of the material cause alone. And where an affection or modification in a particular entity is not preceded by a corresponding affection in another entity, supposed to be its material cause, these two entities must be set down as independent facts without any causal relation subsisting between them. Thus, a cow and a buffalo are considered to be independent entities without any causal relation whatsoever obtaining between them, because any injury done to the one is not conditioned by a similar injury in the other.

Let us see whether the dictum laid down by us in the determination of causal relation is satisfied in the case of consciousness and the bodily organism, which are declared by the *Cārvāka* to be causally related. Now, it is observed that the mind is disturbed by feelings of pain, hatred and the like by some unwelcome speech or disagreeable behaviour of another person, though the body is not affected in the least. Had the body been the material cause of the mind, the latter could not have been disturbed without producing an injurious effect in the former. So the plea of the physical organism being the cause of the principle of consciousness must be abandoned. It may, however, be urged to the contrary that the mind is inflamed with passions and violent impulses, when the body is nourished and developed by nutritious and invigorating food and this points to an intimate causal relation between the two. But this is only an accidental coincidence. Moreover, it does not affect our central position that an effect cannot be modified without a corresponding modification in the cause. The fact that the mind is affected without any affection in the body is sufficient to condemn the whole plea of the *Cārvāka*. The fact that a mental affection sometimes coincides with a bodily modification cannot be construed into an evidence of a causal relation between the two. Because, such coincidence is found even between an external object and a subjective affection ; but nobody with an iota of sanity would think the mental affection to be a product of the object for that. Thus, for instance, a man with a sensitive mind is found to faint away at the sight of a tiger or blood-shed ; but this is a pure coincidence. By similar logic we could regard the body as a product of the mind, as the body is seen to be agitated when the mind is perturbed with passion or grief. These are coincidences, pure and simple. The causal relation can be established if the variation of one is found to follow a corresponding variation of the other, invariably and unconditionally. But passions are not invariably concomitant with bodily affections, as it is not a rare phenomenon that an enlightened man is immune from passions though he may have a developed physique. On the contrary a lean, emaciated creature is seen to have a strongly passionate nature. Certainly a thing cannot be supposed to be the effect of something else, when it is found to occur when that something is absent. Moreover, the relation between a physical change and a mental affection is at best a mediate and conditional one. The emergence of passions, anger or love, is contingent on the association of pleasurable or painful ideas with objects of love or anger. But these ideas are purely subjective manifestations, arising from an inexhaustible and ever-growing fund of memory-impressions deposited in the course of beginningless metempsychosis. So it is seen in the case of an enlightened being, who has completely purged himself of these false ideas, that he is absolutely immune from these solicitations of animal passions, though he might have a powerful physique. A careful consideration of all these facts knocks down the materialist's plea that the mind is a product of the physical elements, no matter whether organised or unorganised.

We have proved the absurdity of the physical organism being the material cause of the mind or consciousness Let us consider whether the organism can be an auxiliary cause of the same. But this is also evidently an absurdity; because an auxiliary cause is that which directly helps the production of an effect. Thus the soil, water and the like are regarded as auxiliary causes of the sprout, because they directly assist in its production. If this dictum is not accepted, anything can be the auxiliary cause of any other thing. But such direct relation is conspicuously lacking between physical growth and rise of passions, as is evidenced in the case of enlightened persons, who are found to be immune from these inspite of their youth and possession of a vigorous physique. In the case of unenlightened persons even, these bodily changes are not directly responsible for the emergence of such passions, etc.; they only stimulate the memory-impressions and subconscious desires that are lying dormant in them and through their medium become the remote causes of the rise of passions. And even if it is assumed for the sake of argument that bodily changes do assist, immediately and unconditionally, the promotion of these passions, it does not necessarily follow that the death of the body will entail the death of consciousness. This will be made clear by an example. Fire is certainly an indispensable factor in the production of an earthen pot (the baked one), but the extinction of the fire in potter's furnace does not necessitate the extinction of the pot. So the possibility of the survival of consciousness after the death of the physical body is not excluded, even though the latter might be regarded (by a concession) as an assisting cause of the former. But we have seen that the whole plea of the materialist that the body is either a material or an auxiliary cause of consciousness is a hollow and unfounded assertion.

It has been further contended that the physical organism and the mind are certainly related as cause and effect, as material and product, because they are found to be invariably concomitant. It is an established proposition that things which are invariably co-existent are in the relation of material and product and this can be brought home by a concrete example, *viz.*, light and its effulgence. But the reason, *viz.*, invariable co-existence, is not acceptable to the Buddhist, as the Buddhist believes in the existence of the disembodied spirit in the immaterial sphere. The common principle of debate is that the probans (the middle term, *hetu*) must be acceptable to both the parties, particularly to the opponent for whose conviction the argument is employed. The breach of this rule constitutes the fallacy of *unproven middle term.* Again, the probans employed may also prove quite the contradictory of the intended thesis, *viz.*, the body may be regarded as the product of the mind. Moreover, the reason of invariable concomitance is inconclusive (*anaikāntika*). Because, invariable co-existence may be due to a reason other than material causation as is the case with fire and liquefied copper. Thus though copper passes into a liquid stage only when fire works upon it, nobody yet thinks fire to be the material cause of the liquid copper. So it can be legitimately supposed that the protoplasmic cell enters into a later development only when it is informed with consciousness; and the co-existence, being thus due to a factual necessity, cannot be made to prove the relation of material and product between the mind and the organism.[1]

It may be argued that though subsequent cognitions may be products of antecedent cognitions, the primal consciousness, which is the source of these derivative conscious states, may be a product of the physical organism and so the theory of beginningless consciousness will have no legs to stand upon. But this is only a dogmatic assumption and has no logic in its support. It may be contended that as the other hypothesis is also an assumption, for which there is no more logical necessity, the present hypothesis may be plausible. Not so, because this hypothesis is opposed to all reason. Thus, if the primal consciousness is derived from the physical organism and subsequent conscious states are purely derivatives of this internal consciousness, then all our cognitions will be purely subjective. But as a matter of

[1] syād etad—yayoḥ sahasthitiniyamas tāv upādānopādeyabhūtau, yathā pradīpaprabhe. asti ca sahasthitiniyamaḥ śarīramanovijñānayor iti svabhāvahetuḥ. tad ayam anyatarāsiddho hetuḥ, virūpe dhātau śarīram antareṇā 'pi manomater abhyupagamāt. nā'pīṣṭasiddhir manomater api dehaṁ praty upādānatva-prasaṅgāt; anaikāntikatā ca hetubhedād api sahāvasthānasambhavāt, yathā 'gnitāmradravayoḥ. tathā hi—vahnisahakāri tāmraṁ dravatvam ārabhate, na kevalam, evam ihā 'pi dehasyo' pādānam kalalādi manovijñānasahakāri deham uttaram ārabhate, ity atas tayoḥ sahasthānaṁ no' pādānopādeyabhāvād ity ato 'nekānta eva.

T. S. P., p, 529.

fact our cognitions are derived from both a subjective and an objective source alike, as is evidenced in sense-perception. But the theory of physical source of primal consciousness leaves no room for this peculiarity, as an effect once produced from a particular cause cannot possibly derive its being from other factors. Thus, smoke being first produced from fire cannot subsequently be produced from other causes.'[1]

Moreover, if the organism be the constitutive cause of the primal consciousness alone and not of the derivative conscious states, what necessity is there that subsequent conscious states should not function independently of the organism? Certainly one cannot have a necessity for a thing, which does not benefit it in any way. But the *Cārvāka* may rejoin : 'Well, according to your theory, the principle of consciousness is independent of the physical organism. But why does it not function in isolation from the body, which renders no service to it?' The answer is that consciousness does function independently of the body in the immaterial sphere. The association of the physical organism is not essential either for the being or for the functioning of consciousness. It is an accidental coincidence, due to a perverted desire on the part of a particular subject for such physical embodiment. If, on the other hand, the organism is supposed to condition even the subsequent career of conscious processes, then there should emerge a multiplicity of consciousness-streams, as the constitutive cause of the subsequent cognitions is present intact in the shape of the physical organism.

[1] athā 'pi syāt—yady apy uttara-kālaṁ mano-dhīḥ pūrvapūrvabuddhi-prabhavā bhavati, tathā 'pi yā prathama-kālabhāvinī tasyā dehopādānatvād ato nā 'nāditvasiddhir iti. tad etad asamyak, na hy asyāḥ kalpanāyāḥ kiñcit sādhakaṁ pramāṇam astī 'ti pratipāditam etat. bādhakam api nāstī 'ti cen, na, vidyata eva bādhakam. yadi dehāt sakṛd utpannā satī manodhīḥ paścāt svajātisamudbhavā syāt, tado 'ttarakālaṁ sarvadai 'va pūrvapūrvamanovijñānasamudbhavai 'va syāt, na vijātīya-cakṣurādivijñāna-samudbhavā. na hi dhūmo 'gneḥ sakṛd udbhūya paścād anyato vijātīyād bhavati.

T. S. P., p. 529.

Thus, whatever cognitions may be produced from the organism, each of them will go on producing their replicas without a break and the result will be an infinite variety of consciousness-streams in each living organism, an issue which is directly contradicted by experience.[1] It may be contended that as the organism is only an ancillary condition and not the constitutive cause of successive conscious states, which however derive their being from the primal internal consciousness, the contingency of manifold consciousness-streams does not arise; and this hypothesis moreover gives the key to the fact of consciousness functioning only in relation to a physical organism. But this is an uncalled-for and irrational hypothesis. For if the organism be the substantive cause of consciousness in its inception, there is no reason why it should function at a later stage in the capacity of an ancillary condition, particularly as the organism persists unchanged as before. If this extravagant hypothesis is accepted, the consequence will be the impossibility of affiliating particular effects to particular causes, as the effects will not have their constitution determined by the causes. Furthermore, if the organism is the constitutive cause of primary consciousness, why should it not be so in respect of subsequent cognitions as well ? Assuredly the organism has not undergone any change in its constitution. And if it is constitutionally identical in its earlier and later stages, it will be either the substantive cause as before or an ancillary condition as later on. Nor can it be supposed that the organism functions as a substantive cause even in relation to subsequent cognitions, subject to its association with the previous cognitions helping as contributory factors. Because, the plea of the organism being the substantive cause of consciousness has been proved to be logically absurd. And even if it is conceded, the primal consciousness too will be the product of a

[1] atho 'ttarakālaṁ dehasyā 'py upakāritvam aṅgīkriyate, tadā 'nekavijñānaprabandhaprasavaprasaṅgaḥ....na cai 'vaṁ anubhavo 'sti.

Ibid, p. 530.

previous cognition working as a helping factor. But in that case the foisting of a physical element upon it will have no logical necessity, as the law of homogeneity of cause and effect and the law of the parsimony of causes equally overrule the hypothesis of the physical cause. All these objections, again, will hold good even if the physical elements are held to be momentary. And so has it been said by the venerable doctor (Dignāga?), " If the primal consciouness is produced from the organism, why should subsequent cognitions be determined by their compeers ? Why should the all-powerful organism cease to function? "[1]

So it must be accepted that non-sensuous consciousness is a beginningless process. But if we are to abide by the dictates of logic not only non-sensuous (*manobuddhi*) subjective consciousness, but consciousness as such must be accounted to be a beginningless principle. Well, as for the primal cognition, is it a sensuous cognition or non-sensuous in character ? The former alternative is unacceptable, because there is no sensuous cognition in swoon, deep sleep and the like although the sense-organs are present intact. The reason is that a sense-organ is incompetent to envisage even external reality unless it is backed by an alert attention. So even if the first advent of consciousness in the baby is supposed to be a sensuous cognition produced by the reaction of the sense-organ on the objective world, the independent existence of previous consciousness has to be postulated. If the primal consciousness were the product of sense-activity alone, it would be found to be so for all times, and the service of consciousness functioning in the background of sense-activity, which is invariably found to be the case in all sensuous cognitions,

[1] ata evā 'nityabhūtapakṣe 'py etad ācāryīyaṁ dūṣaṇaṁ sutarāṁ ślişyati. yad āha—"dehāt sakṛd yad utpannā dhīḥ svajātyā niyamyate | parataś cet, sāmarthasya dehasya viratiḥ kutaḥ ||" (The verse has been emended by me from what appeared to be a faulty quotation, both in metre and matter).

Ibid, p. 530.

would be not only useless but unaccountable. There is no such thing as the plurality of causes ; and if an effect, say smoke, could emerge from a variety of causes other than fire, this would amount to denying *totidem verbis* the law of causation and consequential repudiation of inference. So it must be admitted on the analogy of sense-perceptions in our ordinary experience that the first sense-cognition is the resultant of consciousness aiding and informing the sense-activity ; in default, the law of causation will have to be repudiated.[1]

If, on the other hand, the primary consciousness is supposed to be a non-sensuous, subjective experience, unpreceded by conscious life, the result would be equally disastrous. Pure subjective experience (*manobuddhi*), unmediated by sense-functioning, is incompetent to envisage an external reality, which is the only reality of the *Cārvāka* school. If this dictum is not accepted, organic privation will not operate as a bar and the distinction of blind or deaf persons would be reduced to a nullity. And even if the possibility of independent subjective experience is conceded, it requires to be threshed out whether the primal cognition is an indeterminate simple experience or a determinate judgment. It cannot certainly be determinate, because the characteristic of determinate cognition is verbal association, actual or implicit. Determinate cognition is but a judgment, which means the synthesis or relationing of two discrete ideas and we synthesise when we think in terms of language. Whether actual words or concepts are used, the fact remains that relational thought or judgment is possible only after concepts have been

1 tathā hy ādibuddhir bhavantī akṣabuddhir vā bhavet, manobuddhir vā ? na tāvad ādyaḥ pakṣaḥ suptamūrcchā*nya*-(*dya* ?)-cittānāṁ saty api akṣe 'nuguṇamanaskārābhāvād akṣabuddher anutpatteḥ. ato na kevalam indriyam akṣabuddheḥ kāraṇam, api tu manaskāraviśeṣasāpekṣam iti niścīyate, anvaya-vyatirekasamadhigamyatvāt kāryakāraṇabhāvasya. na cā'pi yato yat prathamataram utpadyamānaṁ niścitaṁ tat tato 'nyasmāt *parastāt* udayam āsādayati ahetukatvaprasaṅgāt.

T. S. P., pp. 530-31.

formed and not before. But concepts or general ideas are mere abstractions and are represented by words, *i.e.*, verbal symbols, which have nothing corresponding to them in reality. And the question arises how this verbal association, which is the invariable concomitant of conceptual thought, comes to be accomplished. Is it due to a knowledge of the conventional relation (*saṅketagrahaṇāt*) between a word and an object, or to the fact that a word is an essential attribute of a concept like consciousness, or thirdly, to a cognition of word and object in one sweep ? The first alternative is out of the question, as this being the first cognition, there can be no previous knowledge of the relation in question. The second alternative is equally doomed to condemnation. Because, words are of two distinct kinds, the particular with its unique individuality (*svalakṣaṇarūpa*) and the generic. The first has no expressive power and so its cognition cannot constitute the determinate knowledge. Nor can it be regarded as an essential constituent of a cognition, as it has as distinct an external reference as any other objective fact, say, blue. Otherwise, the blue and the like will have to be regarded as constituent factors of ideas and the result will be that the whole world of experience will be a collection of ideas and not objective facts. Although in the theory of representational perception, which regards our ideas as copies or likenesses of external objects, the blue-content is a part and parcel of ideas, still as our perceptual knowledge has an external reference, the blue-content is not regarded as an essential attribute of our cognition but of the external object, which impinges its form on the cognition somehow. The word in its generic aspect certainly possesses expressive power, but it is not a constituent factor of cognition, but of the particular word-individual which is cognised in auditory perception. Nor can conceptual thought (*vikalpa*) take cognisance of the individual with all its uniqueness, as it is restricted to general ideas. So conceptual thought has to be set down to a previous memory-impression, deposited by a previous perception in the course of a beginningless career of metempsychosis. The third alternative that words and objects are cognised by a single act of perception is absurd on the face of it ; because, words do not hover over objects or form part of the objective reality, as in that case even the uninstructed would have knowledge of the same.[1]

Moreover, conceptual thought is selective in character and takes note of some one aspect to the exclusion of the rest. And what is the *raison d'etre* of this selective tendency ? It is nothing but a particular habit of thinking, as is seen in the case of a particular object giving rise to different ideas in different persons. Thus, for instance, the body of a woman is looked upon by an ascetic as a mass of dead flesh; by a dog as a covetable morsel of food ; by an amorous person as an object of love. So conceptual thought, which is made possible by a long-standing habit of thinking in a peculiar strain, points to a beginningless existence of consciousness, as a definite beginning, even in some distant past, would raise all the difficulties that beset the inception of consciousness in the present life.[2]

We have seen that consciousness in the sense of intellection cannot be regarded as the product of the bodily organism or physical elements for the matter of that. The reason is that all intellectual thought or judgment presupposes the existence of notions or categories of thought, which are acquired from beginningless experience by a conscious subject. The Buddhist philosopher here differs from Kant in regarding these categories of understanding as a legacy of previous experience and not inherent in the constitution of the mind. The Buddhist however has long anticipated Kant in regarding knowledge as a

1 *Vide* T. S. P., pp. 531 (L. 6)—532 (L. I).

2 kiñ cā 'nityādirūpeṇā 'rthasyā 'viśeṣe 'pi na vikalpaḥ sarvān ākārān yugapad vikalpayati, ākārāntaravyavacchedena pratiniyataikākāropagraheṇai 'va vikalpasyotpatteḥ. ataś cai 'kākāravikalpane kāraṇaṁ vaktavyam, na cā 'bhyāsāt tad anyad vaktuṁ śakyam, yathā kuṇapādivikalpānām. tataś ca pūrvābhyāsavaśena vikalpakasya pravṛtter anādir vikalpabuddhir iti siddham.

synthesis of an *a priori* and an *a posteriori* element, but whereas the great German philosopher regards these *a priori* categories of understanding as supplied by the mind from its own inherent constitution, the Buddhist traces them to a previous experience, shifting however to a continually receding past life. The explanation of this fundamental divergence of thought is to be found in the Buddhist belief in a beginningless existence of consciousness. This epistemological doctrine of the Buddhist is very similar to the Platonic theory that all knowledge is reminiscence.

It has become apparent that material data, whether as a constitutive cause or as a conditioning factor, cannot account for intellectual, synthetic thought and for its explanation we have to postulate the existence of the mind prior to and independent of the organism. So the grand alternative that the primal consciousness as the product of the organism is a simple indeterminate cognition will equally tumble down like a house of cards. If the original consciousness is a simple indeterminate cognition, we shall never have that synthetic knowledge, which is knowledge in the real sense of the term. It is determinate knowledge, which is capable of satisfying pragmatic needs. Nor can simple knowledge be converted into a determinate, synthetic knowledge at any later stage of experience, as all our future experience also will be simple and indeterminate from its very constitution. Determinate knowledge presupposes a relationing of the facts of experience, a synthesis of what is immediately given in experience and what is not so given. Nor can memory be of help, as memory too is conceptual in nature, though perceptual in origin. And two particulars cannot give us the general, and all our knowledge of reality is a combination of a general and a particular idea. This combination or synthesis cannot be effected by a simple, indeterminate cognition and for this we have to posit the relationing or synthesising activity of consciousness. But this relationing is not possible between particulars (*svalakṣaṇa*) and this can be made clear by a study of the process as to how the conventional relation of words and meanings, or meanings and objects, is cognised. Now, when we relate the word 'cow' to the object signified, we do not relate it to the individual cow, which was experienced by us for the first time when an elderly man had occasion to speak of it as a cow. But we come to learn this relation on a subsequent occasion, when the word 'cow' is used in another context with reference to another 'cow.' The previous cow is not before the eyes and so the word cannot be affixed to it Nor can it be affixed to the present cow, as in that case the previous cow will not be denoted by it. So before the relation is understood, it is necessary that we have already had a notion of the cow, that is universal and not this or that cow. So if the first consciousness is a direct experience of the individual and not conceptual, the conventional relation of the word with the object cannot be apprehended. Nor can the second experience be of any better help, as it is equally a simple, non-conceptual experience. Thus relational thought presupposes conceptual thought and conceptual thought is not possible if our consciousness consists of pure, simple indeterminate experience. And conceptual thought (*vikalpa*), which is the precondition of pragmatic activity, is possible if there is an independent thinking principle, prior to the first advent of experience, endowed with a synthetic and selective activity. This selective activity, we had occasion to observe before, is possible if there is a previous habit of thinking and this habit points to the pre-existence of consciousness before the physical organism.[1]

[1] athā'vikalpike 'ti pakṣas tadā na kadācid vikalpikā buddhir utpadyate. proktanītyā saṅketavaśād uttarakālam utpadyata iti cen, na ; nirvikalpakajñāne sthitasya puṁsaḥ saṅketasya kartum aśakyatvāt. tathā hi na yāvac chabdasāmānyam arthasāmānyaṁ vā buddhāv avabhāsate na tāvat saṅketaḥ śakyate kartum. na cā 'vikalpe vijñāne sāmānyaṁ pratyavabhāsate, yac ca pratyavabhāsate svalakṣaṇam, na tatra tena vā saṅketaḥ kriyate, vyavahārāthatvāt tasya. na ca saṅketa-kāladṛṣṭasya svalakṣaṇasya vyavahārakāle 'sti sambhava iti na svalakṣaṇe, saṅketakaraṇāt pūrvam vikalpo 'vaśyābhyupagantavyaḥ. sa cā'bhyāsam antareṇa na siddhyatī 'ti siddhā'nāditā. T. S. P., p. 532.

It might be argued though consciousnes may not be regarded as the product of physical elements, it may have its source in the consciousness of the parents. But then, the parental consciousness may be either the material cause or an auxiliary condition of the consciousness of the son. It cannot be the material cause, as in that case the son's chain of consciousness should inherit all the peculiarities of the material cause in question, to wit, the father's learning, culture and the like. And this is seen to be the case in the father's own chain of consciousness; then why not in the son's consciousness also, as the latter is the product of the former in the same sense. It may be contended that the effect does not inherit all the peculiarities of the cause, as for instance, one light is seen to produce another light, but the thickness, richness and intensity of the flame is not the same in both. But the analogy of the light and the flame is not quite apposite. The peculiar intensity or richness of flame, etc., are but unstable attributes of the light and do not always continue. And the substratum of these attributes is none the more stable, as it is seen to become extinct on the consumption of the fuel, wick, oil and the like. But the case is different with consciousness and its attributes. Education, culture, etc., are seen to persist throughout the career of consciousness and consciousness too never becomes defunct, as it is not dependent for its being on any other cause. Moreover, one flame is not the material cause of another flame, as they are distinct and discrete. So the analogy is entirely out of place. Again, in the case of insects that are born of moisture, how can you account for their consciousness as no parent can be found for them. If however parental consciousness is looked upon as a helping condition, we have no quarrel with you.[1]

[1] atha matam—yathai 'kasmāt pradīpād dīpāntarotpattau na pūrvadīpasaṁskāreṇa sthaulyādilakṣaṇena viśiṣṭasye 'ttarasya dīpasya sambhavaḥ, kiṁ tarhi? nissaṁskārasya pradīpamātrasyo 'tpattiḥ......tadvat tadbuddher iti, tan na, yasmāt pradīpādisaṁskāraḥ svāśraye 'pi tāvat santānaṁ nā 'vabadhnāti, asthiratvāt tasya, tathā hi 'ndhanāpacaye tasyai 'va

So primal consciousness must be admitted to have its source in the previous consciousness of its own series on the strength of experience of the career of consciousness in the present life More so as other likely alternatives, to wit, God, space, physical elements and the like have been found to be improbable, and as consciousness has a historically assignable place, it cannot be regarded as an uncaused category. So pre-existence of consciousness is established beyond doubt. And as regards survival of consciousness after physical death, it can be easily inferred from the nature and function of consciousness. We know consciousness has the power to produce another consciousness and thus the continuity is maintained in our present life and as the consciousness-moment at the time of death has the same attachment and passions and desires that characterise the whole career of consciousness in the present life, there is no reason why it should not culminate in another consciousness. Certainly things having self-same nature and function cannot behave capriciously, as caprices of nature are logically unthinkable. The *Cārvāka* cannot still maintain that consciousness is a direct product of the organism, as the causal efficiency of the organism in respect of consciousness has been exposed to be a hollow pretension on the pain of simultaneous emergence of all possible cognitions. It is a matter of positive demonstration how attention aroused produces memory and memory rakes up pleasurable or painful ideas associated with an object of love or hatred, say, a woman, and finally culminate in a strong passion of love or hatred. Moreover, repeated mental exercises or lack of them in the matter of science and arts are seen to be followed by a heightened or lower intellectual efficiency. Furthermore, when

dīpasyā 'sattvaṁ dṛśyate, na tv evaṁ śrutādisaṁskāraḥ, ato na dīpādivan nissaṁskārasya buddhimātrasya sambhavo yuktaḥ......api ca saṁsvedajātīnāṁ mātai 'va nāsti, teṣāṁ katham anyavijñānajā buddhir ity, alaṁ prasaṅgena, atha sahakārikāraṇam iti pakṣas tadā siddhasādhyatā. T.S.P., p. 534.

the mind is engaged with a particular object, the expected cognition of another object though present to the senses does not take place. All these lead to one and only one conclusion, *viz.*, the independent existence of consciousness, as controlling and directing the physical organism as an apparatus. And as all other alternatives fail, we have willy-nilly to accept that consciousness alone is the substantive cause of another consciousness. And the objection that consciousness located in one organism cannot operate as a cause of consciousness in another organism has no substance in it. Because, consciousness being an incorporeal substance cannot be supposed to be located in a physical organism. Certainly consciousness is not a gravitating object so that a locus may be necessary for its being or functioning.

Nor can consciousness and the organism be regarded as identical in substance by the materialist. The idealist, who denies the existence of anything but ideas, can regard the body as identical with consciousness, but this sounds like a paradox in the mouth of a rank materialist. And how can these two distinct phenomena be identical in character, when they are found to differ in every respect. The body is liable to visual perception. But consciousness is exactly the reverse of it. And how can the two be identical, when they are possessed of contradictory attributes ? And if they are identical, the body would be as much fluxional as consciousness, which disappears in the next moment of its birth. The objection that consciousness in one body cannot be the cause of consciousness in another body is based on an obvious misreading of the nature of bodily organisms. The organism is equally momentary and so there is no one organism as the basis of operations of consciousness. There is no difficulty for consciousness to function though the organism differs every moment ; and if difference of organism does not operate as a bar, why should there be any difficulty if another new organism is adjoined to it in the next birth ?

The objection of Kumārila that consciousness cannot exist in an embryonic form, as there is no sense-organ in it, is based on partial observation. Certainly it is sheer foolhardiness to insist that all cognitions are sensuous. What about dream cognitions, which arise independently of sense-organs? And these cognitions are not objective cognitions (*arthagati*) either, which Kumārila holds all cognitions to be. There is no difficulty, therefore, for consciousness persisting even in fainting fits, though sense-organs cease to function that time. We do not believe that consciousness exists in the form of a potential energy in these states; we hold that it exists in its own nature and so the objections based on it do not arise at all. And there is no proof of its non-existence either. How do you know that there is no consciousness in these states? Is it from absence of self-perception? But this awareness of absence of self perception proves the existence of consciousness in these states. It may be contended that had there been any cognition in these states, a person would remember on awakening that he had such cognitions. But as no memory follows, it is proved that there was no consciousness. But this is the result of a hasty generalisation that all cognitions should be followed by memory, which is not the case. Only those cognitions are followed by memory, which possess intensity and which are repeated and have a special interest, and cognitions which lack these conditions pass into oblivion like the cognitions of a new-born baby.[1]

It may be legitimatelv asked if there is any positive evidence of consciousness existing in these states. The answer is that subjective consciousness is independent of external conditions, such as sense-organs and is produced by its own cause, *viz.*, the preceding consciousness. If there be no consciousness in these

[1] *Vide* T. S., Sls. 1923-1927.

cf. yadi hy anubhūta ity etāvānmātreṇai'va smaranaṁ syāt, syād etat, yāvatā saty apy anubhave pāṭavābhyāsārthitvādiva kalyāt smaraṇam na bhavati, yathā sadyojātādyavasthāyām anubhūtasyāpi cittasya.

T. S. P., p. 541.

states, it would mean death, as death is nothing but cessation of consciousness in physical organism. If it is held that consciousness emerges into being after a lapse, then, there would be no such thing as death, as there is no reason why consciousness should not re-appear in a dead body though it might have lapsed for a time. What demarcates these abnormal conditions from death is the presence of consciousness in the former and its total absence in the latter. If there is total absence of consciousness in these states also, there would be no reason to consider them distinct from death.[1]

But since subjective consciousness as distinguished from objective cognitions (*arthagati*) is independent and absolutely unconditioned by external stimuli, the existence of consciousness in the embryonic stage is not barred out. Moreover, it has been proved that conceptual and imaginative thought are absolutely independent of sense-functions and objective reality. If all our thoughts had been determined by sense-experience, we could have had no such ideas as of sky-lotus and the like, which are subjective fictions, pure and simple. And even the reflective thought that arises in the trail of sensuous intuition is purely an activity of subjective consciousness. So subjective consciousness being absolutely independent of physical environment, the death of the physical organism cannot arrest its continuity. The independent existence of consciousness prior to the organism being thus established by irrefragable logic, we do not insist on the reality of the intermediate, astral body. But there is nothing absurd in this supposition, as non-perception constitutes no evidence against its existence, the astral body being *ex hypothesi* composed of subtler stuff.

[1] svapnamūrchādyavasthāsu cittaṁ ca yadi ne 'ṣyate |
mṛtiḥ syāt tatra co 'tpattau maranābhāva eva vā |
svatantrā mānasī buddhiś cakṣurādyanapekṣaṇāt |
svopādānabalenai 'va svapnādāv iva vartate |

T. S., Sls. 1929-30.

The contention that there can be no continuity of consciousness in different organisms is absolutely unsubstantial, as the association of organisms is accidental, so far as the inherent nature of consciousness is concerned. That the consciousness in cow is different from that in the horse is not due to the difference of organisms, but to the intrinsic difference of nature by which one centre of consciousness is demarcated from another. The continuity of previous consciousness in a newly-born organism is proved by the fact that the child evinces peculiar intellectual and moral characteristics which presuppose a long course of training in previous lives. The pre-existence of consciousness is further proved by the fact that the new-born baby at once seeks for the mother's breast to satisfy its hunger This shows that the child is born with memory impressions acquired in previous lives, otherwise how could it know that the mother's breast contained nourishing food for it ? Again, the child begins to cry when its mouth is forcibly removed from the mother's breast and is satisfied when the breast is applied to the mouth. Certainly it could not acquire these experiences in its present life. Even among animals it is found that the monkey-child clings to the mother's person for fear of death from a fall. How could these phenomena be accounted for unless previous knowledge is postulated ? These activities unmistakably testify that the new-born baby has powers of synthetic judgment and this is possible if the mind can independently bring to bear upon sense-experience some basic ideas, the categories of understanding. And how could these ideas be there, unless it is assumed that they were acquired in a past life ? No determinate thought is possible unless the mind does supply from its own fund these fundamental categories. Sense-experience alone is never capable of giving us that determinate knowledge, which is made possible by synthesis, which again presupposes possession of bas c ideas. This synthetic judgment is possible if the mind can think in terms of words and the knowledge of these words could only be acquired in previous lives.

But it may be contended that if this synthetic thought-activity is the result of memory-impressions of verbal associations of conceptual thought acquired in previous lives, then, why does not the new-born baby remember the actual words or express his thoughts in distinct, articulate language like an eloquent speaker ? But as there is no such memory of verbal expressions and as the baby does not give articulate expression to his thoughts, this hypothesis is absolutely an insensate supposition. But this objection is futile, as it is not an unusual phenomenon that there may be previous experience and subsequent loss of memory. In fact memory is a delicate faculty and suffers lapse, if there is a violent shock in the organism. Thus an attack of typhoid is seen to obliterate memory of previous experience. Here too the memory-impressions have passed through a violent shock during the period of confinement in the mother's womb and so have not had the opportunity to reach the stage of maturation, which makes remembrance possible. So the objection of the materialist on the score of loss of memory does not carry weight. The example trotted out by him that all the people coming from the same village remember the past incidents (in the village) contains only a half-truth, as persons having a bad memory fail to recall these incidents. That this is the case is borne out by the fact that persons of extraordinary spiritual powers do exactly remember their past history and distinctly articulate their thoughts as soon as they are born. The reason is that the confinement in the mother's womb could not impair their mental faculties, which have reached the highest degree of development.

Moreover, some people in their very boyhood are seen to evince strong passions of love, hatred, jealousy, pride and others again display a superior intellectual power, a kindly disposition, dispassionate love and friendship and the like. What might be the cause of this intensity of passions and intellectual and emotional refinement ? Certainly it is neither the environment, nor even the objects, that can be supposed to have a bearing on these emotional idiosyncracies, as enlightened souls are not affected with these passions though the objects may be present in their fulness. They are again seen to emerge with a vengeance when people are not in a mood to philosophise on their worthlessness. These passions are seen to arise even when the objects are lost or dead or not even born. Moreover, these objects cannot be supposed to possess all the fine and good attributes that are associated with them. These good or bad qualities are only creations of subjective fancy, but are superposed on them by the persons concerned owing to their own inherent tendencies. If the objects were really good and beautiful as they are supposed to be, they would appeal to the imagination of all with equal force. So these emotions and passions must be regarded to be purely subjective facts, growing in intensity and volume according to the strength of habits of thinking. But as the intensity of these emotional and intellectual faculties cannot be explained by the habits of present life alone, they must be supposed to have been occasioned by habits of previous lives.

It may be urged that if the presence of objects is not the cause of these passions, then how is it that these passions are seen to emerge when the objects are presented to the senses? The reason is that these objects produce pleasurable or painful sensations and these stimulate the latent memory-impressions, which, when roused, culminate in the stimulation of passions of love or hatred in the minds of those, who are given to indulge in such unfounded speculations. This is seen to be the case with persons who are in the grip of ignorance and who are averse to enlightened thinking. But these objects utterly fail to evoke any response from those, whose minds have been purified by a course of ethical and philosophical discipline. If these passions were the effects of these objective facts, they would have produced these results in the minds of the enlightened and the unenlightened alike.

But the *Cārvāka* may rejoin. 'Well, these passions cannot be construed into evidence of previous births, as it is quite likely that these are originated either by direct experience of the behaviour of others or by communication with those having first-hand experience.' But this is no explanation; even animals, which cannot be supposed to profit by such example or communication, are seen to develop these passions in the presence of the opposite sex of their group. Nor can it be supposed that these passions come out spontaneously; had it been the case, such virtues as enlightenment, mercy, moral elevation and the like, which are known to arrest the career of metempsychosis, would also have come out spontaneously. But it is a matter of common experience that these require to be cultivated by a prolonged course of discipline and training before they become part of our nature.

There are some thinkers who maintain that the passion of love is generated by the prevalence of phlegm, hatred by bile and infatuation is the effect of wind. But this is absolutely an unfounded supposition. It is not unfrequently seen that a phlegmatic person has a violent anger and a bilious man has a loving nature. Moreover, the increase or decrease of phlegmatic humour is not found to be accompanied by a corresponding increase or decrease of love. Certainly, the relation of cause and effect cannot be supposed to exist when the variations of one are not concomitant with the variations of another. So this theory must be abandoned. On the contrary, it must be granted that the strength or weakness, intensity or incapacity of these passions and impulses, which exercise so much influence on the moral, intellectual and spiritual progress of the individual, is derived from the previous habits of life and thought acquired in past lives. The present life and environment cannot be conceivably held responsible for all these good and evil tendencies, for which sufficient latitude in time should be allowed. There is no doubt that a good deal of the ills of the present life is due to environmental conditions, to a hostile or indifferent *milieu*, which are remediable by a better adjustment of the state and society, in other words,—by the present *karman* of man in his individual and collective capacity. But there will ever remain an undeniable residuum, a *soupçon* of individuality, in the life of the individual, which cannot be explained in terms of the present circumstances, to which a man is born. The law of *karman*, it may not be out of place here to observe, emphasises this freedom of will and choice, which lies at the basis of all social and political reform. An individual can do or undo, make or mar his fortune and when the doctrine emphasises the inexorable and relentless character of past *karman*, it only does so with a view to encouraging the individual to put forth greater exertion to undo the evil, that is his present heritage. The evils of heredity too are not insurmountable barriers. They are the creations of his own and so can be altered or undone by his own efforts. The materialist fails to give this encouragement to man, as he makes him a plaything of chance, for which there is no room in the philosophy of *karman*, which the Buddhist along with all other Indian systems of thought propounds as the solution of the evil that is found to hold sway in this imperfect world.

It is established, therefore, that the materialist's theory of origination of consciousness from matter, whether organised or unorganised, is absolutely unsatisfactory, as it fails to account for the variety and wealth of the manifestations of consciousness in various spheres of existence. Not to speak of its failure to give ethical and æsthetic satisfaction it is metaphysically untenable as it leaves a large part of our conscious life and experience unexplained and unaccounted for. It seeks to immolate the rationalistic tendencies of our thought-life at the altar of a false God, the all-powerful matter, for a mess of pottage. The better minds of every age and clime have persistently refused to be seduced by the meretricious charms of this harlot of false philosophy and have tried to give us a philosophy, that satisfies to a far greater extent the æsthetic, moral and intellectual demands of humanity—the demands which lie too deep-seated in our nature to be lightly brushed aside. We have not hesitated to give in the present chapter a full exposition of the honest attempts of two Buddhist philosophers who flourished over twelve centuries before, though some of their arguments seem to have been deprived of their logical value by the advanced researches of modern physiology. But the Buddhist philosophers have no doubt succeeded in making out a very strong case against the materialist and this redounds to their glory, all the more as they could not reinforce their metaphysical arguments from the contributions of modern scientific researches.

References.

Tattvasaṅgraha, Śls. 1857-1964.
Do. *Pañjikā*, pp. 519-550.

CHAPTER XVI

Nirvāṇa

Nirvāṇa is the highest goal, the ultimate objective of human aspiration and the *summum bonum* of rational life and was declared by the Lord Buddha in his clarion voice to the suffering denizens of the three worlds (*traidhātuka*) as the panacea to the ills and sufferings of existence, to which all sentient beings from the amœba to the highest god are subject without exception. And this ideal state, in which all suffering and pain are extinguished totally and irrevocably, was declared by the Master to be within the reach of all mortals, provided they elected to pass through the course of discipline which was styled the eightfold path (*aṣṭāṅgikamārga*). Whatever be the differences of views regarding the nature of *Nirvāṇa*, all schools of Buddhism have accepted it to be the most cardinal principle of their religion and philosophy. '*Nirvāṇam śāntam*' (*nirvāṇa* is the only calm) is the corner-stone on which Buddhist philosophy and religion stand and which gives the distinctive character that marks it out from other religious and philosophical disciplines. The persistent refusal of the Master to descant on the metaphysical implication of *Nirvāṇa*, which was rightly regarded by him as a matter of idle speculation without ethical and spiritual value, has, however, become a fruitful source of polemics among his followers and modern scholars too. The schools, into which later Buddhism became divided, hotly debated with one another on this all-important problem and were sharply divided in their opinions as to whether *Nirvāṇa* meant cessation of passions and sufferings only, or of existence altogether. The emphatic denial of an individual soul, the ego-principle, by all sections of Buddhist thought has naturally given support to this negative conception and the result is that Buddhist *Nirvāṇa* is believed by all and sundry as a state of total annihilation of all existence, conscious or non-conscious. The criticisms of Brāhminical writers, notably Śaṅkarācārya and philosophers of the *Nyāya-Vaiśeṣika* school, have confirmed the belief in the negative character of *Nirvāṇa* and the consequence has been that Buddhism and particularly Buddhist *Nirvāṇa* have become a bugbear to scholars and laymen alike. The present writer has set himself the task of conducting a dispassionate enquiry into the various conceptions of *Nirvāṇa* that are found in the later schools of Buddhist philosophers and it is proposed to evaluate some of these theories on strictly philosophical grounds.

Let us examine the conception of *Nirvāṇa* as found in the *Milinda Panha*, a work of considerable antiquity and believed to represent the philosophical doctrines of the school of Elders (*Sthavira-vāda*). There, in answer to the queries of King Milinda, the Venerable Elder, Nāgasena, enumerates the characteristic features of *Nirvāṇa*. Although some of the qualities, which go to show that there is extinction of all pain and impurities, may be susceptible of a negative interpretation, there are some again, which unmistakably prove its positive character. *Nirvāṇa* is said to allay all thirsts and cravings, even the craving after extinction. *Nirvāṇa* is said to be replete with the innumerable and various fine flowers of purity, of knowledge and of emancipation. *Nirvāṇa* like food is the support of life and puts an end to old age and death. As food increases the strength of all being, so does *Nirvāṇa* increase the powers of *ṛddhi* of all beings. As food is the source of beauty, so *Nirvāṇa* is the source of the beauty of holiness. *Nirvāṇa* like space is not born, does neither grow old nor dies, nor passes away, nor has it rebirth. It is unconquerable, is not liable to be purloined, is not attached to anything. It is the sphere in which *arhats* move; nothing can obstruct it; it is infinite. Like the wish-fulfilling tree, it satisfies all desires; it causes delight; it is full of lustre. As clarified butter is beautiful in colour, so is *Nirvāṇa* beautiful in righteousness. Like clarified butter again, it has the pleasant perfume of righteousness and has a pleasant taste.[1]

The catalogue of some of the quali ies of *Nirvāṇa* in the foregoing paragraph unmistakably points to its being a positive existence, characterised as it is by permanence, blissfulness, freedom and purity. So *Nirvāṇa*, as conceived by the Venerable Nāgasena, does not evidently imply an extinction of all conscious life, but on the contrary points to a much too positive existence, nay, the highest life of purity and perfection and bliss. In the *Viśuddhimagga*, Buddhaghoṣa gives us a disquisition on *Nirvāṇa* which, if carefully analysed, will be found to be far from negativistic. *Nirvāṇa* is characterised as the cessation of lust, of hatred and delusion (Saṁ Ni. *Jambukhādaka Sūtta*). Buddhaghoṣa warns us that mere cessation cannot be the nature of *Nirvāṇa*, as in that case the state of arhatship will have to be regarded as a state of cessation. 'But why has it not been expounded in its specific character ? asks the enquirer. 'Because,' the answer goes, 'it is extremely subtle and the Master was not eager to dilate on this profound mystery. It is a state which can be envisaged only by the noble intuition of the saint.' Again, '*Nirvāṇa* is without origination, as it has no antecedent cause.' (Question) 'But how can it be unoriginated, as it clearly emerges on the practice of the *maggo* (the disciplinary course enjoined as the means to attainment of *Nirvāṇa*)' ? (Answer) 'No, it is not produced by contemplation, it is only attained and realised by it. So it is without origin and because without origin, it is not subject to decay and death, and because it is not subject to origin, decay and death, it is eternal (*nicca*). 'It is devoid of form and colour, because its nature is beyond that of coloured form. In reality it cannot be non-existent, as it is realisable by transcendental intuition, born of unremitting and unflagging perseverance and as it is attested by the words of the

1 The Questions of King Milinda, S. B. E., Vol. II, pp. 189-195. *Milinda-Panha*, pp. 318-322.

Omniscient Master, which run as follows :—"There is, ye monks, an unborn (*ajātam*), un-become (*abhutam*), unmade (*akatam*), un-compounded (*asankhatam*). If, ye monks, this unborn, un-become, unmade, un-compounded, were not, an escape from the born, become, made, compounded, would not be discernible. But because, ye monks, there is an unborn, un-become, unmade, uncompounded, therefore an escape from the born, become, made, compounded, is discernible."[1]

From what has gone before, we can legitimately infer that Buddhaghoṣa refuses to believe *Nirvāṇa* to be an absolute ceasing of existence. *Nirvāṇa* is ceasing of suffering, of lust, of hate and of delusion ; but this does not argue that *Nirvāṇa* is absolute extinction of existence also. Dr. Paul Dahlke has however taunted those who think *Nirvāṇa* as a metaphysical reality with the title of believers, as victims to conceptual thinking, which can never envisage the truth face to face. In support of his position he quotes, "If, ye monks, only so much might permit of being attained of a self that would be permanent, lasting, eternal, unchangeable, eternally the same, then a possibility of a life of purity for the ending of all suffering would not be discernible" (San. Ni. III. 144). The unconditioned (*asankhatam*) in the *Udāna* text has been explained by Dr. Dahlke as non-conditioned, as the Ceasing of Lust, of Hate and of Delusion (San. Ni. IV., p. 162). There are of course not a few passages in the *Tripiṭaka* literature, which can bear such negative interpretation that has been proposed by Dr. Dahlke. The following quotation from the *Ratana Sutta*, Verse 14, also lends support to the negative conception of *Nirvāṇa* and indeed this is one of the current interpretations among the present-day Buddhist monks of Ceylon and Burma, as Mr. Yamakami Sogen tells us.

"Khiṇaṁ purāṇaṁ navaṁ natthi sambhavam,
Virattacittā āyatike bhavasmin,

[1] *Visuddhimaggo*, *Udāna* 8. The translation of the *Udāna* is taken from Paul Dahlke's '*Buddhism*,' p. 219.

Te khinabījā avirulhacchandā,
Nibbanti dhirā yathā 'yaṁ padipo."

"The old is destroyed, the new has not arisen Those whose minds are disgusted with a future existence, the wise, who have destroyed their seeds (of existence), and whose desires do not grow, go out like this lamp."[1]

This negative conception of *Nirvāṇa* is not a newfangled theory or a fiction of later scholasticism. It is older than the *Laṅkāvatāra-sūtra*, as was shown by the learned Japanese scholar, Yamakami Sogen. In the third chapter of the *Laṅkāvatāra-sūtra* we find a review of more than twenty different views of *Nirvāṇa*, which are all refuted on the score that *Nirvāṇa* is undefinable. "The first," says Prof. Stcherbatsky, "evidently alludes to the opinion of the Hīnayānists and the last looks like the opinion of the *Yogācāras*." (*Conception of Nirvāṇa*, p. 31, f.n. 2.) Āryadeva is said to have written a commentary on this section, entitled "The Explanation of *Nirvāṇa* by heretical and *Hīnayāna* schools mentioned in the *Laṅkāvatāra-sūtra*." This work has been translated by Prof. Gueseppe Tucci of the University of Rome. Prof. Stcherbatsky is inclined to believe this commentary to be a forgery by some incompetent Pandit (*ibid*). The first view stated coincides with the negative interpretation and is as follows:—

"There are some philosophers, O Mahāmati, who maintain that by the suppression of the *skandhas* (five aggregates), *dhātus* (*sic*, 18 elements of existence), and *āyatanas* (12 bases), consequent on aversion to sense-objects arising from a constant study of the contrariety of things, the mind and mental affections *in toto* cease to function. And as a consequence, cognisance of the past, present and future objects ceases and all intellections are suspended as a matter of course owing to lack of nourishing

[1] See '*Systems of Buddhist Thought*' by Yamakami Sogen, pp. 132-36.

material just as the light, seed and fire cease to function when all aliment thereto is withdrawn. This is their conception of *Nirvāṇa*; but, *Nirvāṇa*, O Mahāmati, is not attained by (such) a view of annihilation."[1]

Again, in his commentary on the first verse of Chapter XXV of the *Mādhyamika-Kārikā*, Candrakīrti quotes the views of a school of philosophers, who believed in two distinct types of *Nirvāṇa*, to wit, (1) *Nirvāṇa* with some residual substratum (*sopadhiśeṣa*), which an *arhat* attains in his life-time ; and secondly, *Nirvāṇa* without any residuum (*nirupadhiśeṣa*). The first type of *Nirvāṇa* is attained when the entire catalogue of *kleśas* (defilements) beginning with nescience, desires and the like has been abandoned, but there remains behind a substratum (*upadhi*), which here stands for the five aggregates (*pañcopādānaskandhāḥ*), which are the foundation of ego-consciousness. Now in the first type of *Nirvāṇa* though the five aggregates persist, the illusion of an abiding personality has vanished for ever. This purified condition of the five aggregates has been compared to a village of robbers, when all the robbers have been executed. In the second kind, even the aggregates are annihilated and hence it is called *Nirvāṇa* without a residue. This final *Nirvāṇa* is comparable to a village, when not only its inhabitants have been totally annihilated, but the village too has been effaced out of existence.

So has it been said,

> " With his body still at life,
> (The saint) enjoys some feeling
> But in *Nirvāṇa* consciousness is gone
> Just as a light (when totally extinct)"
>
> (Prof. Stcherbatsky.)

The final *Nirvāṇa*, without a residue, is thus attained when all the elements of conscious existence become extinct (*tad evaṁ*

[1] *Laṅkāvatāra*, Ch. III.

nirupadhiśeṣam nirvāṇaṁ skandhānāṁ nirodhād labhyate, M. K. V., Ch. XXV).

I am inclined to believe that Śaṅkarācārya had some such school of thinkers in view whom he characterised as nihilists (*vaināśikas*). Prof. Stcherbatsky tells us that they were an early school of the *Sautrāntikas* who were full-fledged *Sautrāntikas* unlike the school of Dignāga which has been named by Prof. Stcherbatsky the school of *Sautrāntika-Yogācāras*. The older and more orthodox *Sautrāntikas* were perhaps an early offshoot of the *Sthaviravāda* school, who had their followers among the early *Sautrāntikas* and the present-day Buddhists of the Southern school. They are certainly not the Sarvāstivādins, whose direct successors were the *Kāśmīra Vāibhāṣikas*, mentioned by Vasubandhu. The *Vaibhāṣika's* conception of *Nirvāṇa* was positivistic; it is absolutely a positive state of existence, from which passions and defilements of empirical, personalised life have been finally and irrevocably purged out and the chances of recrudescence of the miseries of mundane life have been removed beyond recall. It is a state of perfection *par excellence*. Although there is room for difference of opinion as to whether it is a spiritual living condition or an unspiritual, lifeless objective existence, there is absolutely no divergence about its positive character. This will become manifest in the following sections devoted to examination of the *Vaibhāṣika* and the *Sautrāntika* theories of *Nirvāṇa*.

II

The Conception of Nirvāṇa according to the Sarvāstivādins or the Vaibhāṣikas

The *Sarvāstivādins* maintain the existence of three eternal, incomposite categories (*asaṁskṛta dharmas*), which are immutable and as such remain uniform and unmodified through all time. The rest of the seventy-two categories or elements (*dharmas*) into which the objective and the subjective world of reality have been divided by the *Sarvāstivādins*, are composite (*saṃskṛtas*) and as such subject to constant mutation, though all reals are eternal and imperishable in their noumenal and substantial character (*dharmasvabhāva*). It is for this reason that the system is called *Sarvāstivāda* or "the philosophy of all existents." Though all reals are subject to the law of causation (*pratītyasamutpāda*), the causal operation governs the aggregates and compounds, and not the ultimate elements or atoms. The atoms however are never found in their free, uncompounded state, but are always combined in various proportions. These compounds are subject to constant flux and so change every moment anew, though substantially they remain uniform and unaffected. What change are their states or characteristics or attributes. But the incomposite, simple categories, to wit, *ākāśa*, *pratisaṅkhyānirodha* and *apratisaṅkhyānirodha* are eternal verities, absolutely uniform and unalterable. These two *nirodhas* and *ākāśa* are not negative entities, but are absolutely objective existences. The *Sautrāntikas* however regard them as purely negative ideas, mere conceptual forms, having no objective reference. In the *Sautrāntika's* scheme of reality there is no place for an uncaused category and these three eternal verities of the *Vaibhāṣikas* have been regarded by the *Sautrāntikas* as mere intellectual fictions fondly objectified by an irrational imagination. These *Sautrāntikas* have very severely criticised the *Vaibhāṣikas* for their believing these uncaused fictions as existential categories, which is condemned as rank heresy.

In reply to the strictures of Uddyotakara in one place, Kamalaśīla observes, "your statement, that uncaused categories are twofold, *viz.*, eternal and non-existent, only betray ignorance of the opponent's (Buddhist's) position, as the Buddhist rationalists (*sic*, *Sautrāntikas*) hold uncaused categories to be non-existent illusions. Verily has it been said by the Master—" The *Bodhisattva* while reviewing the entire phenomenal world does not find a single phenomenon, which is exempt from the law of causation. As regards the *Vaibhāṣikas* who regard *ākāśa* and the like as objective existences, they are classed by us with the heretical schools and are not the true followers of the Buddha (*Śākyaputrīyāḥ*). So the advancement of their views in this connexion is not consonant with logical procedure."[1] Again in reply to the charge of Kumārila that eternal entities must be believed by the Buddhists to have occasional efficiency, as *pratisaṅkhyānirodha* and the like become objects of knowledge only after a human exertion, albeit they are eternal,—Śāntarakṣita and Kamalaśīla observe that this accusation of Kumārila is abortive so far as the *Sautrāntikas* are concerned. For according to them, these so-called eternal categories are mere intellectual fictions and as such can have no causal efficiency, which belongs to reality alone. And if the *Vaibhāṣikas* are intended, then, too, Kumārila's charge carries no meaning, as the *Vaibhāṣikas* do not regard these *nirodhas* as nullities (*abhāvas*), as Kumārila imagines. "*Pratisaṅkhyānirodha*," Kamalaśīla continues, " is nothing but dissociation (of the principle of consciousness) from the *āsravas* and *kleśas* (passions and impurities), and as this disjunction is effected by transcendental knowledge (*pratisaṅkhyā*) it is called *nirodha* dependent upon *pratisaṅkhā* (*prajñā*) or the

[1] T. S. P., p. 140, ll. 8-12.

highest knowledge of truth. This is a positive entity, as disjunction is a positive quality of the things that were in conjunction before, since it is logically an established proposition that the number of disjoined entities is exactly in ratio to that of the conjoined entities.

"As regards '*apratisaṅkhyānirodha*, it is not the opposite process as Kumārila thinks. It is altogether distinct from dissociation It is nothing but a circumstance, which makes the future emergence of likely effects absolutely impossible to materialise. This state cannot be realised by knowledge ; it can be effected only by an absolute and irrevocable removal of the causes and conditions responsible for the production of the effects in question. And this is what is called *nirodha* not dependent on transcendental knowledge. "But Kumārila," says Kamalaśīla, "only betrays his woeful ignorance of the Buddhist position, which he has the temerity to criticise." [1] We shall see that these two forms of *nirodhas* have their respective parts to play in the evolution of *Nirvāṇa*.

And this *pratisaṅkhyānirodha* or dispersion of *kleśas* (passions and defilements) is the highest stage, the *summum bonum* of life and is synonymous with *Nirvāṇa* according to the *Vaibhāṣikas*. Vasubandhu observes, "The essential characteristic of it is everlastingness. Its description is beyond the power of the tongue of man. It can only be realised by the self-experience of a perfect man. Generally speaking it may be, for all practical purposes, designated as the highest good, eternally existing, which may be called also *visaṁyoga* or deliverance." [2] Both these *nirodhas* are necessarily involved in *Nirvāṇa*. The *pratisaṅkhyānirodha* by the removal of *kleśas* directly unfolds the state of *Nirvāṇa* and the *apratisaṅkhyānirodha* is also necessary to ensure the non-emergence of these *kleśas* by the perpetual removal of the causes and conditions of the same, pre-eminently

1 T. S. P., pp. 730-31.

2 '*Systems of Buddhist Thought*,' p. 165.

of *avidyā* (nescience). So Śaṅkarācārya is absolutely in the right when he includes the cessation of nescience, etc., in the category of the first *nirodha*.[1] But the truth of the matter is that according to the *Vaibhāṣikas* cessation of nescience and *kleśas* does not connote extinction, but mutual dissociation of the mind and passions from one another and this dissociation is called *nirodha* (obstruction or barrier) inasmuch as it serves as the unfailing barrier against any possible association in future.[2] But Śaṅkarācārya from the very beginning has criticised the views of the *Sautrāntikas* and not of the *Vaibhāṣikas*, although he calls the view refuted as those of the *Sarvāstivādins*. Whether and how far again his criticisms of the *Sautrāntika's* position are logically sound, that is entirely a different question and the value and force of such criticism is to be judged from the *Sautrāntika* standpoint. Whether Śaṅkarācārya erred in the matter of naming is not a very important question so far as the philosophical importance of his comments is concerned, if his criticism can be brought home against a particular school of Buddhistic thought. That he did not criticise the *Vaibhāṣika* doctrine is absolutely clear from the fact of his characterising the three eternal categories as absolute non-entities.[3] Be that as it may, we have found that according to the *Vaibhāṣikas* *Nirvāṇa* is an everlasting existence, uncaused and unproductive by itself. It is an absolute and uniform reality, freed from imperfections and impurities of phenomenal life.[4] We

[1] yo 'yaṁ avidyādinirodhaḥ pratisaṅkhyānirodhāntaḥpātī paraparikalpitaḥ, etc. Br. Sū. II. 2-23.

[2] visaṁyuktir visaṁyogaḥ kleśavisaṁyuktilakṣaṇaḥ. saṁyogaprāptiniyatarodhabhūto vā yo dharmaḥ sa pratisaṅkhyānirodhaḥ.

A. K. V., Kā. VI, p. 16.

[3] trayam api cai 'tad avastv abhāvamātraṁ nirupākhyam iti manyante.

Op. cit., II. 2. 22.

[4] nityaḥ khalu pratisaṅkhyānirodhaḥ, tasya kiṁ sabhāgahetunā prayojanam.

A. K. V., p. 17.

again take the liberty of quoting from the work of the learned Japanese scholar :

" One of the Buddhist elders called Sughoṣācārya (quoted in the *Abhidharmamahāvibhāṣāśāstra*) says :—

" *Pratisaṅkhyānirodha* is the *dharma par excellence* among all *dharmas*, the supreme goal among all goals, the highest of all things, the noblest of all reasons, the greatest of all achievements. And therefore is the title *anuttaram* or supreme. But what is the abode of this supreme *dharma*, *Nirvāṇa* or *Pratisaṅkhyānirodha* ? Is it within or outside the universe ? "

The answer is given—" *Pratisaṅkhyānirodha* is neither quite the same as the *skandhas* nor quite different from them, but its nature is different from the *sāsravadharmas*." (P. 116.)

Prof. Stcherbatsky in his illuminating work, *The Conception of Buddhist Nirvāṇa*, observes that this *Nirvāṇa* of the *Vaibhāṣikas* is a lifeless condition of the elements of existence. "When all manifestations are stopped, all forces extinct, remains the lifeless residue. It is impersonal, eternal death, and it is a separate element, a reality, the reality of the elements in their lifeless condition. This reality is very similar to the reality of the *Sāṅkhya's* undifferentiated matter (*Prakṛti*), it is eternal, absolute death." [1] *Nirvāṇa*, though a *vastu*, is not anything living or spiritual. " The moral law conduces through a very long process of evolution the living world into a state of final quiescence, where there is no life, but something lifeless or inanimate. In this sense the *Vaibhāṣika* outlock resembles the the materialism of modern science." [2]

Candrakīrti in his commentary on the *Mādhyamika-kārikā* refers to two schools of philosophers, of whom one regards the final state of *Nirvāṇa* as a positive existence and another thinks

[1] *Op. cit.*, p. 27.
[2] *Ibid*, p. 29.

it to be an absolute annihilation of the elements of existence. Chandrakīrti criticises these two theories with equal severity. Among the advocates of positivistic *Nirvāṇa*, he counts the followers of Jaimini, Kaṇāda, Kapila and lastly the *Vaibhāṣikas*. [1] We know from Vasubandhu's *Abhidharmakoṣa* that *Nirvāṇa*, which is represented by *pratisaṅkhyānirodha* in its positive aspect and *apratisaṅkhyānirodha* as its negative side, albeit a reality preventing the recurrence of the *kleśas* and their logical consequences, is an incomposite, unconditional (*asaṁskṛta*) category (*dharma*), and is eternal and is neither the product nor the cause of any other *dharma*. We have seen that Śāntarakṣita and Kamalaśīla are emphatic that these two *nirodhas* do not imply extinction of anything ; only there is a mutual dissociation of the elements of existence without leaving any chance for a future combination and as this combination is the cause of the miseries of phenomenal existence, the *Nirvāṇa* becomes a state of absolute purity and perfection, without any tinge of pain and suffering. Prof. Stcherbatsky also endorses the above view in the following words :

"At last the absolute stoppage of all the pure *dharmas* of the highest spiritual beings is reached, an eternal blank is substituted for them. This is *Nirvāṇa*, absolute annihilation of all the *saṁskṛtadharmas*, which is tantamount to the presence of *asaṁskṛtadharmas*." [2]

And this conception of *Nirvāṇa* is in full accord with the metaphysical position of the *Vaibhāṣikas*, who maintain that all the seventy-two categories (*dharmas*) have a twofold nature, " the one representing their everlasting nature (*dharmasvabhāva*) and the other their momentary manifestation (*dharmalakṣaṇa*)." We know from Vasubandhu's *Abhidharmakoṣa* and also from the *Tattvasaṁgraha* that these *Vaibhāṣikas* maintained the imperishable nature of all these *dharmas* in their noumenal state

1 *Op. cit.*, Chapter on Nirvāṇa.

2 *The Central Conception of Buddhism*, p. 53.

and the controversy only related to the nature and relation of their momentary manifestations, whether these manifestations in time connoted the change of attributes or of characteristics or of states of efficiency or only relativity." [1] Patañjali and Vyāsa in the *Yogasūtra* and the *Bhāṣya* respectively synthesised all these different theories and regarded these changes as virtually identical in character.[2] The *Sautrāntikas* vehemently opposed this doctrine of the duality of nature, the division of entities into substantial and phenomenal aspects and they scented in it the reminiscence of *Sāṇkhya* and *Jaina* doctrines. However may that be, the imperishable and uniform existence of realities in their noumenal state is an accepted doctrine of the *Vaibhāṣikas*, and so the mind or intellect (*manas*) being one of the elements of existence must be set down as an eternal verity so far as its noumenal aspect is concerned. And as *Nirvāṇa* does not connote annihilation or extinction of being of any of the categories, and as it means that there is only an absolute dissociation and disjunction of the elements from one another, and consequently of all the manifestations of imperfect life, which were due to the association of these elements in the state of *saṁsāra*, the question relevantly arises as to what part the mind-category (*manodhātu*) plays in *Nirvāṇa*. The mind exists, as extinction in the sense of absolute cessation of being, is denied by the *Sarvāstivādins*. But does consciousness exist ? This is the crux of the problem and the determination of the *Vaibhāṣika's Nirvāṇa* as spiritual or unspiritual hinges on the solution of this problem. Prof. Stcherbatsky observes, "It (*Nirvāṇa*) is, nevertheless, a kind of entity where there is no consciousness... .. The theory is that consciousness cannot appear alone without its satellites, the phenomena of feeling, volition, etc." (Ab. K., ii.)[3] An interesting question is raised, 'The last moment of consciousness (of the *arhat*)

[1] T.S., śls. 1786-1856.

[2] *Yogasūtra*, III. 13.

[3] *The Central Conception of Buddhism*, p. 53.

before entering into unqualified *Nirvāṇa* will not then be a *manodhātu*, because it does not emerge into being? No, it exists in the form of *manas*, but there is no emergence of tainted consciousness which could link it to another birth and another phenomenal embodiment. The reason is that there is a total expulsion of the *karman* and passions, with their possible causes and conditions completely removed.' [1] Now, what is this *manodhātu*? Can it be equated with consciousness? The *manodhātu* can be and has been equated with the several *vijñānadhātus* and this *dhātu* is nothing but the locus or receptacle and *manodhātu* being the substrate of different mental phenomena, as, *e.g.*, *saṁjñā* (concepts), *cetanā* (will), *vedanā* (feeling), etc. has been regarded as a separate principle from these. And this is the reason why these mental phenomena have been classified into separate *skandhas*.[2] It is proved that *manas*, is distinct from these mental phenomena, but it does not throw any light on the nature of *manas*, whether it is of the nature of consciousness, pure and simple, the variations being due to the presence of contents or it is like the soul of the *Naiyāyika* something unconscious and inanimate, the consciousness-states being the accidental products due to the co-operation of objective *dharmas* and the subjective sense-organs. The *manodhātu* has been equated with *manovijñānadhātu* and the

[1] caramaṁ cittaṁ na mano bhaviṣyati, na hi tad asti? na, tasyā, 'pi manobhāvenā 'vasthitatvāt, anyakāraṇavaikalyān no 'ttaravijñānasambhūtir iti.

Ab. K., i. 17.

Yaśomitra comments: tasyā 'pi caramacittasya manobhāvenā 'śrayatvenā 'vasthitatvāt, paunarbhavikakarmakleśakāraṇavaikalyān na punarbhavapratisandhivijñānam ity abhiprāyaḥ.

Ab. K. V., p. 41.

[2] cittād arthāntarabhūte saṁjñāvedane, skandhadeśanāyāṁ pṛthagdeśitatvāt,.........athavā svāśrayād arthāntarabhūte sañjñāvedane, tadāśritatvat.

Ibid, p. 70, ll. 16-18

substrata of the five consciousnesses, beginning with visual consciousness (*cakṣurvijñānadhātu*) and ending in tactile consciousness (*kāyavijñānadhātu*). In discoursing on the graduated arrangement of the *skandhas* in respect of their grossness or fineness, it is said that the aggregate of matter (scil.), sense-data (*rūpa*), is first enunciated, because it is the grossest of all, then feeling, then conception, then the mental faculties and tendencies (*saṁskāra*) and lastly *vijñāna*, because it is the finest of all, being "pure consciousness (without content)."[1] If we are justified in taking Yaśomitra literally at his word, we can regard *manas* as of the nature of pure consciousness and if *manas* remains in its absolute purity in *Nirvāṇa*, as the *Vaibhāṣikas* suppose, then the *Nirvāṇa* of the *Vaibhāṣika* may be regarded as essentially spiritual in nature, since the existence of pure consciousness as in the *Sāṅkhya* conception of *Kaivalya* isolated existence of consciousness would not be barred out. If, however, the principle of consciousness (*manodhātu*) is regarded as the substratum of consciousness, which is the plain sense of many texts, and this substratum be something distinct and different from consciousness itself, as it is indisputably declared to be distinct from feelings and conceptions and sensuous knowledge, being present as the locus or substrate of the same, we shall have to conclude with Prof. Stcherbatsky that *Nirvāṇa* according to the *Sarvāstivāda* school is a "materialistic kind of annihilation," though the word 'annihilation' should not be taken literally in the sense of extinction of being, which the *Vaibhāṣika* emphatically denies and which the learned Professor has taken care to emphasise.[2]

Prof. La Vallée Poussin maintains that *Pratisaṅkhyānirodha* or *Nirvāṇa* is a *dravya* (substance) which the *arhat* enjoys in his

[1] vijñānaṁ tu sarvasūkṣmam *upalabdhimātralakṣaṇatvāt*, yathaudārikaṁ ca vineyānām arthapratipādanaṁ nyāyyam.

Ibid, p. 51.

The Central Conception of Buddhism, p. 98.

[2] *Buddhist Nirvāna*, p. 26.

life-time in the highest trance (*saṁjñāvedayitanirodha*) and which remains when the *arhat* passes out of existence after death. The mind does not exist, nor any consciousness in the final *Nirvāṇa*. We must confess our inability to understand how this conception can be fitted into the metaphysical scheme of the *Vaibhāṣikas*, who like the *Sāṅkhyas* deny absolute extinction of any element of existence. Moreover the highest trance of *saṁjñāvedayitanirodha* on which Proof. Poussin bases his conception of *Nirvāṇa*, does not give us warrant to suppose that *manodhātu* becomes extinct in it. As the name indicates, there is only cessation of ideation and feeling. It is quite evident from Yaśomitra's comment that the mind does not cease to exist, though the possibility of future thought-activity is brought to an end.

III

The Conception of Nirvāṇa according to the Sautrāntikas

The *Sautrāntikas* hold bondage (*bandha*) or phenomenal life (*saṁsāra*) to be an absolutely positive fact, being the outcome of causes and conditions, which are, in their turn, absolutely real. *Nirvāṇa* is the final aim and objective and is the only deliverance from the imperfections and limitations of phenomenal existence. In *Nirvāṇa* the pains and miseries of worldly life, the passions and defilements (*kleśas*) that taint the career of unfree souls, are totally and irrevocably extinguished and so *Nirvāṇa* is characterised as the *summum bonum* (*śivam*) and even as bliss, being the negation of suffering. Whether *Nirvāṇa* is to be understood as denotative of a positive existence or a negative void will be determined in the course of our discourse and should not be anticipated at this stage. The *Sautrāntikas* of course are absolutely emphatic in their denial of a personal individuality or soul-principle, permanent and everlasting, which is the accepted doctrine of all Buddhist schools of thought save and except perhaps the *Vātsīputrīyas*, who postulate the existence of a quasi-eternal spiritual substance over and above the discrete conscious states. We have fully elucidated the grounds of their denial of a personal self in the review of the Soul-theories of the various schools of philosophy and there it has been sufficiently proved that the life of consciousness is confined to a moment's existence only. We have also established that bondage and emancipation do not contain any presupposition of an individual, unitive self as cementing the discrete moments of consciousness ; and the continuity of consciousness is due to recurrence of consciousness units in close, unbroken succession, and does not imply the existence of any real continuum. The chain or continuum is but an apparent, ideal continuum, being an illusion generated by the homogeneity of the moments of consciousness. Bondage only connotes the presence of nescience (*avidyā*) in the subjective centre with all its logical outcomes, birth, decay and death. These different stages of phenomenal life are all governed by the law of causality and so if there is *avidyā* at the bottom, decay and death will follow as inevitable consequences at the top. Bondage is, therefore, nothing but the presence of *avidyā* in the chain of consciousness from an undateable, beginningless time and contrariwise *mokṣa* or *nirvāṇa* is the absolute cessation of *avidyā* with all its paraphernalia. Śāntarakṣita in reply to the criticism of Kumārila declares that *mokṣa* (liberation) is nothing but the purified existence of absolute consciousness, freed from all taints of ignorance.[1] According to Śāntarakṣita and Kamalaśīla, therefore, bondage and liberation, *saṁsāra* and *nirvāṇa*, are positive entities, being the distinctive landmarks in the career of consciousness, the former being represented by consciousness in the grip of ignorance and defiling passions and the latter being free consciousness, purged and purified from the contamination of these masterful passions.[2] These two representative authors, though they give their absolute allegiance to the subjective idealism as propounded by Dignāga and Dharmakīrti, have not hesitated to call themselves *Sautrāntikas* in more than one place and they have taken care to specify the doctrines of the *Yogācāra* school when they advanced them as the final truths. Their allegiance to the *Sautrāntika* school is therefore provisional, but it is unqualified and unhesitating so long as they hold to it. In fact the transition from the *Sautrāntika* to the *Yogācāra* position was an easy and natural passage. The reality of the external objective world was but a logical presupposition in the *Sautrāntika's*

[1] kāryakāraṇabhūtāś ca tatrā 'vidyādayo matāḥ ।
bandl as tadvigamād iṣṭo muktir nirmalatā dhiyaḥ ।

T. S., śl. 544.

[2] teṣāṁ cā 'vidyādīnāṁ tattvajñānād vigatau satyāṁ yā nirmalatā dhiyaḥ sā nirmuktir ity ucyate. cittam eva tu saṁsāro rāgādimaladūṣitam । tad eva tair vinirmuktaṁ bhavānta iti kathyate ।

T. S. P., p. 184.

scheme of metaphysics and so the *Sautrāntika* had to postulate the existence of two worlds side by side, an ideal and a real world. The *Yogācāra* or *Vijñānavāda* as propounded by the school of Dignāga, who adopted the *Sautrāntika* position in logic and epistemology by way of compromise or concession, only explained away this logical presupposition and so the two worlds were reduced to one, the objective reality being unceremoniously shoved aside. So it is very difficult to decide at this distance of time whether the view of *Nirvāṇa* as posited in this connexion represents the orthodox *Sautrāntika* position or the position of the idealist, which is accepted as true philosophy by these thinkers. We have it on the authority of Guṇaratna that the *Nirvāṇa* of the *Sautrāntikas* consisted in the absolute cessation of the consciousness-continuum, the total extinction of the stream of consciousness, induced by an unremitting meditation on the principle of soullessness.[1] We have also indications of this theory from the *Tattvasaṁgraha* itself, which we propose to discuss at length in view of their utmost importance in the course of our present dissertation. Prof. Stcherbatsky tells us that the orthodox *Sautrāntikas* held that "*Nirvāṇa* was the absolute end of the manifestations, the end of passions and life without any positive counterpart."[2] But Śāntarakṣita and his worthy disciple tell us in plain and unmistakable language that *Nirvāṇa* is not discontinuation of consciousness, but its continuation save and except the passions and desires (*kleśas*). We propose to defer the discussion of this tangled problem for the time being.

Is avidyā a positive entity?

We have seen that bondage is nothing but consciousness in the grip of *avidyā*, and *mokṣa* or *nirvāṇa* is but the emancipation of consciousness from the hypnotic spell of this *avidyā*. Now,

1 nairātmyabhāvanāto jñānasantānocchedo mokṣa iti.
S. D. S. T. R. D., p. 47.

2 *The Conception of Nirvāṇa*.

what is the nature of this *avidyā* ? According to the monistic Vedāntists *avidyā* is an indescribable stuff, neither absolutely real nor absolutely unreal, but something different from both of them. It cannot be supposed to have a distinct existence outside consciousness, as it works in and through consciousness alone; nor can it be non-distinct from consciousness, as it is destroyed by knowledge, and knowledge is consciousness in essence. So it is an unclassifiable, nondescript something. It is neither an airy nothing nor a real something. It is not an entity as it disappears totally and irrevocably, but it cannot be regarded as an absolute nonentity like the rabbit's horn or sky-flower, as it has causal efficiency. The nature and functional activity of *avidyā* is illustrated by examples of common illusion like the illusion of a snake on a rope. The snake is not a real snake, but so long as the subsequent knowledge sublating the idea of snake does not emerge, it is as real as anything. But when the rope is known to be a rope and not a snake as falsely perceived before, what happens to this snake ? Well, it vanishes as an airy nothing. The snake is an unreal fiction, but though unreal, it is perceived like a reality and this demarcates it from such fictions as a sky-flower or a barren woman's son, which are never perceived even in illusion. But in its essential character the rope-snake is as hollow and unsubstantial as these fictions of the imagination. It is a product of *avidyā*, an illusion born of another *avidyā*, which, though checkmated and chastised in one case or another, reappears in other forms and under other shapes. *Avidyā* possesses an infinite resourcefulness and is neither baffled nor abashed. The only thing that it cannot stand is the light of true knowledge, which kills it outright, root and branch, with all its resources and magical powers.

Kamalaśīla, however, in common with all realists, refuses to subscribe to such an illusive category, which is neither being nor non-being. He asks, 'Is *avidyā* identical with *Brahman* or distinct from it ? If it is non-distinct from it, *Brahman* and *avidyā* will be identical and the consequence will be the impossibility of emancipation (*mokṣa*). Because, the Absolute being eternal and uniform and *avidyā* being an integral part of its essence, the latter will be indissoluble and emancipation as the result of cessation of *avidyā* will be a meaningless jargon. If on the other hand *avidyā* is distinct from Brahman, it will have no influence on the latter. And even if a relation be conceded, it will be of no avail, as *Brahman* being an eternal, uniform principle will not be liable to any supplementation or detraction from that quarter. So the relation of *avidyā* and the Absolute being out of the question, there would be no *saṁsāra* (birth and death), for whose cessation emancipation would be sought after.

Moreover, it is positively illogical to say that *avidyā* is something which is neither distinct nor non-distinct from the Absolute. A reality must be capable of being defined either as identical or as non-identical with another. There can be no half-way house between two contradictories, as this would constitute a flagrant breach of the Law of Contradiction and the Law of Excluded Middle. Nor can *avidyā* be conceived to be an unreal nonentity, since that would contradict experience. An unreal fiction cannot have any causal efficiency, and causal efficiency alone is the line of demarcation between reality and unreality. If, in spite of this causal efficiency, the Vedāntist insists on calling it an unreality, we Buddhists, shall have no quarrel with him, as the dispute is reduced to a question of nomenclature.

The Buddhist Conception of Avidyā.

Avidyā is, in the judgment of the Buddhist, a positive entity and not a fictitious category as conceived by the Vedāntist It is the inherent tendencies of the mind, the subconscious impulses and drives (*vāsanās*), which make the mind cling to false ideas and notions. And these tendencies and subconscious drives have a causal energy and as vehicles of energy they are an essential part and parcel of consciousness. So in conformity with the law of causal operation the preceding moments of consciousness as informed with *avidyā* produce by their inherent causal energy the succeeding moments of consciousness instinct with false tendencies and impressions, it being an established proposition that the effect inherits the nature of the cause. It is nothing strange, therefore, that the mind should conjure up false ideas as those of an abiding ego-principle, God and the like. But this *avidyā* can be rendered weaker and weaker in each succeeding moment by a graduated course of meditation (*yogābhyāsa*) until the last vestige of the bias of ignorance and superstition is totally removed and a stream of consciousness is let loose, absolutely purified and cleansed of all taints of passions and ignorance. And the emergence of such a pure stream of consciousness is but emancipation (*apavarga*), the highest good, the ultimate goal of aspiring humanity, in which there is no suffering, no limitation, no imperfection, as the sole cause of it has been destroyed once for all without leaving any chance for its recrudescence even at a distant date.[1]

Nirvāṇa, we have seen, is primarily and principally a cessation of the *kleśas*, headed by ignorance and consequential impurities. Now, what is the process, the *modus operandi* of this cessation of the formative principles of phenomenal life, in other words, of the cycle of births and deaths? What is the antidote to these ills of life, (*sic*) of ignorance and passions, which are the mainspring of the perverse will to live ? Śāntarakṣita assures us that these *kleśas* (passions and ignorance), these veils of truth, totally vanish as soon as the truth of non-egoity is realised just as darkness vanishes in the presence of strong light.[2] Now, there are two kinds of veils or positive hindrances to moral and spiritual perfection, to wit, (1) the veil of ignorance and passions (*kleśāvaraṇa*), which impedes the realisation of purity and truth ;

[1] T. S. P., pp. 74-75.

[2] pratyakṣīkṛtanairātmye na doṣo labhate sthitim |
tatviruddhatayā dīpre pradīpe timiraṁ yathā | T. S., śl. 3338.

and (2) the veil covering the ontological reality (*jñeyāvaraṇa*), which again is twofold, *viz.*, one which hinders the thorough-going discerning knowledge of reality as to what is worthy of acceptance and what is worthy of rejection and secondly, what induces the incapacity for exposition of the realised truth to others. The first kind of veil (*sic* of passions) can be got rid of by a realisation of the illusory character of the ego-principle (*nairātmyadarśana*) and the other can be overcome by an unremitting and zealous meditation on this non-egoity carried on for a prolonged period of time. But why should this realisation of non-egoity have such extraordinary efficiency in the matter of removal of passions and imperfections ? Is it a mere dogma or a well-reasoned psychological truth ? For an adequate explanation of this proposition it is necessary to enter into the psychological origin of these passions and cravings for individualised existence, which are held responsible for the miseries of metempsychosis. Now, these passions of love or hatred and the like have certainly their foundation in the perverted belief in the existence of a personal soul, which, however, has been proved to be a baseless illusion. These passions of surety have nothing to do with external objects, as these feelings do not arise in spite of the external world when the belief in a personalised existence is lacking and on the other hand they crop up with a vengeance though the external objects of love or hatred may be absent, when the belief in the masterful ego is in possession of the field. So by the joint method of Agreement and Difference these passions must be causally affiliated to the unfounded belief in the existence of a personal self.[1] It is a matter of logical deduction that in the absence of egocentric bias self-love cannot

[1] tathā hy amī rāgādayaḥ kleśā vitathātmadarśanamūlakā anvayavyatirekābhyāṁ niścitāḥ, na bāhyārthabalabhāvinaḥ, yataḥ saty api bāhye 'rthe nā 'yonisaumanaskāram antareṇo 'tpadyante, vinā 'pi cā 'rthenā 'yonisauvikalpasammukhībhāve samutpadyante, na ca yatsadasattānuvidhāyi yan. na bhavati tat tatkāraṇaṁ yuktam atiprasaṅgāt. T. S. P., p. 870.

arise and attachment to external objects too cannot originate if they were not affiliated to the self as conducive to self-interest and self-gratification. Likewise hatred too will have no *raison d'etre*, as a man comes to resent things or persons that are supposed to thwart his interests, but when a man has no reason to be interested in anything, obstruction of interests becomes unmeaning. The same fate awaits other passions, because they have their roots remotely or immediately in self-love. Thus, ego-consciousness firmly established by repeated illusions from beginningless time extends to external objects, which come to be prized as promoting self-gratification and any obstruction to these objects naturally excites his resentment and hatred. And the whole catalogue of passions comes into being, and as time wears on, they acquire a fresh lease of life and a fresh accession of strength by the sheer right of prescription and the result is all-round confusion and misery.

Now, these evils are not natural growths or attributes of living creatures ; they are exotic growths and excrescences fostered by self-love and so are bound to vanish if egoity is demolished. And this egoity is an ungrounded illusion. The subjectivity of an individual has been shown by us to have no foundation outside the concatenation of momentary psychical units, which are individualized into an abiding self by a false superstition. It may be urged, ' let there be no soul or real individuality, but consciousness is a fact and these passions may be natural attendants of this consciousness, as they live and move and have their being in it. And so they may be ineradicable like consciousness itself. ' But this contention is not based on a logical assessment of the character of these passions. Well, what is the normal function of consciousness ? It is assuredly nothing but to apprehend reality as it is, otherwise the relation of subject and object, knower and known (*viṣayaviṣayibhāva*) cannot be established. And if our intellectual life is not to be condemned as bankrupt, it must be admitted that the normal function of consciousness is to apprehend the reality in its true nature and the true nature of things, both subjective and objective, has been proved to be in a state of perpetual flux without any underlying substratum either in the shape of an abiding self or a permanents ubstance. So consciousness must be supposed to take stock of the principle of non-egoity and non-egoity alone in its normal healthy state. The fact that consciousness gives us the report of an ego-principle must be set down to adventitious defects, which are abnormal accidents like the illusory perception of a snake on the rope.[1] This gives the key to the secret as to why ego-idea goes to the wall in its contest with the idea of non-egoity, though antagonism is the common factor. The reason is that ego-consciousness is a false superstition fostered by abnormal conditions, which are, happily, aventitious phenomena and non-egoity, on the other hand, is based upon truth and so is natural to our thinking principle. It is for this reason that non-egoity invariably triumphs over egoism, because truth is constitutionally stronger than falsehood. With regard to the idealists even, who do not believe in external reality and consequently deny that the normal function of consciousness is to apprehend external reality in its true nature, our explanation also stands. Though these idealists deny external reality and believe the contents of knowledge to be manifestations of consciousness, still they have to acknowledge that consciousness is self-regarding (*sic* self-conscious), otherwise there will be no discrimination and consequently no knowledge. The knowledge of 'blue' and the knowledge of 'red,' though equally manifestations of consciousness, are certainly distinct and distinguishable

[1] tasmād bhūtaviṣayākāragrāhitā 'sya svabhāvo nija iti sthitam. bhūtaś ca svabhāvo viṣayasya kṣāṇikānātmādirūpa iti pratipāditam etat ; tena nairātmyagrahaṇasvabhāvam eve 'ti tan nā 'tmagra' ṇasvabhāvam. yat punar anyathāsvabhāvo 'sya khyātimūḍhānāṁ sa sāmarthyād āgantukapratyayabalād eva.........na svabhāvatvena, yathā rajjvāṁ sarpapratyayasya.

T. S. P., p. 873.

and they can be distinguished, if consciousness can know itself in its manifestations. Consciousness has, therefore, to be admitted as self-regarding (*sic*) as self-intuitive and if knowledge *per se* is not to be condemned as something essentially rotten, it must be accepted that the normal function of consciousness is to know non-egoity in the form of pure consciousness bereft of subject-object distinctions, which is the ultimate reality. So ego-consciousness being an unfounded illusion, the whole catalogue of passions, major and minor alike, must be supposed to be exotic overgrowths and not natural to consciousness. Their extinction is, therefore, inevitable only if the proper antidote in the shape of realisation of non-egoity is applied. That these passions do actually grow and have their being in consciousness is no argument that they are natural and inevitable to consciousness. Mere appearance in some substratum does not argue that it is either natural or inevitable to it. The snake also appears on the rope but it is not believed to be natural. If subsequent disappearance is the reason of its falsity, the same logic applies to these passions, which are experienced to disappear when non-egoity is contemplated.[1]

It may be urged that the antagonism of egoity and non-egoity is not an established truth and is only a dogmatic assumption. Because, it is a matter of experience that even philosophers who are convinced of the truth of non-egoity are as much subject to fits of love and anger as ordinary mortals are and this points to the other way—that conviction of non-egoism is not hostile to the existence or active functioning of these passions. But this objection is only a specious argument. The conviction of non-egoity, which is claimed by us, Buddhists, to be antagonistic to egoism and its derivative passions, admits of varying degrees and grades of perfection. Thus, (1) one comes to believe in the truth of non-egoity from the

[1] *Ibid*, p. 873.

teaching of an expert. The belief is inspired by the teacher's lecture and the truth is accepted more on trust than on conviction (*śrutamayajñāna*). (2) The second stage is reached when a person convinces himself of the truth by logical arguments and this is called intellectual conviction (*cintāmaya*). (3) But when by incessant, energetic meditation on the truth intellectually realised, the mind acquires requisite strength and clarity of vision and ultimately envisages the truth face to face, in all its fullness and richness, all doubts are dissolved and the man is said to have realised the truth of non-egoity. This is intuition born of contemplation (*bhāvanāmayadarśana*). And it is this transcendental intuition of non-egoity that is regarded by us as the antidote to egoity and its satellites, passions of love and hatred and the like. So there is no logical flaw in our position.[1]

So it is only when the profound truth of non-egoity is fully realised by reason of a course of unmitigated and unremitting mediation, the ego-consciousness with all its satellites vanishes into airy nothing without leaving behind any trace or vestige. The ego-consciousness, though an illusion in essence, has however been fostered by a habit of thought, which has no beginning in time, and as a consequence has become almost an integral part of the thought-principle by sheer length of time. It is not at all strange, therefore, that it cannot be uprooted all on a sudden by the mere lecture of a professor. These passions can be made weaker and weaker by a gradual strengthening and fostering of the opposite modes of thought and thus by a long-standing cultivation of spiritual regeneration they can be destroyed root and branch. The neophyte in spiritual discipline has reason to be encouraged by the fact that these passions, exotic growths that they are, cannot raise their head when the mind philosophises on their unreality and worthlessness.[2] So

1 *Ibid*, p. 875.
2 *Ibid.*

there is not the slightest room for doubt or hesitation that realisation of non-egoity will remove these evils of life *in toto* and ultimately land us in the realm of *Nirvāṇa*, the *summum bonum* of life, where there is not the slightest tinge of suffering and impurity.[1]

The realisation of non-egoity, we have seen, is the only way to *Nirvāṇa*. In fact, non-egoity is one of the fundamental truths, nay, the central plank of Buddhist religion and philosophy. But the crux of the problem lies not so much in the way to *Nirvāṇa*, the theoretical and practical discipline enjoined as preparation for reaching the goal, as it is in the conception of *Nirvāṇa* itself. To state the problem in plain words : Is the *Nirvāṇa* of the *Sautrāntika* a positive state or a negative void ? Is there consciousness in *Nirvāṇa* or is it a pure voidity with no consciousness in it ? We have already quoted Kamalalśīla and Śāntarakṣita speaking of *Nirvāṇa* as a pure stream of consciousness with all taint of *avidyā* purged out. In another place Śāntarakṣita states, "This doctrine, that there is no self, will terrify the ignorant heretic. But it was preached to his disciples by the Lord with a view to their ultimate good." Kamalaśīla in this connexion quotes an ancient verse in support of the text which is as follows : "The ego does not exist, nor will it ever come to exist ; likewise nothing pertaining to the self exists or will ever come into existence. This (idea) is a veritable terror to the soft intellect, but it dissolves the fears of the wise."[2] But these texts are not explicit. It is clear that there is annihilation of individualized consciousness in *Nirvāṇa*, and it is quite possible that impersonal consciousness may remain

1 advitīyaṁ śivadvāraṁ kudṛṣṭīnāṁ bhayaṅkaram ।
vineyebhyo hitāyo 'ktaṁ nairātyaṁ tena tu sphuṭam ॥
T. S., Śl. 3322.

śivam iti nirvāṇam ucyate. T. S. P., p. 866.

2 'nāsty ahaṁ na bhaviṣyāmi na me 'sti na bhaviṣyati । iti bālasya santrāsaḥ paṇḍitānāṁ bhayakṣayaḥ'. ॥
T. S., śl. 3322, quoted thereunder.

and this has been plainly stated in more than one place.[1] It is also stated that contemplation of non-egoity destroys *avidyā* and not consciousness *per se*. These passages only indicate that ego-consciousness is a delusion and there is no ego-principle as is supposed in the heretical schools. They only prove that the extinction of ego-consciousness is the ultimate objective and this is realised in *Nirvāṇa*. But there is no indication that extinction of consciousness as such is the desideratum. In another place, Śāntarakṣita tells us that 'true knowledge is knowledge of pure consciousness alone, completely disentangled from the accidental impurities. It has been proved that consciousness *per se* is devoid of subject-object relations and is free from two sorts of delusions and this is the truth that has been promulgated by the Enlightened ones.''[2] All this proves that pure, impersonal consciousness in the abstract is the ultimate reality and *Nirvāṇa* is nothing but the realisation of this truth alone.

But does the above conception of *Nirvāṇa* represent the *Sautrāntika* point of view? A doubt is roused when Kamalaśīla tells us that this doctrine of impersonal consciousness has been established in the chapter on 'Examination of external reality,' where the position of Buddhist idealism (*vijñānavāda*) has been expounded. If this explanation of Kamalaśīla be supposed to imply that the doctrine in question is the property of Buddhist idealists, we have to revise our estimate of the *Sautrāntika* conception of *Nirvāṇa*. Śāntarakṣita and Kamalaśīla are seen to admit the possibility of extinction of consciousness in *Nirvāṇa* as an accepted doctrine of the *Śrāvakayāna* and this perhaps is the orthodox *Sautrāntika* conception. Guṇaratna expressly

1 cittam eva hi saṁsāro rāgādikleśavāsitam | tad eva tair vinirmuktaṁ bhavānta iti kathyate ||

T. S. P., p. 184.

2 etad eva hi taj jñānaṁ yad viśuddhātmadarśanam | āgantukamalāpetacittamātratvavedanāt || avedyavedakārā buddhiḥ pūrvaṃ prasādhitā | dvayopaplavaśūnyā ca sā sambuddhaiḥ prakāśitā ||

T. S., śls. 3535-36.

tells us that in the *Sautrāntika's* conception *Nirvāṇa* consists in the annihilation of the stream of consciousness. The Brāhminical writers have attacked this doctrine of annihilation in severe terms and Śaṅkarācārya, who criticises the *Sautrāntika* position in his *Śārīrakabhāṣya*, has nicknamed these Buddhists as nihilists (*vaināśikas*). That a class of Buddhist philosophers, presumably the *Sautrāntikas*, held the view that in *Nirvāṇa* the consciousness-continuum becomes totally defunct owing to lack of passions and desires, is evidenced from the *Tattvasaṅgraha* and the *Pañjikā* also. And this fact was taken advantage of by the materialist when he claimed total extinction of consciousness after physical death on the analogy of the final consciousness of the Saint.[1] Śāntarakṣita does not challenge the authenticity of the example cited by the materialist. He only makes a reservation in the case of the *Bodhisattva* who does not enter into final *Nirvāṇa* by surrendering the conscious life but on the contrary sedulously preserves his subjectivity to render succour to the suffering world. But this view was held by the Mahāyānic philosophers and was not accepted by the *Śrāvakas*. Śāntarakṣita admits the possibility of extinction of consciousness in the case of *Śrāvakas*, who have no such incentive to maintain their individuality as the *Bodhisattva* has. Śāntarakṣita, we are tempted to believe, only seeks to reach a compromise with the *Mahāyānists* and to glorify his philosophy by maintaining the ideal of Bodhisattva-hood. Whether one can defer the opportunity of entering into *Nirvāṇa* or not to be of service to the suffering creatures, this doctrine does not possess any metaphysical value so long as the possibility of absolute annihilation is kept open. And Śāntarakṣita maintains this possibility. In reply to the charge of the materialist, he only says that the consciousness-moment at death is certainly capable of producing another consciousness as its effect (quite as much the preceding

[1] sarāgamaraṇaṁ cittaṁ na cittāntarasandhikṛt । maraṇajñānabhāvena vītakleśasya tad yathā ॥

T. S., śl. 1863.

moments of consciousness), since it is not purged of attachment, unlike the purified consciousness of the *arhat*. Kamalaśila removes all doubt in the matter, when he says that the argument is conclusive as the emergence of another consciousness, is due to this fact alone (*sic* the presence of passions and impurities in the life of consciousness).[1] This conception of *Nirvāṇa* is absolutely identical with what is found in the *Ratanasutta* and the *Laṅkāvatāra* quoted above. The *Sautrāntika's* conception of *Nirvāṇa* therefore has nothing to distinguish it from that of the *Theravāda*, as both these schools regard *Nirvāṇa* not as annihilation of passions and impurities alone, but of consciousness also. *Nirvāṇa* is a blank and a void. Uddyotakara and Śaṅkarācārya have criticised this conception of *Nirvāṇa* and Jayanta has ridiculed it.

The conception of *Nirvāṇa* as extinction of all existence, conscious or unconscious, has received sledge-hammer blows at the hands of Nāgārjuna, who has broken off the theory into smithereens by his sharp dialectic. The whole *Sautrāntika* philosophy is pivoted upon the law of *Pratītyasamutpāda* (causality, or to be literal, dependent or relative origination) and Nāgārjuna and Śaṅkara and the later Vedāntist dialecticians have thoroughly exposed the hollowness of causality as a metaphysical reality. But, the dialectics of Nāgārjuna and Śaṅkara apart, the theory of *Nirvāṇa* as extinction of all elements of conscious existence stands self-condemned even from the standpoint of the *Sautrāntika* himself. (1) An entitative continuum can cease to exist only if there is an antagonist present to operate against it. Of course, there is no interaction possible between momentary existents and what happens, when two antagonists, say, heat and cold, are brought together, is this : An entity

[1] maraṇakṣaṇavijñānaṁ svopādeyodayakṣamam । rāgiṇo 'hīnasaṅgatvāt pūrvavijñānavat tathā || *ibid*, śl. 1899. 'nā py 'anaikāntikam etāvanmātrahetukatvāc cittāntarotpādasya.'

T. S. P. under above.

deteriorates in its causal efficiency in the presence of another entity and so with progressive loss of causal energy carried to the extreme one of the two entitative series becomes totally extinct.[1] Whatever might be the real nature of oppositional relation, the fact is undeniable that the presence of another entity, supposed to be hostile, is indispensable if there is to be a cessation of an entitative series (*santānoccheda*). Now, there is no such hostile element present, which can occasion the diminution of causal energy in pure consciousness attained by the realisation of non-egoity and consequently there is absolutely no reason for a break in the continuity of consciousness. (2) In the second place, we ask, why should there be any attempt, even if it is possible at all, to get rid of this ideal state of impersonal consciousness ? To use Kamalaśīla's own language, there is absolutely no cause for worry or uneasiness or any sense of limitation in impersonal consciousness, which is admitted on all hands to be an ideal state, free from all suffering and pain and impurity. There is an incentive for transcending the limitations of personalised existence, because it is liable to be associated with pain and impurities. But no such incentive can be supposed to operate against the ideal state of perfection, which pure impersonal consciousness connotes.[2] (3) The admission of the possibility of total extinction undermines the very foundation on which the philosophy of *Nirvāṇa* stands. *Nirvāṇa* is possible of attainment simply because nescience, ego-consciousness and passions are eradicable by a course of moral and spiritual discipline (*sic*), the contemplation of non-egoity, as set forth before. And the reason why non-egoity triumphs over egoity is said to consist in the fact that non-egoity is in the

[1] See *ante*, pp. 51-52.

[2] na ca nairātmyadarśanasya kadācid duṣṭatā, sarvopadravarahitatvena guṇavattvāt............ tan nā 'sya hānāya yatno yuktaḥ, api tu yadi bhaved aparihāṇāyi 'va bhavet, buddheḥ prakṛtyā guṇapakṣapātāt.

T. S. P., p. 874.

constitution of consciousness and egoity is a false accretion, an exotic overgrowth. But the proposition, that consciousness becomes defunct in *Nirvāṇa* because there is no attachment and the like in the purified stream of consciousness, takes for granted that passion is an integral part of consciousness, if not identical with it. And if these passions are integral factors of consciousness, there is no reason why they should be eradicated and if eradication is possible, they should pass into extinction along with non egoity and consciousness itself. But this means that non-egoity and egoity are not antagonistic, and can live in happy concord. At any rate egoity cannot be weaker than non-egoity ; on the contrary the palm of superiority should be given to the former as the continuity of consciousness is entirely dependent upon the continuity of ego-consciousness and its satellites. But this will mean that *Nirvāṇa* is an impossible ideal, a mere catchword and a hoax. The *Sautrāntika* cannot look on with equanimity on this possibility, because the repudiation of *Nirvāṇa* is tantamount to repudiation of Buddhism and its philosophy and ethics. (4) This doctrine of absolute annihilation of the continuum runs counter to the entire *Sautrāntika* metaphysics. As has been aptly observed by Śaṅkarācārya "there cannot be cessation of a continuum, because the members of the series stand in an unbroken relation of cause and effect, and the continuity cannot be interrupted." Vācaspati Miśra explains Śaṅkara's text as follows :—"A number of momentary existents standing in the relation of cause and effect, one emerging as the other disappears, is what constitutes a continuum or series (*santāna*). Now, as for the last moment in the series, whose cessation would entail the cessation of the whole continuum, does this last moment produce any effect or not ? If it does not produce an effect, it will no doubt be the last member, but in that case it will not be a reality, as the reality of a thing consists in its causal efficiency alone. And the unreality of the last moment will retrogressively entail the unreality of all the members of the series, as the cause of an unreal cannot be anything but unreal in itself."[1] If, however, the emergence of a dissimilar series in its place is construed as the cessation of the previous series, as in the case of pot and potsherds, then, too, there is no absolute discontinuity of existence, as another series only takes its place and though there is supersession of one series, the continuity of existence is not suspended. So absolute extinction of consciousness-continuum, leaving no legacy behind in the shape of either a homogeneous or a heterogeneous series, is an impossibility even in the *Sautrāntika's* own system of thought. The cessation of ignorance and its attendant evils is possible because contemplation of non-egoity exercises a hostile influence over it and because pure consciousness follows and takes its place. But on the absolute annihilation of consciousness-continuum there is nothing to succeed and to take its place—a conception, of which there is no warrant, neither logic nor precedent. The theory of *Nirvāṇa* as an absolute extinction of existence is, therefore, not only indefensible in the light of Nāgārjuna's and Śaṅkara's dialectic, which holds that a thing existing on its own account cannot be destroyed and a thing which depends on another for its existence is not real, but it contradicts the central conception of *Sautrāntika* metaphysics, to wit, the conception of causal efficiency as determinant and constitutive of reality. If, however, the *Sautrāntika's Nirvāṇa* is supposed to be an emergence of

[1] sarveṣv api santāneṣu santāninām avicchinnahetuphalabhāvena santānavicchedasyā 'sambhavāt. S. B., Br. Sū. II. 2.22. *Vide* the *Bhāmatī* thereunder.

Also, santater anutpādo 'pavarga iti cet, na, tasyā 'śakyatvāt, santater anutpādo na śakyate kartum, kāryakāraṇabhāvapravāhasya santatibhāvāt.

N.V., p. 77.

nā 'pi santānanivṛttiḥ śakyā kartum antyakṣaṇānupapatteḥ. sa hy antyakṣaṇaḥ kiñcid ārabhate na vā, ārambhe nā 'ntya iti na kāryakāraṇapravāhanivṛttiḥ, pravāhaś ca santāna iti na santānanivṛttiḥ. anārambhe tasyā 'sāmarthyenā 'sattvāt tataḥ pūrve sarva eva kṣaṇā asantaḥ syur iti kasyo 'ccheda iti bhāvaḥ. Tāt. ṭī, p. 242.

pure, impersonal, abstract consciousness, a view which Śāntarakṣita adopts in some places and which has been spoken of as an alternative view by Jayanta, Śrīdhara, and Mādhavācārya,[1] and if the cessation of conscious life in *Nirvāṇa* is construed to be the abandonment of individualised existence or explained away as the opinion of the old *Śrāvakayāna*, then the conception of *Nirvāṇa* (however objectionable it might be from the standpoint of absolutism) of the *Sautrāntikas* will be a logically consistent doctrine in consonance with the fundamental tenets and principles of the school. Otherwise it stands self-condemned and self-contradicted.

[1] (*a*) nirvāṇādipadākhyeyam apavargaṁ tu saugatāḥ । santatyucchedam icchanti svacchāṁ vā jñānasantatim ॥ N. M., p. 512.

(*b*) 'tadubhayanirodhas tadanantaraṁ vimalajñānodayo vā muktiḥ.'

S. D. S., p. 42.

(*c*) nanu bhoḥ ka eṣa mahodayo nāma? savāsanasamucchedo jñānoparama ity eke............nikhilavāsanocchede vigataviṣayākāropaplavaviśuddhajñānodayo mahodaya ity apare.

N. K., p. 3.

PART II

LOGIC AND EPISTEMOLOGY

CHAPTER XVII

PERCEPTION IN DIGNĀGA'S SCHOOL OF PHILOSOPHY

Dharmakīrti in his *Nyāyabindu*, a representative work on Buddhist Logic and Epistemology, has divided all true knowledge into two broad classes, *viz.*, (1) perception and (2) inference. All human activities depend for their success in the last analysis on true and authentic knowledge and Dharmottara, the author of an authoritative commentary on the *Nyāyabindu*, defines this true knowledge in his commentary as knowledge which is capable of verification, or in his own words, which does not disagree with the objective reality represented in it. Correspondence of knowledge with reality is regarded as the test and warrant of its validity and this correspondence is attested when knowledge leads to the actual attainment of the object by creating a volitional urge for the object presented. So the purpose of knowledge is served when it reveals an objective reality in its true character ; and the actual attainment of the object, which takes place by reason of a chain of psychical facts, beginning with desire and volitional urge and ending in actual physical endeavour, is only a bye-product. This intermediate link between knowledge and attainment has only a psychological importance and though they have an important bearing on the problem of truth, the logical value of these intermediate psychical states is only mediate and derivative. Dharmottara explicitly asserts that the function of an accredited instrument of knowledge (*pramāṇa*) is completed when the object is apprehended. The volitional urge and the attainment follow as necessary consequences. It follows, therefore, that an instrument of knowledge fulfils itself by making known an object which is not cognised before. A cognition, which reveals an object which has been known before, is redundant and so is not an independent *pramāṇa*.[1]

Dignāga omitted to put *pratyakṣa* under the rubric of "Valid knowledge" (*samyagjñāna*) as Dharmakīrti has done and Uddyotakara has made capital out of this apparent omission.[2] There is, however, no room for honest doubt that Dignāga proposed to give a definition of *pratyakṣa* as a species of valid knowledge and could not mean anything else. Śāntarakṣita also did not care to supply the word *jñāna* (cognition) in his definition of *pratyakṣa* and Kamalaśīla observes that the word *jñāna* has not been read in the definition as the negation of *kalpanā* (ideal or conceptual constructions) perforce indicates that it must be knowledge, which is alone liable to be associated with conceptual elements.[3] This appears to be a trifling matter and is stated here only with a view to drawing the attention of the readers to the trivial and frivolous character of some of the criticisms of the Brāhmanical writers. Most of these criticisms are misleading as evidence of Buddhist doctrines and unless they are corroborated by the original writings of Buddhist authors themselves, the only course of action for an honest student of Buddhist

1 avisaṁvādakaṁ jñānaṁ samyagjñānam...: ata eva cā' rthādhigatir eva pramāṇaphalam. adhigate cā' rthe pravarttitaḥ puruṣaḥ prāpitaś cā' rthaḥ. tathā ca saty 'ārthādhigamāt samāptaḥ pramāṇavyāpāraḥ, ata evā 'nadhigataviṣayaṁ. yenai 'va hi jñānena prathamam adhigato 'rthas tenai 'va pravartitaḥ puruṣaḥ prāpitaś cā 'rthaḥ. tatrai vā 'rthe kim anyena jñānenā 'dhikaṁ kāryam. tato 'dhigataviṣayam apramāṇam.

N. B. T., p. 3.

The meaning of *pramāṇa* and *pramā* will be made clear later on.

2 "atha svarūpato na vyapadeśyaṁ ity eṣa kalpanāpoḍhaśabdārthaḥ? sarve 'rthās tarhi pratyakṣāḥ prāpnuvanti. N. V., p. 42.

Cf. na hi yathā samyagjñānam adhikṛtya pratyakṣādilakṣaṇaṁ kṛtaṁ Kīrtinā na tathā Dignāgena, yenā 'dhikārāj jñāne vyavatiṣtheta kalpanāpoḍha iti bhāvaḥ. Tāt. Ṭī., p. 154.

3 kalpanāpratiṣedhāc ca jñānasya sāmarthyalabdhatvāt, avatsā dhenur ānīyatām iti yathā vatsapratiṣedhena godhenoḥ, ity ato jñānaṁ noktam.

T. S. P., p. 367.

philosophy will be to hold his judgment in suspension. There has been a good deal of conscious or unconscious misrepresentation and suppression of facts and *suggestio falsi* and this should be regarded as sufficient warning against placing implicit reliance on the evidentiary value of such testimony.[1]

Dignāga's definition of Pratyakṣa

Pratyakṣa has been defined by Dignāga as "*pratyakṣam kalpanāpoḍhām,*" which in simple English can be rendered as "perception is (a cognition) which is free from conceptual constructions." This single adjective has been deemed sufficient to exclude inference, which is invariably associated with ideal constructions (*kalpanā*). It is also competent to exclude errors and illusions (*bhrama*) from the category of perception, as errors and illusions are never in harmony with facts though they may be free from ideal elements. Perception, however, being a species of authentic knowledge presupposes as a necessary condition this harmony of fact with knowledge and as illusions do not admit of verification, which is the only test of this harmony, there is no possibility of confusing them with valid knowledge, much less with perception which is only a subdivision of the same. So we see that the definition of *pratyakṣa,* as propounded by Dignāga, is self-contained and self-sufficient.

[1] It must be observed here that there are a good many Brāhminical writers who possessed first-hand knowledge of Buddhist philosophical works and who have tried to criticise the Buddhist position on fair grounds. Barring a few inaccuracies here and there, the account of Buddhist doctrines, as given by Kumārila, Vācaspati Miśra and Jayanta Bhaṭṭa in their works, appears to be a faithful representation of the Buddhist position and so will continue to attract the attention of students of Buddhist philosophy, particularly so when the original works of Buddhist writers have been lost for the most part.

Dharmakīrti's definition of Pratyakṣa

Dharmakīrti, however, has added another element, namely, *abhrānta* (non-erroneous) to Dignāga's definition with a view to excluding errors from the category of perception. This additional qualification, however, is redundant as we have seen that Dignāga's definition is competent to exclude such contingencies. This addition, however, has been a source of confusion and has led to polemic among the commentators. We have it on the authority of Śāntarakṣita that there were some thinkers who regarded illusions as purely mental facts, having nothing to do with sense-perception; and so these thinkers objected to the inclusion of the adjective 'non-erroneous' (*abhrānta*) in the definition of *pratyakṣa,* as uncalled for. But Śāntarakṣita has stoutly opposed this view on the ground that as illusions occur on the operation of particular sense-organs and cease when this operation ceases, they should be regarded as sensuous aberrations and not pure mental errors. They arise only when there is a defect in sense-organs concerned, and if organic defect is not held to be responsible, these errors would disappear in spite of this defect, if the person is logically persuaded of his error. But however much a man might be satisfied by reasoning, his illusory perception does not disappear so long as the organic defect is not removed. A jaundiced person, though persuaded of the error, does not cease to see things yellow until the jaundice is cured. But mental illusions, such as belief in the existence of supernatural beings or of universals (*bhāvasāmānya*) as objective categories, however obstinate and confirmed by habits, are seen to disappear when the deluded person is properly schooled in philosophic thinking. But the mirage or the double moon will not cease to be presented unless the physical defect is removed. Moreover, the vivid presentation of false objects in illusions cannot be accounted for unless they are regarded as sensuous presentations. Śāntarakṣita, therefore, concludes that illusions being perceptual knowledge and being free from ideal constructions could come within the category of perception, unless the saving clause is added to Dignāga's definition.[1]

Vinītadeva, an older commentator on the *Nyāyabindu*, however, gave a different interpretation of the expression '*abhrānta*.' He interpreted '*abhrānta*' as meaning 'not lacking correspondence with reality' (*avisaṁvādaka*). But this alone would be wide enough to include inference as the latter too does not lack this correspondence. So the other clause "free from ideal constructions" is added for the exclusion of inference, which is invariably attended with ideal elements. "*Abhrānta* should not be construed," says Vinītadeva, "as meaning a cognition which is contrary to and so erroneous in respect of the object. This interpretation of the word '*abhrānta*' would make the definition absolutely futile as all knowledge, let alone perception, is erroneous with regard to its object according to the *Yogācāras* (Buddhist subjective idealists) and accordingly this definition has been so worded as to meet their position also." This interpretation of Vinītadeva has been strongly animadverted upon by Dharmottara. Dharmottara observes that this interpretation of the word '*abhrānta*' as "not lacking correspondence with reality" is itself futile, as from the context which treats of 'true and authentic knowledge' and of perception as a sub-species of the same, we have it that perception must not be incongruent with fact, because authentic knowledge connotes this very congruence and not anything else. So Vinītadeva's interpretation would make the definition tautologous, as

[1] etac ca lakṣaṇadvayaṁ vipratipattinirākaraṇārtham, na tv anumāna-nivṛttyartham. yataḥ kalpanāpoḍhagrahaṇenai 'vā 'numānam nivarttitam. tatrā 'saty abhrāntagrahaṇe gacchadvṛkṣadarśanādi pratyakṣaṁ kalpanā-poḍhatvāt syāt. tato hi pravṛttena vṛksamātram avāpyata iti saṁvādak-atvāt samyagjñānam......tannivṛttyartham abhrāntagrahaṇam, tad dhi bhrāntatvān na pratyakṣam.

N.B.T., p. 9.

the definition in relation to the context would read as follows:

"The cognition which is not incongruent and is free from ideation (*kalpanā*) is not incongruent." But this reiteration of 'not incongruent' does not answer any purpose. So the word '*abhrānta*' should be taken to mean that which is not contrary to the real object presented in it. But what about the position of the idealist? The definition so interpreted will not meet their purpose. The author of the sub-commentary assures us that there is absolutely no difficulty as the definition has been propounded from the *Sautrāntika's* position and not from the idealistic standpoint, though the former is not the orthodox position of the master (*ācārya*).[1]

Is the adjective 'abhrānta' absolutely necessary even from the Sautrāntika standpoint?

If we look deeper into the meaning of the definition, we shall see that the adjective '*abhrānta*' is not necessary. Perception being a species of valid knowledge must be free from discrepancy with fact and this is adequate to exclude 'errors,' as errors are invariably discrepant with reality. The adjective '*abhrānta*' is, therefore, useless whether it is taken in the sense of 'non-discrepant' (*avisaṁvādaka*) as Vinītadeva suggests, or

[1] etac ca lakṣaṇadvayam ityādinā......Vinītadevavyākhyā......dūṣitā. tena tv evam vyākhyātam. "abhrāntam iti yad visaṁvādi na bhavati, evaṁ saty anumānasyā 'py etal lakṣaṇaṁ prāpnotī 'ti kalpanāpoḍhagrahaṇaṁ tannivṛttyartham- yady evam vyakhyāyate, ālambane yan na bhrāntaṁ tad abhrāntam ity ucyamāne sarvaṁ pratyakṣaṁ jñānam ālambane bhrāntam iti na kasyacit pratyakṣatvaṁ syāt. tathā cā 'ha, 'sarvam ālambane bhrāntaṁ muktvā tathāgatajñānam' iti Yogācāramate, tad apy atrā 'cāryeṇa saṁgṛhītam" iti. tad ayuktam.................................. nanū 'ktam Yogācāramatam asaṁgṛhītaṁ syād iti, ucyate. bāhyanayena Sautrāntikamatānusāreṇā 'cāryeṇa lakṣaṇaṁ kṛtam ity adoṣaḥ.
N.B.T.T., pp. 18-19.

in the sense of 'non-erroneous' as proposed by Dharmottara. The idealistic position has been severely left alone and the *Sautrāntika* standpoint can be fully met even without this qualification. The question pertinently arises—what led Dharmakīrti to propose this amendment? We have the answer from Dharmottara's commentary and its confirmation from the *Tattvasaṅgraha*. Dharmottara observes that the twofold qualification is introduced in the definition to combat a prevailing misconception and not for the exclusion of inference, as for this the adjective "free from ideal constructions" is sufficient. If the second epithet was not added, such experiences as of moving trees and the like could be regarded as true perception, as these are free from ideation and capable of satisfying the pragmatic test. But these experiences are absolutely false and so cannot be included in the category of valid perception.[1] Śāntarakṣita and Kamalaśīla too observe that there were certain thinkers among the Buddhists themselves who held even these abnormal experiences to be valid knowledge inasmuch as they satisfied the pragmatic test. But both Śāntarakṣita and Dharmottara rightly point out that what constitutes validity is not pragmatic fitness alone, but that plus harmony of presentation with reality. So such presentations as that of the light of jewel for the jewel itself, or of yellow conch-shell for a really white conch-shell, or of moving trees for trees which are really fixed and stationary are not valid perceptions, though there is actual verification. Mere verification and pragmatic satisfaction cannot however be accepted as the test of

[1] pītaśaṅkhādibuddhīnāṁ vibhrame 'pi pramāṇatām |
arthakriyāvisaṁvādād apare sampracakṣate ||
tan nā 'dhyavasitākārapratirūpo na vidyate |
tatrā 'py arthakriyāvātpir anyathā 'tiprasajyate ||

T. S., ślś 1324-25.

kecit tu svayūtthyā evā 'bhrāntagrahaṇaṁ ne 'cchanti. bhrāntasyā 'pi pītaśaṅkhajñānasya pratyakṣatvāt............pramāṇaṁ cā 'visaṁvāditvāt. ata evā 'cārya Dignāgena lakṣaṇe na kṛtam abhrāntagrahaṇam.

T. S. P., thereunder.

* *

validity ; but verification of presentation with reality is the criterion. What is presented is the light of the jewel or the white conch and what is actually attained is not the yellow conch or the light of the jewel, but something different. In the mirage, too, what is presented is the refracted light of the sun and the determinate experience is of water. In the case of the jewel's light which is mistaken for the jewel itself, the presented datum is the light, though the experience is of the jewel. Here of course there is correspondence of experience with reality. But the test of truth is not correspondence of experience with reality either, but of presentation (*pratibhāsa*) with experience (*adhyavasāya*) and of presentation with reality. And this correspondence is lacking in the case of the jewel's light. The pragmatic utility and partial congruence of such experience, which have given rise to this misapprehension of its validity, are due to previous experience of the white conch, the memory-imposition of which makes this false experience possible. There were some thinkers, who held that discrepancy in respect of colour was immaterial, as the idea of contrary colour was an imposition of the imagination due to memory-association and as there was congruence in respect of the shape and configuration, these experiences should be allowed as valid. But this view is open to grave objection, as no shape or configuration is detachable from its colour and so these should be regarded as identical.[1] Disagreement, therefore, in respect of colour is tantamount to disagreement of the entire presentation with reality.[2]

It has become perfectly clear that Dignāga's definition of perception is complete and sufficient by itself. The addition of the adjective '*abhrānta*' has no logical necessity or justification, as the *sine qua non* of valid experience is agreement with reality in all respects and as experiences of yellow conch-shell and the

[1] This distinction of colour and form and the premium put upon the latter remind us of Locke's familiar distinction of Primary and Secondary qualities.

[2] T. S., śls. 1325, 1327.

like do lack this all-round correspondence, they are excluded *eo ipso* from the category of valid perception. But the misapprehension prevailed in certain quarters and Dharmakīrti felt it imperative to clear this misconception. It is fully evident from the testimony of Dharmottara and of Śāntarakṣita that the introduction of this objective 'unerring' (*abhrānta*) was not made by way of improvement, but was dictated by a practical necessity to rebut a prevailing misconception among a section of Buddhist philosophers, which, perhaps on account of its volume and strength, called for this amendment.

Section B

Kalpanā—What is its meaning?

Dharmakīrti defines *kalpanā* as a cognition, the content (*pratibhāsa*) of which is competent to be associated with verbal expressions.[1] This association takes place when the content and the verbal expression are cognised in one sweep, so the two are felt to be one inseparable whole.[2] The word 'competent' (*yogya*) is advisedly put in to include even the conceptual cognitions of children, who have not yet learnt the use of language, but whose knowledge has reached the state of judgment and so would have been actually associated with articulate words. Even the knowledge of the baby born on the very day is not free from ideation, as the baby, too, recognises the mother's breast and ceases crying when its mouth is applied to it. This recognition presupposes an act of relationing a present sense-datum with a past experience and this recognition of identity has all the competence for verbal association, which is invariably the mode of relational thought in adult psychology. The actual employment of words is, at best, symptomatic of conceptual thought and does not constitute its essential character. The criterion of conceptual thought is found in the indefinite, blurred presentation of the content (*aniyatapratibhāsatvāt*) and this indefiniteness is due to the absence of sense-datum, which alone is the cause of a definite invariable presentation. But as the objective datum in question is not present before the eyes and the conceptual

1 abhilāpasaṁsargayogyapratibhāsapratītiḥ kalpanā.

N. B. Ch., 1.

2 abhilāpena saṁsarga ekasmin jñāne 'bhidheyākāra yā 'bhidhānākāreṇa saha grāhyākāratayā śīlanam.

N. B. T., p. 10.

thought arises independently of this objective reality, the presentation of the content lacks the distinct richness and vividness of direct perceptual cognition. Conceptual knowledge (*vikalpa*) has a past and a future reference and identifies the past and the present datum of experience and so is authentic being based upon and determined by a living fact. Conceptual thought or experience mixed with conceptual thought is independent of a live fact and so is unauthenticated and unreliable as evidence of objective reality.[1] The unreliability of conceptual and relational thought will be made fully clear in a later section and for the present we propose to examine Dignāga's definition of *kalpanā* and to see whether it differs from Dharmakīrti's definition or not.

Dignāga in his *Nyāyamukha*, a work on Buddhist logic,[2] has on the other hand defined *kalpanā* as the association of

1 katham punar etad vikalpo 'rthān no 'tpadyata iti? arthasannidhinirapekṣatvāt. bālo 'pi hi yāvad dṛśyamānaṁ stanaṁ sa evā 'yam iti pūrvadṛṣṭatvena na pratyavamṛṣati tāvan no 'paratarudito mukham āropayati stane. pūrvadṛṣṭaparadṛṣṭaṁ cā 'rtham ekīkurvad vijñānam asannihitaviṣayaṁ, pūrvadṛṣṭasyā 'sannihitatvāt, asannihitaṁ cā 'rthanirapekṣam, anapekṣaṁ ca pratibhāsaniyamahetor abhāvād aniyatapratibhāsam. tādṛśaṁ cā 'bhilāpasaṁsargayogyam. indriyavijñānaṁ tu sannihitamātragrāhitvāt arthasāpekṣam. arthasya ca pratibhāsaniyamahetutvān niyatapratibhāsam.

N. B. T., p. 11.

2 The *Nyāyamukha* is a work on logic composed by Dignāga. It has been referred to by Śāntarakṣita and a passage has been quoted from it by Kamalaśīla expressly and other passages seem also to have been quoted though the name of the author or of the book is not mentioned. The *Nyāyamukha* is lost in Sanskrit but is preserved in a Chinese translation. It is really a matter of gratification that Prof. G. Tucci, Ph D., of the University of Rome, has translated the Chinese version into English. The whole world of Buddhist scholars will be grateful to the learned Professor for having made this important work of Dignāga accessible in one of the most widely known modern languages of Europe.

Vide T. S. and the *Pañjikā*, śls. 1224, 1228, 1237.

class-character (*jāti*), quality (*guṇa*), of action (*kriyā*), of substance (*dravya*) and of name (*saṁjñā*). Critics have found in this definition of Dignāga an inexcusable flaw, inasmuch as class-character and the rest are all imaginary constructions and not objective existences and so cannot be associated with a real object, since association is possible only between two real substances like milk and water. And even these realists, as for instance Kumārila, who believe in the reality of class-character and the rest, have got to admit that *kalpanā* is possible only through verbal association. It is therefore logically economic to hold *kalpanā* to be a verbal association actual or potential. Dignāga, therefore, lays himself open to the charge of looseness of expression or confusion of thought or perhaps both by resorting to this tortuous formulation. Śāntarakṣita has taken elaborate pains to save the master from this unenviable position by resorting to familiar scholastic devices, which the elasticity of Sanskrit idiom easily lends itself to. It will serve no useful purpose to elucidate these textual manipulations and it will suffice to say that Śāntarakṣita with all the aids of scholasticism in his armoury had to admit at last that verbal association alone is sufficient to characterise *kalpanā* and the association of class-character and the like has been mentioned only out of regard for others' views which have found wide currency.[1]

Kalpanā—why shyuld it be unreliable ?

The next question arises as to why should verbal association be tabooed from the category of authentic knowledge ? Verbal expressions are necessary for relational thought and unless relations are wholesale condemned as false appearance, use of words cannot be placed under an indiscriminate ban, as suggested

[1] *Vide* T. S., śls. 1219-38.
parāparaprasiddhe 'yam kalpanā dvividhā matā I *Ibid*, śl. 1221.
satyaṁ lokānuvṛttye 'dam uktaṁ nyāyavide'dṛśam I
iyān eva hi śabde'smin vyavahārapathaṁ gataḥ II *Ibid*, śl. 1228.

by the *Sautrāntikas*. The *Sautrāntika* replies that relational thought, which, of necessity, is carried on by the use of words, cannot be a true measure of reality, since an entity is unique and unrelated (*svalakṣaṇa*), being entirely cut off from the rest of the world of similar as well as dissimilar things. What, however, is perceived in direct experience is this unique, self-characterised real, which has nothing in common with others. All reals are momentary point-instances, absolutely independent of each other and they only emerge into being under the inexorable law of *pratītyasamutpāda* (causality) and exercise a causal efficiency, which is peculiarly individualistic. Relations, therefore, are only ideal constructions (*vikalpas*) and have nothing corresponding to them in the objec ive world. These constructions are purely subjective and independent of both sense-data and sense-organs. It cannot be urged that as this relational thought arises in the train of sense-object contact, it should be valid as much as non-conceptual and non-relational (*nirvikalpa*) cognition. Because, this sequence is purely accidental and is not contingent on sense-object contact, as relational thought is seen to arise even in the absence of such contact. And even in the event of sense-object contact there can be no relational thought, unless and until words expressive of the objects perceived are actually or implicitly associated with the latter. If sense-object contact had competency for the generation of relational thought, it could not fail to do so even in the first instance. There is no reason why an intermediary, *viz.*, the remembrance of word-relations, should be in request for the purpose. And even if the sense-object contact is seen to persist, the determinate, relational knowledge cannot be set down to its credit, as the act of remembrance, which is a non-sensuous and purely psychical fact, would detach the resultant experience from the objective reality.[1]

1 arthopayoge'pi punaḥ smārtaṁ śabdānuyojanam ।
akṣadhīr yady apekṣeta so 'rtho vyavahito bhavet ॥
N. M., p. 92.

It has been urged that the recalling of the conventional relation of word and object is only an auxiliary factor, which merely reinforces the sense-faculty and, therefore, does not obstruct its operation. The relational knowledge is, therefore, purely a case of sense-perception as the sense object contact does not cease to function. If the sense-faculty was inoperative, we could have relational knowledge even if we did shut up our eyes just after the primal contact. But as this is not the case, there is no logic in regarding conceptual experience as untrue.[1] There are varieties of conceptual knowledge and all are not invalid. Conceptual knowledge, which arises as the result of sense-object contact should be regarded as the true perceptual experience and this is endorsed by popular behaviour.[2] But this contention is illogical. The idea of assistant and assistable is only intelligible if there is any actual supplementation from reciprocal services ; but this supplementation, even if conceded. gives rise to logical complications, which are insurmountable.[3] Moreover, a relational knowledge, as for instance, of the staff-bearing-man (*dāṇḍī'ti vijñānam*) is a complex, made up of varying factors and this cannot be the result of primal sense-object contact, but on the contrary presupposes a considerable number of psychical operations. Thus, in the case cited above the complex knowledge arises only after the adjectival factor (the staff), the substantive element (the person), the relation (*e.g.*, the conjunction, *saṁyoga*) and the conventional mode of usage have been perceived severally and jointly and not otherwise.[4] But it is too much to expect all

1 yadi tvā 'locya saṁmīlaya netre kaścid vikalpayet |
na syāt pratyakṣatā tasya sambandhānanusārataḥ |
S. V., p., 174, śl. 128.

2 evaṁ samāne 'pi vikalpamārge | yatrā 'kṣasambandhaphalānusāraḥ |
pratyakṣatā tasya, tathā ca loke vinā 'py ado lakṣaṇataḥ prasiddhaḥ ||
S. V., p., 207, śl. 254.

3 See *ante*, Ch. I.

4 viśeṣaṇaṁ viśeṣyaṁ ca sambandhaṁ laukikīṁ sthitim | gṛhītvā sakalaṁ cai'tat tathā pratyeti nānyathā || N. M. p., 93. The *laukikī sthiti* (the conventional mode of usage) is also a determining factor, by virtue of

this of the first indeterminate experience engendered by sense-object contact.

As regards the distinction of one class of conceptual knowledge from another class, *viz.*, of imaginary constructions, which are independent of objective reality, from relational knowledge, which is supposed to be contingent on an objective sense-datum and is substantiated by verification, it must be observed that the distinction is not based on reality at all. All conceptual knowledge, which moves through the machinery of word-associations, is devoid of objective basis without exception. The logical value of such knowledge is, therefore, really nil. The objective reference and relative vividness of the conceptual thought arising in the trail of sense-experience is due to the preceding non-conceptual cognition, which is generated by an objective reality. The verification and pragmatic satisfaction offered by such knowledge is therefore mediate and derivative and cannot be claimed as a matter of right. The contention of Kumārila and Jayantabhaṭṭa—that verbal association is the condition of perception of class-character as much as the sense-faculty, light, attention and so forth are the conditions of perception of colour, etc., and so remembrance of verbal convention cannot be regarded as a barrier between sense-function and the object is an untenable sophistry. Well, the object is a single entity and, being amenable to perception, is cognised in its entirety by the first sense-perception. There cannot possibly be any part or aspect that may be left uncognised by the original experience.[1] The assertion of the *Naiyāyika* that class-character

which 'the staff' is cognised as an adjectival adjunct to the 'man,' though the relation is the same and the order could be reversed but for this.

[1] ekasyā 'rthasvabhāvasya pratyakṣasya sataḥ svayam | ko'nyo na dṛṣṭo bhāgaḥ syād yaḥ pramāṇaiḥ parīkṣyate || yat tu keṣāñcid vikalpānām idantāgrāhitvaspaṣṭatvādi rūpam tad arthāvinābhāv nirvikalpakadarśanapṛṣṭhabhāvitvāvāptatacchāyāsaṁsargajanitam na tu teṣām arthasparśaḥ kaścid asti, arthātmano nyatātmano nirvikalpenai 'va mudritatvāt.

N. M., P. 93;

and the like are also cognised by the first indeterminate perception is only a dogmatic statement, unsupported by experience and logic alike.

The proposition that the content of determinate knowledge is determined by that of indeterminate perception is an unwarranted supposition, which takes for granted that all our knowledge is derived from sense-data and the mind is only a passive register with no contributions of its own.[1] But this supposition is contradicted by logic, as class-character and the like, which are thought to be cognised in perception, are fictions of the imagination. The relation of class-character with the individual object cannot be either one of identity or of difference. If the two are different and distinct, there is no reason why they should be found together and that for all time. Nor can they be identical, as they are possessed of contradictory characters. The class character or the genus is, therefore, a subjective idea and has no existence outside the subject's consciousness.[2]

All conceptual knowledge refers to false, ideal constructions, having nothing whatever to do with reality. These ideal constructions are fivefold, to wit (1) genus, (2) quality, (3) action, (4) name and (5) substance. These are regarded as ideal constructions, as they proceed on the assumption of difference

1 nirvikalpānusāreṇa savikalpakasambhavāt |
grāhyaṁ tadānuguṇyena nirvakalpasaya manmahe ||
N. M., p. 98.

yad eva savikalpena tad evā 'nena gṛhyate |
iha śabdānusandhānamātram abhyadhikaṁ param |
viṣaye na tu bhedo 'sti savikalpāvikalpayoḥ ||
Ibid, p. 99.

2 tattvānyatvobhayātmānaḥ santi jātyādayo na ca |
yad vikalpakavijñānaṁ pratyakṣatvaṁ prayāsyati ||
T. S., śl. 1304.

also,
vyaktayo 'nā nuyanty anyad anuyāyi na bhāsate |
jñānād avyatiriktañ ca katham arthāntaraṁ vrajet ||
Quoted in the *Pañj.*, *op. cit.*

where there is identity and of identity, where there is difference. Thus, (1) the genus or class-character (*Jāti*) is not anything distinct from the individual, but it is fancied to be distinct. (2 and 3) The same is the case with quality and action, which are really non-distinct from the substratum, but they are imagined to be distinct and hence are called 'false constructions.' (4) Name and the individual, on the other hand, are actually distinct and different, one being a word and the other being a substantive object. But the two are regarded as identical, as is evidenced by such expressions as 'he is Caitra,' 'Caitra' being a mere name. The identification is so complete that a man invariably responds when his name is called out. (5) The last variety is illustrated by such verbal usage as 'He is a staff-bearer' (*daṇḍy ayam*). Here the staff and the man are distinct as poles apart, but there is identification of the two.

Jayantabhaṭṭa, however, takes exception to these forms of understanding being regarded as false constructions on the ground that the relation of identity or of difference actually obtains between the objective facts concerned. But the distinction of class-character and the like has been proved to be false by the dialectic of relations. Now, as regards his contention that name and the individual are never confounded as identical, as the usage is not of the form 'he is the name Caitra' but 'he is Caitra,' it must be said that this is only a cavil and blinks the fact that 'Caitra' is a name none the less. His next objection is that there is no perversion in the usage 'He is a staff-bearer,' as stuff-bearer means the man and not the staff, which is cognised to be distinct as it actually is. But this, too, has no force against the Buddhist, as the Buddhist does not admit any relation outside of the terms. There is no point in the argument that the relation of the staff is predicated and not the staff itself, as the relation and the relatum are not different. Moreover, language does not always conform to the experience of man and to make a contention on the basis of linguistic usage is not psychologically correct. Thus, for instance, it is an allowable expression to say 'The boy is fire' (*agnir māṇavakaḥ*). But our perceptual experience does not conform to the import of language. We do not perceive the boy to be identical with fire, though metaphor gives out such a meaning.[1] There can be no gainsaying that all conceptual knowledge, which proceeds through the machinery of verbal expressions, gives false appearance and not truth.

But it may be asked that if these are only constructions of the imagination and perversion of relations and are all false experiences, then why should not there be any occasion of their being invalidated by a true experience just like the false experience of silver in the mother-of-pearl ? The answer is that conceptual constructions, though false, are not on a level with errors and illusions. An illusion arises when one entity is perceived to be another, as in the case of the sun's rays being perceived as water. But class-character and the like are not distinct entities from the individual and there is no chance of these being cognised as distinct entities. The false conception of identity or difference centres round the individual entity itself and does not refer to a distinct entity. Hence, no experience sublative of the relational knowledge can possibly arise, as such experience can arise if there is confusion of one thing with another. These conceptual constructions are placed in a different category from the categories of truth and error. They cannot be authentic, as class-characters etc., are not objective realities ; nor can they be levelled with errors, as there is no sublative experience possible.[2]

[1] Vācaspati Miśra in his *Bhāmatī* proves that there is no distinction between quality and substance and this is attested by experience which takes them to be identical. It cannot be said that quality here stands for the substance qualified and so there is cognition of identity. Because, our experience does not obey the dictate of linguistic usage. *Cf.* na ca śuklapadasya guṇaviśiṣṭaguṇiparatvāt evaṁ prathe 'ti sāmpratam, na hi śabdavṛttyanusāri pratyakṣam. na hy agnir māṇavaka ity upacaritāgnibhāvo māṇavakaḥ pratyakṣeṇa dahanātmanā prathate. Bhā. under Br. Sū., II. 2. 17.

[2] *Vide* N. M., p. 94.

To sum up: it has been proved beyond the shadow of a doubt, we believe, that determinate perception, which invariably arises in the form of judgment, being essentially relational, only gives us false appearance. Conceptual constructions, *e g.*, class-character and the like are, at best, "working errors" and their pragmatic value is only a meretricious show. Reality is revealed only in the primal simple experience and the truth of such experience is attested by verification of the presentation with reality and pragmatic satisfaction is only symptomatic of such truth.

Is all knowledge determinate and conceptual ?

Bhartṛhari, the grammarian, poet and philosopher in one and the author of the *Vākyapadīya*, a work on the philosophy of grammar and a product of wonderful learning and extraordinary genius, has propounded the theory that the whole universe has been evolved out of 'Word,' which is the eternal, imperishable Brahman.[1] It is for this reason that all knowledge is interpenetrated with words, and a cognition, which is free from word-association, is an impossibility.[2] The contention of the Buddhists that the simple, non-conceptual cognition, free from verbal association, is the only true knowledge, therefore, has no legs to stand upon. Knowledge and word are co-extensive and one without the other is an idle abstraction, which is logically and psychologically absurd. This theory of the grammarians has been vehemently opposed by the philosophers of other schools ; but with the metaphysical side of this doctrine we are not concerned in the present context. We shall only review it as a theory of knowledge and see how far its claims can be psychologically maintained.

1 anādinidhanaṁ brahma śabdatattvaṁ yad akṣaram । vivartate 'rthabhāvena prakriyā jagato yataḥ ॥ Vā. Pad., Ch. I. I.

2 na so'sti pratyayo loke yaḥ śabdānugamād ṛte । anuviddham iva jñānaṁ sarvaṁ śabdena bhāsate । *ibid*, 1. 124.

Harivṛṣabha, the commentator, observes that unless words are actually present in the perceptual cognition, an object cannot be distinctly known and so there would be no memory, as memory comprehends only the thing that was perceived before.[1] Bhartṛhari is emphatic that ' word ' is the life and light of consciousness and consciousness, minus word, is comparable to light without its illumination and as ' word ' refers to something beyond its own self and is, thus, by its very constitution relational,[2] all knowledge is therefore *a fortiori* relational. Jayantabhaṭṭa remarks that this doctrine embodies height of unreason ; how can there be a cognition of word in ocular perception? There may be cases of perception, where the conventional relation of word and the object has not been cognised before ; and even if previously cognised, the relation might be forgotten, or the memory-impression might remain in the subconscious level for want of stimulus. How can there be an impression of word-association in such cases? [3] Harivṛṣabha, however, contends that even the primal cognition is not free from word-association, though the verbal expression may be of a very general kind. Thus, though the particular verbal expression may not be known, the perceived object will at least be referred to in its most generic verbal character, *e.g.*, it is a substance or so. But the full individuality cannot be revealed unless the specific

1 śabdaśaktyanupātinā jñāneno 'pagṛhayamāno vastvātmā vyaktarūpapratyavabhāso jāyata ity abhidhīyate, tādṛśa eva ca smṛtiviṣayo bhavati, anubhavasamānākāratvāt tasyāḥ.

Com. on 1, 124. Vā. Pad.

2 vāgrupatā ced utkrāmed avabodhasya śāśvatī | na prakāśaḥ prakāśeta sā hi pratyavamarśinī ||

op. cit., 1, 125.

3 kathaṁ ca cākṣuṣe jñāne vāktattvam avabhāsate | agṛhīte tu sambandhe gṛhīte vā 'pi vismṛte | aprabuddhe 'pi saṁskāre vācakāvagatiḥ kutaḥ ||

N. M., p. 99.

word-element presents itself.[1] This dispute about the very matter of experience reminds us of the pregnant remarks of Jayantabhaṭṭa in another context. "It is strange that these divergent views should be entertained with regard to the very object of perception. A dispute regarding an unperceived object is set at rest by perceptual evidence ; but what can decide a controversy in the matter of perception itself ? In a dispute about the matter of perception, a man can seek to convince his opponent only by swearing by his own experience." [2]

But Śāntarakṣita does not think that the position is so desperate and seeks to clinch the issue on logical grounds. He argues that the vivid perception of an object presented through a sense-organ, when the mind is occupied in the determinate perception of another object, is clearly a case of simple, non-conceptual experience, free from verbal association. Here obviously a simple cognition synchronises with a determinate, conceptual experience and the former is indisputably an instance of non-relational knowledge. It cannot be urged that there is one determinate experience, as in that case there would be two distinct verbal references, or the previous verbal association would be surrendered in deference to the newcomer. But as this is neither one nor the other, since two verbal references are impossible to abide in one cognition, we have to conclude in fidelity to experience that the determinate knowledge is synchronous with a simple indeterminate cognition. The contention of the

1 yo 'pi prathamanipātī bāhyeṣv artheṣu prakāśo viśeṣanimittāparigrahe 'pi vastumātram idaṁ tad iti pratyavabhāsayati vāgrupatāyañ ca satyāmutpanno 'pi prakāśo viśeṣavāgrūpam asvīkurvan prakāśakriyāsādhanatāyāṁ na vyavatiṣṭhate.

op. cit., Com. under I, 1, 125.

2 pratyakṣaviṣaye 'py etāś citraṁ vipratipattayaḥ | parokṣārthe hi vimatiḥ pratyakṣeṇo 'paśāmyati | pratyakṣe hi samutpannā vimatiḥ kena śāmyati || idaṁ bhāti na bhātī 'ti saṁvidvipratipattiṣu | parapratyāyane puṁsāṁ śaraṇaṁ śapathoktayaḥ ||

N. M., p. 98.

Naiyāyika—that two distinct cognitions cannot synchronise in one perceiving mind and that the idea of synchronism is due to quickness of succession and so is essentially illusory—is opposed to experience. It is a matter of experience how various cognitions do appear simultaneously in the mind of a person witnessing a dancing performance. He sees the movement of the eye-brow of the dancing girl, hears the music, tastes the flavour of spices, smells the fragrance of flowers, feels the cool breeze of the fan waved overhead and contemplates the presents he will make and all these at one and the same time. And does not a man perceive the cooling sensation, fragrance and savour of a delicacy simultaneously when he eats it? Moreover, quickness of succession cannot be a cause of this illusion of simultaneous perception. If rapidity of career could be an obstacle to perception of real succession, we could feel no succession to the movement of thoughts and feelings, which only last for a moment Likewise there would be no distinction of such words as '*rasaḥ*' (taste) and '*saraḥ*' (lake), as sounds are momentary and the order of syllables is one of unbroken succession. The example of the whirling fire-brand producing the illusion of a circle of fire is not apposite either. The illusion is not due to the quick succession of the flames, which as though perceived in succession are mistaken to be grasped in one sweep, as the *Naiyāyika* would make us believe. The fact of the matter is that it is not a case of many cognitions being lumped together by memory; it is one cognition by one sense-organ. If it had been a confusion of memory and perception, the presentation of the circle would have been faint and blurred, as memory only cognises past objects and the representation of past objects by memory would lack the rich colourful vividness of sense-perception. The fire-circle in the fire-brand is not a mental illusion, as the *Naiyāyika* would make out; on the contrary it is a case of perceptual illusion devoid of order and sequence. So synchronism of manifold cognitions being established in perceptual experience, the simple cognition of an object in conjunction with a determinate experience cannot be disputed. Moreover, the appeal to experience is not the only resource of the Buddhist, but there is strong logical proof in favour of indeterminate experience being possible. A determinate experience is always a relational knowledge, in which the individual is related to an 'universal.' But as 'universals' (*jātis*) are pure fictions of the imagination, they cannot be supposed to enter as constituents of the presentative data. They are absolute nonentities and a nonentity cannot be envisaged by perception, which takes stock of a really existent fact only. Again, relational knowledge is possible if there is a previous knowledge of at least one of the relata and this previous knowledge must be non-relational, otherwise *regressus ad infinitum* will become unavoidable. Besides, the whole contention of the grammarian is pivoted on a misapprehension. All reals are unique, momentary individuals, having nothing to do with any other real, preceding or following it. Such reals are from their nature repugnant to word-association, as the conventional relation of word and object is only a fictitious relation which cannot subsist between facts. But the object previously cognised cannot last a moment longer, much less till the time when the word-relation will be comprehended. So words only relate to ideal fictions and not real entities. And the primal sense-perception, which takes stock of reality as it is, cannot, therefore, be amenable to word-association unless it is degraded to the rank of an unreliable vagary. But this is absurd on the face of it, as it sounds the death-knell of all relational activities. Unfailing correspondence and pragmatic satisfaction are, as we have observed before, the test of true knowledge and when these two tests are applicable only to the first non-conceptual experience, the first experience is alone regarded as reliable evidence of reality.

Classification of perception

Dharmakīrti has divided perception into four categories, *viz.*, (1) sense-perception ; (2) mental perception ; (3) self-cognition ; and lastly (4) supersensuous perception of *Yogins*.

The category of 'sense-perception' (*indriya-vijñāna*) stands for the entire class of perception of objective realities, which are presented to consciousness through the medium of sense-organs. The sense-organs being five in number, sense-perception can be classified under five heads, to wit, (*i*) ocular perception (*cakṣurvijñānam*); (*ii*) auditory perception (*śrotra-vijñānam*); (*iii*) olfactory perception (*ghrāṇendriyajavijñānam*); (*iv*) tactual perception (*kāyendriyaja-spraṣṭavyavijñānam*); and (*v*) lastly gustatory perception (*rāsanavijñānam*). The classification is based on the variety of the media or the channels of perception and does not in any sense invest the sense-organs with agentive powers. Their function only consists in creating a connecting link between the subjective consciousness and the objective reality lying outside. This function is exhausted when the object is presented to consciousness and does not continue thereafter. So the first presentation is alone authoritative with regard to the objective reality. But Kumārila would contend that even subsequent cognitions are equally valid, as they only tend to set the first cognition on a ground of certitude; and this certitude being excluded from the category of errors should be regarded as valid knowledge like inference. Śāntaraksita, however, observes that as the certifying knowledge, which arises in the trail of primal cognition, does not exclude any misapprehension, it cannot be put on the level of inference. Mere exclusion from the category of errors cannot be the ground of validity. Inference, too, is valid not because it is distinguished from error, but because it removes error and misapprehension, which were actually present. But in this case of determinate perception, the determinate knowledge does not remove any misapprehension, because no such misapprehension is felt to exist.[1]

Is auditory perception free from verbal association?

Perception has been defined to be a cognition, which immediately takes stock of reality in all its uniqueness and so is free

[1] *Vide* T.S., ślṡ. 1299-1302.

from verbal associations. But auditory perception, which cognises word, cannot be free from word-association and if word-association is condemnation of perceptual knowledge, auditory perception must be *eo ipso* invalid. Moreover, 'words' stand in a different category from all other objects of perception. A word is not a self-contained and self-enclosed entity. It has a reference beyond its own self It not only reveals the object it stands for, but also reveals itself. In this respect, word, light and consciousness stand in a category altogether distinct from the rest of knowables. These three have a double aspect and a double reference. They express themselves and express others.[1] Bhartṛhari too has emphasised this dual character of 'word' and he has sought to bring home this peculiar trait possessed by it by the analogy of consciousness and light. A word reveals not only the meaning, the fact meant by it, but also its own identity, quite in the same way as knowledge reveals the object cognised by it and also its own self. In reality these two aspects or powers do but represent one identical reality and are not factually different. But still they are cognised as distinct functions or powers by reason of an inherent differentiating propensity just as light appears to have two functional powers or energies, to wit, its power of revealing itself, its self-luminosity and its power of revealing aṅ *other*. Thus, word is self-regarding and other-regarding like light and cognition, though these two functional traits are in reality one identical energy or the fact itself, the difference being only an appearance.[2] By

[1] śabdasvalakṣaṇaṁ kiñcid vācyaṁ kiñcid vācakam.

N. B., p. 11.

also, *cf.* nanu jñānaśabdadīpās trayaḥ prakāśāḥ svaparaprakāśā ity āhuḥ.

N. M., p. 542.

[2] ātmarūpaṁ yathā jñāne jñeyarupaṁ ca dṛśyate ।
artharūpaṁ tathā śabde svarūpaṁ ca prakāśate ॥

Vā. P., 1.50.

also, grāhyatvaṁ grāhakatvaṁ ca dve śaktī tejaso yathā ।
tathai 'va sarvaśabdānām ete pṛthag iva sthite ॥

ibid, 1.55.

virtue of this double functional energy a word is distinguished from pure material objects like jar, etc., which possess the power of only being revealed (*grāhyatva*) and also from sense-organs, which are seen to possess and exercise only the energy of revealing (*grāhakatva*).[1] A word, therefore, being possessed of a double facet, in other words being both an expression (*vācaka*) as well as the content of expression (*vacya*), all auditory perception must by its very nature be associated with verbal expression and so cannot be valid knowledge.

Śāntarakṣita observes that the difficulty exists only in the imagination of the opponent. Word, as an objective reality, is as unique and self-contained as other entities are The double aspect of a word, which consists in its being both an expression and the expressed content, does not belong to the unique, self-characterised, momentary word, which alone is real. The expressive power does not belong to a real word *quâ* real word. This relation obtains between two purely ideal fictions and has nothing to do with the real word.[2] Dharmottara also observes that even if the self-identical, unique word-individual is assumed to be possessed of expressive power, there would still be no difficulty, as this twofold character of a word is cognised only when it becomes the subject of conventional relation (*sic*, of word and object).[3] Harivṛṣabha too seems to endorse

[1] yady api ghaṭādayo grāhyā eva cakṣurādīni grāhakāṇy eva, tathāpi tejo yathā upalabdhau viṣayibhāvam āpannam eva viṣayopalabdhau karaṇatvam pratipadyate, tathā śabdo 'pi. te cā 'sya pratipādyapratipādakatvaśaktī nityam ātmabhūte pṛthag iva pratyavabhāsete.

Com. *ad* 1.55, *ibid.*

[2] nāmā 'pi vācakaṁ nai 'va yac chabdasya svalakṣaṇam । svalakṣaṇasya vācyatvavācakatve hi dūṣite ॥ adhyāropitam evā 'to vācyavācakam iśyate । anāropitam arthaṁ ca pratyakṣaṁ pratipadyate ॥

T.S., p. 542.

[3] śrotrajñānaṁ tarhi śabdasvalakṣaṇagrāhi, śabdasvalakṣaṇaṁ kiñcid vācyaṁ kiñcid vācakam ity abhilāpasaṁsargayogyapratibhāsaṁ syāt, tathā ca savikalpakaṁ syāt. nai 'ṣa doṣaḥ. saty api svalakṣaṇasya vācyavācakabhāve saṅketakāladṛṣṭatvena gṛhyamānaṁ svalakṣaṇaṁ vācyaṁ

the view of Dharmottara by saying that a word reveals its own self when it expresses, by reason of its objective reference, its necessary factual incidence in the objective reality. The obvious implication of Harivṛṣabha is that the self-regarding character of a word becomes manifest only when its meaning-reference, its factual incidence, is in evidence and not otherwise.[1] But this relation of word and meaning is not understood in the primal auditory perception and only becomes manifest in the determinate knowledge that follows in its wake. Auditory perception, therefore, has no reason to become a bugbear.

vācakaṁ ca gṛhītaṁ syāt. na ca saṅketakālabhāvidarśanaviṣayatvaṁ vastunaḥ sampraty asti tataḥ pūrvakālaḍṛṣṭatvaṁ apaśyac chrotravijñānaṁ na vācyavācakabhāvagrāhi.

N.B.T., p. 11.

[1] yathā jñāne jñeyam.........gṛhyate, jñānasvarūpaṁ ca svaprakāśatvāt, tadvac chabdo 'py abhidheyatantras tadrūpopagrāhī svarūpam api pratyavabhāsayati. *Prakāśá* ad 1.50, Vā. P.

CHAPTER XVIII

PRĀPYAKĀRITVAVĀDA OR RELATION OF THE SENSE-ORGAN WITH THE OBJECT

Perceptual knowledge arises when the sense-organ operates on the perceivable object in some fashion or other. The sense-organ is located in the physical organism and the object lies outside; and unless some relation is instituted between these two indispensable factors of knowledge, knowledge cannot be supposed to come into being. If this knowledge were independent of such relation, there is no reason why it should not appear always or never at all. There must be a determining factor for this regularity in our psychological life and this determinant is not the sense-organ or the object jointly or severally, because they are present side by side and virtually enjoy an autonomous existence. A *tertium quid* has therefore to be postulated, which can bring these two autonomous realms into occasional relation, that results in the emergence of perceptual knowledge. Philosophers have propounded various theories to explain this phenomenon and these theories, barring differences in details, have been broadly divided into two classes, to wit, (1) *Prāpyakāritvavāda*, which assumes some sort of actual, physical contact between the two; and (2) *aprāpyakāritvavādā*, which denies physical relationship and seeks to explain the relation in non-physical terms. There is again divergence of views in respect of particular sense-organs. In view of the extraordinary importance of the problem we propose to pass under review the various theories of the rival schools of philosophers and the Buddhist position will naturally be dealt with last of all. The *Nyāya*, *Vaiśeṣika* and *Mīmāṁsā* schools hold almost identical views and the differences are of minor importance. The *Sāṁkhya*,

Vedānta and *Yoga* schools are in full agreement in this respect. The *Jainas* hold an intermediate position and the Buddhists are ranged in the opposite camp. We accordingly propose to discuss the theories in the order indicated above and shall take care to point out mutual divergence wherever it exists.

The Nyāya-Vaiśeṣika and Mīmāṁsā schools

The tongue and the skin-surface apprehend objects that are in close contact with themselves ; the taste and touch of objects situated at a distance from these sense-organs are not amenable to perception. There is absolutely no room for controversy with regard to their immediate contactual relationship with their objects so far as these two sense-organs are concerned. About the organ of smell, too, there is practical unanimity that there is actual physical contact with odorous objects. The molecules of a fragrant substance are wafted by the wind directly into the interior of the nasal membrane and odour is perceived by the nasal organ in its own region. This functional peculiarity of the nasal organ is so notorious that authorities on religious law have enjoined the performance of expiatory rites if odours of impure substances are smelt. The implication of such injunctions is that there is actual contact of the impure objects with the nasal membrane and the penance is advised to get rid of sin that accrues on the contact of unholy substances. And we can extend this functional peculiarity to other external sense-organs as well, *viz.*, to the visual and auditory organs by obvious analogy. Moreover, it is absurd to suppose that the sense-organs are the efficient causes of perception of external objects and they can exercise this causal function from a position of sacred aloofness. An efficient cause operating from a respectful distance is contradictory to experience. If it is assumed that organs have an inherent unseen power by virtue of which they take cognisance of objects situated apart, then the non-apprehension of objects separated by a wall and the like would become unaccountable, because energy or power being incorporeal cannot be resisted by a physical barrier. The Buddhists regard the eye-ball as the organ of vision. They contend that the organ of vision cannot be supposed to be made of light or some fiery substance, as in that case a treatment of the eye-ball could not result in the improvement of eye-sight or any injury thereof would not entail deterioration in the power of vision. So the eye-ball possessed of a special energy should be regarded as the seat of the faculty of vision and this applies to all other organs as well. But the *Naiyāyika* regards this objection of the Buddhist as absolutely devoid of substance. The eye-ball is the seat of the faculty of vision, no doubt; but this need not argue that the organic vision cannot go over to the object, as it is not the fleshy ball but something more refined and subtle in nature. The improvement or the deterioration of the eye-ball has a corresponding effect on the faculty of vision. because the former is the medium or the residence of the latter. An improvement of the locus can have a salutary effect on the content. It is also a medically attested fact that treatment in other parts of the body, say in the foot, also results in improved vision.[1] So the medical argument, used by Dignāga, has no cogency.

If the faculty of vision were confined to the eye-ball, it could not possibly go over to the region of the object. But in that case how can it be explained that the eye apprehends distant mountains and trees and not the collyrium painted on the ball? If the sense-faculty is supposed to be something distinct from the fleshy organ, which can travel to the place of the object, the difficulty is at once solved. With regard to the auditive organ, which is believed to be nothing but ether enclosed in the ear-cavity, it cannot of course go over to the region of object, as ether (*ākāśa*) is all-pervading and devoid of locomotion. But

[1] cikitsādiprayogaś ca yo 'dhiṣṭhāne prayujyate | so 'pi tasyai 'va saṁskāra ādheyasyo 'pakārakaḥ || ...cakṣurādyupakāraś ca pādādāv api dṛśyate ||

S. V., p. 147, śls. 45-46.

even in this case also, there is actual physical contact as sound itself travels to the region of the object. There is a theory that sound moves in the fashion of a wave and one sound-wave creates another sound-wave until it reaches the ear-cavity. There is another theory which supposes that a particular sound, when produced, creates other sounds in all directions and so persons standing on all sides can simultaneously come to have sound-perception.

Kumārila is not particular about the physical relation and observes that the *Mīmāṁsā* theory of perception is not affected whichever position is adopted. He, however, observes that there is no difficulty in the theory of contactual relation also. Pārthasārathimiśra in his *Nyāyaratnākara* and *Śāstradīpīkā* has elaborately defended the theory of contactual relation and practically sides with the *Nyāya-Vaiśeṣika* school.[1]

The *Sāṁkhya* school also thinks that sense-faculties travel to the region of the respective objects and in this respect there is practically no difference with the *Naiyāyikas*. There is, of course, difference in regard to the constitution of the organs, which the *Naiyāyikas* hold to be elemental products (*bhautika*) and the *Sāṁkhyas* believe to be evolved from *ahaṁkāra* (the ego-sense), a particular *tattva* (principle) of the *Sānkhya* theory of evolution. The Vedāntists of the Śaṅkara school have accepted the *Sāṁkhya* theory almost *in toto*. Dharmarājādhvarīndra, the author of the *Vedāntaparibhāṣā*, however, holds that even the auditory organ in common with the organ of vision travels to the region of the object. There is no reason to deny locomotion to the auditive faculty, as it is equally circumscribed like the ocular organ. And only on this supposition we can account for the perception of the source of sound, as is evidenced in such judgments as 'I have heard the sound of a drum.' Unless the auditive faculty actually perceives the sound in its place of origin the affiliation of sound to the source would be indefensible. Nor

[1] *Vide* S. V., *pratyakṣa*.
Śā. Dī. (Bom. ed.) *pratyakṣa*.

can we accept the suggestion of Kumārila that such perception is erroneous, as there is no sublative experience to prove the error.[1]

The Nyāya position recapitulated

We have seen that the *Naiyāyika* holds that there is actual physical contact between the sense-organ and the sense-datum and this contact takes place either by the sense-organ going over to the region of the object as in ocular perception, or the object coming over to the locus of the sense-faculty, as in the case of olfactory and auditory perception. With regard to gustatory and tactual perception, however, there is no divergence of opinion. The real controversy relates to the remaining three organs. Dignāga seems to have been the first philosopher who opposed it on the ground that the perception of objects situated at a distance or possessing greater dimension than the sense-organ would be unaccountable if the sense-faculty and the object actually coalesced together. There is no such peculiarity in the case of gustatory and tactual perception, where the immediate contact is an undisputed fact.[2] The eye-ball possessed of ocular faculty is the actual instrument of ocular perception, as medical treatment of the eye-ball is seen to result in the improvement of the faculty.[3] And even if it be conceded that the faculty of vision travels outside, the faculty would be inoperative as in that case one could see an object even after shutting up the eyes immediately after the contact has taken place.[4] But all this is

1 śabde tv ādhikyavicchedau bhrāntyai 'vo 'ktāv asambhavāt ı

S. V., P. 143, Śl. 51.

2 yatho'ktaṁ Dignāgena—'sāntaragrahaṇaṁ na syāt prāptau jñāne 'dhikasya ca ı ' T. T., p. 118.

3 'adhiṣṭhānād bahir nā 'kṣaṁ taccikitsādiyogataḥ.' *loc. cit.*

4 saty api ca bahirbhāve na śaktir viṣayekṣaṇe ı
yadi ca syāt tadā paśyed apy unmīlya nimīlanāt ıı *loc. cit.*

contrary to experience. Uddyotakara in reply observed that the perception of distance is with reference to the physical organism and does not militate against the theory of contactual relation. With regard to gustatory and tactual perceptions, the contact takes place in the organism and hence distance is not felt. Vācaspati Miśra explains that this feeling of distance is actually a case of perversion. People regard their organisms as their own selves and so whatever is outside of this organism is looked upon as something foreign and distant.[1] The perception of greater dimension is possible because the faculty of vision is of the nature of light and light proceeding from a small lamp is seen to pervade a larger amount of space. The perception of dimension is conditional on the dimension of the object and not of the sense-organ.[2]

The Buddhist Position fully Elucidated : the Jaina position

The *Jainas* hold that contactual relation subsists between all other sense-organs and sense-data except the sense of vision. The fact of externality and distance, so vividly apprehended in

[1] śarīram avadhiṁ kṛtvā sāntaranirantare bhavataḥ. na punar indriyaprāptyaprāptinimitte bhavataḥ, yatra śarīram indriyaṁ co'bhayam arthena sambadhyate tatra nirantaragrahaṇaṁ bhavati. tasmāt sāntara iti grahaṇasyā 'nyanimittatvān na sāntaram iti grahaṇād aprāpyakāritā sidhyatī 'ti.

N. V., p. 35.

śarīrāvacchinnāḥ khalv ātmānaḥ śarīram evā 'tmānam abhimanyamānā arthān anubhavanti, tatra ya eva śarīrasambaddha ity anubhūyate tam eva sāntara iti manyate......śarīrasambandhena tatra sparśādau na sāntaratvābhimāna ity arthaḥ.

T. T., p. 119.

[2] yathā vartideśe piṇḍitam api tejaḥ prāsādodaraṁ vyāpnoti......svabhāvataḥ prasarad api na svaparimāṇānuvidhāyinaṁ pratyayam ādhatte, kintu viṣayabhedānuvidhāyinam, viṣayanirūpaṇādhīnanirūpaṇā hi pratyayā ne'ndriyādhīnanirūpaṇāḥ.

T. T., p. 120.

visual perception, cannot be explained, so argues the *Jaina* philosopher, if the visive faculty and the object are supposed to coalesce in any form. With regard to the rest of the organs the *Jainas* are entirely in agreement with the *Nyāya-Vaiśeṣika* school. The real controversy, therefore, centres round the Buddhist position and so we propose to give an exposition of the Buddhist position, as vindicated by Śāntarakṣita.

Śāntarakṣita was perhaps the first Buddhist philosopher, who took up the defence of Dignāga and gave crushing replies to Uddyotakara's animadversions. Śāntarakṣita maintains that the theory of contactual relation is a superfluous hypothesis, and even if it is adopted, we shall have to posit, as an indispensable condition, over and above, that sense-faculties have a natural aptitude for the apprehension of their respective objects; and this alone is sufficient to determine the scope of perception. It may be urged that mere aptitude in the absence of physical contact cannot account for the non-perception of distant objects, as aptitude remains unimpaired even in distance. If physical relationship is regarded as the determinant factor, the position becomes understandable. But this contention, the Buddhist observes, betrays confusion of thought. Why should not there be a physical contact with distant objects? If the loss of efficiency is the answer, it is better and more logical to hold that the sense-organs do not possess this aptitude in regard to distant objects and so distant objects cannot come within their ken. And why should not the faculty of vision apprehend the quality of taste along with the colour, though the two co-exist in one substratum and the physical contact is a factual occurrence? To say that the contact does not take place in respect of taste and hence taste is unperceived may be calculated to throw dust into the eyes of an unthinking person. But we ask, the Buddhist queries—'why should not the contact take place at all?' If the natural constitution of the object is supposed to offer the explanation of the problem, then, the Buddhist pleads, this should alone be postulated as the determinant and to posit physical relationship as an intermediary is superfluous, if not absurd. A magnet attracts a piece of iron from a considerable distance and no physical relationship between the two is observable Of course, Vācaspati Miśra holds that magnets too must be supposed to exercise an energising influence like the faculty of vision, otherwise there would be nothing to prevent attraction of iron even when the latter is situated at too great a distance or intercepted by a partition.[1] But this is only begging the question. If it is supposed that the magnet throws its light (*prabhā*) over the iron-stick and so attraction takes place, we can only remark that such light is not observed by experience and there is absolutely no ground for supposing it to exist. And even if it is conceded, the question pertinently arises why should not the light of a magnet draw on timber and the like, though it may be found in close association with iron? If natural affinity or constitution be the cause, it can hold alike in the absence of such relationship and the assumption of physical contact does not make it more intelligible.

The contention, that in the absence of physical contact a sound will be heard simultaneously by all and sundry irrespective of the distance between the persons, has no force against the Buddhist, as the latter holds that objects are perceived simultane ously by all. But why should there be a variation in the insensity and volume of the sound perceived, according to the distance or proximity of the hearers ? The Buddhist answers that the intensity or otherwise of the quality of perception does not depend on the physical relation at all ; the explanation of this qualitative variation is to be sought elsewhere. The difficulty is not minimised in the theory of contactual relation also. If the sense-faculty apprehends the object in close contact, the question of distance need not introduce any difference and the sense-object should be perceived by all alike. If, however, the

[1] ayaskāntamaṇer api cakṣuṣa iva vṛttibheda eṣitavyaḥ, anyathā vyavadhānaviprakarṣayor api lohākarṣaṇaprasaṅgāt.

T. T., p. 122.

sense-faculty or the object is supposed to suffer deterioration owing to the distance travelled, the Buddhist is not precluded from resorting to some such analogous hypothesis even without physical contact. On the other hand, the theory of contactual relationship fails to explain all cases of perception. If the faculty of vision actually travels forth to meet the object, we cannot account for the simultaneous perception of the moon and the bough of the tree, which are separated by thousands of miles from each other. Uddyotakara's argument that the rapidity of the succession of the two cognitions makes us slur over the temporal distinction in perception is only an eye-wash. We have proved that rapidity of movement is not antagonistic to perception of succession as is evidenced in the cognition of succession of letters in pronounced words. Nay, there would be no idea of succession at all, as our cognitions are all momentary and follow closely one upon the other. Again, the contention of Uddyotakara (N. V., p. 36, Ben. Edn.) that to become an object of perception is to be related to consciousness through the sense-organ does not carry any sense. Relation is not the *conditio sine qua non* of perceptual knowledge. When we say that the real becomes the object of knowledge, we only mean that the real is one of the causes of knowledge and the relation of causality is not necessarily contingent on physical contact, as is sufficiently proved by the behaviour of the magnet and iron.

It may be urged why should the self-identical object cause different kinds of presentation in different persons at different places? Why should the selfsame reality be presented differently, as vague and distinct, intense and feeble? Different presentations should have different causes, else taste and colour could be affiliated to the selfsame sense-datum. But the difficulty is rather on the other side. When actual contact of the sense-organ with the datum is the invariable condition of perception, the object should be perceived alike, irrespective of the relative distance of the percipients. If you suppose that the organic faculty suffers loss of energy in proportion to the distance travelled, the Buddhist can with equal logic and cogency suppose that distance proportionately detracts from the presentative character of the object and hence different presentations of the same object are possible. On the other hand, the contactual theory miserably fails to explain auditory perception in all its varieties. If the sound proceeds in the fashion of a wave and enters into the ear-cavity and is perceived in its own region, there is no reason why there should be any difference in the various sound-perceptions, say, that of the thundering of a cloud and the whistling of a feather twirled within the ear-drum. They should be felt alike as all sounds are apprehended within the ear-drum according to the theory of contactual relationship.

But in reality the thundering of the cloud is perceived to be distinct from and external to the percipient. Uddyotakara's plea, that spatial distinction is felt when the contact takes place outside the physical organism, cannot, however, hold good in the case of auditory perception, as the contact takes place within the ear-drum and hence inside the organism. Kumārila's contention, that perception of distance, and for that matter, of externality in sound-perception, is a perverted illusion, has been nailed to the counter. The conclusion is, therefore, irresistible that the ear and the eye apprehend objects from a distance and that without any movement from any side to bridge over the gulf separating the two. In the case of olfactory perception also, there is the same lack of physical contact, as perception of distance and externality is as much present in it as in others. The doctrine of the *Sāṁkhya* and *Vedānta* schools that the mind moves out to meet the object in its own place is absurd on the very face of it and does not deserve any refutation. Uddyotakara has been misled by the false analogy of the tactual and gustatory organs.

Analogical inference is more often than not an unreliable and unsafe guide and the present case affords a curious commentary on its treacherous and guileful character. Though there is analogy in point of their externality as compared to the mind and their incapacity to apprehend objects separated by an opaque medium, there is fundamental disagreement in other respects *viz.*, their structure, constitution and distribution over the body, and what is the most damaging factor of all is their perception of distance and externality. The external organs of sense, therefore, barring the tactual and gustatory organs, do not differ at all from the mind so far as the absence of physical contact is concerned. The position of Dignāga has, at any rate, the redeeming feature of not making any gratuitous assumption of an invisible and unwarrantable relationship, which instead of straightening matters, rather complicates the situation, so far, at least, as auditory perception is concerned. The Buddhist position, thererefore, has better claims to commend itself to our acceptance, if simplicity in philosophical speculation is regarded as a virtue.

References:

(1) N.V., pp. 33-6.
(2) T.T., pp. 116-22.
(3) N.M., pp. 478-79.
(4) T.S., śls. 220-28.
(5) S.D.S., T.R.D,—p. 260.
(6) S.V., *Pratyakṣa*, śls. 40-51.
Nyāyaratnākara—ad 51.

CHAPTER XIX

Mano-vijñāna or Mental Perception

In pursuance of the classification of perception by Dignāga, Dharmakīrti has included *manovijñāna* as a species of perception in his scheme of epistemology. Kumārilla, we are told by the author of the sub-commentary, very severely animadverted on this additional category of perception as proposed by Dignāga and the rather complex definition of *manovijñāna* in the *Nyāya-bindu* was evidently framed to meet the criticism of Kumārila, who showed that this variety of perception was not only redundant, but also led to preposterous issues. After all, the emendation of Dharmakīrti only satisfied the academic test of the time and even in this emended form, it has very little practical and psychological value. So this variety can be easily dispensed with without prejudice to the theory of perception and it has been actually omitted by Śāntarakṣita in his treatment of perception. This *manovijñāna,* however, should not be confounded with the mental perception (*mānasapratyakṣa*) of the *Naiyāyikas,* which the community of names might suggest. The *mānasa-pratyakṣa* of the Buddhist is entirely a different species of knowledge from its namesake in the *Nyāya-Vaiśeṣika* philosophy, the latter being subsumed under self-perception (*svasaṁvedana*), a distinct category of Buddhist perception.

But what is the reason that led Dignāga to formulate it as a variety of perception, though logically and psychologically it had little or no value ? We can understand the position of Dharmakīrti, as he could not but feel called upon to meet the challenge of Kumārila and gain an apparent triumph over the hated heretic by vindicating *mano-vijñāna* against the latter's criticism. The reason for this is perhaps to be found in the metaphysical scheme of the *Sarvāstivādins*, who included *manovijñāna* and *manovijñāna-dhātu* in the list of the seventy-five categories (*dharmas*), into which the whole universe of knowledge and reality was reduced by the *Sarvāstivādins*.[1] We have it further from the sub-commentary that the conception of *manovijñāna* as a species of perception was a necessary deduction from the import of a scriptural text, a *Buddhavacana*, which declares, "Colour is cognised, O monks, by a twofold cognition, the sense-perception and the mental perception induced by it."[2] But Kumārila justly pointed out that if this mental perception was cognisant of the selfsame object as the sense-perception, it would be useless as it did not give any new experience. If, on the other hand, it was supposed to be cognisant of the external object without the mediacy of the sense-organ, such distinctions as of blind and deaf from normal persons would become impossible, as even a blind man could *ex hypothesi* perceive colour by this *manovijñāna* and privation of sight would be no bar. In order to avoid these contingencies Dharmakīrti observes that this mental perception does not cognise the self-same object of sense-perception, but only the exact facsimile of it which springs into existence immediately in the second moment in the object-series.[3] And this mental perception is brought into being by the cumulative force of (1) the sense-perception, which is its immediate substantive cause (*samanantarapratyaya*), from which the former derives its conscient character and (2) the objective datum, which leaps into being in the second moment, as an exact facsimile of the object

1 *Vide* Yamakami Sogen's '*Systems of Buddhist Thoughts.*' P.152 and Prof. Stcherbatsky's '*Central Conception of Buddhism,*' p. 97 and p. 100.

2 dvābhyāṁ bhikṣavo rūpaṁ dṛśyate cakṣurvijñānena tadākṛṣṭena manovijñānene 'ti. N.B. T.T., p. 26.

3 tataś cāntare pratiṣiddhe samānajātīyo dvitīyakṣaṇabhāvy upādeyakṣaṇa indriyavijñānaviṣayasya gṛhyate tathā ca satī 'ndriyajñānaviṣayakṣaṇād uttarakṣaṇa ekasantānāntarabhūto gṛhītaḥ. N.B.T., p. 13.

of sense-perception. So mental perception being the joint product of sense-perception and an objective datum, it cannot come into play without the mediacy of the sense-perception and consequently a blind man has no chance of perception of colour, as the visual perception, its antecedent cause, is absent. Nor can it be superfluous, as its object is entirely distinct from that of sense-perception. This mental perception, however, must be supposed to come into play only after the sense-organ has totally ceased to function ; otherwise there would be no means of distinguishing one from another.[1] After all is said and done, the question however necessarily arises as to the utility of admitting this additional category of perception in the scheme of knowledge. Dharmakīrti's ingenuity has saved it from the charge of absurdity, but its superfluity is patent on the face of it. Does this *manovijñāna*, which has been defended by Dharmakīrti with such a flourish of logic, add an inch to our stock of knowledge of extra-mental reality ? Certainly not, as sense-perception is sufficient for that purpose. Nor is it necessary to reinforce the sense-perception, since there is no warrant for us to suppose that sense-perception, unaided by any extraneous agency, is not competent enough to give us all the knowledge we require of the external objective world. It is on the contrary the most effective and satisfactory instrument for that. The position of the *Naiyāyikas*, who regard mental perception as a separate category of perception, is, however, intelligible, as mental perception is requisitioned for the apprehension of pleasure and pain, which are in their opinion blind qualities of the self unlike the Buddhist's theory, which makes them live facts being self-intuitive and self-revealing. Moreover, knowledge according to them reveals only the object of

[1] yadā ce 'ndriyavijñānaviṣayopādeyabhūtaḥ kṣaṇo gṛhītas tade 'ndriyajñānenā 'gṛhītasya viṣayāntarasya grahaṇād andhabadhirādyabhāvaprasaṅgo nirastaḥ. etac ca manovijñānam uparatavyāpāre cakṣuṣi pratyakṣam iṣyate. vyāpāravati tu cakṣuṣi yad rūpajñānam tat sarvaṁ cakṣurāśritam eva, itarathā cakṣurāśritatvānupapattiḥ kasyacid api vijñānasya.

N.B.T., p. 13.

knowledge and for its own revelation and knowledge, it requires another knowledge to comprehend it. And this subjective comprehension is called by them mental perception. But the Buddhist has no necessity for such mental perception, as feelings of pleasure and pain and all consciousness are, in their theory of knowledge, regarded as self-regarding and self-cognisant. The futility of admitting *manovijñāna* as a separate category of perception was apparent to that astute Buddhist philosopher, Śāntarakṣita, who thought it discreet to slur over it. Kamalaśīla, however, in this connexion observes that mental perception is a well-known piece of doctrine and so a definition of it has not been given in the text.[1] But this is only a tribute to scriptural authority and only proves that it has no epistemological or pragmatic value of its own to claim a separate consideration.

But desperate efforts were made to justify this variety of perception and its function and utility were sought to be proved beyond cavil. There were some thinkers who maintained that this mental perception was to be postulated for making the rise of *vikalpa* (the interpretative conceptual thought) a possible event. Sense-perception, belonging as it is to a different category of experience, cannot be supposed to have generative efficiency in regard to conceptual thought, which, being a purely intellectual fact, would require, according to the law of homogeneity of cause and effect, as its generative cause, another purely intellectual entity. Thus, *manovijñāna*, notwithstanding its inefficiency in regard to acquisition of fresh knowledge, has an important part to play as an intermediary between the indeterminate sense-perception and the determinate interpretative knowledge which makes selective activity possible. But this is an idle hypothesis, as the author of the sub-commentary observes, since sense-perception is alone competent to generate such knowledge. The very validity of sense-perception depends on this generative efficiency of itself and it can be regarded as an

[1] siddhāntaprasiddhatvān mānasasyā 'tra na lakṣaṇaṁ kṛtam. T S.P., p. 396, under śl. 1330.

efficient cause of knowledge only if it exercises a function, and this functioning is nothing but the generation of conceptual knowledge itself. If you suppose a *tertium quid* between the two cognitions, you will only make the indeterminate sense-perception an inefficient, abortive fact, which is absurd.[1] But the apologia of the sub-commentary, too, is equally a hopeless failure. The author admits that this mental perception has no service for us; but he goes on to say that this is unquestionably of use to *Yogins*, who are enabled to discourse on mystic matters by comprehending these truths in the mental perception.[2] But this, too, is not convincing enough as for the comprehension of such truths the supersensuous mystic perception of the *Yogin*, which has been postulated as a separate category of perception, is sufficient in itself. Dharmottara seems to offer the key to the solution of this tangle by observing that mental perception is an accepted doctrine for which there is no logical warrant. A definition has been proposed in the text only to show that it would be free from logical difficulties, if it conforms to the definition.[3] It is clear, therefore, that *manovijñana* has no epistemological importance and can be jettisoned without harm. The inclusion of it in the scheme of perception is made only in deference to scriptual authority and not for any logical or epistomological necessity.

[1] kiñ ce 'ndriyavijñānasya kathaṁ prāmāṇyaṁ, yadi svavyāpāraṁ karoti. svavyāpāras 'tu svasmin vikalpotpādakatvaṁ nāma. tataś ca vijātīyād api vikalpasyo 'dayād iti yatkiñcid etat.

N.B. T.T., p. 31,

[2] na mānasapratyakṣeṇā 'smadvidhānām arthakriyāvāptir bhavati, api tu vītarāgādeḥ. te ca tasmin kṣaṇe mānase co 'padarśitaṁ viṣayaṁ pratipadya dharmadeśanādikām arthakriyām āsādayanti 'ty anavadyam.

N.B. T.T., p. 29.

[3] etac ca siddhāntaprasiddhaṁ mānasapratyakṣam, na tv asya prasādhakam asti pramāṇam. evaṁjātīyakaṁ tad yadi syān na kaścid doṣaḥ syād iti vaktuṁ lakṣaṇam ākhyātam asye 'iti.

N.B.T., pp. 13-14.

The causal factors in perception

Before we proceed to discuss the next variety of perception, *viz., svasaṁvedana*, we feel it necessary that something should be said about the causes and conditions of perception, as conceived and designated by the *Sautrāntikas*. We had occasion to speak of *samanantara-pratyaya* in connexion with *manovijñāna* and unless there is a clear conception of *samantarapratyaya* or of all *pratyayas* for the matter of that, the understanding of the theory of perception will of necessity remain incomplete. We hope the apology is sufficient for our embarking upon a consideration of this topic, which would otherwise appear as irrelevant in the scheme of epistemological problems. We however abstain from giving a detailed examination of the theory of *Pratītyāsamutpāda* (the Buddhist theory of causation, literally, of dependent or contingent origination)—a theory, which in its richness of details, in its various applications and abstruse metaphysical character, will remain for ever an object of admiration as a triumphal monument of Buddhistic dialectic. In the present context we shall however be content with giving a brief exposition of the nature of the different *pratyayas*, so far as their bearing upon the psychology of perception demands.

The *Sautrāntikas* have postulated four different causal factors, which are necessary to produce perceptual cognition. No one single cause can give rise to this cognition and for this the combination of all the four causes is a *conditio sine qua non*. This combination of all the causal factors, which invariably and immediately eventuates in the production of the effect concerned, has been termed *sāmagrī* (the entire causal complex) in the Buddhist and in the *Nyāya-Vaiśeṣika* system of philosophy. These four causes are named and explained as following :—

(1) *Ālambanapratyaya*—the object of perception is termed the *ālambanapratyaya* or the basal cause, which is the objective

basis of knowledge. Thus red, blue, pen and the like are the instances in question. These are responsible for the variation of contents of knowledge and are objectively referred to.

(2) *Samanantarapratyaya* is the immediate antecedent in a particular series (*santāna*), which is similar in every respect to the effect, the consequent entity and which disappears immediately leaving behind a legacy of its own character in the consequent (*samaś cā'sāv anantaraś ce 'ti*). The *samanantara-pratyaya* of a particular cognition is the immediate cognition preceding it, which communicates its cognitive character to its immediately succeeding cognition. It is different from the content of the cognition, which is its *ālambana*, in this that the character of the *samanantarapratyaya* is uniform, whereas the content is variable. It can be best illustrated by a case of mental perception (*manovijñāna*), the *samanantarapratyaya* of which is the sense-perception (*indriyavijñāna*), which is responsible for the cognitive character of the former—a quality which is common to both. Dharmottara has expounded this particular *pratyaya* in the following language: "It is similar or co-ordinate in respect of its cognitive quality (*jñānatva*) and is the immediate precedent (*anantara*), as there is nothing intervening and is termed the *pratyaya*, as it is the cause thereof."[1] So *manovijñāna* is the joint product of sense-perception as its immediate co-ordinate cause and of an auxiliary cause, which is, in this instance, the immediate duplicate of the object of sense-perception, leaping into existence in the second moment in the series concerned.

(3) The third *pratyaya* is the auxiliary cause or the set of auxiliaries, as the case may be (*sahakāripratyaya*). The auxiliary causes are rather co-operative factors, all acting together towards a common effect and are not to be understood

[1] samaś cā 'sau jñānatvena, anantaraś cā 'sāv avyavahitatvena, sa cā 'sau pratyayaś ca hetutvāt samanantarapratyayaḥ.

N.B.T., p. 13.

in the Buddhist theory of causal operation in the sense of reciprocally helpful factors, as the causal factors are all momentary and as such can neither be the generators nor receivers of supplementation to be afforded by such help.[1] Thus, light, attention, etc., are the co-operating causes of sense-perception, as light reveals the object in a clear perspective and attention makes the cognition possible. As these sets of causal factors cannot be subsumed under any other category, they are treated as a distinct causal category *sui generis*.

(4) The fourth and the last causal category is the *adhipati-pratyaya*, the dominating or determinative cause. The other causal factors, to wit, the object, light, attention and the immediate consciousness (the antecedent cause) though present in full, cannot determine the specific character of the perceptual experience to follow. They are sufficient to account for the production of perceptual experience as such, colourless and undifferentiated in itself. But the specific character of the perceptual knowledge, in other words, the specific objects to be cognised, can be determined by the sense-organ in operation. Thus, the organ of sight is the determining factor in the perception of form and colour and the auditory organ in that of sound. The perceptual character is the common feature and the variable contents of perceptual knowledge are determined by the extra-mental reality. But the particular character of the object and the consequential specification of the perceptual experience can therefore be determined by the action of sense-organs alone. This determining factor is called the *adhipatipratyaya*, the dominating cause, as in ordinary language all that determines or regulates is said to be the dominant factor.[2]

[1] divividhaś ca sahakārī, parasparopakāry ekakāryakārī ca. iha ca kṣaṇ ke vastuny atiśayādhānāyogād ekakāryakāritvena sahakārī gṛhyate.

N. B. T., p. 13.

[2] loke niyāmakasyā 'dhipatitvopalambhāt. S. D. S., *Bauddha-darśana*, p. 39.

CHAPTER XX

SELF-COGNITION (*Svasaṁvedanam*)

"*Sarvaṁ cittacaittānām ālmasaṁvedanam*"—All consciousness, cognitions (*citta*) and feelings (*caitta*) irrespectively are known by themselves, that is to say, they are self-transparent and self-luminous. Consciousness is diametrically opposed to matter in this that it is of the nature of illumination like the luminary in the firmament, whereas matter is veiled and hidden by a constitutional darkness. The being of consciousness is its illumination, its self-luminosity, and so it cannot be unknown. Consciousness, thus, differs from dead, unfeeling and unthinking matter, which has no light in itself. The immateriality of consciousness carries with it the prerogative of self-revelation and does not connote any subject-object relation in its constitution, which its very immateriality precludes. Matter alone can be divided and consciousness can be consciousness only if it refuses to be split up into compartments, which the subject-object relation involves.[1] So self-luminosity of consciousness does not connote bifurcation of consciousness into a subject and and an object, which would be absurd in a single unit. Consciousness and self-consciousness, therefore, are interchangeable

[1] vijñānaṁ jaḍarūpebhyo vyāvṛttaṁ upajāyate |
iyam evā 'tmasaṁvittir asya yā 'jaḍarūpatā ||
kriyākārakabhāvena na svasaṁvittir asya tu |
ekasyā 'naṁśarūpasya trairūpyānupapattitaḥ ||

T. S., śls. 2000-2001.

na hi grāhakabhāvenā 'tmasaṁvedanam abhipretam, kiṁ tarhi ? svayam-prakṛtyā prakāśātmatayā, nabhastalavartyālokavat.

T. S. P., *ad* 2000.

terms.[1] Now, in the text of Dharmakīrti quoted above the word '*citta*' stands for consciousness in general, inclusive of all cognitions, thoughts and ideas. The word '*caitta*' stands for feelings, which are classed apart from cognitions on the ground that feelings do not contain an external, objective reference like the latter, but are conversant with internal mental states and are purely inward in reference.[2] Barring this difference, they are all conscious states, the conscient character being common to cognition and feeling alike In this respect, the Buddhist philosopher is in complete agreement with modern psychologists. The word, '*sarvam*' (all) is advisedly put in with a view to including all the states of consciousness, feelings and cngnitions alike and not merely pleasurable and painful feelings, which, on account of their manifestness (*sphuṭānubhavatvāt*) are alone apt to be mistaken as self-revealing and self-transparent. There is no state of consciousness, which is not cognised of itself which, in other words, is not self-revealed. And this alone constitutes its difference from matter that consciousness shines in its own light and matter, being veiled in its nature, is revealed by the

1 *Cf.* "We can know nothing until we know intelligence, for the knowledge of all things depends on it, and not it on this knowledge." Descartes, Reg. VIII (XI, p. 243). "Or......all forms of perception, imagination and conception, that is all forms of knowledge are forms of consciousness or thinking, and hence consciousness is known in knowing any. thihg." Norman Smith, *Studies in the Cartesian Philosophy*, p. 90.

2 cittam arthamātragrāhi, caittā viśeṣāvasthāgrāhiṇaḥ sukhādayaḥ. sarve ca te cittacaittāś ca...sukhādaya eva sphuṭānubhāvatvāt svasaṁviditāḥ, nā 'nyā cittāvasthā ity etadāśankānivṛttyarthaṁ sarvagrahaṇaṁ kṛtam. nāsti sā cittāvasthā yasyām ātmanaḥ saṁvedanaṁ na pratyakṣaṁ syāt.

N. B. T., p. 14 (A. S. B. Edn.)

Cf. tatrā 'rthadṛṣṭir vijñānaṁ tadviśeṣe ca caitasā' ity abhyupagamāt.
M. K., P. P. V., *ad* 1. 1.

also, 'cittam arthamātragrāhi, caittā viśeṣāvasthāgrāhiṇaḥ sukhādayaḥ vijñānaṁ upalabdhir vastumātragrahaṇaṁ, vedanādayas tu caitasā viśeṣagrahaṇarūpāḥ.' A. K. V.

light of consciousness. Matter, thus, can shine only in borrowed light and if this light itself be veiled, we cannot conceive how the object can be revealed at all. An object is revealed only when it is cognised, to be precise, when it becomes part and parcel of the cognition and if this cognition remains veiled and unknown, the object cannot possibly be known. The proposition of the realistic philosophers, *i.e.*, the *Naiyāyikas* and the *Mīmāṁsakas*, that cognition makes known the object by keeping itself in the background like the sense-organ, has, therefore, no sense in it and contains a contradiction in terms. The analogy of the sense-organ is absolutely out of place, because, it ignores a fundamental difference between cognition and the sense-organ. The sense-organ is the efficient cause, *the causa essendi*, of cognition, whereas cognition only reveals the object already in existence. It has no generative efficiency, it is what is termed *a causa cognoscendi* in regard to the object.[1]

An object is known when it enters into an intimate relation with consciousness ; and what is the nature of this relation? This relation presupposes that consciousness and the objective reality, though enjoying absolute autonomy of existence in their own right, sometimes depart so far from their sacred aloofness that they come together and form a coalition between themselves. And this coalition *eo ipso* presupposes that either of these participant factors should sacrifice some amount of their independence. Otherwise if they are insistent on maintaining their *status quo* of absolute independence, no relation can take place and consequently no cognition will result. The contention of Bhadanta Śubhagupta, that consciousness being cognisant in nature will take stock of the reality as it is without any surrender of independence on the latter's part, only

[1] tad idam viṣamaṁ yasmāt te tathotpattihetavaḥ |
santas tathāvidhāḥ siddhā na jñānaṁ janakaṁ tathā ||

T. S., śl. 2008.

fights with words.[1] This taking stock of reality means that consciousness is no longer pure consciousness but has become consciousness of something, that is to say, has got a distinctive content in its being ; and on the side of the objective reality too a momentous change of character has taken place, it is no longer a brute objective fact but has become an object of some consciousness. It will therefore be of no avail to posit the character of cognisancy on the part of consciousness or the character of cognisability on the part of the object. Consciousness minus its objective content is at best a pure cognisancy and the objective reality outside the consciousness is only an indeterminate cognisability.[2] And if the *status quo* is maintained intact, the consequence will be that no knowledge will take place. An intimate relation must take place resulting in the combination of the two factors in a synthetic whole.

What again is the nature of this relation? It must be such as can fully account for the inseparability of the two factors in a cognition. It cannot be, for aught we know, a relation of causality, because there is no such restriction that the cause and the effect should be bound together. The potter and the pot, the carpenter and the table, though causally related, do actually exist apart. If the object be the cause of the cognition in any sense, it can at most be an efficient cause, unless the materiality of consciousness is maintained, which, though a possible metaphysical doctrine, is not evident in the psychological process

1 Bhadanta Śubhaguptas tv āha, vijñānam anāpannaviṣayākāram api viṣayaṁ pratipadyate tatparicchedarūpatvāt tasmān nā 'śaṅkā kartavyā kathaṁ paricchinatti kiṁvat parircchinattī 'ti. āha ca, kathaṁ tadgrāhakaṁ tac cet tatparicchedalakṣaṇam. vijñānaṁ tena nā 'śaṅkā kathaṁ tat kiṁvad ity api.

Quoted in T. S. P., p. 562.

2 tatpariccheddarūpatvaṁ vijñānasyo 'papadyate । jñānarūpaḥ paricchedo yadi grāhyasya saṁbhavet ॥ anyathā tu paricchedarūpaṁ jñānam iti sphuṭam । vaktavyaṁ na ca nirdiṣṭam ittham arthasya vedanam ॥

T. S., śls. 2009-10.

and so has no bearing upon this psychological issue. The causal relation therefore is no explanation of the inseparability of the two factors in cognition. We can explain this peculiarity however, if we suppose that the two are essentially identical, and for this it is supposed that the object is known because it imprints its likeness or image on the consciousness and as this likeness is but a part and parcel of consciousness, the two are invariably found together. There is no other means of cognising an external object except through its likeness imprinted on the consciousness. All our cognitions therefore are copies or configurations of the objects and external objects can be known only through these copies or representative symbols. You can say, if you choose, that this is only a vicarious sort of knowledge as objects are known only through their representative symbols and not directly. We plead guilty to the charge but we shall only emphasise that this is the only possible way of knowing external reality and you cannot make a grievance that a medium has got to be postulated for that. Even in the theory of direct perception of objective reality, the medium of the sense-organ has got to be postulated and if this should be no obstacle to our knowledge of external reality as it is, the medium of representative symbols should not be condemned on that score.

From the very peculiarity of the cognitive relation we get it that consciousness and its content are so interrelated that to know the one means the knowing of the other. It is impossible that the thing can be known apart from and independent of consciousness, as consciousness is its very essence quite as much as the feeling-tone is of the feeling itself.[1] The subject-object relation does not exist at all and so the objection that the same thing cannot be the subject and the object is futile. The fact of the matter is that consciousness does not require any other consciousness to make it known, but it is not unknown either

[1] paricchedaḥ sā tasyā 'tmā sukhādeḥ sātatādivat |

T. S., 2001.

when an object is cognised and this is described as the self-perception of consciousness. It does not mean that consciousness is dichotomised into a subject and object, which is absurd on the face of it. It only seeks to bring home the fact that consciousness and its content being inseparable, the one cannot be known without the other.[1]

The knowledge of external reality in perception therefore is made possible only on the hypothesis of consciousness being impressed with a likeness of the external object and it is for this reason that consciousness and its content are felt together, because the two have coalesced in one consciousness-unit. This synchronism of the two factors in perceptual knowledge can be explained by no other theory. There is a school of Buddhist philosophers who maintain that the object and the cognition both are the co-ordinate effects of a common collocation of causal factors (*sāmagrī*) like light and colour-form and so their synchronism does not connote that the object is taken into the body of cognition by a representative symbol. They exist independently of one another, being co-effects of a common causal complex. That one thing (*sic.* cognition) is the subject and another is the object is to be explained by the constitutional peculiarity of the two factors themselves. Jayantabhaṭṭa also quotes this view at length. But as Śāntarakṣita and Kamalaśīla point out, this theory assumes the very fact which is to be explained. The crux of the problem is how can consciousness function as the subject ((*viṣayī*) with regard to the objective factor ? This can be explained if the two coalesce together and this can be possible if knowledge is believed to be a configuration of the external reality which is our theory.[2]

[1] svarūpavedanāyā 'nyad vedakaṁ na vyapekṣate | na cā 'viditam astī 'dam ity artho 'yaṁ svasaṁvidaḥ ||

T. S., śl. 2012.

[2] " nā 'nyo 'sti grāhako jñānac cākṣuṣair viṣayair vinā | ataś ca sahasaṁvittir nā 'bhedān nīlataddhiyoḥ || pūrvikai 'va tu sāmagrī prajñānaṁ viṣayakṣaṇam | ālokarūpavat kuryād yena syāt sahavedanam || "

Quoted in the T. S. P., p. 569.

It therefore follows from the very peculiarity of the cognitive relation that knowledge and its content are known in one sweep. And this is a matter of logical demonstration. Knowledge by its very immateriality is distinguished from the material objects and these objects are expressed and revealed when consciousness operates on them. The light of consciousness makes the dead matter shine and if this consciousness is supposed to be hidden and veiled in and by itself, we cannot explain how knowledge can arise at all. Dharmakīrti has very pertinently observed elsewhere, "Perception of an object is impossible if perception itself is unperceived." [1] Māṇikyanandi too observes, "Certainly admirable is the person who thinks an object is perceived but not the perceptual knowledge which sheds light on it like a burning lamp." [2] If cognition cannot shine in its own light but only in the borrowed light of another cognition, how can the second cognition, which equally lacks original light like the first, make it shine? Certainly there must be light somewhere and in its own right and if it is supposed to belong to some remote cognition, what is the harm if it is conceded to the first? If you deny original light to any cognition whatsoever, perception of objective reality will become impossible, as darkness cannot be removed by darkness. And the alternative of shining in borrowed light is exposed to the charge of *regressus ad infinitum*.

na jñānātmā parātme 'ti nīladhīvedane katham । nīlākārasya saṁvittis tayor no ced abhinnatā ॥

T. S., śl. 2032.

1 'apratyakṣopalambhasya nā 'rthadṛṣṭiḥ prasiddhyati.'

2 ko vā tatpratibhāsinam artham adhyakṣam icchaṁs tad eva tathā ne'cchet. 1.11. pradīpavat. 1.12., P. M. S.

also, tathāhi—na tāvad arthasya svānubhavakāle 'pi siddhiḥ, tadabhivyaktisvabhāvasyā 'nubhāvasya tadānīm asiddhatvāt kadā siddhir bhaviṣyatī 'ti vaktavyam. tajjñānajñanājātau (*sic*) arthajñānajñānotpattikāle siddhir bhaviṣyatī 'ti cet, etad atisubhāṣitam. yo hi nāma svānubhavakāle na siddhas sa katham asvānubhavakāle setsyati.

T. S. P., p. 561.

Thus, if a cognition is unrevealed in and by itself and is only revealed by another cognition before it can reveal the object, that other cognition being equally unrevealed will again require a third and the third again a fourth and so on to infinity. The upshot will be that the object will not be known—a position extremely absurd.[1] The contention that a cognition reveals its object though lying unknown by itself like the sense-organ has been proved to be a colossal hoax. A cognition reveals other objects, which are foreign to it, only because it is self-revealing like light. The subject-object relation does not exist and so there is no dichotomy in consciousness. It is immediate in all knowledge and is not known like an external object. Its nature is to be revealed and revealing. It shines, it sheds lustre and all things coming in its contact are revealed. To say that I do not perceive consciousness in perceiving an object is

[1] kim ca yadi jñānāntareṇā 'nubhavo 'ṅgīkriyate, tadā tatrā 'pi jñānāntare smṛtir utpadyata eva jñānajñānaṁ nāmo 'tpannam iti, tasyā 'py apareṇā 'nubhavo vaktavyaḥ, na hy ananubhūte smṛtir yuktā, tataś ce 'mā jñānamālāḥ ko 'nanyakarmā janayatī 'ti vaktavyam. na tāvad arthas tasya mūlajñānaviṣayatvāt, nā 'pī 'ndriyālokau tayoś cakṣurjñāna evo 'payogāt. nā 'pi nirnimittā, sadā sattvādiprasaṅgāt. T. S. P., p. 565. And if the original perceptional knowledge is supposed to generate subsequent cognitions as cognisant of the previous cognitions, the process will have no end. Nor can the presence of an objective datum intercept this movement, as an objective datum stands outside, being foreign to consciousness. And if it could stop the psychic process in spite of its foreignness, there would be no case of knowledge itself, as objects are always lying adjacent to consciousness. The result will be that there will be no knowledge of another object. And if this knowledge of another object is conceded, the question arises as to whether the final cognition of the previous knowledge is self-revealed or not. If it is not self-revealed, it will be unrevealed as there is no other cognition to cognise it, and being unrevealed it cannot reveal the object. The result will be a universal blindness with no light of knowledge to redeem its monotony. If to avoid this contingency, the last cognition is believed to be self-transparent, there is no warrant to deny this of the first original cognition. T. S., ślś. 2026-28, pp. 565-66.

tantamount to saying that I do not know if I have a tongue or not.[1] Argument will be lost upon him—a human statue in stone, who perceives an object but is not conscious that he perceives it. ' To be perceived ' means ' to be revealed by perception.' It is a complex of two factors, perception and the objective reality, which by mutual association have acquired a new status and are no longer simple entities as before. To say therefore that the object is known and not the fact of knowledge is to talk nonsense.[2] The contention, that awareness is only implicit in objective perception and so knowledge is not always of the form ' I know the object,' but is simply of the object, does not prove that knowledge is unknown. Implicit or explicit, awareness is always self-awareness. The reference to the subject and the object in a judgment is a question of emphasis and is possible only if there is a recognition of the fact of knowledge. The self-transparency of knowledge is the presupposition of all knowledge and cannot be denied without denying the very possibility of knowledge.[3]

The problem of self-knowledge has been debated in European philosophy with such an avidity and keenness as remind us of similar discussions in India. There are some psychologists who hold that knowledge of self is an impossibility, because " knowledge is a subject-object relation ; the subject knows the

1 bodhe 'py anubhavo yasya na kathañcana jāyate ।
taṁ katham bodhayec chāstraṁ loṣṭaṁ narasamākṛtim ॥
jihvā me 'sti na ve 'ty uktir lajjāyai kevalaṁ yathā ।
na budhyate mayā bodho boddhavya iti tādṛśī ॥ —*Pañcadaśī*
Ch. III, 19-20.

2 viditaviśeṣaṇasya vedanasyai 'va bodhasvarūpatvāt tadanubhavābhāve viditasyā 'py anubhavābhāvaprasaṅgāt bodhānubhavo 'vaśyam aṅgīkartavyaḥ. *Vyākhyā, ibid.*

3 *Cf.* na ca nilīnam eva vijñānam arthātmānau jñāpayati cakṣurādivad iti vācyam. jñāpanaṁ hi jñānajananaṁ janitaṁ ca jñānaṁ jaḍam san no 'ktadūṣaṇam ativartete. evam uttorottarāṇy api jñānāni jaḍānī 'ty anavasthā. tasmād aparādhīnaprakāśā saṁvid upetavyā. *Bhāmatī*, p. 35.
N. S. P., A. Sāstry's edn.

object ; but when we speak of the subject knowing itself, are we not using language which is meaningless? Knowing is a relation, and a relation needs two terms, while here we have one term only. *Ex vi terminorum* what the subject knows must be an object, and therefore it cannot be the subject itself. The subject of knowledge is like the eye which sees all things but itself is invisible." As a result of this dialectic it follows that "All introspection is retrospection." "The object which the knower has before him in introspection is truly an other, something that has been shed from his own life and is now a *caput mortuum*, a fragment of the past, and no part of the present living subject of knowing and doing."[1] This view is apparently based on abstract logical grounds and fails to account for the fact of unity of conscious life. If the subject is *eo ipso* unknown and unknowable, what is there to cement the discrete experiences and thoughts into one subjective whole ? After all, there has been no doubt felt about the emergence of a feeling or thought by a subject, nor has there been any confusion in their subjective reference. A thought or experience is immediately felt as one's own experience. Knowledge of the self by the self does not mean any duality—the self is immediately felt in all knowledge, objective or subjective. It is not felt as an object, as an other. We shall make nonsense of all our knowledge if we suppose that consciousness is unconscious of itself. J. F. Ferrier is nearer the truth when he formulates the dictum, "Along with whatever any intelligence knows, it must, as the ground or condition of its knowledge, have some *cognisance of itself*."[2] But it will be misleading and also perversion of truth if self-cognisance is understood to be cognisance of self as an object. This would imply that there are two objects in all knowledge, *viz.*, the self and the matter in hand. We have no warrant to suppose it to be so. As has been pertinently observed by Prof. Sorley,

[1] Sorley, *Moral Values and the Idea of God*, p. 202.

[2] *Institutes of Metaphysic*, 2nd ed., p. 81. The italics are mine.

" I may be entirely occupied in the examination of an object of perception, or in thinking about it, without the reflexion entering my mental state that I am so perceiving or so thinking. That reflexion is always there at call—so to speak a potential element of any cognitive state ; but it is not in all cases an actual element in it."[1] The truth seems to lie in the golden mean. Consciousness is neither unconscious of itself nor always explicitly and emphatically self-conscious. The former position would fail to explain the unity of psychic life and the latter would put all our knowledge on the level of judgments. Prof. Sorley concludes, " Surely the true condition of all our knowledge is not a superadded consciousness of self, but the fact of its being a consciousness by self."[2] Of course the Buddhist and the Vedāntist who advocate the self-shining nature of consciousness do not maintain that self-consciousness as a judgment is the condition of all knowledge. They only emphasise that implicitly or explicitly the ground of all empirical knowledge is consciousness, which is never known or hidden in its nature. Self-consciousness as the connotation of all consciousness is an immediate felt fact and is rather the form than the content of knowledge. In self-judgments the self appears as the object, but this objectivity is only a heightened form of self-consciousness and need not imply any alienation of the self. It only means that attention is turned back internally upon itself, upon the thought as thought.

As has been aptly observed by M. Bergson, " There is one reality, at least, which we all seize from within, by intuition and not by analysis. It is our own personality in its flowing through time—our self which endures. We may sympathise intellectually with nothing else, but we certainly sympathise with our own selves."[3] Prof. Sorley observes, " It is an apprehension which is immediate—which is lived in the moment that it is known, although it is preserved in memory and clarified

1 *Op. cit.*, p. 205.
2 *Op. cit.*, p. 207.
3 *Introduction to Metaphysics*, Eng. tr., p. 8.

by reflexion." Further, "This is more difficult to name: for in naming it we are apt to speak of it as if it were one element amongst the others. But it may be described as the sense of life or the sense of self. It is not one factor amongst others —such as sensation or impulse or feeling. For it is something through which all these are—through which they have being. And it is through it that each person has his own individual being and no other, so that my perception of this sound, say, is entirely distinct from yours, even although no perfect analysis can find no dissimilarity between their respective contents."[1] Again, "The idea of self is founded upon immediate experience of self as a unity or whole of conscious life. We do not approach it from the outside: We have inside acquaintance, because we are it."[2] Although the Buddhist does not believe in the existence of an enduring self running through all the diverse experiences, still these opinions of the immediacy of consciousness are fully in accord with his views. The problem of the self as a permanent unity is a different problem and is irrelevant to our present enquiry. We have however dealt with this problem in our critique of the Buddhist non-soul theory and we have expressed our differences. Be that as it may, we cannot help thinking that the besetting sin of philosophers has been to lay stress on the objective content and so to ignore the self-revealing character of consciousness. Prof. Sorley evidently contradicts himself when he denies consciousness of self as the ground of all consciousness. "We should need clear evidence to convince us," observes Prof. Sorley, "that the consciousness of one object always requires to be accompanied by the consciousness of another object, even although the other object is self."[3] The point is that consciousness as such is never known as an object, as if it were one factor among other factors. It is hasty analysis

[1] *Op. cit.*, pp. 263-64.
[2] *Op. cit.*, 265.
[3] *Op. cit.*, p. 207.

to speak of the self or consciousness as a part of the objective judgment. Judgment is itself possible because consciousness supplies 'the spiritual bond' to quote Goethe.[1] And this is admitted by Prof. Sorley himself in other places as quoted by us.

Citsukhācārya is certainly on the right track when he says that the judgment, 'The pot is known by me' is no evidence of the self being known as an object. The 'me,' is the subject of the knowledge and not its object. The language too is unmistakable. In the proposition the predicate is "knownness" and it is predicated of the object, the pot. Knownness does not qualify the subject, but the object. So the self is never known objectively. And all cases of self-knowledge will be found to be knowledge of something as an object by the self and never of the self by the self, though the *prima facie* view of self-judgment would point the other way. The objection of the *Nāiyāyika* that consciousness, if it is self-consciousness, must necessitate the judgment, 'I know this or that'—is based on a faulty reading and analysis of knowledge. We have seen that the judgment 'I know this' does not connote that the self is objectively cognised as 'this' is cognised. The judgment 'I know this' presupposes a series of psychical activities. In the first flush of experience, the contents are given in a lump—as a whole. "Analysis brings out into relief elements which are in the whole and are important for understanding the whole." The judgment is thus the result of analysis of the immediate experience and it must be noted that analysis can never reach the inner life; "in the centre it is always at a loss; for when the centre or subject is reached there is nothing further to analyse, and the mere analyst is tempted to say that there is nothing there at all."[2]

1 *Cf.* "To understand the living whole
They start by driving out the soul;
They count the parts, and when all's done,
Alas! the spirit-bond is gone." *Op. cit.*, p. 250.

2 *Op. cit.*, p. 264.

The contention of Rāmānuja that all knowledge is judgmental in character and self-knowledge is possible only in association with an other is based on superficial psychology and slipshod logic. We have seen that knowledge of sense-data is possible only because consciousness owns them up and consciousness or self is never in need of a foreign light for its manifestation. And even in sense-perception the data are not apprehended as isolated or distinct units ; their distinctness is due to our own processes of abstraction and analysis, which take place after the experience has taken place. Judgment is thus only a clarified form of the immediate experience, made possible by a series of psychological processes, such as analysis, reflection, selection and synthetic reintegration. So the plea of the *Nāiyayika* that self-consciousness must emerge in the form of a judgment is based on a short-sighted view of experience. In the first flush of experience, remarkably in sense-perception, the contents are known in a lump. In the second place, the contents are distinguished and analysed and objective judgments in the form of 'this is blue,' etc., are made possible. In the third place, when attention is turned back upon the subjective pole, the judgment emerges in the form of self-consciousness, such as 'I know the blue object,' etc. But it would be a faulty analysis if we suppose that either in the first or in the second stage the element of consciousness is not conscious of itself. As in the third stage where we get the explicit knowledge of the self as the subject, the objective elements are not unknown, though the subjective side is prominently felt, as attention is focussed upon it, so in the first two stages the subjective side is neither slurred over nor unfelt, though attention is focussed upon the objective contents and the subjective side is not emphasised. The question of immediate indeterminate knowledge and of judgments, both objective and subjective, is a question of analysis and attention ; but the logical postulate of all knowledge in all stages is the presence of consciousness as the form and the form is never unknown, though attention may be diverted to the contents and the presence of consciousness as the form or the spiritual bond may not be emphasised. It is the presence of consciousness as the form and as the spiritual bond in all processes of knowledge that is emphasised by the Buddhists and the Vedāntists and they insist with unerring logic that this form is the life and soul of all knowledge and its existence is never unknown. On the contrary they assert that this self-shining nature of consciousness is its special prerogative and it is this which distinguishes it from matter, which for its revelation is dependent upon consciousness. But consciousness is not dependent upon matter for its self-revelation ; and association of contents in our wakeful experience is only an accident. The *Nāiyāyika* or all realists for the matter of that have made a grave blunder in supposing consciousness to be the product of objective elements operating upon the self, which is regarded as but an unconscious receiving apparatus. But this would make the explanation of the unity of conscious life impossible and so the postulation of a permanent self as the cementing bond of psychic life will have no meaning.

Pleasure and pain, which have been grouped under '*caittas*' (secondary mental phenomena) are equally conscious states and as such self-transparent and self-intuited. Dharmottara observes that the feelings of pleasure or pain are experienced immediately on the perception of external objects. The perceptual knowledge emerges with a distinctive feeling-tone, be it pleasurable or painful, and this is felt internally and has no external objective reference. The experience of pleasure or pain, therefore, is purely subjective like the perceptual knowledge itself and so there is no excuse to identify it with the external object, though the external object may be rightly regarded as the occasioning condition of such experience. The fact of the matter is that consciousness and its feeling-tone are one and the same thing. Pleasure and pain are the characteristic features of consciousness itself. It is quite possible that there may be a neutral state of consciousness, which is neither pleasurable nor painful.

Yaśomitra and Guṇaratna have admitted this possibility and have accordingly divided *caittas* into three categories, (1) pleasurable, (2) painful, (3) neutral.[1] The contention of the *Naiyāyikas*, that pleasure and pain are not essentially conscious states but are felt objectively as much as external objects, is psychologically untenable. Of course, Jayantabhaṭṭa admits that pleasure and pain are internally perceived, but he would have us believe that they are objective perceptions none the less. The pleasure and pain are objective realities existing inside the soul-substance in the form of universal archetypes and so are felt as much objectively as external objects are perceived. An experience is distinguished as pleasant because pleasure is the object of this experience quite as much as a jug becomes an object. The feeling-tone cannot be regarded as the essential character of consciousness, as the feeling-tone is variable. So it must be conceded that pleasure and pain enter into the constitution of knowledge as objects and are not integral parts of consciousness, as pure consciousness without a feeling-tone is also experienced.[2]

Śāntarakṣita observes in reply to this contention of the *Naiyāyikas* that unless pleasure, etc., are regarded as the integral parts of perceptual knowledge and as such essentially conscious states, the immediate perception of pleasure or pain simultaneously with the perceptual knowledge cannot be accounted for. Even if it is held that pleasure and pain are felt by a distinct mental perception this mental perception can arise in the second moment and so the simultaneous perception of pleasure and perceptual

1 citte bhavāś caittā vastuviśeṣarūpagrāhakāḥ sukhaduḥkhopekṣālakṣaṇāḥ. T. R. D., p. 40.
also, yathā hi tisro vedanā bhavanti sukhā, duḥkhā, aduḥkhasukhā ve 'ti. Abhi. K. V., p. 14.

2 tad idānīṁ sukhajñānam apy anubhūyamānaṁ sukhena viṣayabhāvajuṣā ghaṭādine 'vo 'parajyata iti gamyate na svarūpeṇai 'va sukhātmakam, tato bhinnarūpasya bodhamātrasvabhāvasya jñānasyā 'nyadā dṛṣṭatvād iti. N. M., p. 75.

experience cannot be accounted for. The pleasure or pain is felt immediately the external object is perceived and this immediacy can be explained if the feeling-tone is regarded as the part and parcel of the perceptual cognition. Nor can the feeling of immediacy be accounted as an illusion due to the rapidity of the successive cognitions, as we have proved before that rapidity of succession cannot be a bar to perception of succession. Moreover, if pleasure and pain are objectively perceived, we can expect that the *Yogins* should feel happy or miserable when they supersensuously intuit the pleasure and pain in other persons. Not only that, one should feel happy or miserable when one infers the pleasure or pain of another person. The existence of the pleasure and pain in the subject is not essential.

Jayantabhaṭṭa's explanation of the Naiyāyika position.

Jayantabhaṭṭa, we are inclined to believe, anticipated this difficulty and so posited the existence of pleasure and pain in their universal archetypal forms in the subjective centres. These archetypal universals are ubiquitous and so can exist in the being of the self. And these archetypal universals become evident when they come into relation with particular causes of pleasure and pain and this relation is brought about under the influence of the law of harmony or mutual affinity (*yogyatā*).[1] But this attempt on the part of Jayantabhaṭṭa to deny the character of consciouness to feelings does not seem to be convincing. On the other hand it makes some unwarrantable assumptions. The existence of archetypes or universals is not above doubt and in the second place the assumption of these universals of pleasure

[1] nanu sukhotpādāt pūrvam anāśrayaṁ sukhatvasāmānyaṁ kathaṁ tatra syāt, kaś cā 'pi sukhahetubhiḥ kārakaiḥ saṁsargaḥ, asaṁsṛṣṭaṁ ca kathaṁ kārakaṁ syāt ? ucyate. sarvasarvagatāni sāmānyāni sādhayiṣyanta iti santi tatrā 'pi sukhatvādīni. yogyatālakṣaṇa eva cai 'ṣāṁ sukhahetubhiḥ kārakaiḥ saṁsargaḥ. N. M., pp. 75-76.

and pain in the soul-substance does not seem to be justified by any logical necessity. Not only is there no logical justification, but it does not make these psychical states any more intelligible. And to give it a semblance of justification Jayanta has to postulate a relation of harmony or affinity with particular objective realities known to induce pleasurable or painful sensations. This is not all; Jayanta is compelled to commit one absurdity after another. Once he lets in a particular universal, he finds himself under the painful obligation of postulating as many universals as there are conscious states. Thus, pleasure, pain, knowledge, volition, hatred, desire and many others are to be assumed to exist in their universal forms. And what does this existence of universals avail ? They cannot make themselves felt unless and until particular objective facts are perceived, and to justify these two factors he postulates a sort of mysterious relation under the name of 'affinity' or 'harmony,' which is not intelligible to the plain understanding. The Buddhist theory does not make any one of these assumptions, which have been requisitioned by the *Naiyāyika* to escape the unmistakable fact of the self-transparency of knowledge, which the *Naiyāyika* feels called upon to deny. But the self-transparency of consciousness is based upon the irrefutable testimony of experience and an undeniable logical necessity and the denial of this leads to an infinite variety of absurd situations, little suspected by the *Naiyāyika*. It redounds all the more to the credit of the Buddhists that modern psychological researches fully corroborate the Buddhist theory, as feelings are regarded as conscious states as much as cognitive and volitional facts.

CHAPTER XXI

THE THEORY OF PERCEPTION AS PROPOUNDED BY DHARMAKĪRTI AND DHARMOTTARA

Perception according to Dharmakīrti consists in the apprehension of an object in its own specific character (*sva-lakṣaṇa*) having nothing in common with other objects similar or dissimilar and is thus completely free from association with names and verbal expressions—an association which presupposes and is made possible by relational thought. The object of perception is the reality which is immediately revealed to the mind and not such other ideas as generality (*sāmānya*), quality (*guṇa*), action (*kriyā*), substratum (*dravya*), or name (*nāman*), which are not a part of the presented sense-data but are supplied by imagination (*vikalpa*). The criterion of reality from unreal creation of fancy or imagination is this : that which by its position of nearness or distance affects the presentative character of perception is alone real. Thus, a jug or rather its presentation is seen to vary as faint or distinct according to its situation in relation to the percipient. But an idea, which is supplied by memory-association or conjured up in imagination, does not undergo any variation whether the object represented be situated near to or distant from the perceiving subject. This reality is alone endowed with practical efficiency (*arthakriyā-kāritva*) and not the fancied or inferred object, which is not presented through sense-medium. The test of reality therefore is practical efficiency alone and not any thing else.

The Theory of Perception of Dharmakīrti, or of the *Sautrāntika* school for the matter of that whose system is expounded by Dharmakīrti in his *Nyāyabindu*, is rather an intricate one. All existents being momentary in character, the thing that is in contact with the sense-organ at one moment is not contemporaneous with the idea that springs up in the mind at the second moment. Thus perception is impossible inasmuch as the mind cannot come in direct relation with the extra-mental reality but through the medium of sense-organs only. In view of this difficulty it has been postulated that a sense-object has the power to leave behind an impress of its image in the consciousness through the sense-channel. By virtue of this peculiar efficiency a sense-object is regarded as an object of perception.[1] What really is immediately perceived is not the external object but a copy or image of it imprinted on the consciousness. And this mental image is regarded as a faithful representation—an exact copy of the extra-mental reality existing in its own right. It is evident therefore that external reality can never be an immediate object of perception but can at best be mediately known—in other words, it can only be inferred by its supposed likeness presented in the idea. Perception of an external object is therefore only the perception of the idea believed to be a copy or picture of the same.

In this connection an interesting but extremely difficult question has been raised as to the immediate cause of perceptual knowledge (*pramāṇa*). Our consciousness is seen to be ever active varying with a constantly variable content. The conscious character is however common to all the different cognitions

[1] bhinnakālaṁ kathaṁ grāhyam iti ced grāhyatāṁ viduḥ |
hetutvam eva ca vyakter jñānākārārpaṇakṣamam ||

Quoted in S. D. S., p. 16 and Tāt. ṭī., p. 153.

Cf. na hi mukhyato yādṛśaṁ jñānasyā 'tmasaṁvedanam tādṛg evā 'rthasye 'stam, kiṁ tarhi svābhāsājñānajanakatvam evā 'rthasya saṁvedyatvam.

also, 'sākārajñānapakṣe ca tannirbhāsasya vedyatā | '

T. S. P., under śls. 2034-35.

Compare Dharmottara: "nīlanirbhāsaṁ hi vijñānaṁ yatas tasmād nīlasya pratītir avasīyate. yebhyo hi cakṣurādibhyo vijñānam utpadyate na tadvaśāt tajjñānaṁ nīlasya saṁvedanaṁ śakyate 'vasthāpayitum. nīlasadṛśam tv anubhūyamānaṁ nīlasya saṁvedanam avasthāpyate."

N. B. T., p. 19.

forming the sumtotal of consciousness, the differentiating factor being the varying contents. What is the cause of this variation of contents in consciousness ? Certainly, the *Sautrāntika* observes, it is nothing but the objective reality lying outside the mind but coming in contact with it.

But this objective reality lying outside the mind, cannot, as has been shown above, be directly cognised by the mind because of its momentary character. It is only the image or copy of it that is directly cognised and the supposed likeness of the percept, that is the idea in the mind, to the extra-mental reality is to be regarded as the cause and warrant of its validity (*arthasārūpyam asya pramāṇam, tadvaśād arthapratītisiddheḥ*) ; and the cognition as such is regarded as the resultant of the same. Thus, the cognition of 'blue' has a particular form which is different from that of the cognition of 'red.' The conscient character is common to both ; what varies is only the form, that is, the content. So the immediate cause of a particular cognition (*pramāṇam*) is the form or the likeness impressed on it and not sense-organs as supposed by the *Naiyāyikas*. It is the particular form or likeness which determines the character of a cognition and not sense-organ, which is common to cognitions of red, blue, white and so forth.[1]

1 See Pt. I, pp. 78-9. Dharmakīrti in the *Nyāyabindu* and so also Dharmottara emphatically maintain the possibility of sense-perception of an objective reality. The mental likeness is regarded as the means of objective perception and not as the object or its substitute. In fact if the objective reality were deemed to have only an inferential status as in Cartesian or Lockian epistemology, the division of perception into sense-perception, etc., would be unmeaning. Dharmakīrti's theory of sense-perception in my judgment seems to have greater affinities with that of the Critical Realists of America than with the naïve realism of the Cartesian school. This is evident from the emphasis laid by Dharmakīrti on the mediumistic character of the psychical content. *Cf.* arthasārūpyam asya pramāṇam, tadvaśād arthapratītisiddheḥ.

Here the objective likeness of the mental content is regarded as the medium or instrument of perception and not as the object, exactly in the

A difficulty has been raised in this connection by rival schools of thinkers. The cognition and its likeness (*sārūpyam*) are not two distinct things but one. So Dharmakīrti makes the same thing *pramāṇa* (cause of knowledge) and *pramāṇaphala* (the resultant cognition), which is absurd. *Pramaṇa* is the cause of cognition and the effect of it is the cognition itself revealing a particular object.[1] To make the same thing both cause and effect only betrays confusion of thought.

In reply to this objection Dharmottara says that the relation of *pramāṇa* and *pramā* is not a causal relation but one of determination. When in contradistinction to the perception of a red object we have a cognition of blue, we feel that the particular cognition refers to a thing which is different from the red that was perceived immediately before. What enables us to

same fashion as sense-organ is regarded as the instrument by the upholders of the presentative theory of perception. The difference lies in this: the mental likeness is substituted for the sense-organ as the instrument or medium of perception, but the instrumental character is never lost sight of. That we are in direct touch with the objective reality lying outside is apparent from the text of Dharmakīrti himself, where he speaks of the object of perception as the self-characterised unique real (svalakṣaṇa), whose proximity or distance causes variation in the presentative character of perceptual knowledge. This text would be reduced to nonsense if the object of perception be believed to be the mental content. This fact distinguishes Dharmakīrti's theory of perception from that of Kant, who believes the thing-in-itself (svalakṣaṇa of Dharmakīrti) to be unknown and unknowable and from that of the naïve realists, who makes human knowledge a closed circle out of all touch with external reality. I have therefore not hesitated to characterise the realism of Dharmakīrti's school as Critical Realism in contra-distinction to the naïve Realism of the Cartesian school. In fact the theory of perception of the Sāṁkhya and Vedānta schools too should be believed to be presentative, as direct contact with reality is emphasised. If and how far this theory of perception can be logically justified is a different question, which cannot be discussed in the present context.

[1] 'pramāṇasya phalam arthaprakāśaḥ arthasaṁvedanam'—Hemacandra's *Pramāṇamīmāṁsā*, 1.1.35.

differentiate the cognition of blue from the cognition of red is the peculiar blue-form experienced in the percept. Thus the cognition is ascertained to be one of blue and not of any other, only when the particular likeness imprinted on it is perceived.[1]

So the objection that the same cognition cannot be both *pramāṇa* and *pramā* has no force as the relation supposed is not one of cause and effect but that of determinant and determinable.[2] They are one as relating to one single cognition, but different only on account of one aspect having a determining force and the other being determined.[3]

We have seen how the selfsame cognition can alternately discharge the dual function of *pramāṇa* and *pramā*, in other words, how a cognition can be both the condition and the result of itself. It is effected by a change of emphasis. Thus when the emphasis is laid upon the particular form of the cognition, the form is regarded as the condition of perceptual knowledge and when the emphasis is transferred to the quality of consciousness endowed with a particular content, the consciousness is said to be determined or conditioned by the likeness imprinted on it, which is thus regarded as the determining condition. The Buddhists had recourse to this rather cumbrous theory because they did not acknowledge the existence of a separate spirit-entity standing aloof behind the mental apparatus and

[1] sadṛśam anubhūyamānaṁ tadvijñānaṁ yan nīlasya grāhakam avasthāpyate niścayapratyayena tasmāt sārūpyam anubhūtaṁ vyavasthāpanahetuḥ, niścayapratyayena ca taj jñānam avasthāpyamānaṁ vyavasthāpyam ....vyavasthāpakaś ca vikalpapratyayaḥ pratyakṣabalotpanno draṣṭavyaḥ.

N. B. T., p. 19.

[2] nā 'sato hetutā nāpi sato hetoḥ phalātmatā |
iti janmani doṣaḥ syād vyavasthā tu na doṣabhāk ||

P. Mīm., 1.1.35.

[3] ekajñānagatatvena pramāṇaphalayor abhedaḥ, vyavasthāpyavyavasthāpakatvena tu bhedaḥ.

Ibid, under 1. 1. 38.

illumining the psychical processes going on therein. The *Jainas* are at one in this respect with the Buddhists, as they also denied the existence of a spirit-entity as separate and distinct from the mind.[1] The logical consequence of this identification of consciousness with the varying mental states has been the doctrine of momentary consciousness—consciousness reduced to a series of transitory mental states in perpetual flux. The notion of continuity has been explained away as an illusion, being due to the homogeneity and the free unimpeded career of the conscious states. The *Jainas* have avoided this consequence by their peculiar doctrine of relativity (*anekāntavāda*), which possesses the miraculous efficiency of reconciling all contradiction.

The *Sāṁkhyas* and the Vedāntists have avoided this pitfall by positing the existence of a spirit-entity standing aloof, detached and unaffected by the varying psychical processes though animating them all the while with the light of knowledge. The consciousness in the psychical states is only apparent ; it is at best borrowed from the eternal spirit-entity (*sākṣī*). But with the Buddhists and the *Jainas* there is no soul distinct from the mind. Vijñānabhikṣu is very severe upon the Buddhists for their identifying consciousness with the passing psychical states with the result that consciousness has been reduced to a congeries of momentary conscious units having no real nexus between.[2]

[1] The *Jainas* hold that all knowledge exists in an accomplished state in the soul and it becomes manifest only when the veil of passion is removed from it. The veil of passion envelops the soul and not the mind, as the soul and mind are not distinct but identical ; *cf.* "nā 'pi manasas tair āvaraṇam ātmavyatirekeṇā 'parasya manaso niṣetsyamānatvāt."

P. M. S. Laghu-Vṛtti of Anantavīrya, p. 19 (A.S.B. En.).

Also *cf.* 'cittavyatirekeṇā 'tmano 'niṣṭatvāt.' Kamalaśīla, T. S. P., p. 119.

[2] *Cf.* Vijñānabhikṣu—

"naivā 'lpamatinā śakyo viveko vṛttibodhayoḥ ।
tārkikā yatra saṁmūḍhāḥ Sāṁkhyānāṁ śreṣṭhatā yataḥ ॥
jñānātmatvaśrutau mūḍhā ime bauddhās tamasvinaḥ ।
vṛttibodhāvivekena menire kṣaṇikām citim ॥"

Sāṁkhyasāra, Ch. III. ślş. 16-17, *uttarabhāga*.

Be that as it may, a question has been raised as to why a perception free from determination (*nirvikalpa*) is alone regarded as reliable evidence of reality, though it has no practical utility unless and until it is made determinate. It can be converted into useful knowledge only when determinative reflection (*vikalpa*) is brought to bear upon it and this determinative process is considered to be purely intellectual having nothing to do with reality proper. Indeterminate perception however has no practical value unless and until it is determined as perception of some thing. And this determination is rendered possible only by the reflective, intellectual activity, which certifies 'it is blue that is perceived and not red or any other thing.' Unless and until it is determined as such, the experience is as good as non-existent (*asatkalpa*), because it cannot lead to any activity and so there is no acquisition of any thing. As perception, determined by an intellectual activity is alone endowed with practical efficiency, it is determined perception (*savikalpa pratyakṣa*) that should alone be regarded as valid experience (*pramāṇa*); and if *vikalpa* is invalid by its very nature, how can it refrain from infecting it with its own invalidity ?[1]

To this Dharmottara says that there are two kinds of *vikalpa* and though both the varieties are equally unreliable and invalid by their very constitution, there is a vital difference in their functional character. There is a kind of *vikalpa* which interprets the perceptual experience and makes it clear and intelligible. It does not assert its independence but functions in the background. The other variety of *vikalpa* is

[1] nanu nirvikalpakatvāt pratyakṣaṁ eva nīlabodharūpatvenā (na) 'tmānam avasthāpayituṁ śaknoti. niścayapratyayenā 'vyavasthāpitaṁ sad api nīlabodharūpaṁ vijñānam asatkalpam eva. tasmān niścayena nīlabodharūpaṁ vyavasthāpitaṁ vijñānaṁ nīlabodhātmanā sad bhavati tasmād adhyavasāyaṁ kurvad eva pratyakṣaṁ pramāṇam bhavati............ yady evam adhyavasāyasahitam eva pratyakṣam pramānaṁ syān na kevalam.

N. B. T., p. 20.

pure imagination without any touch with external reality. This latter variety is absolutely unreliable as evidence of reality. But the reflective thought, which arises in the trail of perception and is generated under its influence (*pratyakṣabalotpanna*), stands in a different category. It does not assert its independence as pure imagination does. but only serves to determine the perceptual knowledge as knowledge of something. The *nirvikalpaka* perception is a simple, homogeneous, unitary cognition, in which the subject and the object, perception and perceptual matter, are not distinguished but given in a lump, as it were. But such knowledge is entirely useless and has no pragmatic value. It is only when perceptual knowledge is interpreted by a subsequent act of reflection, which analyses it into a subjective and an objective element and imposes a relation upon them, that it can be made useful in our practical life. It is however the primary, homogeneous experience (*nirvikalpa pratyakṣa*) that can be accepted as reliable testimony of the external reality and the reflective thought and the relational knowledge, which is the result of it, are purely subjective facts and are no index to the objective reality—the thing-in-itself (*svalakṣaṇa*). But the purely subjective character of this reflective process, which is necessary for the interpretation of perception, does not in any way detract from or add to the evidentiary value of perceptual knowledge. The analytic-cum-synthetic process, which is involved in the reflective activity, gives us purely perceptual data and not imaginary things. It is perception all the while even when interpreted by reflective thought. This interpretation only serves to put the perceptual knowledge in a clear light and neither supersedes nor overshadows it. The contention that perceptual knowledge together with *vikalpa* should be held as valid testimony therefore falls to the ground. *Vikalpa* is purely subjective and though requisitioned to interpret perceptual experience does not enter into the composition of the perceptual data. The apprehension therefore that *vikalpa* should infect perceptual knowledge with its own invalid character is without a foundation and only betrays lack of clear vision. The *vikalpa*, which is imagination pure and simple, is absolutely without touch with reality. It only gives us purely fictitious data, in which our knowledge is of the form 'I imagine the blue' and not 'I perceive the blue.' It is not attended with that sentiment of belief and sense of security which invariably distinguish perceptual knowledge.[1] This distinction in this functional character is fundamental and must be kept in view for our proper understanding of Dharmakīrti's theory of Perception.

[1] *Op. cit.*, P. 20. 11. 7 *et seq.*

CHAPTER XXII

INFERENCE

The Buddhist philosophers of the school of Dignāga admit only two *pramāṇas* (sources or media of valid knowledge), *viz.*, perception and inference. Of these two we have already dealt with the nature, scope and function of perception and we propose to treat of inference in this chapter. Inference has been divided by Dignāga and Dharmakīrti and their followers into two kinds, *viz.*, (1) Inference for the sake of one's own self and (2) for the sake of others. The former is defined as the deduction of the probandum, *i.e.*, the inferrable thesis, from the reason endowed with threefold characteristics, which are as follows :—

(1) The reason or the middle term must abide in the subject or the minor term.

(2) The reason must abide only in cases which are homologous.

(3) The reason must not abide in cases which are heterologous.

The inferrable thesis is the subject, of which the probandum is sought to be predicated. And the homologue is one which invariably possesses the probandum along with the probans or reason. The heterologue is one which is the opposite of the homologue, that is to say, which does not possess the probandum and the probans at any time.

Now, if a particular reason or probans (*hetu*) is understood to possess these threefold characteristics, it will invariably and unmistakably lead to the knowledge of the probandum. But what is the means of knowing that a particular probans would possess the triple characteristics ? Dharmakīrti says that only the following 'reasons' (*hetu*) would satisfy this triple condition :—(1) a reason which is identical in essence with the probandum (*svabhāvahetu*) ; (2) which is an effect or product ; and (3) thirdly non-perception. In other words, in cases of co-existence, only that probans is the ground of valid inference, which bears a relation of essential identity to the probandum and in cases of succession, the reason must be shown to stand in the relation of causality to the probandum, *i.e.*, as the effect of it. Non-perception (*anupalabdhi*) is of service only in negative inference, that is to say, when the non-existence of a thing or a quality is to be inferred. But non-perception can have logical value only if all the requisite conditions of perception are present in full except the object, or in other words, when the object is amenable to perception and all other conditions of perception are present intact. Well, but why should these three alone be specified as the ground of valid inference and not any other ? The reason is that a thing can prove another thing only if there is a natural relation between the two, in other words, if the relation is unconditional and invariable. And what sorts of relation can be invariable and unconditional ? The answer is, that only the relations of causality and fundamental identity can be invariable and unconditional. The *Naiyāyikas* think that invariable relation is understood from observation of concomitance in presence and absence. But mere concomitance, though observed in hundreds of cases, is not sufficient warrant for its invariability unless and until the relation between the probans and the probandum can be clearly reduced either to causality or essential identity.[1] We defer the discussion of this all-important problem for the present, as it requires fuller treatment, to which a separate section will be devoted.

The triple characteristic of a valid reason is the *conditio sine qua non* of true inference and a breach of these conditions

[1] kāryakāraṇabhāvād vā svabhāvād vā niyāmakāt ।
avinābhāvaniyamo 'darśanān na na darśanāt ॥

Pramāṇavārttika, quoted in Tāt. ti. P., 158.

severally and jointly will give rise to various cases of fallacies.[1] But there are fallacies of thesis (*pakṣābhāsa*) also. It is therefore relevant to enquire into the nature of the thesis (*pakṣa*), or the conclusion in the language of Aristotelian logic. The thesis or conclusion has been defined as 'a (proposition) which is desired by the arguer himself to be established only as the probandum and which is not contradicted by other evidence.' The clause 'only as the probandum' excludes the case of unproven reason, as, *e.g.*, in the syllogism, 'word is non-eternal, because it is visible,' the reason 'visibility' is unproven, as it does not belong to the subject and so has got to be proved. But though unproven like the probandum (non-eternality), it is advanced not as a probandum alone but as a probans also. The clause 'by the arguer himself' is intended to exclude all other possible facts save and except what is intended by the arguer himself. Various other facts may be predicable of the subject, but that alone should be regarded as the thesis which is intended by the arguer himself. The clause 'which is desired' is significant. It shows that the thesis is not what is expressed in so many words alone, but even what is implied should also be accepted as the intended thesis. Thus, for instance, when the *Sāṁkhya* argues, "The eye and the rest are for the sake of another, as they are compounds, like beds and cushions and the like," it is not expressly stated that the phrase 'for the sake of another' means 'for the sake of the self' (*ātmārtha*). But though not expressly stated, that is the implied subject and so should be understood as such.[2] If the thesis is contradicted either partially or wholly by any such evidence as perception, inference, conceptual knowledge (*pratīti*) or one's own statement, it would constitute a case of unsound thesis.[3]

[1] *Vide History of Indian Logic*, under Dignāga and Dharmakīrti.

[2] N. B., Ch. III, pp. 110-11. *Cf.* anukto 'pi vādinā ya eve 'cchayā viṣayīkṛtaḥ sa evā 'yam sādhya iṣyate.

T. S. P., p. 672.

[3] N. B., Ch. III. For an exposition in English, *vide* H. I. L, pp. 312-13.

II

The Subject-matter of Inference or the Thesis or Conclusion.

In the previous section we have seen what according to Dharmakīrti should be properly regarded as a correct thesis or conclusion. But Dharmakīrti does not vouchsafe any information as to the exact character of what should be regarded as the conclusion. Inference proceeds through the machinery of three terms, the subject, the predicate (the probandum) and the probans. There must also exist an invariable and unconditional relation between the probans and the probandum. These are the conditions precedent of all inference. But what is the objective and the proper matter of inference ? This problem was attacked by Dignāga in his *Pramāṇasamuccaya.* Dignāga argues, "There are some logicians who think that the object of inference is the predicate (the probandum), which is invariably connected with the probans. Others again think it is the connexion that is inferred and neither the subject nor the predicate, because they are known from other evidence. But both these views are untenable. If the probans is known to be invariably connected with the probandum the latter is already known at the time the connexion was apprehended. If it is contended that the predicate was not known as related to the subject, well, let then the subject thus qualified be regarded as the probandum. The connexion too cannot be the subject-matter of inference, because it does not contain the two terms, the probans and the probandum, in its fold like the subject. Moreover, the relation is not stated as the probandum in the syllogism either by name or through a case-ending. And the probans is not shown to be connected with the relation. Moreover, the relation is tacitly included in the probandum and need not be stated. So it is neither the subject, nor the predicate, nor again the relation that is inferred ; but it is the subject as qualified by the predicate, which is inferred on the strength of invariable relation between the probans and the probandum observed elsewhere." [1]

Uddyotakara does not subscribe to the position of Dignāga; but his arguments are all sophistical and do not carry conviction. He denies that there is any relation at all between smoke and fire, because he argues that smoke without fire and fire without smoke are observed and this would be impossible if there was an invariable relation between the two. And even if causal relation is conceded, fire can at best be conceived to be the efficient cause (*nimittakāraṇa*) of smoke, but an effect is not necessarily bound up with its efficient cause. Nor can there be a locus or subject, say the hill, where the smoke and fire could be inferred to be associated together, because Dignāga does not admit any whole in the shape of the hill. And even if the hill as a locus be perceptible, the hill and the smoke are not necessarily found together. If the perception of the hill be a necessary condition of inference, there can be no inference, when a man sees a column of smoke ascending high up in the sky.[2] But all these arguments of Uddyotakara serve to deny the possibility of inference and this denial does not affect the position of the Buddhist alone, but also of Uddyotakara himself. And it goes against the verdict of popular experience. Uddyotakara, too, realises this undesirable consequence of his sophistry and so hastens to restrain himself. He avers that there is no contradiction of ordinary experience and inference based upon experience. But there is no logical necessity that the smoke must

[1] kecid dharmāntaraṁ meyaṁ liṅgasyā 'vyabhicārataḥ | sambandhaṁ kecid icchanti siddhatvād dharma-dharmiṇoḥ || liṅgaṁ dharme prasiddhaṁ cet kiṁ anyat tena mīyate | atha dharmiṇi tasyai 'va kimarthaṁ nā 'numeyatā || sambandhe 'pi dvayaṁ nāsti ṣaṣṭhī śrūyeta tadvati | avācyo 'nugṛhītatvān na cā 'sau liṅgasaṅgataḥ || liṅgasyā 'vyabhicāras tu dharmeṇā 'nyatra dṛśyate | tatra prasiddhaṁ tad yuktaṁ dharmiṇaṁ gamayiṣyati ||

Tāt. ṭi., p. 180.

[2] *Vide* N. V., pp. 50-51 and Tāt. ṭi., pp. 180-81.

be perceived in a locus, say, the hill, when a volume of smoke is perceived at a great distance from the source of its origin, high up in the sky rising in an ascending column ; in that case the subject-matter of inference is only smoke with fire predicated of it without any reference to the locus. So the proposition of Dignāga that the object of inference is the hill as qualified by the fire is not universally true, though in the generality of cases, Vācaspati concedes, Dignāga's contention may hold good.[1]

Kumārila refers to this view of Uddyotakara and justifies it from the charge of *petitio principii.* If the thesis is of the form 'smoke is possessed of fire,' the probans 'smoke' is taken as a part of the thesis, and so there can be no inference owing to the lack of another probans. Kumārila says that there is no such apprehension, as the subject is a particular individual smoke and the probans is the smoke-as-universal.[2] But though he vindicates the view of Uddyotakara from the charge of logical inconsequence, Kumārila however accepts the position of Dignāga without reservation and carries it to greater logical precision.

Though Kumārila's conception of the thesis is substantially identical with that of Dignāga, Kumārila's arguments, however, are more elaborate and cogent and so we do not hesitate to reproduce them even at the risk of some repetition. Neither

[1] yadi dhūmenā 'gneḥ anumānaṁ na bhavet, nanu loko virudhyata iti cet, nāsti virodho dhūmaviśeṣeṇā 'gniviśeṣaṇasya dhūmasya pratipādyatvāt......anumeyo 'gnimān ayaṁ dhūma iti. *Ibid.*

Cf. yatra tāvat parvatanitambavartinī dhūmalekhā satatam udgacchantī dṛśyate tatrā 'sāv eva tadviśiṣṭo 'numīyata iti lokaprasiddham eve 'ti kim atra vaktavyam. yatra tu bhūyiṣṭhātayā tasya dhūmasya dūratvena deśo na lakṣyate, dhūma eva tv abhraṁlibo limpann ivā 'bhramaṇḍalam avalokyate, tatra deśānumānaprayāsālasatayā dṛśyamāno dhūmaviśeṣa evā 'gnimattayā sādhyate. Tāt. ṭī., p. 182.

[2] prameyatā......dhūmasyā 'nyaiś ca kalpitā | (śl. 47)......nanu dhūmaviśeṣyatve hetoḥ pakṣaikadeśatā | nai 'tad asti, viśeṣe hi sādhye sāmānyahetutā | śl. 50½-51½ S. V., *anumānapariccheda.*

the predicate ' fire,' nor the subject ' hill ' can be severally or jointly be the legitimate object of inference, as the ' hill ' is known from perception and the 'fire' too is known at the time that the universal relation between fire and smoke was apprehended. So inference would be useless, as it would not add to our stock of knowledge. In an inference, where impermanence is sought to be proved of ' word ' on the ground of its being ' a product,' the syllogism cannot be of the form ' Impermanence exists, since it is a product.' Because, ' being a product ' is not an attribute of ' impermanence ' (*anityatva*). Nor can it be of the form ' word exists, because it is a product ' there being no invariable concomitance between word and being a product, as the fact of being a product exists in an earthen jar but word does not. Equally absurd would be the syllogistic form, ' word and impermanence exist, because of being a product,' as the probans ' being a product ' belongs to word alone and not to both.

The possibility of the subject or the predicate being the thesis is thus ruled out of court. Nor can the thesis be supposed to consist in the necessary connexion between the subject and the predicate. Had it been so, the connexion would have been expressed in the thesis either by a whole word or a genitive case-ending in some such form as ' the hill's fire exists' (*parvatasyā 'gnir asti*), or ' the connexion between the hill and the fire exists ' (*agniparvatasambandho 'sti*). Nor is there an invariable concomitance between the probans and the 'connexion' as probandum. Again, connexion as such cannot be the subject of the conclusion, as it does not possess the probans and the probandum inside itself like the hill, which possesses both smoke and fire. And the connexion as particularised (say of hill and fire) cannot be known before the inference is arrived at, and even then, ' the possession of smoke ' cannot be an attribute of ' the connexion ' (*pakṣadharma*). So this alternative, too, should be dropped down. What then is the subject-matter of inference ? The answer is that 'the hill and fire related as subject and predicate, adjective and substantive, is the thesis and so the idea of relation being implicitly contained in the related whole, as a logical presupposition, does not require to be explicitly formulated, though it is the all-important factor, being previously unknown. The reason is that relation in itself without reference to concrete terms is useless. The object of inference is thus a judgment, a relational whole with two factors, the subject and the predicate. But which is the subject and which is the predicate ? There are some thinkers who hold that the relation of subject and predicate is one of substantive and adjective and is interchangeable according to option, though the fact is undeniable that one element in a subject leads to the inference of another element. Thus, in the inference of impermanence of word on the ground of its being a product, the thesis can be expressed either as 'word is impermanent' or as 'there is impermanence in word.' Similarly in the familiar instance of hill and fire, the thesis can assume either form : 'The fire is in the mountain' or 'the mountain has fire,' the subject and the predicate being left indeterminate concepts and their relation as reversible.

Let us take a concrete syllogism and see the position of the subject and the predicate. 'Word is impermanent, because it is a product, whatever is a product is impermanent, as for instance a jar.' In this syllogism, 'word' is the subject and the substantive element. Let the syllogism again be as follows :—

'Impermanence is in-word, because it is a product, etc.'

In the latter syllogism, as the fact of being a product cannot be construed with 'impermanence,' it has to be construed with 'word' though it is a part of the adjectival clause, and hence subordinate. But in the first syllogism, there is no difficulty of construction, as 'word' is the subject and the probans 'being a product' is directly construed with it. It may be urged that the probans (smoke) is invariably connected with the probandum (fire) and so the existence of smoke can prove the existence of fire. In that case how can it be construed with the subject (hill) ? But this need not cause any difficulty —the universal proposition shows the invariable concomitance between fire and smoke independently of the subject and though the probandum (fire) is construed as an adjective of the hill, the connexion of the probans and the probandum in and through the hill is not difficult to understand. Moreover, the hill is apprehended prior to fire, and fire is known only by a process of inference and so the hill should be regarded as the subject, with 'fire' predicated of it. And though the subject 'hill' was known as such, the hill as qualified by fire was not known. Inference, therefore, is not a repetition of previous information ; on the contrary it constitutes a distinct advance in knowledge.[1]

We have seen that Dignāga's speculations on the nature of the thesis were fully accepted by Kumārila. Later *Naiyāyikas*, notably Jayantabhaṭṭa, accepted the position as final. Uddyotakara's animadversion is rather sophistical and we do not know that any later *Naiyāyika* has accepted his finding. Even Vācaspati Miśra had to admit the cogency of Dignāga's arguments and only in special circumstances could he find a justification for the extraordinary conclusion of Uddyotakara. Uddyotakara's debate is inspired more by spite than logical justice and this is proved by the verdict of posterity, notably of Jayanta, who has given unqualified support to Dignāga's and Kumārila's position. It is rather curious that Uddyotakara himself accepts the position of Dignāga in his comments on 1. 1. 33. There is absolutely no logical necessity to rebut the finding of Dignāga, which is, on the contrary, in close conformity with the position of Vātsyāyana. Dignāga only drew out the logical implications of Vātsyayana's

[1] S. V., śls 28-48. deśasya parvatādes tu svarūpe pāvakād ṛte | gṛhīte 'gniviśiṣṭasya punar jñānaṁ na duṣyati || tasmād dharmaviśiṣṭasya dharmiṇaḥ syāt prameyatā | sā deśasyā 'gniyuktasya. *Ibid*, 46-48.

view.[1] Vācaspati skips over this portion of the *Vārttika*, perhaps in full consciousness of the palpable inconsistency, which he could not expose as a commentator.

[1] sādhyanirdeśaḥ pratijñā 1. 1. 33. prajñāpanīyena dharmeṇa dharmiṇo viśiṣṭasya parigrahavacanaṁ pratijñā. (*Bhāṣya*)—na brūmo dharmimātraṁ sādhyam api tu prajñāpanīyadharmaviśiṣṭo dharmī 'ti. N. V., p. 108, *et seq.*

CHAPTER XXIII

MEMBERS OF A SYLLOGISM (AVAYAVA)

Akṣapāda enumerates five members or sentences as constituting a syllogism, *viz.*, (1) proposition (*pratijñā*), (2) reason (*hetu*), (3) an explanatory example (*udāharaṇa*), (4) application (*upanaya*) and (5) conclusion (*nigamana*).[1] These sentences are not detached, unconnected statements ; but on the other hand, they are closely knit together by mutual requirement and they form a coherent group or a complex judgment.[2] There was a wide divergence of opinion regarding the number of premises and Dharmakīrti denied that the conclusion formed a part of the syllogism. Vātsyāyana refers to a view which held that the members of a syllogism were ten. The Vedāntists admitted only the first or the last three members.[3] The advanced *Jainas* held that two propositions formed a syllogism and the Buddhists too were at one with the *Jainas* so far as the number was concerned, though the form and nature of the syllogism were different in each school. But of this we shall have occasion to speak more fully later on. Now, those who insisted on the ten-membered syllogism, were of opinion that, psychologically speaking, five other factors should be added to the syllogism of the *Naiyāyika* to make it fully representative. These were, in their opinion,

[1] pratijñāhetūdāharaṇopanayanigamanāny avayavāḥ.

N. S., 1. 1. 32.

[2] avayavatvenai 'kavākyatā darśitā, sā ca padānāṁ parasparāpekṣitasambandhayogyārthapratyāyanena bhavati.

Tāt. ṭi., p. 266.

[3] tatra pañcatayaṁ kecid, dvayam anye, vayaṁ trayam
udāharaṇaparyantaṁ yadvo 'dāharaṇādikam ||

Vide *Advaitasiddhibālabodhinī*, p. 173.

(1) enquiry (*jijñāsā*), (2) doubt (*saṁśaya*), (3) belief in the competency of the premises advanced to prove the thesis (*śakyaprāpti*), (4) the practical utility (*prayojana*) and (5) removal of doubt (*saṁśayavyudāsa*). But Vātsyāyana and the later commentators point out that enquiry or interrogation, though psychologically an antecedent condition of discussion or proof, has no bearing on the fact of proof and so is outside the pale of syllogistic argument, which aims at proving a thesis. Doubt, too, is a purely psychical fact and though it inspires the enquiry and as such initiates the argument, it has no probative value. Belief in the competency is a question of psychological attitude and by itself has no logical consequence. Utility or practical application of the truth ascertained is only a bye-product of the syllogistic argument. And removal of doubt, which is effected by a *reductio ad absurdum* of the opposite thesis, has a remote logical bearing no doubt, but it cannot for that matter be regarded as a part of the syllogism, because its function is only to approve and confirm the truth of the conclusion logically deduced from the premises. It is outside the syllogism, being requisitioned from outside to corroborate the newly discovered truth and is thrown outside as soon as the truth is confirmed. Proposition and the rest, however, are true members of a syllogism, as each of them is essential to the deduction of the conclusion and to the conviction of the disputant; and neither of them can be omitted as each contributes a quota of meaning, which is not expressed by another.[1]

[1] *Vide* Vā. bh. *ad* 1. 1. 32. *Cf.* parapratipādakā ye vākyāṅgabhūtā itaretarāpratyāyitenā 'rthenā 'rthavanto vākyāngatām upayanti te 'vayavāḥ.

N. V., pp. 107-8.

Cf. te ca jijñāsādaya utpannāḥ prakaraṇasyo 'tthāpakāḥ svarupeṇa, na punaḥ svajñānena, yena svaśabdapratipādyāḥ santaḥ prakaraṇe 'py aṅgam bhaveyuḥ......tasmāt sarvathai 'va jijñāsādivācakapadaprayogo 'narthaka iti bhāvaḥ.

Tāt. ṭi , p. 267.

Now,

(1) Proposition is the statement of the thesis to be proved, *e.g.*, ‘ word is impermanent ’ (*pratijñā*).

(2) Statement of reason consists in adducing a fact capable of proving the probandum, *e.g.*, because it (word) has a definite origin (*hetu*).

(3) Example is a familiar instance which is known to possess the prabandum by virtue of the probative reason which it possesses in common with the subject or the minor term, *e.g.* a thing having a definite origin is seen to be impermanent, as, for instance, a pot (*udāharana*).

(4) Application of the reason to the subject after its probative value has been attested in the example, *e.g.*, word has a definite origin quite as much as the pot which is known to be impermanent (*upanaya*).

(5) Conclusion is the re-statement of the thesis with the statement of reason attached to it, *e.g.*, ‘ therefore word is impermanent, because it has a definite origin’ (*nigamana*).

The whole syllogism with all its members fully stated amounts to this :—

(1) Word is impermanent,
(2) Because it has a definite origin.
(3) A thing having a definite origin is seen to be impermanent, as for instance a pot.
(4) Word has a definite origin.
(5) Therefore, word is impermanent.

Dharmakīrti is perhaps the first philosopher who questioned the cogency of the proposition. A Proposition has no probative value. The conclusion is proved by virtue of the second and third, or the third and fourth members, the fourth and the second member being identical in import. These two members are alone relevant and the conclusion, too, follows irresistibly from these two and, as such, need not be stated in so many words. A statement is necessary when a fact cannot be known otherwise, and it is redundant here as the fact is known from the drift of the two members. Moreover, the conclusion is only an inane and useless repetition of the thesis and so should be expunged. But even the thesis by itself without any reference to the conclusion is redundant, because the subject of dispute is an accepted datum and is known from the context. Vācaspati and Jayantabhaṭṭa, on the other hand, contend that the five-membered syllogism is psychologically the most sound and satisfactory medium of argument. Vācaspati argues that the arguer (*vādin*) has to state what is wanted by the opponent, otherwise his statement will fail to receive attentive consideration at the hands of the opponent. The thesis, *e.g.*, 'word is impermanent,' is what is wanted to be proved both by the opponent and the arguer and unless this is stated, the reason 'because it is a product' will be completely irrelevant. Of course, the Buddhist can contend that his syllogism would completely satisfy the intellectual demand. Thus, 'whatever is a product in time is impermanent and word is a product in time' is a perfect syllogism, as it brings home by a logical necessity the conclusion that 'word is impermanent,' and this should satisfy the intellectual demand. Vācaspati maintains that the statement of the thesis has a psychological value as it directly enlists the attention of the opponent to the subject-matter of dispute and so the whole argument becomes effective. The Buddhist syllogism lacks this initial advantage and will fail to rouse the attention of the opponent. This defence of Vācaspati is not convincing enough. The arguer advances a syllogism only when there is an occasion for it and the opponent too cannot but give attention to the argument if he is serious of purpose, otherwise the *Naiyāyika's* thesis, too, would receive short shrift at the hands of a frivolous opponent.[1] Jayanta contends that the arguer

[1] *Vide* Tāt. ṭi., pp. 274-75. *Cf.* prakṛtārthāśrayā sā 'pi yadi vā na virudhyate | na vādy akāṇḍa evā 'ha parasyā 'pi hi sādhanam ||

T.S., Śl. 1436.

should try to bring home an argument exactly in the order in which he has himself reasoned out the conclusion. The arguer first observes the subject and the reason (probans) and then remembers the universal concomitance, etc. Although the subject is observed without the probandum, the probandum (impermanence, etc.) should be stated in the thesis to disarm a feeling of uncertainty as to the subject-matter of proof, for which a reason would be requisitioned. Psychologically speaking, Jayanta is perfectly correct. But the Buddhist contends that a syllogism should be chosen with a view to its logical cogency and psychological order should have no bearing on it. If psychological factors should have a determining value, even a statement of approval or direction which initiates the debate should be incorporated in the syllogism.[1] If logical cogency is regarded as the criterion, then the proposition should be excluded in the same way as 'enquiry,' 'doubt,' etc., advocated by the exponent of the ten-membered syllogism have been discarded by the *Naiyāyika*.

The third member, application of the reason, too, is a superfluity and has no independent probative force, as it only reiterates the meaning of the second member, the statement of reason.[2] To this charge of Dignāga, Bhāvivikta and Uddyotakara have given this reply. The statement of reason, *e.g.*, 'on account of being a product' (*kṛtakatvāt*) only serves to assign a reason and does not testify that the reason exists in the subject or not. The application (*upanaya*) emphasises the subsistence of the reason in the subject and as such has a different function and value from the mere statement of reason. The value of *upanaya* may be shown in another way. The *upanaya* does not reiterate the reason as such ; it applies the reason with its invariable

[1] *Vide* N. M., pp. 571-72 ; also, T. S., śls. 1432-33.

[2] "upanayavacanaṁ na sādhanam, uktahetvarthaprakāśakatvāt, dvitīyahetuvacanavat" ity ācārya-Dignāgapādaiḥ pramāṇite Bhāviviktādayaḥ............āhuḥ.

T. S. P., p. 421.

concomitance as shown in the example and thus leads to the conclusion. The statement of reason unbacked by invariable concomitance with the probandum is inane and ineffectual; hence the application is necessary.[1] But Śāntarakṣita contends that if *upanaya* is deemed necessary for pointing out the subsistence of the reason in the subject, the necessity and function of the statement of reason should be stated. Mere assignation of a reason without reference to the subject is absolutely out of place and uncalled for. It must therefore be admitted that assignation of reason has a reference to the subject and so has the same value with *upanaya*. Therefore, either of them should be jettisoned. Nor is it necessary for bringing into relation the invariable concomitance with the reason assigned, because this relation is understood *eo ipso* from the two premises (*sic*), the statement of reason and example with universal concomitance. And these two premises, *e.g.*, 'whatever is a product is perishable, as a pot' and 'word is a product,' constitute a perfect syllogism and nothing further is necessary. Vācaspati and Jayanta fully realised the cogency of the argument as put forward by Śāntarakṣita and the weakness of Uddyotakara's defence. But they appealed to psychological evidence. They argue, 'well, our argument should be advanced in the order of our own experience, by which we arrived at the truth. Now we first observe the subject, say, 'the hill' and then the reason, 'smoke.' Next we remember the invariable concomitance of smoke and fire as observed in a furnace and immediately this invariable concomitance is understood in relation to the smoke in the hill and the direct upshot of this is the deduction of the conclusion. The five members only embody the order of our own subjective ratiocination and as such constitute the most satisfying syllogism.' This defence, on the ground of psychology of ratiocination, reflects great credit on the part of Vācaspati and Jayanta and is more satisfactory than the apologia of Uddyotakara and Bhāvivikta. Logic

[1] *Ibid*, also *vide* N.V., pp. 137, 138.

and psychology indubitably occupy some common ground, especially in its most deliberate and elaborate processes, namely, conception, judgment and reasoning. Psychology tries to explain the subjective processes of conception, judgment and reasoning and to give their natural history; but logic is wholly concerned with the results of such processes, with concepts, judgments and reasonings and merely with the validity of the results, that is, with their truth or consistency, whereas Psychology has nothing to do with their validity, but only with their causes. Besides, the logical judgment is quite a different thing from the psychological; the latter involves feeling and belief, whereas the former is merely a given relation of concepts. If belief has any place in logic, it depends upon evidence; whereas in psychology belief may depend upon causes which may have evidentiary value or may not.[1]

So psychological evidence as to the subjective processes of reasoning should not be allowed to dictate terms to the constitution of a logically sound syllogism. Logic, as has been pointed out above, is concerned with validity and cogency, whereas psychology is interested in the natural history of mental phenomena. So though psychologically the proposition and the application may have a *raison d'etre*, they cannot on that account be suffered to enter as factors into a syllogistic argument, whose chief interest and guiding principle should be logical cogency and probative value, which is conspicuously lacking in the premises under consideration.

And as regards the conclusion (*nigamana*), this also does not require to be stated, as it follows by a sheer logical necessity from the universal proposition as stated in the example and the statement of reason in the application (*upanaya*). Moreover, on the *Naiyāyika's* own showing it is perfectly redundant being only a purposeless reiteration of the proposition (*pratijñā*).[2]

1 *Vide* Carveth Reid's *Logic*: *Deductive and Inductive*, pp. 9-10.

2 tatrā 'cārya-Dignāgapādair uktam "nigamanaṁ punaruktatvād eva na sādhanam" iti. T.S.P., p. 421.

Cf. 'upanayanigamane nā 'vayavāntare, arthāviśeṣād'—quoted in N.V., p. 137.

Uddyotakara however maintains that the conclusion is not a useless repetition of the proposition or the thesis, as the latter only states what is yet to be proved and the former is the statement of a proven fact. Nor is the statement of the conclusion unnecessary, because it serves to dispel a likely error or doubt. Unless the conclusion is stated, the opponent may still waver as to whether 'word is perishable or not.' The clear statement of the conclusion disarms all such doubt and satisfies the opponent completely. But Śāntarakṣita points out that this defence only seeks to gloss over a glaring defect with a show of explanation. The fact of the matter is that there can be no possibility of a doubt, if the reason endued with triple condition is advanced. The conclusion irresistibly follows from this and none else. If on the other hand the triple character be lacking, the statement of the conclusion by itself cannot remove the doubt about its validity.[1] Aviddhakarṇa contends that the premises scattered and piecemeal cannot establish a unitary judgment, that is, the conclusion, unless they are shown to be mutually related and this reciprocity of relation is shown by the conclusion. But this too is a hopeless apology because though the premises are stated piecemeal, they have a mutual compatibility and relevancy, as the probans by reason of invariable concomitance establishes the probandum by a logical necessity and through this concomitance, the premises are knit together by a logical bond. Thus, the statement of the conclusion is unnecessary even for the purpose of showing the mutual relation of the premises, as they are related by virtue of their own relevancy.[2]

1 trirūpahetunirdeśasāmarthyād eva siddhitaḥ ।
na viparyayaśaṅkā 'sti vyarthaṁ nigamanaṁ tataḥ ॥

T.S., śl. 1440.

Cf. nā 'pi nigamanād vacanamātrān niryuktikāt tu sā vinivartate. T.S.P., *ibid.*

2 Aviddhakarṇas tv āha—" viprakīrṇaiś ca vacanair nai 'kārthaḥ pratipādyate । tena sambandhasiddhyarthaṁ vācyaṁ nigamanaṁ pṛthak ॥ " T.S.P., p. 422. *ad* T.S., śl. 1441.

The Buddhist therefore reduces the syllogism to two members, the universal proposition with the example tagged on and the minor premise. The *Jaina* logician by advocating internal concomitance of the probans and the probandum without reference to an example expunges the example from the universal proposition and thus brings it into line with Aristotelian syllogism. From the doctrine of ten-membered syllogism reduced to five in the *Nyāyasūtra* and still further reduced to two in Buddhist logic, we can trace the history of the evolution of syllogism. Naturally the psychological and the logical factors were mixed together in the doctrine of ten-membered syllogism. In the *Naiyāyika's* syllogism there has been a bold attempt to shake off the psychological incubus, but still the psychological influence did not cease to be at work. In the Buddhist syllogism as propounded by Dignāga and Dharmakīrti the psychological factors were carefully eliminated and the syllogism received a perfectly logical shape. But the survival of the example was a relic of the ancient sway of psychology and this was destined to be unceremoniously brushed aside by the onslaughts of *Jaina* logicians, who propounded the doctrine of internal concomitance (*antarvyāpti*). We are inclined to believe that the growth and evolution of syllogistic argument was purely indigenous and the theory of Greek influence, advanced by the late Dr. Satish Chandra Vidyābhūṣaṇa, has no more substantial basis than pure conjecture to support it. The points of contact are rather flimsy coincidences and too laboured to produce conviction. We confess that we stand unconvinced of Aristotelian influence in spite of the ingenuity of the learned Doctor. It is highly improbable that the five-membered syllogism was worked out from Aristotle's syllogism of three members. The universal proposition does not seem to have received the attention, it deserves, at the hands of the old *Naiyāyikas*. It was Dignāga who emphasised this important point. The learned Doctor goes out of his way to detect here also Greek influence, but this looks like seeing tiger in every bush. The whole theory of Dr. Vidyābhūṣaṇa appears to have been formed from *a priori* considerations and then coincidences, far-fetched and accidental, were pressed into requisition to confirm his theory conceived on *a priori* grounds. We should on the other hand believe Vātsyāyana who derived the five-membered syllogism from the syllogism of ten members and this was due to the growing clarity of logical vision, which ultimately culminated in the two-membered syllogism of Dignāga's school, with the conclusion suppressed. Here it was an improvement on Aristotle's syllogism. The survival of the example in Indian syllogism except in *Jaina* logic, appears to be decisive proof of indigenous growth of the syllogistic form of argument in India.[1]

1 *Vide* H.I.L., Appendix B, pp. 497-513.

CHAPTER XXIV

UNIVERSAL CONCOMITANCE (VYĀPTI)

The problem of Logic is pre-eminently the discovery of universal concomitance of the probans (*hetu*) and the probandum (*sādhya*), because this is the pivot and ground on which inference is based. We can infer the existence of fire from the existence of smoke in all places and times, only if we can persuade ourselves by unflinching logic that smoke cannot exist without fire. But what is the guarantee that smoke and fire will be associated together without any break ? We cannot certainly arrive at this truth from perceptual observation, because all the individual cases of fire and smoke, present, past and future, near and distant, are not amenable to observation; and even if it had been possible, it would have rendered all inference nugatory. Nor can this invariable concomitance be known with the help of inference, because inference is itself possible only if there is an invariable concomitance at its back and for this, again, another inference would be in request and for that a third and so on *ad infinitum*. The upshot will be that no inference would be possible. So the problem of problems that logic has to face and solve is to enquire into and discover the grounds of this universal concomitance.

The Materialists of the *Cārvāka* school and later on Bhartṛhari and Śrīharṣa emphatically denied the possibility of ascertaining this universal connexion and consequently the validity of inference as a medium of authentic knowledge. The Buddhists affirm that inference of the probandum is possible if the probans is ascertained to be endowed with triple characteristics set forth above. And these triple characteristics can be easily established if the probans can be shown to stand in the relation of causality or essential identity to the probandum in question. But this fundamental position of the Buddhists has been questioned by these sceptics. There is no knowing that fire will produce smoke for all eternity or the oak will have the essential attributes of a tree for all time to come. The powers and attributes of things are not unfrequently observed to undergo essential change of nature in different seasons and places and circumstances. Dates grown on a particular soil have a distinct taste and nutritive properties from dates grown in other countries; water is generally cool, but the water of the well has a tepid temperature and the ice-glaciers of the Himalayas have a freezing touch. Fire has an excessively hot touch in summer, but has got a bearable heat in the cold season. Moreover, even things observed to have definite causal efficiency are seen to be inoperative in regard to other substances. Thus, fire observed to have burning capacity is seen to be inoperative on asbestos and mica. So appeal to the Uniformity of Nature, too, is unavailing, because it is not given to man to divine the secrets of Nature.[1] The sun rises in the east every morning, but there is no guarantee that it will not rise in another direction or not rise at all. Causality, too, is of no avail, because it is quite supposable that the secret nature of the objects and consequently their effects and influence may change without any change in their sensible qualities. "This happens sometimes, and with regard to some objects: why may it not happen always and with regard to all objects? What logic, what process of argument secures you against this supposition?" And the relation of cause and effect is not understood by any process of reasoning or argument (*tarka*), but from experience. Certainly

[1] avasthādeśakālānāṁ bhedād bhinnāsu śaktiṣu | bhāvānām anumānena prasiddhir atidurlabhā || nirjñātaśakter dravyasya tāṁ tām arthakriyāṁ prati | viśiṣṭadravyasambandhe sā śaktiḥ pratibadhyate ||

Vāk Pa., Ch. I, śls. 32-33.

there is nothing in what we call the cause which can make us infer an event, the effect. Were this the case one could infer from the first appearance of an object the event that would follow.[1] But only a number of instances can make us understand the relation. And there is nothing different in a number of instances from every single instance except this: that when in a number of instances the same thing is followed by a particular event, the mind is, by a customary habit, taken, on the appearance of one, to the thought of another, its attendant. The connexion takes place in the mind and cannot be supposed to subsist between the objects and so cannot be known *a priori*.[2] The relation of causality or of essential identity (*tādātmya*), on which the Buddhist logician bases the universal concomitance, has, by itself, no special virtue to commend itself in preference to repeated observation of co-presence (*sahacāra*), which the *Naiyāyika* claims to be guarantee of the validity of inferential knowledge. Even causation in the last resort is nothing but a belief in the Uniformity of Nature and this Uniformity of Nature is but an unproved postulate. No guarantee can be offered that the course of Nature, though seen to be perfectly regular in the past, will not change in the future. "Being determined by custom to transfer the past to the future in all our inferences, where the past has been entirely regular and uniform, we expect the event with the greatest assurance, and leave no room for any contrary supposition."[3] Purandara, evidently a philosopher of the *Cārvāka* school, observes that ordinary inference, which we make in our practical life and

[1] na ca kākatālīyatvādiśaṅkāvyudāsārthaṁ dvitīyādidarśanāpekṣe 'ti vācyam, dvitīyādidarśane 'pi śaṅkātādavasthyāt.........evaṁ bhūyodarśanam api saṁśāyakam, tarkas tv anavasthāgrasta eve 'ti kathaṁ vyāptigrahaḥ. *Tattvacintāmaṇi, Vyaptigrahopāya.*

[2] bhūyodarśanatas tāvad udeti matir īdṛśī I niyato 'yam anene 'ti sakalaprāṇisākṣikā II

Quoted in N. M., p. 122.

[3] Hume.

experience, is not denied by the *Cārvākas*. The *Cārvāka* questions the ultimate validity of inference as an instrument of metaphysical thought. Śāntarakṣita rejoins that if ordinary inference is admitted, you admit the validity of inference as such. Inference, whether ordinary or super-ordinary, is based on causal relation and identity of essence and if this basic relation is taken to be a fact, there is no reason to doubt the authenticity of inference even in metaphysical speculations.[1] Gaṅgeśa in the *Tattvacintāmaṇi* maintains that universal concomitance is known from observation of co-presence of two facts, provided this knowledge is not vitiated by a doubt or uncertainty as to its invariability. If there is a definite knowledge that the co-presence is variable, the universal concomitance is out of the question. But if there is no definite certainty of an exception the universal concomitance can be presumed and this presumption amounts to certitude when all doubts are resolved by a *reductio ad absurdum* of the contrary supposition. It may be contended that the *reductio ad absurdum* too is a sort of inference, being based upon a knowledge of universal concomitance between the contradictories and so there will arise a vicious infinite series. Thus, when one argues, that smoke must be concomitant with fire, because smoke is the product of fire, and a product cannot exist without its cause, the arguer assumes a wider universal proposition that cause and effect are inseparably related and for this second universal proposition a third will have to be assumed and so on to infinity. The sceptic will doubt that though a product, smoke can exist independently of fire. But Gaṅgeśa says that no such doubt is possible. You can doubt so long as you do not contradict yourself. It is not possible that you doubt the invariability of causal relation, when you invariably adopt fire to produce smoke. Your own practice and behaviour are proof positive that you do not and cannot doubt the invariable character of causal relation. If out of cussedness

[1] T. S., ślS. 1482-83.

you insist on doubting, your practice contradicts your doubt and self-contradiction is the limit of doubt.[1] But this argument of Gaṅgeśa would not satisfy a sceptic. The sceptic would observe in return that the logician here confounds a metaphysical doubt with a logical doubt. The doubt of a philosopher may be deeper than our ordinary empirical doubts. We can quote with profit Hume in this connexion, " My practice, you say, refutes my doubts. But you mistake the purport of my question. As an agent I am satisfied on the point ; but as a philosopher, who has some share of curiosity, I will not say scepticism, I want to learn the foundation of this inference."[2] European logicians have relegated the task of solution of these doubts to metaphysics. " Now these doubts and surmises are

[1] vyabhicārajñānavirahasahakṛtam sahacāradarśaṇaṁ vyāptigrāhakaṁ, jñānaṁ niścayaḥ śaṅkā ca......tadvirahaś ca kvacid vipakṣabādhakatarkāt..., tarkasya vyāptigrahamūlakatvenā 'navasthe 'ti cet, na, yāvadāśaṅkaṁ tarkānusaraṇāt. yatra ca vyāghātena śaṅkai 'va nā 'vatarati tatra tarkaṁ vinai 'va vyāptigrahaḥ...tad idam uktam, tad eva hy āśaṅkyate yaṣminn āśaṅkyamāne svakriyāvyāghāto na bhavatī 'ti. na hi sambhavati svayaṁ vahnyādikaṁ dhūmādikāryārthaṁ niyamata upādatte, tatkāraṇaṁ tan ne 'ty āśaṅkyate. *Tattvacintāmaṇi*, *Vyāptigrahopāyasiddhānta*.

[2] We, however, do not undertake to conduct an enquiry into the merits of the sceptical position adopted by Hume and Śrīharṣa, which enquiry will be entirely irrelevant to our purpose, *viz.*, the discussion of logical problems. It will, however, suffice to observe that the doubts and problems raised by these thinkers were not understood at their true value both in India and Europe for a long time. We can profitably quote Kant's opinion about Hume, which, I doubt not, applies with equal force in the case of Śrīharṣa and his critics. " But the perpetual hard fate of metaphysics would not allow Hume to be understood. We cannot, without a certain sense of pain, consider how utterly his opponents, Reid, Oswald, Beattie and even Priestley, missed the point of the problem. For while they were ever assuming as conceded what he doubted, and demonstrated with eagerness and often with arrogance what he never thought of disputing, they so overlooked his inclination towards a better state of things, that everything remained undisturbed in its old condition." *Prolegomena*, p. 6.

metaphysical spectres which it remains for Metaphysics to lay. Logic has no direct concern with them, but keeps the plain path of plain beliefs, level with the comprehension of plain men." [1] From the metaphysical standpoint, therefore, all our inferences are of a hypothetical character, being based in the ultimate analysis on the belief in the Uniformity of Nature, which belief again is inspired by our uncontradicted experience in the past. "Nevertheless, it seems undesirable to call our confidence in Nature's Uniformity an hypothesis, it is incongruous to use the same term for our tentative conjectures and for our most indispensable beliefs. 'The universal Postulate' is a better term for the principle which, in some form or other, every generalisation takes for granted." [2]

Apart from these metaphysical doubts, which lay axe at the very root of all inference, the empirical validity of inference is not doubted even by the greatest sceptic. The importance of universal concomitance both in subjective inference (*svārthānumāna*) and syllogistic argument (*parārthānumāna*) was emphasised by Dignāga perhaps for the first time and ever since it has been recognised as an indispensable part of syllogistic argument. Though the *Nyāyasūtra* does not contain any reference to this all-important factor of inference and there is room for supposition that the argument in *Nyāya* is based on analogy, there are indications that Vātsyāyana was conscious of the necessity of universal concomitance. Uddyotakara, however, interpreted the *Sūtras* (1.1.35-36) in such a way that he brought it into line with the triple condition emphasised in Buddhist logic. Dignāga was perhaps the first logician to insist on the universal concomitance being stated in a syllogism and the violation of this rule was stated to give rise to two fallacies of the example, *viz.*, (1) non-statement of concomitance in agreement (*apradarśitānvaya*) and non-statement of concomitance in

1 Carveth Read, *Logic : Deductive and Inductive*, p. 10.

2 *Op cit.*, pp. 264-65.

difference (*apradarśitavyatireka*). Jayantabhaṭṭa fully endorses the Buddhist position in this respect and observes that mere statement of the example is due to laziness ; on the other hand, it should be stated only with a view to point out the universal concomitance.[1]

Now, what is the means of apprehending this universal concomitance? The Buddhist answers that the concomitance is known to be universal and invariable if the relation between the probans and the probandum can be shown to be either one of causality or essential identity and not from mere observation of co-accompaniment of two factors. If the concomitance be based upon causality or essential identity, the relation cannot but be conceived to be invariable, as an effect cannot be conceived to be independent of a cause and hence the effect is the proof of the cause ; and as regards two things, whose nature is fundamentally identical, there can be no separation between the two, as that would be tantamount to forfeiture of their own essential character, which is inconceivable. So long as the supposition of the contrary possibility is not ruled out of court by a *reductio ad absurdum*, the doubt as to their concomitance being a case of accidental coincidence will not be removed. And the *reductio ad absurdum* can come into operation only if the facts in question are known to be related as set forth above. Jayantabhaṭṭa, however, charges the Buddhist with partial observation and narrowness of outlook. If nothing outside causality be supposed to be the ground of universal concomitance, then numerous cases of invariable concomitance and consequential inference would be left unaccounted for. Thus, for instance, the forthcoming appearance of stars is inferred from sunset, the rise of tidal waves from the rise of the moon, impending rainfall is inferred from

[1] udāharaṇavacanam ahi paṭavad ity evam ālasyād eva prayuñjate, tad dhi vyāptipradarśanāyai 'va vaktavyaṁ yat kṛtakaṁ tad anityaṁ dṛṣṭam yathā ghaṭa iti. N.M., p. 569.

the movement of ants carrying off their larvæ, the existence of shade on the other side of light on the surface and suchlike cases of inference are approved by all and sundry. But the concomitance in these cases cannot be traced to causality. If the Buddhist raises doubt about the invariability of such cases of concomitance, we shall answer that there is some invariable relation between the two, no doubt, but there is absolutely no justification to restrict this relation to causality and identity alone. Moreover, such doubts are possible even in the case of causality, why should smoke issue from fire alone and not from water? If uncontradicted experience be the answer, the *Naiyāyika* also can point to this uncontradicted experience of concomitance in agreement and difference as evidence.[1]

The Buddhist in reply observes that mere concomitance in presence and absence cannot constitute sufficient evidence of its invariability; unless the contrary possibility is debarred by a *reductio ad absurdum* doubt will persist. And the *reductio ad absurdum* can arise only if the relation is understood to be one of causality or identity, because no other relation can be conceived to be invariable and uniform. Mere concomitance is incompetent to prove this invariability. For an instance in point, the case of material bodies and the fact of their being inscribable by an iron stylus can be adduced. It may have been observed in hundreds of cases that material bodies are liable to be inscribed by an iron stylus, but this is no guarantee that it would hold good universally and an exception is found in the case of diamonds, which though material are not liable to be scratched by an iron stylus. As regards the cases adduced by the *Naiyāyikas*, it should be observed that there must be a causal relation, though indirect, between the two sets of connected phenomena. They

[1] tasmin saty eva bhavanam na vinā bhavanaṁ tataḥ | ayam evā 'vinābhāvo niyamaḥ sahacāritā || kiṁkṛto niyamo 'syā 'sminn iti ced evam uttaram | tadātmatādipakṣe 'pi nai 'ṣa praśno nivartate || jvalanāj jāyate dhūmo na jalād iti kā gatiḥ | evam evai 'tad iti cet sāhacarye 'pi tat samam || N. M., p. 121.

must be co-effects of the same set of causes and conditions, otherwise the invariability of their relation cannot be explained. If the relation of causality or identity cannot be discovered offhand, we should conduct researches to find out such relation. It will not do to rest content with observation of mere concomitance. So long as such relation is not discovered, the universal proposition can at best be regarded as an empirical generalisation.

Prof. Carveth Reid has enumerated five cases of Uniformities of Co-existence, which cannot be supposably subsumed under a wider Principle of co-existence corresponding to Causation, the principle of succession. These are as follows :—

(1) "The Geometrical ; as that, in a four-sided figure, if the opposite angles are equal, the opposite sides are equal and parallel .... The co-existent facts do not cause one another, nor are they jointly caused by something else ; they are mutually involved : such is the nature of space." The Buddhist logician, however, has postulated for the explanation of such cases of co-existence the relation of essential identity.

(2) " Universal co-existence among the properties of concrete things. The chief example is the co-existence of gravity with inertia in all material bodies." The Buddhist would include this case under essential identity of nature.

(3) " Co-existence due to causation ; such as the position of objects in space at any time .... the relative position of rocks in geological strata, and of trees in a forest, are due to causes." The Buddhist has also noticed such co-existence between the co-effects of a common cause, as between smoke and transformation of fuel, between colour and taste in a fruit.[1]

(4) "The co-existence of properties in Natural Kinds ; which we call the constitution, defining characters, or specific

[1] ekasāmagryadhīnatvād rūpāde rasato gatiḥ ।
hetudharmānumānena dhūmendhanavikāravat ।
Quoted in T.S.P., *ad* śl. 1425, p. 417.

nature of such things—oxygen, platinum, sulphur and the other elements ; —all these are known to us as different groups of co-existent properties. It may be conjectured, indeed, that these groupings of properties are also due to causation, and sometimes the causes can be traced ; but very often the causes are still unknown."

(5) "There are also a few cases in which properties co-exist in an unaccountable way, without being co-extensive with any one species, genus, or order : as most metals are whitish, and scarlet flowers are wanting in fragrance."[1]

But the Buddhists would suppose that the source and determinant of concomitance in these cases also must be either causation or identity of essence, though such may not be patent to our limited understanding. Because if one thing could be a condition of another thing without a definitive relation, there would be no restriction in inference and anything could be inferred from any other thing.[2] In support of the Buddhist position we again quote Prof. Carveth Reid, "All these cases of co-existence (except the Geometrical) present the problem of deriving them from Causation ;.........and, indeed, if we conceive of the external world as a perpetual redistribution of matter and energy, it follows that the whole state of Nature at any instant, and, therefore, every co-existence included in it, is due to causation issuing from some earlier distribution of matter and energy." "Geometrical Co-existence.........is deduced from the Definitions and Axioms." "When Co-existence cannot be derived from Causation, they can only be proved by collecting examples and trusting vaguely to the Uniformity of Nature. If no exceptions are found, we have an empirical law of considerable probability...........If exceptions occur, we have at most an approximate generalisation, as 'Most metals are whitish,'

[1] *Op. cit.*, pp. 165-66.

[2] sambandhānupapattau ca sarvasyā 'pi gatir bhavet.

T. S., śl. 1423.

or 'Most domestic cats are tabbies.''[1] The objections of the *Naiyāyikas* are refuted by this argument, because without causal connexion or essential identity we cannot convince ourselves of the impossibility of the contrary and this alone is determinant of universal concomitance.

Now, the question arises, what is the guarantee that smoke will not abide in a place devoid of fire? And unless all doubts of exception, of the possibility of the particular concomitance being regarded as a case of accidental coincidence, are not totally removed, the knowledge of universal concomitance cannot take place. We have already quoted Gaṅgeśa who says that doubt of universality is removed by a *reductio ad absurdum* of the contradictory supposition in cases where the contradictory is possible. But in the case of an Exclusively Affirmative Inference (*kevalānvayyanumāna*) there is no contradictory and so doubt regarding the subsistence of the probans in the contradictory is impossible. Here the *reductio ad absurdum* is not resorted to, because no occasion arises. And in cases where doubt is removed on pain of self-contradiction, there is absolutely no necessity of having recourse to this negative reasoning, as there is no other doubt to remove. So knowledge of concomitance of probans and probandum unqualified by a doubt or certitude of its variable character is the guarantee of the certitude of invariable unconditional concomitance. Gaṅgeśa, perhaps, casts a fling at the *Jaina* Logicians who hold that knowledge of the unconditionality of the probans is always made possible by an appeal to negative reasoning (*reductio ad absurdum*, *vipakṣabādhakatarka*) and this is the determinant of invariable concomitance; because negative reasoning is possible only where there are negative instances and is necessary only where there is doubt. In an Exclusively Affirmative Inference it is out of the question, as there is no negative instance. For example, in an inference of the type, 'This is nameable, because it is knowable,' there is nothing, which is not knowable, which can be known inasmuch

[1] *Op. cit.*, pp. 275-76.

as *if* it is known, it becomes knowable. So reduction to absurdity of the contrary instances being impossible, the universal concomitance should be held to be cognised by other means than the *reductio ad absurdum*. But the *Jainas* contend that there is no such case as an exclusively affirmative inference, because though an actual contradictory may not be in existence, any imaginary contradictory will serve the purpose of showing the absence of the probans as concomitant with the absence of the probandum.[1] It is curious that Jayanta does not admit an exclusively affirmative reason (probans) and thinks that negative concomitance is the most satisfying and decisive factor, though it may not be actually stated in a syllogism. Mere concomitance in agreement is a halting proof. In default of an actual contradictory, the absence of concomitance should be stated in respect of an imaginary concept like the rabbit's horn. So no probans can be held to be exclusively affirmative and universal, and unconditional concomitance can be proved by means of negative argument only, as concomitance in mere agreement has no probative value.[2]

[1] Vādīndra Paṇḍita has elaborately proved that Exclusively Affirmative Inference is an impossible fiction and he has taken the same line of argument as set forth above. He has raised an interesting dilemma, which reduces the opponent to an absurdity. 'Well,' the opponent may argue, 'when the probans has no counter-instance (*vipakṣa*), and so exists only in the homologous cases, it is a case of Exclusively affirmative inference.' But this is only a pretence. Is the counter-instance known or unknown? If known, you cannot deny it. If unknown, you cannot assert that it is non-existent! *Vide Mahāvidyāviḍambana*, p. 97.

[2] kevalānvayihetuś ca na kaścid upalabhyate.

N. M., p. 676.

Also, na kevalānvayī nāma hetuḥ sambhavati. *Ibid.*

Again, sādhanadharmasya vipakṣād vyāvṛttim abhidhitsatā sādhyābhāve sādhanābhāvo darśayitavyaḥ...yo hy avidyamānavipakṣo hetuḥ so 'pi sutarāṁ tato vyāvṛtto bhavati, tadabhāvāt tatrā 'vrtter iti......yatrā 'nityatvaṁ nāsti tatra kāryatvam api nāsti yathā śaśaviṣāṇādāv iti. Also, vyatirekaniścayam antareṇa pratibandhagrahaṇānupapatteḥ.

Op. cit., p. 122.

The *Jaina* logicians further contend that the triple characteristic and the fivefold characteristic of the probans, respectively maintained by the Buddhist and the *Naiyāyikas* as the *conditio sine qua non* of valid inference, are absolutely inane and ineffectual, because the triple or the fivefold condition, if unbacked by knowledge of the impossibility of the contradictory supposition, cannot be a sufficient guarantee of universal concomitance. This can be brought home by a concrete example, 'X is certainly of a swarthy complexion, because he is a son of Mitrā like the other sons of Mitrā (who are known to be swarthy).' In this syllogism, the probans 'being the son of Mitrā' is present in the subject X, and so the first condition is satisfied (*pakṣa-sattva*). It is also a known fact that other sons of Mitrā are swarthy, and so the second condition 'existence of the probans in the homologues' is fulfilled ; it is also known that those who have not a swarthy complexion are not sons of Mitrā, and so the third condition, 'absence of the probans in the heterologous cases' is satisfied. But though the triple condition is satisfied in full, the inference is not valid, as there is no logical imcompatibility in the fact of Mitrā's son possessing a fair complexion.

It is, therefore, perfectly reasonable to hold this 'logical incompatibility of the contradictory supposition' to be the only legitimate character of a valid probans, when the triple character is absolutely abortive in the absence of this condition and this condition alone is found to prove the thesis, though the triple character may be absent. The triple character of the Buddhist and the fivefold attribute of the *Naiyāyika* are only logical offshoots of this condition alone, *viz.*, the incompatibility of the probans with the contradictory and all their cogency and validity are derived from this factor alone. So it is only a roundabout procedure to regard them as the essential condition of a legitimate probans and sometimes this is misleading and erroneous. It is not infrequently seen that inference is made without any reference to the subsistence of the probans in the subject (minor term), as for instance the Brāhmanhood of the son is inferred from the Brāhmanhood of the parents.[1] And even the Buddhist has to admit that in negative inference, *e.g.*, in the heterologue, reference to the subject is absolutely unnecessary. The mere knowledge of negative concomitance, of the absence of the probans consequent on the absence of probandum, is alone necessary in such cases.[2] The Buddhist, therefore, cannot insist that the triple character is either fundamental or universal.

The Buddhist however has contended in protest that the triple condition is the only legitimate ground of universal concomitance and, consequently, of inference. The second condition 'subsistence in homologues' (*sapakṣasattva*) does not mean 'mere subsistence,' but 'subsistence in homologues, solely and exclusively,' which is tantamount to its absolute non-existence in the heterologues or contradictory instances. And in the syllogism in question, the non-existence of the probans, 'being the son of Mitrā,' in the contradictory instances is doubtful, as there is no logical incompatibility in Mitrā's son being not swarthy. The question of complexion, swarthy or otherwise, depends upon other factors, *viz.*, food, merit and the like and not upon Mitrā's motherhood.[3] Hemacandrasūri, one of the foremost *Jaina* philosophers, observes in reply to this defence of the Buddhist that the Buddhist here completely gives up his position when he seeks to put such restriction upon the second condition. 'Subsistence in homologues alone, solely and exclusively' is tantamount to negation of the contradictory and this is our position. We, *Jainas*, maintain that the probans must be shown to be incompatible with the contradictory of the probandum in question and this is the only legitimate and

[1] pitroś ca brāhmaṇatvena putre brāhmaṇatānumā |
sarvalokaprasiddhā na pakṣadharmam apekṣate ||

of Kumārila, quoted in Pra. mi., II. 1. 17.

[2] tasmād vaidharmyadṛṣṭānte ne 'ṣṭo 'vaśyam ihā 'śrayaḥ |
tadabhāve tu tan ne 'ti vacanād api saṅgateḥ ||

quoted in T. S. P., p. 145.

[3] T. S., śls. 1416-18.

self-sufficient condition. And when the Buddhist has to fall back upon this negative interpretation, it is legitimate and fair that he should take up our position and waive all false allegiance to the triple character, simply because it is propounded by Dignāga and Dharmakīrti.[1] Moreover, the triple character as the definition of a valid probans is rather too narrow, because it fails to meet the exigencies of such arguments as, 'whatever is existent is momentary.' In this syllogism there is no homologue, as the attribute of momentariness is predicated of all existent things without exception. The subject or the minor term is a comprehensive class including all existents in its denotation and the universal concomitance is understood in the subject itself. If existence in a homologe was a necessary precondition of the knowledge of concomitance, there could not possibly be any such knowledge of concomitance between momentariness and existents. But the truth of this concomitance and the resultant inference form the very foundation of the Buddhist theory of flux. The Buddhist logician therefore has got to admit that the triple character is not a universal condition.[2]

We have fully refuted the objections of the *Naiyāyikas* and proved that an imaginary datum has as much logical value as a real object ; and where an actual contradictory (*vipakṣa*) may be impossible, the imaginary concept will do duty for it. So universal concomitance can be understood only by ruling out the contradictory supposition, though the contradictory may be a fiction. The contention of the *Naiyāyikas* that there is no contradictory of such concepts as 'knowable,' 'cognisable,' etc., is absolutely devoid of sense and substance. Because, words are used to remove a doubt or misconception in the mind of the hearer, and not without a purpose. And the use of language finds its

[1] atha sapakṣa eva sattvam anvayo na sapakṣe sattvam eve 'ti cet, astu, sa tu vyatireka eve 'ty asmanmatam aṅgīkṛtaṁ syāt. vayam api hi pratyapīpadāma, anyathānupattyekalakṣano hetur iti.

Pr. mi. v., *ad* 1-2-12.

[2] *Antārvyāpti*, SBNT., p. 110.

justification in the removal of such doubt and the like. Such propositions as 'colour and form is cognisable by visual perception,' though tautologous, have still got to be used if there is a doubt or misconception regarding this truth. One may argue, 'there is no reason that colour should be cognisable by visual perception only, consciousness is one indivisible entity and as such can cognise colour through the auditory sense also.' And only to rebut such doubt the former propositon is employed. So such words as 'cognisable,' 'knowable' and the like have got a definite meaning and this definiteness means the exclusion of what it is not, *viz.*, 'unknowable.' The excluded thing may be a fact or a fiction. So there is no such thing as a purely affirmative concept and consequently exclusion of negative instances necessary to bring home the truth of a universal proposition is not impossible, as the *Naiyāyika* contends.[1]

It follows therefore that incompatibility with the contradictory should be regarded as the only logical attribute of a valid probans and the triple or quantuple character without this is powerless to prove the necessary connexion. The *Jaina* Logicians and later on Ratnākaraśānti, a Buddhist, call this fact 'internal concomitance' (*antarvyāpti*) as opposed to the *Naiyāyikas* who hold that universal concomitance is apprehended outside the subject of inference, *e.g.*, in a kitchen and not in the hill. This conception of universal concomitance is characterised as 'external concomitance' (*bahirvyāpti*). The *Jainas* emphasise that the relation of probans and probandum must be a natural constituitional relation, appertaining to the inherent nature of things and so wherever may concomitance be apprehended, the concomitance must be understood in respect of the probans and the probandum *per se* without reference to the place of occurrence, which is an accidental coincidence.

[1] T. S., śls. 1166-80. *Cf.* 'ajñeyaṁ kalpitaṁ kṛtvā tadvyavacchedena jñeye 'numānam.' Dignāga, quoted in T. S. P., p. 359, and *Nyāyaratnākara*, p. 605, *ad* śl. 145, S. V.

Though this doctrine of internal concomitance has been established by Ratnākaraśānti with ardour and emphasis, and he has left no stone unturned to reconcile this theory with the logical position of Dignāga, it is absolutely certain that the orthodox Buddhist logicians did not accept this theory for a long time to come. On the other hand, the Buddhist logicians attacked this doctrine with all the emphasis at their command. And this is quite natural, because the doctrine of internal concomitance is antagonistic to the doctrine of the triple condition of the probans advocated by Dignāga and also the fallacy of the inconclusive-reason-peculiar-to-the-subject. That this was the case can be inferred from the fact that Śāntarakṣita has attacked this theory as propounded by the *Jaina* logician Pātrasvāmin and tried to uphold the position of Dignāga.

Pātrasvāmin argues, 'The valid probans is that which is incompatible with the contradictory and it is immaterial whether the two examples, positive and negative, are present or not. Incompatibility with the contradictory is the foundation of inference and if it is present, the triple characteristics are unnecessary and if it is absent, these are absolutely futile.[1] Śāntarakṣita observes, 'let this incompatibility be the determinant of unconditional, invariable concomitance. But where is this unconditional concomitance apprehended ? Is this relation apprehended between the probans and probandum in their widest and most general character without reference to the particulars ? Or is it understood in the subject under dispute ? Or in the homologue ? Now, in the first alternative, the existence of the probandum in the subject (minor term) cannot be proved, because the probans is not said to be present in the subject. For

[1] anyathānupapannatvaṁ yasya tasyai 'va hetutā ।
dṛṣṭāntau dvāv api stāṁ vā mā vā tau hi na kāraṇam ॥
anyathānupapannatvaṁ yasya tasya trayeṇa kim ।
nā 'nyathānupapannatvaṁ yasya tasya trayeṇa kim ॥

T. S., śls. 1368-69.

instance we can point out the concomitance of visibility with impermanence, which, though unconditional and invariable as far as it goes, cannot prove the quality of impermanence in a word. If the subsistence of the probans in the subject is to be expressly stated, we get the triple character in full. Because by the incompatibility-with-the-contradictory we have got universal concomitance both in agreement and difference and from the subsistence of the probans in the subject we have the first condition. So the *Jainas* do not gain anything by formulating this unitary character, which is nothing but an abbreviated formula of the triple characteristics. If however it is supposed that the universal concomitance is understood in and through the subject itself, the employment of the probans in an inference becomes redundant, as the existence of the probandum in the subject will be proved by the knowledge of the concomitance. " The Buddhists think that a valid probans is what is not found to be dissociated from the probandum in an example. But we *Jainas* think that the probans is what is not capable of coming into existence without the probandum in the subject of inference. So our inference has a double aspect like the man-lion deity, as there is in it the room for exclusion of the contradictory (*vipakṣavyāvṛtti*), the condition of *arthāpatti* (Presumption) of the *Mīmāṁsakas* and the *pakṣasattva* (the subsistence of the probans in the subject) of the Buddhists. It is an entirely different thing from the inference of the Buddhists and the presumption of the *Mīmāṁsakas*." [1] But this conception of inference will make the value of the probans absolutely nugatory. If the probans cannot come into existence without being conjoined to the probandum, then the very apprehension of the probans in the subject will entail the apprehension of the probandum also, as the probans is

[1] vinā sādhyād adṛṣṭasya dṛṣṭānte hetute 'ṣyate | parair mayā punar dharmiṇy asambhūṣṇor vinā 'munā || arthāpatteś ca śābaryā bhaikṣavāc cā 'numānataḥ | anyad evā 'numānaṁ no narasiṁhavad iṣyate ||

T.S.P., *ad* śl. 1388.

invariably associated with the probandum. And if the probandum is not known, the probans also cannot be known, because the probans is supposed to be constitutionally associated with the probandum and this inseparable relation with the probandum is the very life and soul of the probans. If however the probandum is known by any other means, the probans will have no function and value, as the probans is requisitioned only to prove the probandum and if the probandum is proved otherwise, what shall we do with the probans ?[1]

If the universal concomitance is supposed to be apprehended in an external example without reference to the subject, then, the existence of the probandum in the subject will not be proved, because the concomitance, which is the foundation of inference, is not apprehended in its universal reference. So it is proved that no inference is possible unless the probans is possessed of the triple character, enunciated by Dignāga and Dharmakīrti. And as in subjective inference the probans is reduced to nullity in the theory of internal concomitance, so will be in syllogistic argument the statement of the subsistence of the probans in the subject ; in one word, the minor premise will be redundant. In a syllogism, the universal proposition expressing the universal concomitance is first stated and then the minor premise, showing the subsistence of the probans in the subject, is employed. But this would be unnecessary and unjustifiable in the theory of internal concomitance, because this theory takes for granted that the concomitance is apprehended in the subject and so the subsistence of the probans in the subject would be cognised along with, or previous to, the concomitance. The statement of the universal concomitance will therefore itself involve a knowledge of the minor premise and as such the express statement of the minor premise will become redundant. But in the theory of external concomitance (*bahirvyāpti*), the statement of the minor premise is necessary, because the concomitance is apprehended outside the

1 T.S., śls. 1386-88.

subject in outside examples, *e.g.*, kitchen and the like, and if the minor premise is not stated, the knowledge of the probandum in the subject will become impossible.[1]

In reply to this elaborate charge of the orthodox Buddhist logicians, the upholder of internal concomitance maintains that all this attack proceeds upon a misconception of the nature and process of the knowledge of universal concomitance on the part of the opponents. It must be admitted by all that universal concomitance is understood without any reference either to the subject or to the homologue whatsoever. The advocate of external concomitance holds that inference is rendered possible if it is preceded by a knowledge of the subsistence of the probans in the subject (minor premise, *pakṣadharmatājñāna*) and the remembrance of the universal concomitance (*vyāptijñāna*), and this position is fully endorsed by the exponent of internal concomitance also. The knowledge of the minor premise (*pakṣadharmatā*) alone unbacked by a knowledge of universal concomitance (as in a case of lapse of memory) does not lead to any inference. In the circumstances it may be contended that whereas the concomitance with the probandum of the probans is remembered in respect of the subject, and as such the knowledge of the probandum in its relation to the subject is derived from the act of remembrance, the possibility of inference as an independent instrument of knowledge is excluded, as its function, namely, the deduction of the probandum, has been exercised by memory. If to avoid this contingency it is contended that the universal concomitance is remembered without any reference to the subject, we ask why should the subject be ignored or passed over when the universal concomitance is remembered in respect of the probans factually existing in the subject ? You will have to concede that this concomitance is cognised in respect of the universals, say, for instance, the universal-smoke and the universal-fire, and that the subject or the

[1] A.V., p. 107.

homologue does not enter as determinant factors into this knowledge. On the contrary, reference to the subject or the homologue would render the probans too particularistic to make inference permissible. The subject or the homologue is only a medium of this universal knowledge and cannot be supposed to delimit the concomitance to their own individual extent. The minor premise, in which the probans is found to exist, has a value in determining the incidence of the probandum, but it has no function so far as the universal concomitance *qua* its universal character is concerned. Reference to the individual on the other hand would only circumscribe the concomitance and thus render inference either futile or impossible. Moreover, this individualistic reference cannot be pressed as a universal characteristic because universal concomitance is known to be cognised in negative instances without any reference to a particular individual as the substratum of such concomitance. If the knowledge of the subsistence of the probans in the subject (the minor premise) is deemed to be a necessary factor of knowledge of universal concomitance the opponent cannot maintain that such concomitance is ascertained in the homologue, because the knowledge of the minor premise is lacking in this case. And if this reference to the subject is insisted upon as a factor of the concomitance, then inference will be rendered nugatory, as the knowledge of the probandum in the subject will be derived from memory. It follows therefore with irresistible logic that reference to the subject is unnecessary in universal concomitance, whether it is held to be cognised internally between the probans and the probandum or externally in an outside homologue and so inference has a scope and a function assured in the doctrine of internal concomitance much to the discomfiture of the opponents.

The interests of subjective ratiocination (*svārthānumāna*), we have seen, are not in jeopardy in the theory of internal concomitance. The probans has a utility of its own and so inference is not jettisoned. And the contention of the opponent that the statement of the minor premise, showing the subsistence of the probans in the subject, will be useless in syllogistic argument (*parārthānumāna*) is equally hollow and unsubstantial. It is urged that the customary form of a syllogistic argument is that the universal proposition is stated first and then comes the minor premise. In the theory of internal concomitance, the universal concomitance is known in the subject and so the knowledge of the subsistence of the probans in the subject being an antecedent condition of knowledge of universal concomitance, the statement of the universal proposition will carry with it a reference to the subject and so the statement of the minor premise will be redundant and useless. Nay, the statement of the probans will alone be sufficient, as the probans, by virtue of its concomitance with the probandum, will induce a knowledge of the probandum.[1]

In reply to this contention of the advocate of external concomitance, the adherent of internal concomitance observes that the order of syllogistic premises has nothing to do with our subjective experience. Whatever be the customary arrangement of propositions in a syllogism, we have nothing to quarrel with. Because, after all, it is a question of arrangement of words, and words have no bearing on objective facts and much less on concomitance and the like, which are relations of facts. Words are employed only to indicate these factual relations and so verbal order has no essential relation with factual order and the order of our ratiocinative process.[2] Whatever be the arrangement of premises, the knowledge of the probans subsisting in the subject is the first step in the ratiocinative process and then the universal concomitance is ascertained by a *reductio ad absurdum* of the contradictory proposition. And this is exactly the

[1] **tadbhāvahetubhāvau hi dṛṣṭānte tadavedinaḥ |**
vyāpyete viduṣāṁ vācyo hetur eva hi kevalaḥ ||
P.L.S.V., *ad* III. 93.

[2] **saktasya sūcakaṁ hetor vaco 'saktam api svayam.**
A. Vyā. S., p. 108.

psychological process involved in all cases of inference irrespective of the order of propositions in a syllogism. Moreover, the syllogistic order is not the same in all schools of thought, and if the order of ratiocination is made contingent upon the verbal order, there will be no uniformity in inferential knowledge as a psychological fact. The statement of the minor premise is therefore not redundant in the theory of internal concomitance.

In the opponent's view, too, the probans is first cognised and then its concomitance with the probandum is apprehended in the externally found homologue. Such also is the case in the theory of internal concomitance. The probans is first cognised in the subject and then the concomitance is arrived at by its own proof, *viz.*, the *reductio ad absurdum* of the opposite thesis. We therefore hold that invariable concomitance is a factual relation inherent in the probans and the probandum and is arrived at internally, that is to say, without reference to an external homologue or the subject. It may be contended that in an external example the probans and the probandum are seen to be associated together and so their concomitance is easily apprehended. But these two are not found in association in the subject and so their concomitance cannot be comprehended. But this contention blinks the fact that though found in association, the two facts are not correlated as probans and probandum in an external example and this correlation is understood after the comprehension of their concomitance. Moreover, this co-association may be pressed only in cases like that of fire and smoke, but the case of the concomitance of existence and *momentariness* is not a matter of perception. In this case at least the *reductio ad absurdum* has to be appealed to as proof of the concomitance of the two qualities. There can be no difficulty, therefore, for the concomitance being comprehended in the subject. Again, observation of co-association can be of little avail. If such observation had any efficacy, we need not have waited for a number of instances, as each observation is absolutely alike and non-distinct from the other and there being no special virtue in a mere repetition of the instances, the first instance should have been sufficient for the purpose. Mere observation of co-association cannot be regarded as an adequate security of invariable concomitance and its failure in the case of diamonds and the fact of inscribability can be adduced as an instance in point. It must be admitted that unless and until the contrary supposition is barred by a *reductio ad absurdum*, there can be no assurance of invariable concomitance and this fact alone is sufficient and necessary.

Śāntarakṣita contended that if the universal concomitance is not apprehended with reference to the subject, the probans will fail in its probative value. Because this would only mean that the subsistence of the probans in the subject would not be a necessary condition and the consequence would be that word could be inferred to be perishable on the ground of visibility. But the objection is neither sound nor fair. There is no invariable concomitance between visibility and impermanence of word and so no inference is allowed, and reference to the subject has nothing to do with it. Furthermore, the statement of the probans endowed with invariable concomitance can only prove the probandum in any and every possible subject, but the particular subject has got to be mentioned for determinate reference. The objection that the statement of the subject will make the probans useless has already been refuted. Neither can it be urged that in the absence of *pakṣadharmatā*, an inference would be legitimate on the basis of a probans existing outside the subject, because the occasion for debate cannot arise unless the probans is apprehended in relation to a particular subject.[1] The

[1] asiddhe dharmiṇah (ṇi ?) sattve vivādānavatārataḥ ।
tatra siddhasya ca vyāptigrahaṇe, sādhyadharmiṇi ।
vyāptigrahaḥ kathaṁ na syād dṛṣṭānte 'pi na vā bhavet ॥

A. Vyā. Sa., p. 111.

Also, sādhyadharmādhārasandehāpanodāya gamyamānasyā 'pi pakṣasya vacanam. P. M. S., III. 29,

subsistence of the probans in this subject is an implied fact. It follows therefore that reference to an external example is absolutely redundant and unprofitable, because invariable concomitance is comprehended only when the contrary supposition is absolutely barred out and so long as this does not occur, a thousand instances of co-association will not help us in the least.[1]

Nor is there any logical necessity for the statement of the example in a syllogistic argument, and the omission of the example on the other hand will make the syllogism scientific and less cumbrous. The example is usually tagged on to the universal proposition, the major premise, but there is no logical or psychological warrant for this addition of a superfluous and otiose adjunct. It may be contended that if universal concomitance is comprehended in the subject of inference and not in an outside example, say kitchen, then the probandum will be proved in the subject along with the concomitance by the proof of the latter and an appeal to the probans will be superfluous. The result will be that 'inference' as an independent proof will have no scope, as the predication of the probandum, for which it would be in request, would be accomplished by the knowledge of universal concomitance and its proof. But if the said concomitance is held to be cognised in an outside example without any reference to the subject, the adduction of the probans will have a meaning and a purpose for bringing home the predication of the probandum in respect of the subject and inference will have its own sphere of action. Our reply is that if the probandum is proved by means of the instrument of universal concomitance and resort to inference is, thus, rendered unnecessary, we have nothing to complain about. On the contrary we have every reason to congratulate ourselves on the positive gain and the economy of logical procedure that we are relieved of the

[1] bādhakāt tadasidhhiś ced vyartho hetvantaragrahaḥ |

A. Vyā. Sa., p. 109.

necessity of having recourse to the probans. It is not an obsession with us that we shall have to resort to the probans at all events. We must have courage to throw away this convention, if there is no sanction of logical necessity behind it. And if the probandum is not so proved of the subject by the instrument of universal concomitance, the probans will not be superfluous and inference will have its vested rights preserved intact. That such is the case has been proved beyond cavil or doubt in the foregoing paragraphs. So there is absolutely no cause for this consternation about our theory of internal concomitance.[1]

Neither can reference to an example be needful for the comprehension of concomitance, because the *reductio ad absurdum* of the contrary supposition is alone sufficient for the purpose. Nor can it be in request for the attestation or verification of the same, because concomitance has reference to universals and examples being individual instances can have no relevancy in that respect. Nor again can it be supposed to be necessary for recalling the fact of concomitance to memory, because the mention of the concomitant probans is the sufficient stimulus for that. An example, on the other hand, would raise the spectre of doubt, because an example can but serve as evidence of concomitance in its own particular case and it does not afford any guarantee for its universal truth. If to lay this spectre you think it necessary to state the universal proposition as proof of universal concomitance, we submit, let this alone be stated and why should the example, an otiose appendage as it is, be tagged on to it ? It may be urged that mention of a concrete example is

[1] yadi hi dharmiṇi vyāptiḥ siddhyanty eva sādhyasiddhim antarbhāvayati, nanu lābha evai 'ṣaḥ, vyāptiprasādhakād eva pramāṇāt sādhyasiddheḥ sattvahetvapāśrayaṇaprayāsasya nirasanāt. na hi vyasanam evai 'tal liṅgāntarānusaraṇaṁ nāma. atha na vyāptisādhakāt sādhyasiddhiḥ, na tarhy antarvyāptau hetuvaiyarthyam iti kim akāṇḍakātaratayā bahutaram āyāsam āviśasi.

A. Vyā. sa., pp. 109-10.

necessary for bringing home the universal truth to a dull understanding. It may be so, we submit. But in that case, the statement of example should be confined within a manual of logic and should not be stated in a logical disputation, because only an expert is eligible for debate. Besides, a debate or a logical disputation is not the occasion for the instruction of pupils, as its objective is only to score a victory by an effective refutation of the opponent's thesis.[1] It has been contended that this admission of the incompatibility of the probans with the contradictory and the implied necessity of its reference to the subject on the part of the exponent of internal concomitance virtually amounts to the postulation of the triple-charactered probans advocated by the orthodox Buddhist logicians; and so the unitary probans transpires to be but an abbreviated formula and the gain is only verbal and apparent. We admit the plausibility of the objection. The triple character is but a corollary of incompatibility-with-the-contradictory and the latter alone is the validating condition of the so-called triple character, which, without this saving grace, becomes but an effete and inane adjunct. We therefore regard this factor alone as the adequate qualification of the probans and not the triple character, which draws all its validity from the former.

It may be urged that if incompatibility with the contradictory, that is to say, total absence from heterologous instances, is deemed the sufficient qualification of a valid probans and subsistence in homologous cases, the second characteristic according

[1] na hi tat sādhyapratipattyarthaṁ tatra yathoktahetor eva vyāpārāt. III. 33. tadavinābhāvaniścayārthaṁ vā, vipakṣa-bādhakād eva tatsiddheḥ. 34. vyaktirūpaṁ nidarśanam, sāmānyena tu vyāptiḥ, tatrā 'pi tadvipratipattāv anavasthānaṁ syād dṛṣṭāntāntarāpekṣaṇāt. 35. nā 'pi vyāptismaraṇārthaṃ tathāvidhahetu-prayogād eva tatsmṛteḥ. 36. tat param abhidhīyamānaṁ sādhyasādhane sandehayati. 37. bālavyutpattyarthaṁ ca tattrayopagame śāstra evā 'sau na vāde 'nupayogāt. 40. P. M. S., Ch. III. *Cf.* na hi vādakāle śiṣyā vyutpādyāḥ, vyutpannānām eva tatrā ' dhikārāt.'

L. V. *ad* III, 40, *ibid.*

Buddhist logic, is not an indispensable condition, then there would be no case for the fallacy of 'the uncommon inconclusive probans' (*asādhāraṇānaikāntika-hetu*). The fallacy is supposed to arise when the probans belongs exclusively to the subject (*pakṣa* or *dharmin*) and so does not exist in a homologous instance, as for instance, the probans 'audibility.' According to Dignāga, such inference as 'word is impermanent, because it is audible' is not valid, as the quality of audibility is the exclusive property of word and its concomitance with impermanence is not attested in a homologous instance. If the testimony of a homologous instance is deemed unnecessary, as is done by the advocate of internal concomitance, this argument would be legitimate and valid. But this is in express contravention of the position of Dignāga. The *Jaina* logicians, who professed no allegiance to Dignāga, did not regard this discrepancy as a case of disloyalty; on the contrary, they gloated over this triumph over Dignāga for obvious reasons. The *Jaina* logicians regarded the above inference as perfectly legitimate and valid, because they think that audibility is incompatible with permanence, the contradictory of impermanence, and this incompatibility is the only satisfying condition of validity.[1] But Ratnākaraśānti, who appropriated this theory of internal concomitance from the *Jainas*, had to face this charge of treason against Dignāga, whose authority he could not disown being a Buddhist by profession. Accordingly he has endeavoured to bring it into line with Dignāga's conception of valid probans; and he has succeeded in doing so only by explaining away Dignāga's theory of triple character. He observes that the doctrine of triple character only emphasises the fact of invariable concomitance in agreement and difference and that this concomitance in its dual aspect has got to be ascertained to ensure the validity of the probans. It is silent and indifferent with regard to cases where this twofold concomitance has to be

1 *Vide Pramāṇamīmāṁsā*, 1. 2. 2.

ascertained. The obvious implication is that it should be ascertained wherever it is possible. If the aspect of agreement is ascertained in the subject on the strength of the impossibility of the contradictory proposition, there is no ground for complaint. The opponent has got to admit it in such cases of inference as 'All that exists is momentary.' In this inference, 'momentariness' is predicated of all existents without exception and as such there is no homologue external to and apart from the subject, where the agreemental aspect could be verified. The agreement therefore must be admitted to be comprehended in the subject on the strength of the absurdity of the contrary possibility. Subsistence in a homologue in and by itself has no cogency, unless it is ratified by the absurdity of the counter-issue. So the fallacy of the uncommon inconclusive probans is no fallacy in reality. It has been formulated by the Master only as a concession to persons of dull intellect, who labour under the delusion that concomitance can be ascertained only in an external example outside the scope of the subject. But this is not really so, as concomitance is apprehended in a universal reference.[1]

The uncommon probans has been characterised as inconclusive only with reference to these deluded persons. As a matter of fact, concomitance is comprehended without reference to the homologue and so the absence of the homologue cannot render a probans inconclusive, though it might be uncommon. If we probe deeper into the question, we shall see that the probans, 'audibility,' is not only not inconclusive, but also is not uncommon either. It has been characterised as uncommon only in deference to the logical superstition of dull-headed persons. A probans is called uncommon when it is found to belong solely and wholly to the subject of dispute. But in

[1] A. Vyā., pp. 112-13:

asādhāraṇatāṁ hetudoṣaṁ mūḍhavyapekṣayā ।
abravīd agrahād vyāpter, nai'vaṁ sarvopasaṁhṛtau ॥ *Ibid.*

the case of audibility, the subject of dispute is the perceived sound and the probans 'audibility' belongs to perceived and unperceived sounds alike, just like the smoke-in-the universal, which is not the property of the hill alone, but also of the kitchen and the like. So *concomitance in a universal reference.*[1] being cognisable between audibility and impermanence, there is absolutely no reason to characterise it as uncommon. An uncommon probans cannot have a universal reference, and if its concomitance is supposed to be comprehended in the subject, which is its only locale, the probandum will be proved of the subject along with the concomitance and so the probans will be futile as an instrument of inference. In such cases, there can possibly be no concomitance and in the absence of concomitance, the probans will have a doubtful cogency either this way or that and so will be inconclusive. But when universal concomitance is possible, audibility should be regarded as a conclusive probans. When the subject of dispute is an individual sound, another sound will serve as the example and if all the sounds are made the subject, the *reductio ad absurdum* will make an example of one among them, though it may not be accepted as a full-fledged example. In other words, the absence of an undisputed example will not operate as a bar. It is seen that audibility and the like are neither uncommon nor inconclusive. The objection based upon this fallacy has no force against the theory of internal concomitance and it should not be regarded as conflicting with the position of the venerable Master Dignāga.

We have seen that concomitance is comprehended by means of *reductio ad absurdum* of the contradictory thesis and examples have no bearing upon it. *Reductio ad absurdum* is a species of *tarka* (hypothetical reasoning) and *tarka* is not regarded as an independent means of proof.[2] We shall bring this chapter to a

1 sarvopasaṁhāravatī vyāptiḥ (*ibid*, p. 113). 'sarvasmin dharmiṇi hetoḥ sādhyena vyāptipradarśanaṁ sarvopasaṁhāraḥ.' T. S. P., p. 245 *ad* śl. 746.

2 *Vide infra*, the Chapter Prasaṅgānumāna.

close after discussing whether *tarka* is a proof or not. Vātsyāyana has called it not-proof (*apramāṇa*). It is not a vehicle of certitude. It is not a knowledge of the type 'this is so and not otherwise.' When two conflicting alternatives present themselves, *tarka* only shows the incompatibility of one and approves of the other. It only reinforces the independent means of truth and as such is only an assistant in the matter of ascertaining the truth. It approves the matter of proof and does not prove it.[1] Uddyotakara regarded it as a kind of cognition different from doubt and certitude alike and has gone the length of declaring them fools who subsume it under inference. There is a vital difference between the two, as *tarka* has no reference to the probans or its subsistence in the subject (*pakṣadharmatā*). Inference is invariably pivoted upon this knowledge of the probans in relation to the subject. But *tarka* is not fettered like this. It may prove something regarding a particular subject on the basis of an attribute found in the other, as for example in a reasoning like this, 'certainly there are human beings here, because we see that horses are used as beasts of burden.' Now, a horse as bearer of burden is no attribute of human beings, but nevertheless it signifies their existence.[2] The difference between inference and *tarka* is, therefore, very manifest and so they should not be confounded. Gaṅgeśa, too, has characterised *tarka* as not-proof (*apramāṇa*).[3] Thus, the tradition among the *Naiyāyikas* is uniformly consistent with regard to the neutral character of *tarka* and about its lack of probative value. We have not come across any speculation on *tarka* in any Buddhist work. But Ratnākaraśānti always characterised it as *vipakṣabādhakapramāṇa* (the

[1] Ny. bhā., 1.1.40. tattvajñānaviṣayābhyanujñālakṣaṇānugrahabhāvitāt prasannād anantaraṁ pramāṇasāmarthyāt tattvajñānam utpadyata iti. *Cf.* 'pravṛttasya prayojyasya taddhitopāyoktir anujñā.' *Vedāntakalpataru*, p. 70. Abhyanujñā = approval.

[2] N. V., p. 142, and Tāt. ṭī., p. 301.

[3] *Tattvacintāmaṇi*: Vyāptigrahopāyasiddhānta—'tarkasyā' pramāṇatvāt.'

proof refuting the contradictory) and Ratnakīrti treated this proof of contradiction as a full-fledged syllogistic argument in his *Kṣaṇabhaṅgasiddhi*. The obvious implication is that it is regarded as a proof and as a species of inference. In fact, if *tarka* is to be treated as a *pramāṇa*, it must be included under inference as there is no third proof according to the Buddhist logicians. Uddyotakara and Vācaspati Miśra possibly had these Buddhists in view when they characterised this identification of *tarka* with inference as a delusion. The *Jainas* however regard it as a separate *pramāṇa*.

Hemacandra Sūri has fully refuted the views of the *Naiyāyikas* on *tarka*. The *Naiyāyikas* cannot regard *tarka* as a separate *pramāṇa*, because that would contradict their doctrine of four *pramāṇas*. Nor can they subsume it under inference, as inference is contingent on the knowledge of universal concomitance and for this the accepted *pramāṇas* have no competency. They have to requisition *tarka*, but to make it consistent with their central epistemological doctrine of four *pramāṇas*, they give it a half-hearted recognition. Older *Naiyāyikas* hold that perception, reinforced and supplemented by *tarka*, is competent to visualise the universal concomitance. But this doctrine is the result either of confusion or of wilful perversion. Mere perception is incompetent to envisage the concomitance and it is presumed to acquire the competency only when *tarka* aids and informs it. Is it not fair and legitimate therefore to give *tarka* the credit and the glory for this generalisation, which perception by its very constitution and nature is incapable of arriving at? Perception is generated by the impetus of sense-data upon our sensitivity and is absolutely delimited to the same, being destitute of ratiocinative faculty. The *Naiyāyika* is guilty of a dual injustice and this only to maintain a pet superstition. He gives credit to perception which it does not deserve and denies it to *tarka* though it is its rightful due. The *Naiyāyika* would plead that he does so because *tarka* has no validity of its own. But this is a mere dogmatic assertion and has no logic in it. Why should it be invalid? It has all the incidents of validity in it, to wit, (1) absence of discrepancy with fact and (2) a legitimate object in the shape of universal concomitance. To dub it invalid despite these two characteristics of truth and validity betrays a wilful perversity that will not bow to reason. So *tarka* must be given an honourable niche in the palace of *pramāṇas*. It is the instrument of knowledge of universal concomitance and perception and the like do but give the occasion for it. The *Naiyāyika* only puts the cart before the horse when he seeks to throw *tarka* into the background, supposing it to subserve as a vassal the interests of the false master, perception. But the truth is in the contrary version.[1]

We have seen that the doctrine of *antarvyāpti* (internal concomitance) is originally the creation of *Jaina* logic and the doctrine has been supported and accepted by *Jaina* logicians from beginning to end, from Siddhasena Divākara[2] of the 6th century down to Hemacandra Sūri of the 12th century, to name only two masters. Śāntarakṣita has made frantic attempts to refute this doctrine and this was natural and inevitable, because the doctrine is, we have seen, antagonistic to the doctrine of triple probans and the fallacy of the uncommon inconclusive reason, propounded by Dignāga. Jayantabhaṭṭa refered to this doctrine of *antarvyāpti*, but his presentation of it is not in consonance with the orthodox view.[3] Moreover, he is silent as to the exponents of this doctrine, as to whether they are Buddhists

1 *Pramāṇamimāṁsāvṛtti* 1.2.5.

2 *Vide History of Indian Logic*, see Jaina Logicians.

3 Jayanta says that universal concomitance is a relation of universals and when the same is comprehended in reference to a particular subject, it is designated as internal concomitance. To take a concrete case, when fire is inferred in a hill on the strength of the concomitance comprehended outside the hill in a forest and the like, the concomitance in the forest is called external concomitance. Again, this very concomitance is regarded as internal concomitance, when fire is inferred at some other time in that very forest. But Jayanta's representation is not in conformity

or *Jainas*. Later on Ratnakīrti[1] and his worthy disciple, Ratnākaraśānti, more fully than the former, adopted this doctrine and incorporated it into the corpus of Buddhist logic.

with the conception of *antarvyāpti* set forth above. It ignores the supreme fact of importance in *antarvyāpti* that the concomitance is comprehended by means of the *reductio ad absurdum* of the contradictory supposition, *viz.*, the existence of smoke in a fireless place. It fails to recognise that *antarvyāpti* is not a relative concept, but an absolute relation between two universals without any reference to the subject, possible or actual. When, this concomitance is cognised, there is no possibility of a contradicted or counterbalanced reason, for which Jayanta pleads so energetically. So the position of the antagonist, that if the concomitance of coldness and being a product is apprehended to the exclusion of fire, which though a product is not cold, then *antarvyāpti* will not have been cognised, stands.

yadi tv analam utsṛjya ghaṭādāv anvayagrahaḥ ।
nā 'ntarvyāptir gṛhītā syāt sādhyasādhanadharmayoḥ ॥

N.M., p. 110.

Cf. sāmānyena ca vyāptir gṛhītā satī siṣādhayiṣitadharmyapekṣāyāṁ sai 'vā 'ntarvyāptir ucyate. yai 'va ca nagalagnānumānasamaye tadvyatiriktakāntārādiprādeśavartinī abhūt sai 'va kālāntare kāntāravartini vahnāv anumīyamāne 'ntarvyāptir avatiṣṭhate. *Ibid.*, p. 111.

[1] Ratnakīrti has not expressly advocated the claims of *antarvyāpti*, but he has adopted the exact principle on which it is based and also the same line of argument as found in Ratnākaraśānti's monograph. He expressly declares that the concomitance of 'existence' (*sattva*) with 'momentariness' (*kṣaṇikatva*) is not attested by perception in the familiar example, *ghaṭa* (earthen jar). The concomitance is proved by means of *Prasaṅga* and *Prasaṅgaviparyaya*, which two are cases of inference (*anumāna*). He also admits that the universal concomitance is capable of being comprehended in the subject of inference, provided the arguer has the energy to appeal to the evidence at every step. In this case, reference to an outside example is unnecessary and unprofitable. *Cf.* anumānāntaram eva prasaṅga-prasaṅga-viparyayātmakaṁ ghaṭe kṣaṇabhaṅgaprasādhakaṁ pramāṇāntarm asti. SBNT., p. 21.

Also, nanv ābhyām (prasaṅga-prasaṅgaviparyayābhyām) eva pakṣe 'pi kṣaṇabhaṅgasiddhir astv iti cet, astu, ko doṣaḥ. yo hi pratipattā prativastu yad yadā yajjananavyavahārayogyaṃ tat tadā taj janayatī 'tyādikaṃ upanyasitum analasas tasya tata eva kṣaṇabhaṅgasiddhiḥ. *Ibid*, p. 26.

We have seen that Ratnākaraśānti has made bold and almost frantic efforts to reconcile this doctrine with the fundamental logical position of Dignāga and his followers. It is a truism to say that the world is much indebted to the Buddhists and *Jainas*, whose logical and philosophical contributions have distinctly extended the frontiers of human knowledge. It will be nothing short of folly and perhaps madness to form an estimate of the development and worth of Indian logic without a close and serious study of the *Jaina* and Buddhist works still available to us.

Reference :

1. Nyāyasūtra, 1-1-5 ; 1. 1. 33-40.
2. Do. Bhāṣya of Vātsyāyana.
3. Nyāyavārttika of Uddyotakara.
4. Do. Tātparyaṭīkā of Vācaspati Miśra.
5. Tattvasaṅgraha of Śāntarakṣita.
6. Do. Pañjikā of Kamalaśīla.
7. Parīkṣāmukhasūtra of Māṇikyanandi.
8. Do. Laghusūtravṛtti of Anantavīrya.
9. Pramāṇamīmāṁsā of Hemacandra Sūri.
10. Ślokavārtika—anumānapariccheda of Kumārila.
11. Vākyapadīya, Ch. I, of Bhartṛhari.
12. Mahāvidyāviḍambana of Vādīndra (G. O. S.).
13. Antarvyāptisamarthana of Ratnākaraśānti.
14. Kṣanabhaṅgasiddhi of Ratnakīrti.
15. Tattvacintāmaṇi of Gaṅgeśa.

N.B.—The term *antarvyāpti* which we have rendered in English as internal concomitance, may be more happily expressed as 'Intrinsic Determination' following Dr. McTaggart. *Cf.* "If it is true that, whenever something has the quality X, something has the quality Y, this involves that, besides the relation between the two propositions "something has the quality X" and "something has the quality Y," there is a relation between the qualities X and Y. I propose to call this relation Intrinsic Determination.........The quality X will be said to determine intrinsically the quality Y whenever the proposition that something has the quality X implies the proposition that something has the quality Y." *The Nature of Existence*, Ch. XII, p. 111.

CHAPTER XXV

PRASAṄGĀNUMĀNA

In view of the importance of *Prasaṅgānumāna* as a logical weapon used with telling effect in the philosophical literature of medieval India and in view of the divergence of opinion regarding its validity as an instrument of knowledge, we propose to give an exposition of the nature and function of *prasangānumāna.* It is a hypothetical negative argument devised to point out logical defects in the position of the adversary. The word '*prasaṅga*' has been given as the synonym of '*tarka*' by Vācaspati Miśra and '*tarka*,' though included in the list of the sixteen logical categories enunciated in the first aphorism of the *Nyāyasūtra,* is not regarded as an independent instrument of valid knowledge by the *Naiyāyikas.* It is regarded as an indirect proof, requisitioned to strengthen the desired conclusion by showing that the contradictory is not a supposable alternative. *Tarka* has been defined by Jayanta as "Presumptive evidence in favour of one of the two doubtful alternatives by showing the reason conducive to the establishment of the thesis."[1] "In *tarka,* or indirect proof, we start with a wrong assumption and show how it leads to absurdities .... The admission of a false minor necessitates the admission of a false major."[2] "The older *Nyāya* admits eleven kinds of *tarka* which the modern reduce to five, of which the chief is the *reductio ad absurdum,* called *pramāṇa-bādhitārtha-prasaṅga.* The other four are *ātmāśraya,*

[1] 'sandigdhe 'rthe 'nyatarapakṣānukūlakāraṇadarśanāt tasmin sambhāvanāpratyayas tarkaḥ.' N.M., p. 8.

[2] *Vide* Prof. Radhakrishnan's *Indian Philosophy,* Vol. II, p. 114. *Cf.* 'sa cāyaṁ tarko vyāpakābhāvavattvena nirṇīte dharmiṇi vyāpyasyā 'hāryāropād vyāpakasyā 'hāryāropalakṣaṇaḥ' (C. K. Tarkālaṅkāra's ṭīkā on *Nyāya-Kusumāñjali,* p. 5).

or *ignoratio elenchi* (?); *anyonyāśraya*, or mutual dependence; *cakraka*, or circular reasoning, and *anavasthā*, or infinite regress. Even the *reductio ad absurdum* is regarded as a case of fallacious reasoning, since it derives a conclusion which is absurd.'' *Prasaṅgasādhana* can be subsumed under the last variety of *tarka*, *viz.*, the '*reductio ad absurdum*,' subject to a necessary qualification. *Prasaṅgasādhana* differs in a very material respect from '*reductio ad absurdum*,' *viz.*, that whereas the latter is requisitioned to prove the justice or correctness of a particular syllogistic argument by showing the contradictory supposition to be false, the former is employed for exactly the opposite purpose. According to modern *Nyāya* '*reductio ad absurdum*' has a twofold utility; first, it serves to establish the universal proposition, the major premise, in which the invariable concomitance of the middle term with the major term is enunciated (*vyāptigrāhaka*); secondly, it serves to prove the correctness of the conclusion established (*viṣayapariśodhaka*). The last variety corresponds to the '*reductio ad absurdum*' of European logic, which "consists in showing that the supposition of the contradictory of the given conclusion is false and so, by opposition, the given argument is correct.'' The logical procedure is the same, *viz.*, showing the absurdity of the contradictory supposition. The logical principle and procedure are also the same in the case of *prasaṅgānumāna* and *tarka*; the difference lies in the application. The former is employed for demonstrating the falsity of a given argument—thereby showing the logical necessity of the contradictory position being accepted. In fact, *prasaṅgasādhana* can be included under '*pratibandhī*,' a variety of *tarka* enunciated by older *Naiyāyikas*.

The ordinary rule of debate requires that the middle term must be acceptable to both the parties (*ubhayasiddha*) and that the probandum ((*sādhya*) must be a fact. But the requisite conditions of *prasaṅgānumāna* are that (1) the probans (*hetu*) is false and assumed for argument's sake on the statement of the opponent and is not accepted as true by the arguer (*vādin*) himself, and (2) consequently the probandum is a false issue, which is forced upon the adversary ; (3) the main implication of such argument is of course the truth of the contradictory position, which decisively invalidates the assumption of the adversary. This form of argument has been very frequently employed with advantage by Buddhist philosophers against their adversaries. It is, however, significant that Dharmakīrti in his *Nyāyabindu* is very emphatic on the point that the probans must be approved by both the parties in a debate. He has, therefore, included in his catalogue of fallacious reasons those middle terms which are not accepted by either of the parties (*vādin* or *prativādin*). It is plain, therefore, that *prasaṅga-hetu* (a falsely assumed middle term) has no place in the scheme of Dharmakīrti's logic, and probably also in Dignāga's system,[1] which has been mainly followed by Dharmakīrti. In the *Nyāyapraveśa* and the *Hetutattvopadeśa* of Jitāri also,[2] a middle term, which is not approved by common consent, has been declared to be a fallacious reason.

Although the attitude of the orthodox Buddhist logicians is not friendly to such forms of argument, it is not undeniable that it has played a very prominent part in the evolution of philosophical thought in India. Candrakīrti, in the course of his comments on the first verse of the *Mādhyamika Kārikā* of Nāgārjuna, has taken elaborate pains to elucidate the *Mādhyamika's* position in logic. Notwithstanding the fact that the

1 *Vide Nyāyamukha*, translated into English from the Chinese version of the same by Prof. G. Tucci. It is gratifying that the present writer's conjecture has been confirmed, as Dignāga is insistent on the middle term being accepted by common consent.

2 The *Hetutattvopadeśa* of Jitāri is lost in the Sanskrit original, but it has been reconstructed from Tibetan by my pupil, Mr. Durgacharan Chatterjee, M.A., P.R.S. The constructed text with the Tibetan version and copious critical notes and an informing introduction is ready for printing. When published, it would be welcomed as a really scholarly work.

metaphysical position of absolute scepticism, which he adopts, precludes him from admitting the truth of, and so advancing at his own initiative, any of the premises of a syllogistic argument, the *Mādhyamika* can, Candrakīrti argues, refute the arguments of his antagonists without prejudice to his philosophical predilections by the aid of *Prasaṅgānumāna*. He, however, declines to be committed to the necessity of the contradictory proposition being established, as a *Mādhyamika* cannot have *ex hypothesi* any position of his own. He thinks that his duty consists in showing contradiction in the adversary's position and not in proving any particular thesis of his own. In fact, he has no thesis in philosophy save and except that nothing can be proved.[1] A divergence of opinion regarding the necessity of the contradictory position being accepted, which is the third condition of *prasangānumāna*, seems to have been responsible for the two main divisions of Nāgārjuna's followers into the *Prāsaṅgika* and *Svātantrika* schools, the latter insisting on the necessity of independent arguments for the refutation of the contradictory implication of a *prasaṅgānumāna*. So in this respect the historical importance of *prasaṅgānumāna* cannot be over-estimated. Śrīdhara in his *Nyāyakandalī* makes mention of *prasaṅgasādhana* which is the same thing as *prasaṅgānumāna*, *sādhana* and *anumāna* being synonymously used. He says "*Prasaṅgasādhana* is not employed for establishing one's thesis but for bringing home an undesirable contingency in the opponent's position. And an undesirable contingency can be brought home by means of the data which are admitted by the opponent himself. It is not necessary that the argument, in order to be valid, should be recognised as valid and true by the arguer himself. The opponent cannot make a grievance of it and refuse

[1] tataś ca parapratijñāpratiṣedhamātraphalatvāt prasaṅgāpādānasya nāsti prasaṅgaviparyayāpattiḥ. tathā cā 'cāryo bhūyasā prasaṅgāpattimukhenai 'va paroktāni nirākaroti sma. *Vide Prasannapadā* of Candrakīrti under Kar. I of M. K., p. 6 (B. T. S.).

to be convinced, though he himself admits every word of the argument to be true." [1]

Śāntarakṣita, who is believed to have flourished in the 8th century, and his disciple, Kamalaśīla have made use of *prasaṅgānumāna* in several places in the *Tattvasaṅgraha* and the *Pañjikā*. In course of refuting the *Mīmāṁsā* argument 'that the *Vedas* are eternal and self-evident truths, as they are not the handiwork of any human author,' Śāntarakṣita points out that the *Vedas* would become unmeaning, if they were independent of an author, as the truth or falsity of a statement is relative to the veracity or mendacity of the speaker, and the speaker being absent, the truth or otherwise of the Vedic statements would become impossible of ascertainment. Kamalaśīla in his *Pañjikā* observes in this connexion that the argument (of Śāntarakṣita) is a *prasaṅgasādhana* and not an independent argument, as the conclusion is obviously contrary to experience (the *Vedas* having a determinate meaning), and the reason, *akartṛkatva* (independence of human authorship), is not approved by both the parties. But these two contingencies are allowable in a hypothetical argument of the type of *reductio ad absurdum*.[2]

The *Naiyāyikas*, however, do not subscribe to the aforesaid position of the Buddhists. They do not recognise *prasaṅgasādhana* as a logically justifiable form of argument. They are insistent in their demand that the middle term must be a real datum, attested by experience and approved by both the parties and not

[1] prasaṅgāpādanañ ca na svapakṣasādhanāyo 'pādīyate, kintu parasyā 'niṣṭāpādanārtham. parāniṣṭāpādanañ ca tadabhyupagamasiddhair eva dharmādibhiḥ śakyam āpādayitum. tatra pramāṇena svapratītir anapekṣaṇīyā ; na hy evam paraḥ pratyavasthātum arhati tavā 'siddhā dharmādayo, nā 'ham svasiddheṣv api teṣu pratipadya iti. N. K., p. 197.

[2] prasaṅgasādhanam etad draṣṭavyam, anyathā hi svātantryeṇa sādhane dṛṣṭavirodhaḥ syāt, tathā hy 'agnihotraṁ juhuyāt svarga-kāma' ityādivākyād arthapratītir bhavanty upalabhyata eva, na ca dṛṣṭam apahnotuṁ śakyate, na cā 'kartṛkatvam ubhayasiddham ity asiddhaś ca hetuḥ syāt, prasaṅgasādhane tu dvayam apy aduṣṭam. T. S. P., p. 437, under ślś. 1502-3.

a mere hypothetical entity. Any infringement of the above dictum will make the fallacy of 'unproven middle term' inevitable. Śaṅkarasvāmin, an older *Naiyāyika*, emphatically avers that whether the argument be a hypothetical or an independent one, the probans must be attested by one's own personal experience ; otherwise it (the probans) will fail to be appropriate. Kamalaśīla observes that the penalty of the violation of this principle will be the fallacy of unproven middle term.[1]

Jayantabhaṭṭa, the author of the *Nyāyamañjarī*, has an occasion to speak of *prasaṅgasādhana* in connexion with his animadversion on Kumārila for his denial of an omniscient *yogin*. Kumārila declares that even the supersensuous perception of a *yogin* is not competent to envisage the real nature of *dharma* (duty). Jayantabhaṭṭa in opposing Kumārila says, "If yogic perception be an established fact, your argument is vitiated by self-contradiction ; if it is non-existent, the middle term is unproven in respect of an unreal subject (*āśrayāsiddha*). You have yourself stated the dictum in rebutting the doctrine of subjective idealism (of the Buddhists) that no inference is possible from unreal data merely on the strength of other people's belief. And as a (supposed) middle term, accepted only by the adversary, cannot prove the probandum, so also a (supposed) minor term, accepted only by the opponent, is not an acceptable datum.' [2]

1 Śaṅkarasvāmin is an older *Naiyāyika*, who is completely ignored in the Brahmanical works except in the *Nyāyamañjarī*, where he is referred to only in one place and so would have been totally forgotten but for the quotations of his views in the *Tattvasaṅgraha* and the *Pañjikā*. The opinion referred to is embodied in the following verse: svātantryeṇa prasaṅgena sādhanaṁ yat pravarttate | svayaṁ tadupalabdhau hi satyāṁ saṅgacchate na tu ||

T. S., śl. 614.

'anyathā hy asiddhatādoṣaḥ syāt.' T. S. P., under the above.

2 parasaṁsiddhamūlam ca nānumānaṁ prakalpate |
uktam bhavadbhir eve 'daṁ nirālmbaanadūṣaṇam ||

"It may be argued that it is a case of *prasaṅgasādhana* and *prasaṅga* means the demonstration of a defect in an opponent's position by means of the data accepted by the latter... But this cannot be approved. Because, *prasaṅgasādhana* is a form of argument, which is as unreal as a fresco-painting without on a wall. Certainly a dissertation on the fragrance or otherwise of a sky-flower cannot be a justifiable procedure." [1]

The refusal of the *Naiyāyikas* to regard *prasaṅgānumāna* as a valid means of cognition stands on a par with their denial of *tarka* as an independent means of knowledge. Hemacandra Sūri in his *Pramāṇamīmāṁsa* and Ratnakīrti in his '*Kṣaṇabhaṅgasiddhi*' have elaborately criticised the *Naiyāyika* position and they have made no scruple to declare that the denial of validity to *tarka* is due to the cussedness of the *Naiyāyika* and has no logic in its support. Without taking sides, we can legitimately hold that *prasaṅgasādhana* has been wielded as a potent logical weapon in the tangled controversies of the medieval age and is regarded as the only acceptable form of argument by the *Mādhyamika* school. Whatever be the logical merits of it as a valid syllogistic reasoning, the historical importance of *prasaṅga sādhana* cannot be underrated by any scrupulous student of Indian thought. [2]

sādhyasiddhir yathā nāsti parasiddhena hetunā |
tathai 'va dharmisiddhatvaṁ parasiddhyā na yujyate ||
N. M., p. 102.

1 tatrai 'tat syāt prasaṅgasādhanam idam, prasaṅgaś ca paraprasidddhyā parasyā 'niṣṭāpādanam ucyate...nai 'tad evam.

prasaṅgasādhanaṁ nāma nāsty eva paramārthataḥ |
tad dhi kuḍyaṁ vinā tatra citrakarme 'va lakṣyate ||
na hi nabhaḥkusumasya saurabhāsaurabhavicāro yuktaḥ.
Nyāyamañjarī, pp. 102-04.

2 For a convenient understanding of the nature and function of *prasaṅgasādhana* as an invalidating form of argument we propose to give a concrete illustration in Aristotelian syllogistic form as follows:—

(A) The *Mīmāṁsaka's* argument—

All statments that have no authors are infallible.
Vedic statements are those that have no authors.
∴ Vedic statements are infallible.

(B) The Buddhist's argument—

All statements that have no authors are unmeaning
Vedic statements are those that have no authors.
∴ Vedic statements are unmeaning.

The syllogism (B) is a *prasaṅgasādhana* in relation to the syllogism (A), as the latter (A) is invalidated by the former (B).

N.B.—I think a word of explanation is necessary for my using the terminology of European logic for elucidating the concepts of Indian logic. There is a fundamental difference between Indian *Nyāya* and European syllogism in that the former is not content with formal consistency alone, but insists on the material truth of the premises and the conclusion, whereas formal consistency is the only criterion of Aristotelian syllogism. In fact, the whole controversy in connexion with *prasaṅgasādhana* would not have arisen at all, if formal consistency had been regarded as the satisfying test of an argument by Indian logicians. But my apology for the use of European terms is that they are the nearest equivalents of Indian logical concepts and in this I have only followed in the footsteps of veteran scholars like the late Dr. Satishcandra Vidyābhūṣaṇa, Dr. Ganganath Jha, Prof. Sir S. Radhakrishnan, Prof Stcherbatsky and others. The readers are requested to bear this distinction in mind to guard against obvious misunderstanding.

CHAPTER XXVI

NEGATIVE JUDGMENT

There is a wide divergence of opinion among philosophers regarding the nature and status of negative judgment and the problem can be studied with profit by way of division into an epistemological and a metaphysical aspect ; and though these two aspects are intimately inter-related, the epistemological aspect of the question will be primarily discussed by us and the metaphysical aspect will be considered in so far as it will be found to be germane to the determination of the negative judgment as an epistemological problem. The *Nyāya-Vaiśeṣika* school, at least in its later offshoot, believes in the ontological reality of negation as an additional category and the knowledge of negation in the primary stage is derived by it from sense-perception. Kumārila does not think negation to be an independent reality, but only as an aspect of the positive locus in which it is cognised. The metaphysical issue apart, the knowledge of negation is not believed to be perceptual in character, but rather as a kind of experience to be classed apart from the accepted modes of knowledge, for which a distinctive instrument of knowledge, *viz.*, non-perception, is postulated. The Buddhist philosopher, so far at any rate as the original formulation is concerned, has sought to derive the knowledge of negation from inference.

Prabhākara does not believe in the metaphysical reality of negation and the epistemological problem simply does not exist in his view. Negation according to him is nothing but the absence of a knowable fact and the knowledge of negation is but the absence of the knowledge of this fact. To take a concrete example, the proposition, ' there is no pen on the table,' simply means that the pen, an objective fact, is not present and consequently no knowledge of the pen arises. It has been argued that though the pen is not present, the absence of the pen at any rate exists and for the knowledge of this absence, which is as much an objective fact as the pen, we must posit an instrument just as we have to postulate the visual organ for visual knowledge. Prabhākara scouts this attitude as uncritical inasmuch as it seeks to make out that absence of cognition is a positive cognition and that absence of a fact is the presence of a fact—the absurdity of which is obvious on the face of it. The Mīmāṁsists of the Bhāṭṭa school have, however, laid emphasis upon the differences in the modes of knowing and this has led them to a different conclusion. According to them the negation of a particular object is nothing but a determination of the locus and is not anything distinct from it, as the *Naiyāyikas* would make out. But though not distinct from the locus, the *Bhāṭṭas* would insist upon its being regarded as a character or a mode of the locus quite distinct and different from its positive character or mode. Every reality is believed to be possessed of a dual nature—one positive and the other negative. The negative aspect is cognised only through reference to a perceivable object felt to be uncognised in the locus, whereas the perception of the positive aspect is entirely independent of any such foreign reference. The conditions of negative cognition are thus seen to vary from those of a positive fact and this makes the postulation of a separate cognitive instrument a necessity. But Prabhākara contends that variation in the mode of knowledge cannot be regarded as sufficient warrant for the postulation of a separate cognitive instrument (*pramāṇa*) unless it can be shown that there is a corresponding variation in the objective order, which Prabhākara refuses to believe.[1] We shall return to this question at a later stage.

Kumārila has given the most careful consideration to this problem and it will be found in the course of our enquiry that

[1] *Bṛhatī* with *Pañcikā*, pp. 118 *et seq.*

rival philosophers have totally failed to assail the arguments of Kumārila, which have been substantially adopted by them. The Buddhist logician had to re-state his position in the light of Kumārila's hostile criticism and the *Naiyāyikas* had substantially to agree with the latter in his findings subject to this reservation, *viz.*, that negative judgment is believed by them to be perceptual in nature. To revert to the epistemological problem, what is the means of our cognition of the absence of a particular object, say, a jar ? Kumārila gives the answer in the following words : the judgment 'there is no jar on the ground' can be arrived at only if we are assured that all instruments of cognition, competent to envisage a positive fact, are not in operation to cognise the positive fact. This non-operation of cognitive instruments is to be regarded as the instrument of the cognition of the absence of the jar. To be precise, the non-production of the cognitive activity of the subject, further defined as the non-perception of a perceptible fact, is here the means of cognition and the judgment of the absence is the resultant knowledge. Unless the validity of negative judgments be admitted, the mutual distinction of entities would not be cognised and consequently all selective activity, which makes practical life and conduct possible, would come to a cessation. But what is the means of ascertaining the validity of negative judgments and what again is the ground of this validity ? These questions arise inevitably and demand a solution.

The negative judgment can be proved to be true and valid if it can be shown that it corresponds with an objective fact— in other words, if there is such a thing as negation in its own right and not as a subjective construction as the Buddhist and idealists would have it. Kumārila therefore legitimately starts with an enquiry into the validity of negative judgments and the question of its conditions and content are discussed after this. The question of validity is necessarily bound up with the question of fact, correspondence to which constitutes the truth of a judgment and so a consideration of this metaphysical problem should not be looked upon as an illogical divagation from the logical issue. Kumārila maintains that negation is as much a part and parcel of an objective fact as the fact of its positive existence. Unless negation be admitted as a necessary element in an existent, the distinction of one thing from another would be impossible and distinction means negation of what it is not, *Determinatio est negatio.* The admission of negation as an element in existent facts is not only necessary for distinction, but its reality is also proved by other arguments. Negation is amenable to division into four kinds, *viz.*, the negation of the effect in the cause (*prāgabhāva*); the negation of the cause in the effect (*pradhvaṁsābhāva*); the negation of things in one another, *i.e.*, mutual exclusion (*anyonyābhāva*); and absolute negation, *e.g.*, of colour in air (*atyantābhāva*). Certainly these divisions and classifications are not applicable to fictions. Moreover, the concept of negation is common to all these distinctive kinds of negation and so identity and difference are found as elements in its constitution and this is the characteristic of positive facts also. We must therefore accord an objective status to negation, otherwise we shall face the risk of denying validity to all selective and exclusive usages and the result will be a condemnation of all our activity. So negation and affirmation are equally elements in an existent and even when one is perceived the other also is felt. Determinate cognition of a thing is possible if there is a cognition of the negative element serving to separate it from the rest. And the cognition of negation is possible only through reference to an existent positive fact, either as its object or as its locus.

Having thus established the objective reality of negation Kumārila now addresses himself to the question as to how the knowledge of negation arises. What is the instrument or condition of this cognition? Is it the same as that of perception, or of inference or any other? The cognition of negation cannot be regarded as perceptual in character since no relation can be conceived between negation and the sense-organ. The element of negation is something destitute of form and colour and these are invariably found to be the conditions of perception. The philosophers of the *Nyāya-Vaiśeṣika* school have postulated a relation between negation and its locus, *viz.*, of the substantive-adjective type. It is contended that when we negate a pen on the table, the table is not regarded simply as table, but as a table qualified by the absence of the pen. The absence of the pen serves to determine the locus as an adjectival element, and so when the sense-organ is connected with the locus, it becomes automatically connected with the adjectival element present in it and thus the condition of perception being present in the shape of the sense-object contact, the perception of the negative element becomes irresistible. But this contention of the *Naiyāyika* is inspired more by his love of a pet theory than by his regard for truth. The adjectival relation of negation to the locus can be maintained only if another relation can be demonstrated. What is the nature of an adjective? It is nothing but what is predicated of the subject and a thing can be predicated of another only if there is a relation between the two. In the case of a negative judgment the negative element is predicated of the locus as the subject, as for instance, in the judgment 'the table is without a pen;' and if the clause 'without a pen' is to be looked upon as the adjectival factor of the table, it must be shown in what precise relation the adjective stands to the subject as its qualifying condition. That such relation is the *conditio sine qua non* of substantive-adjective or subject-predicate relation in a judgment will be quite manifest from an analysis of other similar judgments. To cite concrete examples: 'The flower is red,' 'The man is with an umbrella' and so on. Now, the adjective 'red' is predicated of the flower, because there is a factual relation of inherence between the two. The quality of redness is actually present in the relation of inherence in the flower and the proposition only states this relation. The other example too exhibits the relation of conjunction (*saṁyoga*). In all these propositions it is quite apparent that the adjectival element is predicated of the subject only on the basis of an actual relation. It will not be fair to say that the relation is simply one of subject and predicate, substantive and adjective because this relation is only secondary to, and derivative from, the original relation and presupposes the original relation as its condition precedent. But no such relation can be made out to exist between the locus and negation and so there is absolutely no *raison d'être* of the secondary relation.

In the second place, the negative judgment being a judgment presupposes the previous knowledge of its constituent terms and their relation. To revert to our old example, 'The table is without-a-pen ;' here, the clause 'without-a-pen' is predicated of the table and this predication presupposes the previous knowledge of the predicate. Now what is the source of this previous knowledge? It may be said to be perception, because the judgment is at once borne upon us when we look at the empty table, according to the *Naiyāyika*. But the *Naiyāyika* cannot reasonably maintain that the judgment is entirely perceptual. The knowledge of the table may be derived from sight, but this is not possible of the absence of the pen. The *Naiyāyika* posits the simple indeterminate apprehension (*nirvikalpaka*) of terms as the condition precedent of a perceptual judgment. If the negative judgment be perceptual in nature, the perceptual cognition of the adjectival term should be shown to be antecedent to it. But this is impossible in the case of the negative term, because negation is intelligible only if it is understood as negation of something and as such there can be no simple non-relational cognition of it. The Mīmāṁsist however has an easy explanation in his theory of non-perception as a separate *pramāṇa*, which is *ex hypothesi* believed to be capable of giving this relational knowledge of the negative factor. The *Naiyāyika* is precluded by his theory of perception from giving this explanation, as determinate perceptual judgment, which negative judgment is believed to be, is possible only if there is a previous simple apprehension of the adjectival term. But this is impossible from the very nature of negation.

Now what is this non-perception which is postulated by the Mīmāṁsist to account for negative judgments? A negative judgment is formed in the mind when the locus (of negation) is cognised and the object to be negated is remembered and this knowledge of absence is purely due to a mental activity and not conditioned by a sense-organ.[1] That is to say, the knowledge of negation is never sensuous but always mental. What is the organon of this knowledge? Pārthasārathi Miśra elucidates this question thus :—' Non-perception is not mere absence of perception but non-perception of a thing competent to be perceived. When the locus is perceived and the object of negation is remembered, the non-perception, as defined above, sets the mind to activity and the mind so activated produces the knowledge of negation just as a sense-organ functions in regard to its object. The knowledge of negation seems to follow upon the sense-organ in function and this has caused the *Naiyāyika* to regard it as sensuous. But the sense-organ is employed upon the locus and has no competency with regard to negation. The judgment follows as the result of the combination of the two factors—the locus and the negative element, which combination takes place in the mind entirely unaided by the sense-organ so far at any rate as the negative element is concerned.[2] The negation and its relation to the locus is cognised by non-perception as defined above and the sense-organ only gives us the cognition of the locus. The negative judgment that follows should be affiliated to non-perception as its condition and not to sense-activity,

[1] gṛhitvā vastusadbhābaṁ smṛtvā ca pratiyoginam |
mānasaṁ nāstitājñānaṁ jāyate 'kṣānapekṣayā ||

S.V., śl. 27, p. 482.

[2] gṛhite cā 'śraye pratiyogini ca smṛte 'kṣasthānīyena dṛśyādarśanasahāyena manasai 'vā 'bhāvajanmopapatteṛ ne 'ndriyasyā' bhāve śaktiḥ śakyā kalpayitum. āparokṣyaṁ tu bhāvāṁśa eva nā 'bhāvāṁśe tad asti...... dṛśyādarśanam akṣaṁ ca sahitam abhāvaviśiṣṭaṁ bhāvaṁ bodhayati, tatra bhāvāṁśe 'kṣasya vyāpāraḥ, abhāvāṁśatatsambandhayos tv anupalabdhir vyāpriyate. N.R., pp. 482-83.

because the latter is incompetent to envisage negation and its relation, for which non-perception as the conditioning factor has to be postulated. When two factors co-operate to bring about a single judgment, the result is to be affiliated to that factor alone which is capable of cognising the relation. For instance inference is brought about by the co-operation of perception of the subject (*pakṣa*) and the knowledge of invariable concomitance (*vyāptijñāna*). But the knowledge of the conclusion is not believed to be perceptual in nature, because the perceptual cognition of the subject is not competent to envisage the relation of the probandum with the subject. With coequal logic the negative judgment, though produced by the co-operation of two factors, perception and non-perception both, should be affiliated to the latter, because the relation was incompetent to be cognised by the perceptual cognition of the locus. The contention of the *Naiyāyika* that negative judgment is given by the sense-organ aided by competent non-perception and hence is perceptual in character betrays slipshod observation, inasmuch as this would lead him to characterise inferential knowledge also as perceptual in character—an undesirable consequence in all conscience.[1] The *Naiyāyika* has been guided by considerations of economy to subsume non-perception under perception by reducing the former to the status of an auxiliary.[2] But why should he not extend the economy further afield and reduce inference to a mode of perceptual knowledge by regarding the condition of inference as an auxiliary to sense-organ?

1 yatra hi viśeṣaṇaviśeṣyasambandhaḥ pratyakṣaḥ tatrai 'va viśiṣṭasvarūpasya pratyakṣatvam, anyatra tu yenai 'va pramāṇena sambandhagrahaṇam, tad eva viśiṣṭasvarūpasya pramānam. tathā cā 'gnisambandhasyā 'numānikatvāt viśiṣṭarūpam ānumānikam ity uktam. atrā 'py abhāvasambandhasyā 'bhāvapramāṇaga nyatvād abhāvaviśiṣṭabhūtalādibodho 'bhāvapramāṇaka eva. *Loc. cit.*

2 tathā ce 'ndriyāṇām abhāvapratyakṣe jananīye yogyānupalabdheḥ sahakāritāmātreṇa nirvāhe 'tiriktapramāṇakalpanam anucitam.
Din., p. 264 (Bom. edn.).

We propose now to consider the question whether negative judgment can be equated with inferential knowledge. Now non-perception has been included by the Buddhists in the list of *hetus* (probanses) and knowledge of negation is regarded as the product of the knowledge of this probans—in other words, as inferential in character. This is at any rate a *prima facie* plausible interpretation of the Buddhist position though we shall find that the Buddhists have given an altogether different orientation to their solution of the problem which is different from the position criticised by Kumārila. If the negative judgment is believed to be reached by inference, we shall have to find out the probans. To take a typical case of negative judgment, 'there is no jar on the ground,' which of the constituent terms of the judgment may be regarded as the probans? The 'jar' is not the probans, as the jar is not cognised and an uncognised term cannot be a probans of any thing. The cognition of the jar, on the contrary, would make its non-cognition impossible and as a consequence the negative judgment will not be reached. Nor can the locus, the ground, function as the probans, as the locus cannot be understood as the property of the negation, as a qualifying adjunct, unless negation is known to be present, but in that case inference will have no object, as negation, the professed objective of inference, is already known. Thus there will be no minor premise if we seek to make the locus the probans of negation. Not only this, the major premise, the universal proposition, too, cannot be made out, as the concomitance of the locus and negation cannot be proved. The jar may be present or absent in the locus and its presence or absence does not make any difference to the ground *qua* locus. The locus may be cognised together with the jar and also independently of it in its absence. The relation of the locus to absence of a particular object is thus seen to be accidental and variable and so with regard to absence in general, unqualified and unconditioned by any object. The cognition of the locus therefore cannot be maintained to be the ground of inference of negation.

Moreover, the position that negation is always inferred leads to contradiction, irrespective of the consideration whether there is a competent probans possible or not. Inference is possible only if there is a knowledge of universal concomitance of the probans and the probandum at its back and if negation is to be inferred, its concomitance with a probans has to be demonstrated as possible of knowledge. And the knowledge of concomitance can be possible only if there is a knowledge of the terms and knowledge of negation as a term in universal concomitance cannot be reached through inference, as the inference in question presupposes the knowledge of negation in the universal concomitance as its condition. In the final analysis the knowledge of negation has to be reached independently of inference through the aid of some other *pramāṇa* and so the position of the Buddhist falls to the ground that negation is judged through inference.

The Buddhist logician however is not dismayed by this array of arguments and considers the knowledge of negation as capable of a syllogistic demonstration and there is neither lack of the universal proposition nor of the minor premise, as a competent probans is always found in the shape of non-perception. Now, non-perception is not a negation of perception, but perception of only one of the terms that are capable of being perceived together. For instance, when the jar on the ground is perceived, we perceive 'the jar' and 'the ground' together and when the jar is absent, we perceive the ground alone; this perception of the solitary ground is an act of positive perception and this positive perception is construed as the non-perception of the jar. The non-perception of the jar is invariably concomitant with negation of the jar and the relation constitutive of this invariable concomitance is found on examination to be a relation of identity of essence (*tādātmya* or *svabhāva*). The question may be raised, how can there be identity between negation and non-perception? Non-perception, as interpreted by the Buddhist, is a positive perception and a psychical event, whereas negation is an objective fact. How can there be identity between an objective and a subjective fact, between an object and its awareness, unless the position of extreme subjectivism is adopted ? The answer is however simple. The *Sautrāntikas* believe in the external world, no doubt, but they do not believe in the objective existence of negation. Negation according to them is a conceptual construction and a logical fiction, and so when negation is predicated, it is to be understood merely as the knowledge of negation (*asadvyavahāra*) and not as an objective fact. But the question may arise, that though negation be a subjective construction, the awareness of negation cannot be equivalent to awareness of a positive fact, to which non-perception or, to be precise, competent non-perception, has been reduced. The answer is that though perception of one of the terms of a complex situation, for instance of the ground-surface alone as bereft of a jar, is not numerically identical with cognition of negation, still the former has the competency (*yogyatā*) to be converted into the negative judgment and this competency is not anything distinct from the positive perception. The equation is between competent positive perception and negative judgment and thus the relation of identity being established between these two pieces of knowledge, the inference of negation is admissible. The knowledge of negation is thus not anything distinct from the perception of one aspect of a complex situation, of one of the several terms capable of being cognised in association at one sweep if they are present together, and this perception being a positive experience is felt of itself, as all knowledge is self-revealing. If the knowledge of negation were conceived to be the absence of knowledge of a perceptible fact, this would make a *regressus ad infinitum* inevitable, as absence, whether of a knowledge or of a fact, could be known through competent non-perception and that being again of the nature of absence could be known through another non-perception and so on to infinity. But this objection cannot be advanced against the conception of non-perception interpreted as a positive perceptional experience.[1]

[1] tasmād ekasya yā dṛṣṭiḥ sai 'vā 'nyādṛṣṭir ucyate |
sā ca svatantrasaṁsiddhiḥ svarūpeṇā 'jaḍatvataḥ || T. S , 1683.

The Mīmāṁsist is not satisfied with this explanation of the Buddhist and regards it only as a pretence and delusion, which will be exposed if the nature of non-perception is subjected to a critical analysis. Now, non-perception cannot be taken in an unqualified absolute sense, nor can negation be understood absolutely without reference to a context, even if such things are admitted to be conceivable. The negation to be inferred is to be understood as the negation of a particular object and this cannot be supposed to be inferred from unqualified non-perception, because unqualified non-perception is not incompatible with the presence of the object to be negated. There may be presence of a jar and the absence of a pen and the like in the same place. So non-perception has to be interpreted as non-perception of the thing, the negation of which is to be inferred. That is to say, the absence of a jar can be inferred from the non-perception of a jar. But what is this non-perception of the jar? If it is identical with the perception of the locus, say the ground-surface, then there will be no knowledge of negation, as the locus is perceived even when the jar is present. If you say that this non-perception consists in the perception of one of the possibly co-presentable factors, this too does not make negation intelligible, as it is not a peculiar characteristic of negation that one of the terms is perceived. The perception of the term in question takes place also when both the terms are perceived. To take a concrete example, the jar and the ground are perceived together and if negation of the jar consisted in the perception of the ground, the said negation should be cognised even when the jar is present, as the presence of the jar does not preclude the perception of the ground. Thus the attempt on the part of the Buddhist logician to equate negative cognition

tathā yai 'vai 'kajñānasaṁsargiṇor anyataropalbdhiḥ sai 've 'tarasyā 'nupalabdhir na tū 'palabdhyabhāvo nāma kaścid upalabdhivyatirekeṇā 'nupalabdhisaṁjño 'sti, yatas tasyā 'nupalabdhyantarāpekṣyayā 'navasthā syāt. yā cā 'sāv anyataropalabdhiḥ sā svasaṁvedyai 've 'ti nā 'navasthā.
N. R., pp. 486-87.

with cognition of one of the possibly co-presentable terms fails to explain the *raison d'être* of negative judgment and he will have to admit that non-perception of the jar means the non-origination of the perception of the jar. And non-origination being a negative fact has to be inferred on the basis of non-perception and the latter too will be subject to the same difficulty. The result will be a vicious infinite series. The same difficulty confronts the fact of negation, when its concomitance with non-perception has to be understood. Moreover, inferential knowledge is generated by the knowledge of the probans endowed with triple condition and when non-perception is admitted to be nothing but a case of non-origination of perception and non-origination is not an effect, how can this be considered to be generated by the knowledge of the aforesaid probans? Non-perception therefore has to be admitted as generative of the knowledge of negation on its own account without its being a logical probans—in other words, negative judgment is to be believed in the last analysis as non-inferential knowledge.[1]

Non-perception has been proved to be a separate source of knowledge and the possibility of its functioning as a logical probans has been totally demolished on the basis of infinite regressions to which it leads as an inevitable consequence. The same result can be reached through other considerations also, calculated to prove the absence of all the conditions of inference. The impossibility of the knowledge of universal concomitance of non-perception with negation has been demonstrated up to the hilt. This means the lack of the universal proposition, without which no inference is admissible. But this is not the only drawback, the minor premise too (*pakṣadharmatā*) will be found to be equally an impossible phenomenon on examination. Now, what can be the subject (*pakṣa* or minor term), of which non-perception as the logical probans can be predicable? It cannot be 'negation,' because this is the very objective of inference.

[1] *Vide*. S. V., śls. 38-44 and N. R. thereunder.

Moreover, negation cannot be understood, as has been shown above, without reference to the place and time and the object to be negated. And if for the sake of argument 'negation' as qualified by these conditions is admitted to be known as the subject of the predicate of 'non-perception' as the logical probans, there will be no matter left for inference to prove, as the knowledge of the minor premise will give us the knowledge of negation, for which inference would be in request. Nor can the locus (of negation) be accepted to be the subject, because non-perception cannot belong to it, as it is directly perceived and as such cannot be thought to be unperceived without involving self-contradiction. Nor can the object of negation, *e.g.*, the jar whose negation has to be proved, be accepted to be the subject, because no relation can be conceived between the object and non-perception. Non-perception cannot be regarded as the attribute of the object, say, the jar, because the jar is a real objective fact and never fails to be perceived when it is present together with the conditions of perception. It cannot be contended that non-perception may be an attribute of the absent jar, because the contention is suicidal to the opponent's position. If the jar is known to be absent antecedently to inference, the problem is solved and inference will have no subject-matter. It may be maintained that the subject is the jar as such without any reference to its positive or negative aspect, its presence or absence, and of this subject, negation can be proved by a regular syllogistic argument: for example, 'The jar is not on the ground, because it is not perceived though competent to be perceived.' But this is only a hoax, simply because the probans, '*is not perceived*,' is an unproved assumption and it has been shown how it leads to infinite regression. It may be urged that 'negation' can function as the subject, inasmuch as they are related as subject (*viṣayī*) and object (*viṣaya*), negation being known through non-perception. But this too will not help the cause of the opponent. The relation in question is understood after negation is known through non-perception and not before and so it cannot be a contributory factor to the knowledge of negation. Nor can any other type of relation be maintained between negation and non-perception. Even if it is conceded for argument's sake that a relation is possible, still the knowledge of the minor premise, in which the relation is stated, will give us the knowledge of negation and inference will have no scope.[1] The absurdity of the opponent's position that negation is known through inference has been exposed thoroughly and the question has been discussed threadbare. The Buddhists found themselves in an awkward predicament and Dharmottara has substantially admitted the justice and cogency of Kumārila's contention by trying to make out a case in favour of Dharmakīrti. But we shall presently see that his defence has served to expose the weakness of the Buddhist position by deprviing it of all logical value.

Dharmottara was absolutely convinced of the cogency of Kumārila's arguments and realised that the Buddhist position was entirely indefensible as it stood. He therefore tried to give an altogether different orientation substantially accepting the justice and correctness of Kumārila's animadversions. The interpretation of non-perception as perception of one of the possibly associable factors cannot be converted into perception of absence and even if it were possible, there would not be a whit of necessity for inference as a medium of the knowledge of absence, which is already derived from perception. The absence of the effect means the presence of the cause and the cause-as-present is known through perception, and so there is nothing to be known through inference or any other mode.[2] Dharmottara admits that knowledge of the absence of the jar follows upon the perception of the vacant ground and so the former should be set down as the result of perceptual experience and what is derived from perceptual experience does not stand in need of being proved by

[1] *Op. cit.*, śls. 50-53.

[2] kāryādīnām abhāvo hi bhāvo yaḥ kāraṇādinā ।
sa cā 'paraviviktātmā pratyakṣeṇai 'va gamyate ॥

T.S., śl. 1671.

inference. The knowledge of absence or negation therefore should not be regarded as inferential in character. But inference comes into play when an undisputed pragmatic usage is made of this perceptual knowledge. And pragmatic usage of negation may be of three distinct, but allied, varieties: firstly, the logical conviction that a thing is non-existent; secondly, linguistic usage expressing this fact of non-existence through a proposition; and thirdly, practical behaviour following upon it. Although non-perception is competent to give rise to knowledge of negation, the result cannot be susceptible of pragmatic applications unless non-perception is reinforced by a knowledge of the competency of the object to be perceived, because even imperceptible things may escape perception, but this failure of perception is not capable of being construed as evidence of their absence. Of course the deliverance of perceptual evidence that a particular object is absent in a particular context of place and time is competent to give rise to these pragmatic uses, but the knowledge of absence is placed on a footing of absolute certainty when it is re-certified by inference. Thus, the absence of the pen on the table is known through perception of the empty table, no doubt. But the knowledge of this absence is made absolutely certain when the inferential knowledge brings up the rear in the following order: 'Certainly the pen does not exist upon the table. Were it present, it could not but be perceived as it is competent to be perceived like the table.' Though this process of inference does not give us the knowledge of an unknown fact, it certainly makes this knowledge absolutely free from doubt and as such makes it an instrument for practical behaviour and linguistic usage. [1]

This defence of Dharmottara virtually amounts to a confession of the futility of non-perception as an instrument of inference. He has tried to prove the obvious, which Kumārila and others have not denied. The main contention of Kumārila is that non-perception has got to be admitted as an independent means of knowledge of absence without being a logical probans

[1] N.B.T., pp. 32-34.

at the primary stage and this contention is admitted to be valid by Dharmottara. The admission of non-perception as an independent probans by Dharmakīrti has therefore no logical sanction behind it and only subserves the interests of perception. The *Naiyāyika* was fully conscious of the subservient character of non-perception and has accordingly relegated it to the rank of an auxiliary factor, as *tarka,* which is denied independent validity and probative value by them. The attempt on the part of Śāntarakṣita and Kamalaśīla to reduce non-perception to the status of the non-perception of the effect and thus to make knowledge of negation as inferential knowledge of the absence of the cause from the absence of the effect, has equally failed to save the Buddhist position. " The absence of the jar," argues Kamalaśīla, "is proved from the bare perception of the empty ground and this bare perception is nothing but the non-perception of the effect, *viz.*, knowledge of the jar." Knowledge of the jar is produced by the jar when it is present together with other conditions of perception and so the absence of the knowledge of the jar must be set down as due to the absence of the jar in the same or similar context. Therefore non-perception, which is set down as the natural correlate of absence of a perceptible fact (*svabhāvānupalabdhi*), should be equated with non-perception of an effect (*kāryānupālabdhi*).[1]

We must confess that this argument of Kamalaśīla does not improve the Buddhist position in the least. It leaves the problem, as to how the knowledge of negation whether of a fact or knowledge is ultimately derived, absolutely cold. The knowledge of the absence of the jar cannot be inferentially derived from knowledge of the absence of the perception of the jar and even if it were possible, the knowledge of the absence of perceptual

[1] yatrā 'pi kevalapradeśopalambhād ghaṭābhāvasiddhiḥ, sā 'pi ghaṭopalambhākhyakāryānupalabdhir eva......... tasmāt sarvai 'va svabhāvānupalabdhir asadvyavahārahetuḥ, paramārthataḥ kāryānupalabdhir eva draṣṭavyā.

T. S. P., p. 481.

knowledge cannot at any rate be reached through inference. So the Buddhist has got to admit that knowledge of absence, at least in the primary stage, is not derived from inference. In fact, the Buddhist does not believe in the ontological reality of negation and so the knowledge of negation is believed to be an intellectual construction, following in the trail of the perception of the empty locus. But though an intellectual construction, it cannot be placed upon the same footing with the determinate judgmental knowledge of perceptual facts, albeit knowledge of negation follows upon the perception of the bare locus. For there is a pronounced difference between a positive judgment and a negative judgment, although all judgments are intellectual constructions in the view of the Buddhist logician. The positive judgment, which follows upon the perception of a positive fact, has got an objective reference and serves to clarify the perceptual experience by emphasising the objective content as a distinct element in it, whereas the negative judgment is entirely devoid of an objective reference, at least one that is derived from the primal perceptual experience. The perceptual experience, which eventuates in the negative judgment, was cognisant of the locus which is a positive fact, and did not contain any reference to negation. Negation, both as content and as a judgment, has no existence outside the subjective experience, whereas the objective reference of positive perceptual judgments is remotely grounded in an objective fact, directly perceived in the indeterminate simple experience preceding it. The Buddhist philosopher could justify his position if he placed negative judgments in the same category with knowledge of word-imports (*apoha*), which, notwithstanding their pragmatic efficiency, have been regarded by him as unmitigated subjective constructions.

We made a brief reference to Prabhākara's theory of negation just in the beginning of our present dissertation and we propose to resume the discussion in view of its pronounced affinities with the Buddhistic position. Śālikanātha

Miśra in his *Prakaraṇapañcikā* has given an elaborate treatment of this problem and after representing the orthodox Mīmāṁsist's position he sets out the position of his school, which is entitled to careful consideration in view of its ingenuity. Negation according to Prabhākara is nothing but the presence of a positive fact. The negation of the jar on the ground does not connote the presence of an additional fact save and except the ground itself. The cognition of the locus is interpreted as the cognition of the absence of the jar, but this absence is never a fact and as such is not amenable to cognition. The cognition of the locus takes place both in association with an object existing in it and also by itself when any such object is not in existence. The cognition of the locus by itself may or may not be followed by a reference to an object which is not present in it, but which, if present, would be surely perceived. When the cognition of the locus is accompanied by a reference to an absent perceivable object, the knowledge of its absence is seen to follow upon it. This knowledge of absence is nothing but the knowledge of the solitary locus with reference to a perceivable object. Kumārila admits the knowledge of the empty locus together with a memory-reference to a perceivable object as the condition of the knowledge of the absence. But Prabhākara would stop short with this condition alone and regard it as the knowledge of the absence. The condition of Kumārila, that is to say, the knowledge of the locus by itself followed by reference through memory to a perceivable object is construed as the knowledge of the negation and this knowledge has for its content the locus alone. Negation is only a designation of this perception of a positive fact followed by a reference to a perceivable object and is not an additional entity. Negation is not believed to be a presentable datum and if it were conceived to be presented it must be held to be identical with the locus itself. The negation of the pen is nothing but the presentation of the table or any other positive fact, without which no negation is conceivable. Kumārila too admits the presentation of a positive datum as the condition of the knowledge of negation and we may legitimately enquire as to what sort of a positive datum is regarded as the condition. Is it the positive datum perceived together with the object of negation? This is certainly absurd, as in the presence of the object the knowledge of its absence cannot arise. Nor can the positive datum, cognised together with negation as its qualifying adjunct, be conceived to serve as the precondition of the knowledge of negation. For, the knowledge of negation would be already achieved by the knowledge of the adjectival element and there would be no other negation to be cognised with the help of it. So it must be admitted that the knowledge of the positive datum without reference to any other element, positive or negative, is the condition of the knowledge of negation, but this condition has nothing further to produce as its effect. The cognition of the positive datum alone, as distinguished from the object of negation, should be recognised as the cognition of negation. The judgment 'there is no jar on the ground' when analysed, will be found to mean nothing but this: that the ground by itself is cognised in spite of the fact that the jar is susceptible of perception. The Buddhist also regards the perception of the positive fact by itself as tantamount to perception of negation and in this there is entire agreement between Prabhākara and the Buddhist philosophers. But the Buddhist goes a step further. The knowledge of negation *qua* the perception of the positive fact is perceptual in character and as such is based upon an objective datum. The negative judgment which follows upon this perceptual cognition is only an intellectual construction and 'negation' as its objective is purely an illusion, as there is no such thing as objective negation. Negation superadded to the positive perceived fact is only an ideational fiction quite as much as universals and other concepts, which have been proved to be mere ideas without any objective basis[1] and has nothing corresponding to it in the objective order

[1] *Ante*, Chapter VI.

But Prabhākara being an uncompromising realist cannot be expected to believe in unfounded ideas and he denies knowledge of the negation in the sense of its being anything in excess of the knowledge of positive datum. Prabhākara denies knowledge of negation together with negation as an objective category and though the Buddhist denies the latter, he leaves room for the possibility of negative judgments as subjective constructions, since realism of the *Sautrāntika* accepts the reality of particulars alone.

We now propose to discuss the *Naiyāyika's* view of negation. The *Naiyāyikas* believe in the objective existence of negation, but does not think it necessary to posit another *pramāṇa* (cognitive instrument) for its cognition. Negation according to the *Naiyāyika* may be perceived by the sense-organ when it is situated within its province, and when it is placed outside its province it may be cognised by inference or verbal knowledge. In any event it does not necessitate the postulation of a distinct kind of knowledge. The main ground of difference between the *Naiyāyika* and the Mīmāṁsist consists in the contention of the former that negation is directly perceived by the sense-organ, whereas the latter denies the possibility of sensuous cognition of negation. The Mīmāṁsist contends that no sensuous cognition can take place unless a recognised relation between the sense-organ and the perceivable object can be shown to exist and this very condition of perception is absent in the case of negation, as negation is neither a substance nor an attribute with which alone the sense-organ can be related. The relation of the subject-predicate or substantive-adjective type between negation and the locus has been shown to be impossible, as such a relation is only incidental to an original relation behind it and no such original relation is capable of being shown by the *Naiyāyika*. The sense-organ is profitably employed upon the locus and has no competency with regard to negation, as it is neither related to the locus nor to the sense-organ.

Udayana in his *Nyāyakusumāñjali* has made a desperate attempt to show that the perception of the locus is absolutely irrelevant to the perception of negation and so the explanation of the Mīmāṁsist that the sense-organ is employed only upon the locus falls to the ground. Udayana cites the concrete case of the cognition of the cessation of sound in support of his position. Suddenly a noise ceases and we directly experience it. The experience of the sudden cessation of noise is certainly perceptual just as the experience of noise is perceptual. The sense-organ was active a moment before and cannot be supposed to have ceased to function just when the noise ceases. If the activity of the sense-organ were absolutely irrelevant to the experience of the cessation of the sound, a deaf man also could have an experience of it. The supposed absence of relation between the auditory organ and the extinction of sound cannot be made the ground of denying the perceptual character of the experience. The relation is always inferred from the experience and is an epistemological device to explain the origin of experience and is never uniform and identical. The relation in the case of perception of substance is different from the relation with attributes. The visual organ is supposed to be related to the jar in the relation of conjunction (*saṁyoga*), but to its redness in the relation of conjoined inherence (*saṁyukta-samavāya*) and so on, simply because the attribute redness is never perceived apart from the substance. But in the case of fragrance, which is an attribute, it is perceived apart from the substance and the relation between the olfactory organ and fragrance is supposed to be simply inherence (*samavāya*). So with regard to sound, which is believed to be an attribute of ether (*ākāśā*) by the *Naiyāyika*, the relation between the auditory organ and sound is regarded as pure inherence. These relations are sometimes simple, at other times complex and all these are epistemological hypotheses, varying according to the nature of the objects to be perceived. Nor are these relations universally accepted. The philosophers of different schools have differently conceived them in accordance with their philosophical persuasions; but so far as the psychological status of experience is concerned there is absolutely no difference of views. None denies that visual knowledge is perceptual. The absence of the recognised relations in the case of negative knowledge should not cause difficulty, as we can easily conceive of a suitable relation. If the lack of uniformity in relations is no objection to the perceptuality of visual, auditory and olfactory experiences, no objection should be raised if the relation in negative cognition is different from the accepted kinds. The relation of negation with the locus is a peculiar relation, designated as the substantive-adjectival relation. The negation is adjectival to the locus, exactly like the positive object residing in it. The jar on the ground distinguishes it from the ground that is without it and so the absence of the jar distinguishes the ground from the ground that is possessed of a jar. The jar is thus the distinguishing feature of the ground and so also the absence of the jar and the relation between the two terms is thus seen to be one of distinguisher and distinguished, qualifier and qualified, adjective and substantive. The relation between the sense-organ and negation will be a corresponding relation of the substantive-adjectival type.

The objection of the Mīmāṁsist, that the substantive-adjectival relation is only a derivative relation from an original relation existing between the terms and can never be an original relation, is based upon an accident. There is no logical necessity that the adjective should stand to the substantive in an additional relation. Of course the quality of redness is actually seen to inhere in the flower and the umbrella is conjoined to the bearer, but this relation of inherence or conjunction is not constitutive of the adjectival relation, but rather accidental. The relation of inherence or conjunction is found to exist from direct experience and so also the adjectival relation ; and we do not see any reason why the one should be regarded as the primary and the other secondary. After all a relation is posited to bring two terms together and if the terms are not naturally related, the position of a further relation will be useless. In the case of negation, it is by its very constitution related to the locus and hence it does not stand in need of a foreign relation, which will bring the terms together. Moreover, if negation were supposed to be related to the locus by way of conjuction or inherence, it would become a positive entity like substance or attribute and we shall have no criterion to distinguish existence from non-existence.[1] We cannot appreciate the logical propriety of the Mīmāṁsist's objection that negation cannot be perceived as an adjectival element in the absence of an additional relation at its back. Is not negation the distinguishing characteristic of the locus? Do we not distinguish an empty bag from one that is full ? And if we do distinguish, what is the criterion of distinction ? Certainly the absence of contents distinguishes the empty bag from the full one and so to deny that absence can be the qualifying adjective will be tantamount to denying the plain verdict of experience and this means self-contradiction. The Mīmāṁsist cannot deny this adjectival relation of negation to the locus and he will have to fall back upon an original relation to explain this. If the Mīmāṁsist can trot out an original relation, the *Naiyāyika* too may accept it provided it does not violate logical propriety. The relation of negation and the locus is regarded as one of identity (*tādātmya*) by the Mīmāṁsist and if this relation were logically consistent with the terms, we could also accept it and satisfy the scruples of the Mīmāṁsist. But identity between an existent and a non-existent is inconceivable and if the non-existent were simply an aspect of the existent the non-existent could be perceived in the same fashion as the existent. The *Naiyāyika* does not believe in the relation of identity between negation and the positive locus as the foundation of the substantive-adjectival relation simply because the foundational relation supposed by the

[1] abhāvo yady atiriktasambandhavān syāt sattāvān syāt ity avyavasthā. Ny. Ku. P., p. 108,. Ch. III.

Mīmāṁsist involves self-contradiction. The substantive-adjectival relation can subsist between two terms without any other relation. In fact this relation cannot be denied by the Mīmāṁsist, as we have shown above, on pain of self-contradiction and to fall back upon the relation of identity as the basic relation equally leads to a quagmire. Moreover, this search for a foundational relation is entirely unprofitable. The Mīmāṁsist has not succeeded in making out the logical necessity why one relation should be regarded as more fundamental than the other and the argument from the analogy of cases where the two relations are found together is at best of an empirical value. It has been shown that experiences are not uniform and they are all of equal logical value, unless it can be found that one is sublated by the other. If the adjectival relation is not fundamental, why should the other relation be so ? If the relation of inherence is self-sufficient, why should the adjectival relation be condemned ? And if relations as such are condemned as illogical makeshifts, an infinite regression and a consequent denial of the validity of all judgments will be the inevitable consequence—in other words, philosophy will wander into the *cul de sac* of scepticism, to which the Mīmāṁsist of all persons cannot be a party.

The Mīmāṁsist declares that the cognition of negation is non-perceptual and our feeling of its being an immediate perceptual experience is only a psychological error due to confusion with the perception of the locus.[1] But the argument seems to move in a vicious circle. Why should the felt immediacy be erroneous, because the sense-organ is not in contact with negation and why should such contact fail, because the felt immediacy is erroneous? Nor can the Mīmāṁsist deny sensuous cognition of negation on the ground of its lack of

[1] *Cf.* āparokṣyaṁ tu bhāvāṁśa eva nā' bhāvāṁśe tad asti. N. R., p. 483. bhūtalādes tv aparokṣatvād abhāvasyā 'pi tattvabhrama evā 'yuṣmatām. Mān. Me., p. 60.

sensible qualities. The Mīmāṁsist believes that time and space are perceived though they have no sensible qualities. Why should he then go out of his way to condemn the felt immediate experience of negation as a psychological error? We open our eyes and see that the air is colourless. The absence of colour is felt to be visually perceived. Why should you condemn it as false perception? Why again do we not have this experience with our eyes shut up? The eye certainly functions and it cannot function upon the locus, the air, as it is visually unperceivable. If it is not engaged in the perception of negation, it will have no employment. If it is supposed to be engaged upon the surrounding objects, we do not see how the seeing of other objects can have a bearing upon the negative cognition. But it has been contended by the Mīmāṁsist that the visual organ has got to function in order to complete the conditions of competent non-perception, which is the instrument for the cognition of negation. What are the conditions constitutive of competency? Competency is constituted by the presence of all the conditions of perception save and except the object and the consequent sense-object contact. One can be sure of the absence of the jar upon the near ground-surface only if one is fully persuaded that there is full light, alert attention, the fit visual organ in function and still the jar is not perceived. If any one of these conditions be absent, the absence of the jar cannot be categorically affirmed, as non-perception may be due to the lack of an essential condition of perception and not to the absence of the object. The visual organ thus has got to function in order to fulfil the conditions that go to make the non-perception of the object, say the jar, a fit and competent instrument for the deliverance of the negative cognition. The *Naiyāyika* opines that this explanation is rather tortuous and deliberately makes a plain situation complex. The visual organ may be believed to cognise the absence of the object and thus have an utility of its own.

The *Naiyāyika* further argues that perceptual knowledge is invariably seen to be caused by an uncognised instrument and non-perceptual knowledge is always conditioned by some knowledge of fact. The negative cognition is caused by an instrument unperceived by us and this instrument is not, whatever else it might be, a knowledge of fact. We should regard negative cognition to be perceptual in character as it is not conditioned by a knowledge of fact. The Mīmāṁsist is not satisfied by this analogical argument and thinks that the universal proposition, 'all knowledge that is caused by a non-cognitional instrument (*jñānākaraṇakajñāna*) is perceptual in character, is vitiated by the case of memory, which, though caused by memory-impression (*saṁskāra*), which is not a cognition, is not perceptual in character.

The next argument of Udayana also proceeds upon analogy. All knowledge of external objects is seen to be generated by the mind when it is influenced and directed by a positive cognitive instrument. Thus the visual knowledge of external objects is seen to be produced by the mind under the direction of the visual organ, which is a positive instrument. In verbal knowledge of external objects, the mind is guided by the knowledge of the word and conventional relation, and so also in inference the mind is under the guidance of the knowledge of the probans, with universal concomitance—all positive facts. In our external knowledge of absence too the mind should be under the influence of a positive cognitive instrument, *viz.*, the sense-organ and not non-perception, which is a negative fact. The cogency of this argument is not admitted by the Mīmāṁsist. What cognitive instrument is employed to bring about a kind of knowledge can be determined from the nature of the knowledge that follows and from the nature of the object to be cognised. And the relation of a particular cognitive instrument to a particular species of knowledge is a relation of causality and it can be determined exactly in the same way as other causal relations are determined. It might be a fact that our knowledge of external positive entities is achieved by a positive cognitive instrument. But there is no logical necessity that the same condition should prevail in negative cognitions too. It might be argued with equal plausibility that negative cognition should be generated by an instrument other than a sense-organ, because this is found to be the case in our inference of negation. These are arguments by analogy, pure and simple, and have no logical necessity, as the contrary possibility is not barred out by a *reductio ad absurdum*.

The *Naiyāyika* further argues that the competency of the sense-organ in respect of negation should be admitted exactly like its competency in respect of the relevant positive entity. The jar is cognised by the visual organ and the absence of the jar too should be believed to be so cognised. It is no argument that a positive cognitive instrument is competent to cognise positive objects alone. What about the verbal knowledge of negation? When we hear a trustworthy person say that John is not at home, we at once have a knowledge of John's absence. What is the instrument of our knowledge of absence in this case? Certainly the aforsaid proposition, not anything negative. So also when a man proves by argument that the sun does not move or that the Arabs are not civilised and so on, our knowledge of negation is certainly inferential. The *Mīmāṁsaka* may contend that in all these cases inference or verbal communication serves to give rise to an idea of non-cognition of the positive fact, *e.g.*, of the conditions of motion in the sun or of civilization among the Arabs and the negative judgment is thus the result of non-cognition. Inference or verbal knowledge only serves to communicate this fact of non-cognition and has no bearing upon the negative judgment following upon it.

The *Naiyāyika* next fights on the issue of illusory cognition of negation and its opposite in places where the opposites are present. The pen may actually exist on the table, but we may miss it through a defect in the sense-organ and think that there is no pen on the table. Contrariwise through a defect in the organ we may see a ghost though there is none. The error is not confined to the visual organ alone. We may miss a sound through a defect in the organ of hearing, say partial deafness, and we may judge that there was no sound. It is common knowledge that the malaria patient after having taken a strong dose of quinine seems to hear continuous sounds, though there are none. What are these illusions due to ? Certainly these aberrations are caused by defects in the sense-organs. And if defective sense-organ can envisage illusory negation, we do not see any earthly reason why the healthy organ should not cognise real negation. But the Mīmāṁsist argues that the function of the organ comes into request only to fulfil the conditions of competency of non-perception and in erroneous cognitions of negation the defective sense-organ is responsible for the illusion of this competency and does not proceed further. The negative judgment follows as the result of non-perception.

As regards the charge that the negative judgment cannot be maintained to be perceptual in nature as it is not preceded by the simple perceptual apprehension of the negative term, which is found to be the invariable condition of perceptual judgments, the *Naiyāyikas* admit the truth of the accusation, but they deny that this lack of condition makes the negative judgment non-perceptual in character. A judgment is made possible by the antecedent knowledge of terms in isolation and when there is no such antecedent simple apprehension of the terms, the judgment cannot take place. This rule holds good only in the case of those terms whose isolated apprehension is possible, but it does not apply to those relative terms, which are by their very nature incompetent to be cognised by themselves without reference to some other terms, with which they are constitutionally bound up. Negation, for instance, is one such term and is understandable only with reference to the object to be negated. So a simple isolated apprehension of negation is impossible and whenever it is comprehended, it is comprehended in relation and never out of it. This objection, the *Naiyāyika* contends, is suicidal and the Mīmāṁsist too cannot give a more satisfactory explanation. The rule that a judgment is preceded by simple apprehension of the terms is not confined to perceptual judgments alone, but to all judgments. Even inferential and verbal judgments are in the ultimate analysis traceable to simple non-relational knowledge of the terms. And if the rule were absolute and did not brook exception, the Mīmāṁsist too would have to find an explanation of the anomaly presented by negative judgments. The Mīmāṁsist cannot make out that negation is apprehended in isolation at any stage and he will have to admit that negative judgment is reached at one sweep and not step by step. The contention, that perceptual judgment alone is subject to this contingency and the difficulty will not arise if negative judgment is recognised as non-perceptual in character to be reached by non-perceptual evidence, is not tenable, as all judgments have been shown to be ultimately traceable to perceptual knowledge of terms. If an exception is allowed in favour of negative judgments, the *Naiyāyika* too will have the benefit of it, and the question of its etiology is irrelevant. If 'non-perception' is believed to be capable of giving simple knowledge of negation, the sense-organ too may be credited with such capacity. The question is whether negation permits of being simply apprehended and if the possibility is admitted, the instrument in question, be it sense-organ or non-perception, will be supposed to yield this requisite knowledge.

Now to sum up the results : The main contention of the Mīmāṁsist is that the sense-organ is employed elsewhere to constitute the competency, without which non-perception is incompetent to give knowledge of absence. The *Naiyāyika* would make the sense-organ yield this knowledge, although he also admits the instrumentality of non-perception. The difference seems to be a question of emphasis. The *Naiyāyika* will make non-perception only an auxiliary factor to the sense-organ and the Mīmāṁsist would make it the self-sufficient condition and for this very purpose he will relegate the sense-organ to a subordinate rank as serving to prepare the ground for non-perception to take effect. The sense-organ is only in request to assure the subject that non-perception is present inspite of the presence of the conditions of perception. Udayana has made a vigorous plea in favour of the sense-organ being the instrument of negative judgment and he seeks to demolish the contention that the sense-organ is employed upon the locus. The perception of locus is not indispensable to the cognition of negation of those objects, which can be perceived without reference to the locus. Sound, for instance, is perceived without reference to its locus. Sound is cognised by the auditory organ which is incompetent to cognise its locus, ether (*ākāśa*), which is not amenable to perception. Smell, again, is perceived without reference to its locus, which, though cognisable by other organs, is not liable to be cognised by the olfactory organ. In the case of negations of these perceptible objects the knowledge of the locus is either impossible or unnecessary. Accordingly the sense-organ will have no employment upon the locus and still it is seen to be in function, otherwise the negation of these objects will not be cognised. For instance, the extinction of sound is cognised only by a person who possesses a sound auditory organ and when that organ is in actual operation. Similarly with regard to the extinction of smell the function of the olfactory organ is seen to be necessary for knowledge of such extinction and yet the sense-organ cannot be supposed to be employed elsewhere. The Mīmāṁsist has sought to explain these difficulties by regarding these negative cognitions as the result of inference. 'The subject, who was perceiving the sound but suddenly ceases to perceive it, infers the absence of the sound from the absence of sound-cognition, which could not but take place if the sound were there.' The Mīmāṁsist therefore can maintain his position only by explaining away these simple experiences as inferential judgments. But what about the sense-organs all this while ? The Mīmāṁsist will have to admit that they remain active, otherwise the non-cognition of sound or smell may be attributed to the aberration of the sense-organs and thus knowledge of negation will be precarious. The *Naiyāyikas* contend that the activity of the sense-organ is necessary for the negative cognition, but the Mīmāṁsist will explain it away as a constitutive factor of the competency, which makes non-perception an effective instrument of negative cognition. The quarrel seems to be endless as neither party will yield. But to a dispassionate critic it appears that both parties have made a good case for themselves and the difference seems to be reducible to a question of attitude and emphasis. The *Naiyāyikas* seem to have the support of psychology in their favour and their position will readily command the assent of the avarage man. But the quarrel of philosophers is not at all a simple affair. The Mīmāṁsist has made capital out of the peculiar character of negation, which is neither a substance nor an attribute, nor even a relation. It has no shape, no colour, in short, none of the sensible qualities and the commonplace, work-a-day man will find it difficult to believe that such an amorphous thing is capable of being directly perceived. But the Mīmāṁsist thinks time and space to be amenable to perception and it does not lie in him to impugn its perceivability on the ground of its lack of sensible qualities. The Buddhist and Prabhākara, particularly the latter, have cut the Gordian knot by declaring negation to be *non est* and the problem of epistemology is simply given a wide berth. We purposely refrain from entering into the metaphysical issues. We have laid bare the epistemological problem with the solutions offered by the rival philosophers and we hope this comparative study has served to put the Buddhist position in a clear perspective.

References

1. The Ślokavārttika—Chapter on Abhāva.
2. Nyāyaratnākara — Do.
3. The Prakaraṇapañcikā—pp. 118-25.
4. Nyāyabindū—Chapters II and III.
5. Nyāyabindu ṭīkā—Do.
6. Nyāyakusumāñjali—Ch. II, pp. 16-30; Ch. III, pp. 98-107.
7. Tattvasaṅgraha— Śls. 1648-98.
8. Do. Pañjikā—Do.
9. Mānameyodaya—pp. 58-64.
10. Tattvacintāmaṇi—pp. 673-719.
11. Nyāyāmañjarī—pp. 49-63.
12. Bṛhatī—pp. 118-23.
13. Pañcikā—Do.
14. Nyāyamañjarī—pp. 49-63.

INDEX

References are to pages